The Official History of
Ballymena United
Football Club

Neil Coleman

BALLYHAY BOOKS

Published by Ballyhay Books,
an imprint of Laurel Cottage Ltd.,
Donaghadee, Northern Ireland.
Copyrights reserved.
© Neil Coleman 2015.
Contributed texts are copyright of individual contributors.
Photographs are reproduced by permission.
All rights reserved.
No part of this book may be reproduced or stored on any media
without the express written permission of the publishers.
Printed by Gutenberg Press, Malta.
ISBN 978-1-910657-04-1

But for one woman's patience, love, support and continued drive this book wouldn't be the completed article you see today. Thank you Niki.

This book is dedicated to my family and also all the long suffering supporters with whom I've shared terraces, buses and pints over the years, this is our story and one we can be proud of.

Special thanks go out to the following; The Management Committee of Ballymena United FC, Clifford Adams and family, Stephen Alexander & the Ballymena Times, Iain Black, Ballymena Central Library, Belfast Central Newspaper Library, Scott Boyd, John Duffy, Martin Harris, the Hickson family, Jonathan Irwin, Jonathan Houston, Tim Johnston & Carolyn Scott of Ballyhay Books, Alan O'Loan, Paramount Ballymena United Supporters' Club, Paradise Ballymena United Supporters' Club, Lawrence Patterson, Ivan Russell, Shaun O'Neill & the Ballymena Guardian, Spirit of 89 Ballymena United Supporters' Club, Don Stirling, John Taggart.

Foreword

When Neil Coleman approached me to write a forward for his book on Ballymena United I was absolutely delighted to be asked to make a small contribution to the history of the club I have been associated with for many years.

As I was scanning through a draft of the book, one of the things that caught my eye was the names of some of the players, not the household names who everybody knows, but the ones that came and went without really making much of an impression.

I can remember, in the days before transfer windows, lifting players at the airport on a Saturday morning and taking them to wherever Ballymena United were playing on that particular day, running them back to the airport after the game and in some cases never seeing them again! Thankfully this nonsense was brought to a halt very quickly, and United, who have a history of signing very good English and Scottish players all through the years, who served the club well and contributed to to their success in various competitions, went back to bringing in players in a more conventional manner.

In recent times Ballymena United have started introducing a number of younger members into various working committees, who with their enthusiasm, willingness to work and total awareness of the power of social media are proving to be invaluable in fund raising activities, club administration and generating positive publicity for the Sky Blues.

Getting information out to the supporters and wider public hasn't always been high on United's things to do list! This is perfectly illustrated by an incident that happened at a time when the fans' regular source of information was the local press. Ronnie Burns had just joined United, but was unable to play on that particular day as his clearance hadn't arrived from the IFA. The regular PA announcer was ill and Jackie Fullerton who was attending the game was asked to broadcast the team to the spectators, Jackie, always willing to help his hometown club, a fact sometimes not fully appreciated by the clubs hierarchy, duly read out the list of players featuring that day. He then welcomed Ronnie to the Showgrounds and explained to a puzzled crowd the reason why he wasn't playing. Job well done, or so you might think. At the next committee meeting a member remarked that this idea of giving out information before a game worked very well and was worth pursuing, only for another member to state in no uncertain terms "sure the people don't want to listen to that oul nonsense".

The subject of publicity brings me unto the press and the invaluable service they provide in keeping club names to the forefront in media terms. I have heard them subjected to blistering criticism at times, but in my dealings with them on behalf of Ballymena United over many years, I have always found them helpful and amenable to positive suggestions. I think it's just a matter of you treat them right and they will reciprocate.

Talking of that reminds me another anecdote from the annals of the United Boardroom. The manager was bemoaning the fact that Ballymena United were, in his opinion, not getting enough publicity for their efforts. He proceeded to ask the then Chairman what he felt the club could do to generate more headlines, back came the laconic answer "win trophies!"

Finally just a few words about personal highs and lows at the club. The eighties were probably the best time for United and their fans, three Irish Cup wins and three European trips, the most fascinating of which for me was East Germany. Remember this was before the Wall came down, and we went on a bus tour of Berlin which took us through the notorious Checkpoint Charlie, something I found to be a chilling experience.

The lowest point for me was United being thrown out of the Irish Cup for a breach of Cup regulations in 2011, with a lucrative semi-final tie against Linfield at stake the club fought against the IFA ruling through various appeals but in the end we were unsuccessful and left to wonder what might have been.

Finally, I would like to congratulate Neil Coleman on his mammoth efforts in compiling this comprehensive record of Ballymena United, it was something that needed doing and I'm sure it will make for many an entertaining debate among supporters as they give their opinions of the Sky Blues best and worst teams throughout their history.

Don Stirling

Contents

Prologue

On 7th April 1928, the *Belfast Newsletter*, in reporting that Crusaders had decided to apply for admission to the Irish League, briefly mentioned that a meeting had been called "to consider the advisability of forming a team" in Ballymena[1]. A similar note was included in the *Ireland's Saturday Night* on the same day[2]. The meeting was subsequently confirmed and advertised in both Ballymena newspapers a week later[3] and was scheduled to take place in the Protestant Hall on 17th April.

A further reference to the meeting was included in the same edition of the *Ballymena Weekly Telegraph* in the regular 'Notes on the Game' section by 'Half-Back'. The columnist, after providing a particularly gloomy summary on the recent activities of the Summerfield club (the intermediate side, who were the leading team in the district at this point, had lost 4-2 and 4-1 over the Easter period with the players, management and facilities coming under criticism), stated that "Ballymena should be represented in the ranks of the Seniors in Association Football"[4]. This desire for top level football was symptomatic of the current civic pride throughout the town. A new Town Hall building was completed in 1928; at a cost of more than £30,000 along with three new weaving factories had also been built at "great expense"[5]. Money was evidently being readily spent in this spirit and the proposed new club looked set to follow suit, with Half-Back disclosing that those behind the venture had already researched the probable expenses involved in its formation and running.

Half-Back's next instalment provided a detailed report of the meeting, which was said to have drawn a large attendance. Mr. Albert McClelland took the chair and led with a confident assurance that the applications for senior football league

---

1   *Belfast Newsletter (hereafter BNL), 7th April 1928*
2   *Ireland's Saturday Night (hereafter ISN), 7th April 1928*
3   *Ballymena Observer (hereafter BO), 13th April 1928; Ballymena Weekly Telegraph (hereafter BWT), 13th April 1928*
4   *BWT, 13th April 1928*
5   *Belfast and Ulster Directory 1928, pg. 1514*

admission and use of the jumping enclosure and grandstand at the Showgrounds would be successful. Both of these statements were met with applause by the large gathering, McClelland asked if the formation of a senior club would be desirable and if so would the financial support necessary, for which a sum of £1,500 was quoted as being required, be forthcoming. The former was unsurprisingly almost unanimously agreed on by attendees and the general opinion regarding the latter was that the finance could indeed be raised. Interestingly, discussion then moved onto forming a company to include the sale of public shares, which would allow followers of the game to show their "practical sympathy". Whilst it was not a unique situation, it was certainly unusual for a new club to consider company status immediately. The motion was also agreed on though and before the meeting was concluded, an executive committee was appointed, its first task was to follow up with the Irish League and the County Antrim Agricultural Association on the aforementioned applications and to identify a list of potential shareholders[6]. The immediacy of the progress made was remarkable; it is worth remembering that this meeting was held a mere ten days after the first indication of a local senior club forming had appeared in the Belfast press!

This pace was maintained as the remaining actions from the inaugural meeting were dealt with soon after. The next editions of the Ballymena newspapers carried an advertisement for 4,000 ten-shilling shares in the new Ballymena Football and Athletic Club Limited Company[7]. The facilities at the Showgrounds were secured next with the Co. Antrim Agricultural Association offering a rent of £120 per annum. This very favourable rate could possibly be attributed to the fact that chief-promoter of the new club, Albert McClelland, was also a member of the Agricultural Association and having a foot in both camps would have undoubtedly helped the club's application. This also explains how he was so confident on the issue beforehand[8]. Finally, Ballymena were selected to replace Barn, who had failed to be re-elected, in the Irish League for the start of the 1928/29 season. They had faced competition from Belfast clubs Crusaders and Brantwood (whilst Derry's application was not considered as it had been received three days too late) but the selection went strongly in favour of Ballymena, as they received 32 votes compared to the four for Brantwood and one for Crusaders[9]. This strong endorsement from the Irish League committee have been seen as a

---

6   BWT, 21st April 1928
7   BO, 27th April 1928; BWT, 28th April 1928
8   BWT, 12th May 1928
9   BWT, 2nd June 1928

very encouraging sign, as the League had experienced a strong Belfast domination since its formation before the partition of Ireland.

These administrative accomplishments coincided with the club having raised just short of their desired £1,500 by mid-summer through the sale of almost 3,000 shares[10]. The annual returns for the company in the first year of its existence can be used to give some insight into who purchased these. It is strikingly apparent that the shareholdings were overwhelmingly made up by local men. There were only five female investors, making up approximately only 2% of the total, and of all the given addresses only one was outside Ballymena town and district. It is the consideration of why these individuals would consider investing in their new local club which provides the more interesting conclusions though. Whilst dividends were unlikely, as they were with most clubs at this time[11], the opportunity for indirect financial gain may have been a compelling motive. A prominent example of this is the fifteen shareholders, with an approximate 11% stake in the club between them, who listed occupations closely tied to the sale of alcohol. A further three men, who described themselves as a 'merchant' or 'clerk' could also be cautiously linked to this trade as a comparison of their names and addresses against the 1911 census suggests that they were in fact 'wine merchants' and a 'spirit store clerk'. These investors may well have hoped to benefit from thirsty supporters, particularly on match days by sharing their personal association to the club with their business. Whilst other theories of potential financial gain can be somewhat speculative, for example perhaps the two shoemakers may have hoped to supply football boots for the team. Historians[12] have stressed the importance of the 'drink interest' in football club investments and so we can fairly safely say that this was also the case with Ballymena. It is also worth noting though that the president of the town's 'Catch-My-Pal' organisation, a society for abstinence, also made a heavy investment. His own motive may well have been to divert business away from these opportune alcohol traders![13]

The annual returns also suggest that genuine enthusiasm for local sport may also have been a key motivation for some. Nine shareholders had acted, or would go on to act, as president of the Ballymena Bowling Club and two, James Cathcart and John Kyle Neave, actually played the game at international level[14]. Neave,

10   David Laverty & Neal Garnham, 'Football in inter-war Northern Ireland: Ballymena Football and Athletic Club Limited – religious and political exclusivity or civic inclusivity?' in The International Journal of the History of Sport, Vol 27, No. 13, September 2010, pg. 2216
11   Neal Garnham, Association Football and Society in Pre-partition Ireland, pg. 54
12   See Tony Mason, Association football and English society, 1863-1915 & Steven Tischler, Footballers and Businessmen: The Origins of Professional Soccer in England
13   Records of Ballymena Football and Athletic Club Ltd (PRONI VOM/40/2/478)
14   Ballymena Bowling Club: The First Hundred Years, pg. 12 & 36

who is listed as a 'gardener' in the annual returns, was also a groundsman for Ballymena Cricket Club and alongside Charles Forsythe had played in their 1925 County Antrim Trophy final team[15]. Interestingly, with regards to Ballymena Rugby Club, a Mr J. Owens suggested on 27th April 1928 that they should apply for admission to their respective senior League. Whilst he had no apparent personal link to the new football club, it seems likely that he had taken inspiration from the motion carried by the association rules club 10 days previously. William Weir, who was one of the aforementioned presidents of the bowling club, later served in the same capacity for the rugby club in 1934/35[16].

Through looking at the correlation of the shareholders against the memberships of other organisations, an intriguing religious situation is observed. It is worth clarifying at this point that the previously mentioned inaugural meeting which was held in a Protestant Hall should not be confused as an attempt to underline a Protestant identity (as had been the case with Linfield Football Club who held general meetings in the Sandy Row Orange Hall for this reason[17]). The location was being used for all "meetings of importance" at this time[18] as it was the most appropriate large venue until the opening of the new town hall. In fact, in spite of the setting, it is probable that that initial meeting would have had a number of Roman Catholics in attendance given their eventual representation in the club's shareholdings. Three priests, living in parochial houses in nearby villages Ahoghill, Portglenone and Cloughmills, purchased a combined 10 shares. As well as this, Patrick Murphy, who was the president of Ballymena Catholic Club and was later made a Knight Commander of the Order of St. Gregory (a papal knighthood) in 1947[19], bought 100 shares and took on directorship in the club. An identifiable Protestant presence was provided by an elder of Wellington Street Presbyterian Church, president of the North End Unionist Club, district treasurer of the Apprentice Boys of Derry[20] and secretaries of Loyal Orange Lodges 512 and 637[21] (Braidsvale Purple Star and Ballymarlow respectively)[22]. Later in 1928, at the opening of the new town hall, chairman of the local district council William Shaw (who would go on to serve as Ballymena's first mayor in 1932) observed that "nowhere is there more friendly co-operation than in the field of

15   George Glass, *Ballymena Cricket Club: The First 150 Years*, pgs. 15 & 17
16   George Burton (ed), *Ballymena Rugby Football Club, 1887-1987*, pg. 12
17   Garnham, *Association Football and Society in Pre-partition Ireland*, pg. 99
18   Eull Dunlop, *Ballymena Town Hall, 1928 and Other Aspects of the Civic History*, pg. 5
19   *Infocus, Official Newsletter of Ballymena Borough Council*, VI (Autumn 2009), pg. 9
20   *Belfast and Ulster Directory 1928*, pg. 1516
21   Grand Orange Lodge of Ireland, *County Antrim Grand Orange Lodge Reports, 1925-6*
22   *Records of Ballymena Football and Athletic Club Ltd* (PRONI VOM/40/2/478)

sport" referring to Ballymena's cross-community relations[23]. Indeed it seems that Ballymena Football and Athletic Club was a prime example of this and since Shaw held 50 shares in the club was adequately placed to make such a statement. This evidence goes against what has previously been argued by historians Alan Barnier and Paul Darby[24], who played down the non-playing involvement of Catholics in Northern Irish football. In this case it seems that a strong sense of local pride and a love of the game were much more important to those involved than their religious and political differences.

Remarkably the club had gone from ascertaining the probable support for a new club to preparing for their first game in the senior League in just over 4 months. The programme notes for the opening of the town hall, later in 1928, stated that "the inhabitants of Ballymena are at times slow to manifest any great spontaneous outburst of enthusiasm, unless the occasion merits it"[25]. Ultimately, the formation and establishment of Ballymena Football and Athletic Club had fitted that bill.

Senior football had finally, yet hurriedly, arrived in Ballymena.

David Laverty

---

23   Eull Dunlop, Ballymena Town Hall, 1928 and Other Aspects of the Civic History, pg. 19
24   See Alan Barnier and Paul Darby, 'Divided Sport in a Divided Society: Northern Ireland' in Divided Societies, pgs. 66-70
25   Eull Dunlop, Ballymena Town Hall, 1928 and Other Aspects of the Civic History, pg. 10

Chapter One

The Early Days (1928-1934)

 1928/1929

Advertisements were placed in the press for both professional and amateur players to assist Ballymena for the forthcoming season, with two key figures from local football circles brought in to assist the relentless recruitment drive in the summer of 1928. Former Cliftonville half-back James Cathcart was appointed to find suitable quality players and was assisted by Sam McDowell former secretary of Willowfield and Larne Olympic.

The club's first two signings revealed by the local press were to be pivotal members of the forthcoming success of this new team. Harryville native John 'Jock' McNinch, a tough tackling full-back, was signed from local intermediate side Summerfield whilst forward James 'Hoody' McCambridge had senior experience with Larne and had played in the Irish Cup final a few months before.

Early expectations were high with the *Ireland's Saturday Night* noting "If Ballymena do not do well in

JOHN M'NINCH,
Ballymena F.C.

TOPICAL TIMES

their first season, no fault can be laid at the doors of the officials". Team building continued in earnest with Sydney Webster - a junior international inside left from Dundela, James Mitchell – an exciting young forward fresh from a spell at Scottish side Heart of Midlothian and Gordon McDairmid an experienced defender joined from Free State League side Dundalk, having had Irish League experience with Bangor and Belfast Celtic. Completing the forward line was Jamie Shiels a spritely unknown forward signed from junior team Ballymoney Blues. Despite having no previous senior experience, he would go on to take the league by storm during the team's first season.

The Ballymena officials' biggest signal of intent during their recruitment drive were the signings of two Glasgow born brothers of Ulster parentage; Davy and John Reid. Davy had been a regular in the Everton team alongside the famous Dixie Dean, competing at the top end of the English First Division for seven years and making over 100 appearances in that time. He had spent the previous season on loan at Distillery who looked certain the secure his signature on a permanent basis, before being surprisingly unveiled as captain of the new Braid side. Older brother John, a fellow defender, had played a number of seasons in the English Third Division with fellow Merseyside club New Brighton and returned home to Ireland to join his sibling at the 'Light Blues'.

No less than two dozen players were registered ahead of the season opener. William Clarke - a reliable goalkeeper signed from Ards Rangers would eventually make his name as a winger for the club and John Morrow another local lad secured from Summerfield were a couple that would competitively represent the club during the season. Entrusted with the training of this new group of players was local gentleman William Bartholomew, a former British Army veteran who had fought with the 2nd Battalion Royal Irish Rifles in France during the First World War and a talented amateur boxer in his youth. The trainer's appointment by the committee would prove very popular amongst the playing staff.

Ballymena Football & Athletic Club's bow into senior Irish football was a prestigious affair as they welcomed reigning league champions Belfast Celtic to the Ballymena Showgrounds on Monday 20th August 1928 for the club's first competitive match. The introduction of senior football to the town drew a packed crowd but the home supporters were the ones that went away disappointed as they lost 3-0 to their more established opponents. The team lined up as follows: Clarke, McNinch, McDiarmid, J. Reid, D. Reid, McCambridge, Morrow,

Mitchell, Shiels, Woodrow, Webster. Despite the defeat the first foray into senior football only served to whet the appetite of the Ballymena public for more.

The team's first point and goals came only five days later as they visited neighbours Larne and secured a 2-2 draw. James McCambridge claimed the honour of scoring Ballymena's first senior goal playing against his former club. Davy Reid scored the other goal to win their first point of the league season. The games continued to come thick and fast for the Light Blues, a 3-3 home draw with rivals Coleraine was followed four days later with an early exit in the first round of the Gold Cup to Ards.

It was the same County Down side that would provide the opposition for the club's first victory on 8th September. United had strengthened their back line with the signing of former Irish international goalkeeper John Gough from struggling Queen's Island and came out 2-1 winners with goals from Shiels and McCambridge – two players who would feature regularly in Ballymena's 'goals for' column throughout their debut campaign.

Aided by winger Richard 'Dickie' Shaw from Irish Cup holders Willowfield and half-back Sydney Howard from Distillery – a remarkable twelve game unbeaten run continued until early December. The national press were suddenly beginning to take notice of the 'Ballymena Babes' with a stunning 4-2 win over Linfield at the Showgrounds and three weeks later a 7-3 trouncing of Queen's Island, which pushed Ballymena into the lofty realms of third position in the table at the half-way point of the league season.

Defeat to Belfast Celtic (who would finish the league campaign unbeaten) halted the unbeaten streak and paved the way for an inconsistent finish in the league. A surprising Christmas day defeat to struggling amateurs Cliftonville followed by a Boxing Day victory over Glentoran summed up the erratic second half of the season. The Light Blues were also defeated in the first round of the County Antrim Shield at home to eventual winners Linfield early in the New Year.

Further recruitments were brought in to strengthen the team as veteran Scottish international winger Joe Cassidy (a former Scottish League and Cup winner with Glasgow Celtic)

Joseph Cassidy

joined in February 1929 and made an instant impact with a goal in the 7-0 rout of Queen's Island. 'Trooper Joe' as he was affectionately known at Parkhead also won a military medal whilst serving the British Army during the First World War.

Despite ending the club's first league campaign on a sour note with a 6-0 defeat to Linfield at Windsor Park; Ballymena finished a highly respectable sixth in the table, emulating the same benchmark that the previous year's rookies Coleraine set – an achievement that few onlookers believed to be possible.

The Irish Cup was to bring unprecedented success to the town as winning the famous trophy at the first attempt was likely to even be beyond the wildest dreams of Chairman Albert McClelland. In the first round a replay was needed to overcome league rivals Glentoran, but the team surprised all by cantering all the way to the final having overcome Intermediate League side Broadway United (4-1) and Coleraine (3-0) in the quarter-final and semi-final respectively.

All roads led to Solitude, for the Irish Cup final against Belfast Celtic on Saturday 30th March, 1929 as Ballymena's first cup final team lined up as; Gough, McNinch, McDairmid, J. Reid, D. Reid, Howard, Clarke, Mitchell, Shiels, McCambridge, Cassidy. Watched by a paying gate of £1,018 who witnessed history as Ballymena triumphed 2-1 in a close encounter with the ever reliable Jamie Shiels and James McCambridge scoring the goals that brought the Irish Cup to Mid-Antrim.

A civic reception at Ballymena town hall followed, with McClelland being presented with a replica of the Irish Cup by the Irish Football Association to commemorate Ballymena winning the prestigious trophy in their first season in existence. The replica cup was returned to the Showgrounds many years later by members of the McClelland family and still currently resides in the board room of the Showgrounds after being used as the club's Player of the Year award for a time.

The season wasn't over for the Light Blues yet. Before the dust settled on the historic Irish Cup win, Ballymena were still in strong contention for the end of season City Cup. Despite winning nine of their first eleven games in the competition they still found themselves in second place going into the penultimate match at Windsor Park against leaders Linfield. The winner of the game would determine the destination of the City Cup. Unfortunately it was one game too far for the Braidmen who went down by three goals without reply, handing the trophy to the South Belfast Blues.

Ballymena pictured with the Irish Cup in May 1929 at the Ballymena Showgrounds
Back row: William Bartholomew (Trainer), John Reid, John McNinch, John Gough, Gordon McDairmid, Sydney Howard.
Front row: William Girvan, James Mitchell, David Reid, Jamie Shiels, James McCambridge, Joseph Cassidy.

Winning the Irish Cup secured two further prestigious fixtures as Scottish Cup winners Kilmarnock visited the Showgrounds on 29th April with the home side losing 1-0 - this was incidentally the first time a match programme had been produced by the club. The final match of the season was dubbed the 'Dublin Invitational Challenge' as Free State Cup winners Shamrock Rovers hosted the Braidmen in an exhibition game at Tolka Park. Goals from Joe Cassidy and Jamie Shiels sealed a 2-1 win for the Northern side.

Ballymena v Kilmarnock match programme: the first of such issued by the club. Thanks to Alan O'Loan

Shiels confirmed his place as one of the deadliest forwards in Ireland with 42 goals in only 37 games in his debut season in senior football while 'Hoody' McCambridge provided an impressive 32 goal return and earned a place in the Irish League team for a representative game against the League of Ireland in March.

⚽ *1929/1930* ⚽

Despite the rising stock value of Ballymena's playing assets, the Irish Cup winning team remained largely intact for the 1929/30 season. Only John Reid failed to agree terms with club officials and started the season with Bangor, while question marks remained over the future of his brother Davy whose disagreement with the club's directors rumbled on until the season was already underway. John Reid's replacement was veteran English defender Alf Bassnett who joined from Lincoln City and had won the English First Division with Burnley in 1921. James Kirkwood from Willowfield was the only other summer signing of note, but he failed to claim a regular spot in the team after the opening weeks.

Expectations had risen amongst the media and supporters and there was now curiosity as to whether Ballymena could push on from the success of their first senior season. The opening match of the new campaign produced a 2-2 draw with Portadown, with goals from Joe Cassidy and James McCambridge. It took five games for the Light Blues to secure their first win and by this stage they had already exited the Gold Cup at the first hurdle to Belfast Celtic. Eventually a 2-0 victory away to Ards was secured through an unlikely source – young winger Thomas Hanna scored both goals in only his fourth appearance for the club but surprisingly never appeared again in the team.

Following a resolution with the club's directors, commanding captain Davy Reid returned to the team alongside two Scottish wingers, Thomas Kilpatrick from Ayr United and Jamie Murphy from Kilmarnock. The team suddenly regained their form though as the autumn progressed with five wins from six in the league including a 2-1 win over pacesetters Glentoran at the Oval and two victories against Derry City, who had now been accepted into the Irish League in place of Queen's Island.

On Christmas Day the selection committee (charged with picking the team in the absence of a manger) handed a debut to new signing Johnny Dalrymple, a local of the town who won full International honours in 1922 and a host of domestic medals with Distillery. It was over the festive period that the club produced two of the best results of the season with 14 goals in two games. Ballymena secured a stunning 7-4 victory over future league champions Linfield with hat-tricks for McCambridge and Cassidy and one for Jamie Shiels, followed two days later by an emphatic 7-1 win over Cliftonville to sign off 1929 by moving into fourth place in the table.

Following on from the club's success the previous season, Ballymena progressed to the final of the Irish Cup after impressive wins over Derry City (4-1) and Belfast Celtic (3-2) in the opening two rounds of the competition. This set up a tense semi-final showdown with border club Newry Town at Solitude which Ballymena won 3-1 with goals from Cassidy, McCambridge and Murphy in front of a modest £219 gate which confirmed a second successive Irish Cup final appearance for the boys in light blue.

McCambridge's impressive form earned him a place in the Ireland senior team against Wales at Celtic Park on 1st Feburary 1930 – becoming the first player of the club to be capped at full international level. In front of a crowd of 25,000, his impressive performance in the resounding 7-0 win (in which Linfield's Joe Bambrick scored six of Ireland's goals!) allowed 'Hoody' to retain his place for the next British Home Nations international against Scotland three weeks later, which Ireland went on to lose 3-1 at Parkhead.

Shortly after the Scotland game, McCambridge secured a high-profile move to Everton for £1,750 after weeks of speculation. He played 71 times, scoring 49 goals during his time at the Braid and became the first player the club had

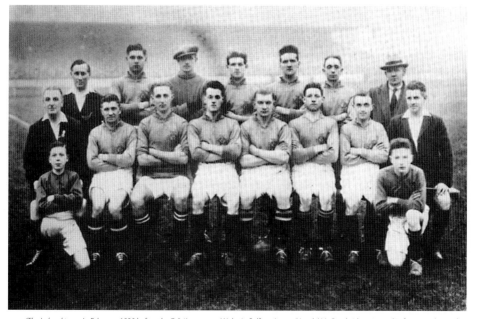

'The Ireland team in February 1930 before the 7-0 victory over Wales in Belfast. James 'Hoody' McCambridge pictured in front row (second player in from right side). Courtesy of Northern Ireland Football Greats

transferred to professional football on the mainland. As part of the transfer the club also negotiated an exhibition match against the Merseyside club in April at the Showgrounds which Ballymena won 2-1 thanks to goals from Jamie Shiels and Joe Cassidy against an understrength Everton line-up.

The loss of the talented inside forward seemed to destabilise the team ahead of their Irish Cup final against Linfield at Celtic Park. The in-form Bambrick was the player whom the Ballymena defence could not handle as the Irish League's leading goalscorer scored all four goals in the final as Linfield won 4-3 in front of over 20,000 spectators – a record Irish Cup final crowd with gate receipts of over £1,500. The '*Ireland's Saturday Night*' described the game as a 'scrappy affair' as Jamie Shiels scored twice and Davy Reid once for Ballymena, with the Light Blues unfortunately finishing the game with only ten men after Thomas Kilpatrick went off injured with a nasty head injury with the scores level at 3-3.

1930 Irish Cup final advertisement in the Ballymena Weekly Telegraph

Following the disappointment of the Irish Cup final defeat, the club's selection committee of Messrs Ernie Staunton, James Cathcart and William Leetch collectively resigned following a difference in opinion between directors and selectors in the first signs of trouble behind the scenes at the Showgrounds.

Ballymena's end-of-season City Cup campaign provided little excitement - a mediocre 13 game campaign reached its high point with a 3-0 victory over Belfast Celtic at home. Supporters did finish the season with something to cheer as Scottish side Kilmarnock returned on 30th April for another high-profile friendly at the Showgrounds. This time the home side won 3-1 with Murphy scoring twice with Gilmour getting the other. Ballymena also accepted the offer from League of Ireland champions Bohemians for an exhibition fixture at Daylmount Park, which the Dublin side won comfortably 5-2.

All was not well in the background at the club, as the directors submitted a request in May 1930 to go into voluntary liquidation at the end of only the club's second season in senior football. After two successful seasons the decision was a major shock to all involved in local football as a exiting future was envisaged for the club. The liquidation proposal was quickly overturned a week later after immediate consultation with key supporters of the club who refused to see the club die.

Jamie Shiels again finished as top goalscorer at the club with 30 goals taking his tally to 72 goals in two seasons but the diminutive leader of the forward line was overlooked by both international and inter-league selectors as James McCambridge, Joe Cassidy, David Reid and Jamie Murphy all appeared for the Irish League in representative games during the 1929/1930 season.

⚽ 1930/1931 ⚽

Putting the summer uncertainty behind them the club approached their third season with renewed optimism as the committee enlisted the experience of veteran Irish international defender Billy McCandless in July 1930. Previously an Irish transfer record moving from Linfield to Glasgow Rangers for £2,500, winning eight Scottish League titles and countless other medals at Ibrox and returned home to join the Light Blues as a player-coach. McCandless replaced the outgoing defensive stalwart Gordon McDairmid who moved to the Free State League with Dundalk after two successful seasons at the Showgrounds.

*New player-coach Billy McCandless
(courtesy of Northern Ireland Football Greats)*

Other movement included goalkeeper John Gough who left the club and Englishman Alf Bassnett who had not been retained, returning home to take up a position of player-manager of a Birmingham league team. Bassnett's replacement was local centre-half Robert Stewart from Glentoran whilst Richard Shaw also returned to the team for a second spell after spending the previous season with Willowfield.

The season started in inauspicious form with a 4-3 defeat at Solitude to Cliftonville, but three days later Ballymena produced a formidable display with a four goal victory over Distillery. Back to back seven goal wins in the first week of September against Newry Town (Gold Cup) and Portadown (League)

outlined the team's credentials as a free scoring outfit. Ballymena would go on to score six or more goals on seven different occasions throughout the season!

In November, Ballymena pinched prolific goalscorer James Gilmour from rivals Coleraine – the Scottish striker had scored 79 goals in the last two seasons for the Bannsiders. Gilmour marked his Ballymena debut in typical fashion, scoring the winning goal in a 2-1 win against Distillery at Grosvenor Park.

The Braidmen kept pace with the chasing pack in the Irish League championship race throughout the autumn, cementing their place in fourth position by losing only once in 13 games – that being against runaway league leaders and eventual champions Glentoran. League form from December onwards became increasingly erratic as defeat to Linfield on Boxing Day moved Ballymena down to fifth place – a position that would be the club's final position at the end of the league campaign but with their highest points tally to date.

John 'Jock' McNinch the Ireland international'

One of the positives of the 1930/1931 season was the form of home grown full back John McNinch, which was noted by the *Ballymena Observer* as "having improved immensely following the arrival of Billy McCandless". This merited selection for the full Ireland team in February for the British Championship game against Scotland in Belfast. The Irish team drew 0-0 and McNinch won various plaudits both locally and nationally for his performance which led to interest from top English clubs Liverpool and Preston North End, the latter made an offer for McNinch's services but Albert McClelland and his fellow directors were reluctant to lose such an integral player after experiencing the negative impact of losing McCambridge to Everton had on the team the previous season – so John stayed with the Light Blues.

Ballymena's reputation as cup specialists was reaffirmed with a third Irish Cup final in three seasons and Linfield again were the opponents as the Braidmen

Captain Billy McCandless leads his players out at the Showgrounds. Courtesy of Ballymena Observer

sought revenge with the encounter last season still fresh in the memory. Ballymena had defeated Cliftonville, Bangor (via a replay) and Derry City to progress to the showpiece final at the Oval. On 28th March 1931, the reported crowd of 20,211 at the Oval watched the Belfast Blues win the cup against Ballymena for a second year in succession. The scoreline this time was much more one sided – as Linfield won 3-0 against their provincial opponents. The game as a spectacle was badly affected by blustery conditions, however Linfield managed three second half goals from Hewitt, Houston and McCracken as Ballymena's punchless attack failed to reply after a promising first half display.

The cup final would be the last time Ballymena supporters would see Joe Cassidy in their colours as he returned home to Scotland with the greatest sympathies of both the club and its followers to be with his family following the untimely death of his young son. Cassidy's three years' service to the fledgling club had won many admirers in the local game and he would eventually be offered a contract at Morton – having bizarrely been tipped during the close season for the vacant manager's position of the Turkish national team.

Ballymena's efforts in the low-key City Cup ended with an eighth place finish assisted by four wins in a row to end the season on a positive note. In the other cup competitions Ballymena had bowed out of the Gold Cup at the quarter-final to Linfield and in the first round of the County Antrim Shield to Ards.

Other noteworthy moments of the 1930/31 season included the beginning of inside-forward Billy McCready's long association with the club in January 1931 when he started the final game of the Irish League season against Belfast Celtic after joining from Summerfield. Jamie Murphy also finished as the leading goalscorer with 36 goals during the season – which included 5 hat-tricks!

⚽ *1931/1932* ⚽

The summer of 1931 saw the biggest turnover in playing staff at the Showgrounds to date to enable significant reduction in the wages budget. The whole starting forward line from the previous campaign moved on with regular goalscorers Jamie Murphy and Jamie Shiels failing to agree terms. Both moving to Dublin to sign for Shelbourne and Dolphin respectively. James Gilmour was also freed by the club but was strangely not picked up until Christmas when he joined Ards.

Arguably the biggest blow to Ballymena was the loss of influential captain Davy Reid, who also joined the exodus to the Free State League becoming player manager of struggling Dublin based side Drumcondra.

In early July, Secretary Samuel Eagleston and Treasurer John Watt travelled to Glasgow in search of suitable replacements for the outgoing players and signed five Scots to help improve the Mid-Antrim side; Andrew Haddow a centre forward (from Dundee United), outside-left David Hodge (Morton), goalkeeper James King (Airdrieonians), outside-right Walter Cox (Falkirk) and forward Thomas Lamont (Alloa Athletic). On the eve of the season former Irish Cup winner James Mitchell also returned to the Showgrounds after a spell with Waterford United in addition to Stranraer forward Robert Stoddart.

The new-look Braid side – now littered with Scottish influence - failed to gel quickly on the pitch, losing four of their opening five league games. After a 2-0 defeat to Linfield at Windsor Park dropped to their lowest league position in four seasons, sitting in fourteenth position at the foot of the table come mid-September.

In September, Ballymena made a double signing from Coleraine with another Scot, defender Davy Flannigan and local forward

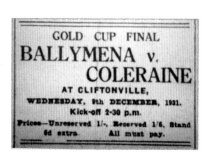

GOLD CUP FINAL

BALLYMENA v. COLERAINE

AT CLIFTONVILLE,
WEDNESDAY, 9th DECEMBER, 1931.
Kick-off 2·30 p.m.
Prices—Unreserved 1/-, Reserved 1/6, Stand
6d extra. All must pay.

1931 Gold Cup final advertisement in the Ballymena Observer

John Barr joining the club. The introduction of the two men had an instant impact for struggling Ballymena as they went on a seven game unbeaten streak and progressed to the final of the Gold Cup for the first time in style – beating Distillery and Ards in the opening two rounds. A stunning John Barr hat-trick against holders Linfield at Celtic Park secured a 3-0 win in the semi-final which maintained the club's fantastic record of appearing in a final in every season to date.

Action from the 1931 Gold Cup final between Ballymena and Coleraine. Courtesy of Ballymena Observer

The Gold Cup final on 9th December 1931 pitted the Braidmen against derby rivals Coleraine at Solitude in the competition's first all provincial final in front of an enthusiastic 10,000 crowd. It proved a disappointing showing for Ballymena, losing 3-0 to the Bannsiders (who played in unfamiliar amber and black hoops) for their first ever trophy in senior football.

Jock McNinch had established himself as Ireland's first choice full-back during 1931, as he won two more international caps to bring his total appearances to three and became the most capped player in the history of senior football in Ballymena. The first of the two games in September against Scotland which Ireland lost 3-1 at Ibrox stadium followed by a comprehensive win in early December against Wales at Windsor Park finished 4-0 to the home side. Jock would eventually lose his place in the team to Glasgow Celtic's Billy Cook.

On Boxing Day, the game between Ballymena and league leaders Linfield attracted the biggest attendance of the season. A crowd of 10,000 descended on the Showgrounds however the size of the crowd would prove unmanangable as

Linfield's Joe Bambrick leaps above Ballymena's McNinch and Davison at Windsor Park. Courtesy of Ballymena Observer

the game was abandoned 17 minutes into the second half for encroachment of the spectators onto the pitch. Without any pitchside boundary it was reported that supporters were so close to the pitch that throw ins were being taken beyond the line because players couldn't get near it! Unfortunately Ballymena were leading 1-0 at the time the game was abandoned, but in the replayed fixture in March, the Braidmen won 2-0.

For the first time in the club's short history, Ballymena failed to reach the Irish Cup final – losing out in a quarter-final replay to eventual cup winners Glentoran at the Oval. The club also exited the County Antrim Shield at the same stage losing to Belfast Celtic; it was a competition in which the club had failed to make any headway in the last four seasons.

Despite the numerous personnel changes and a poor start to the league season the team's form was impressive in the new year and following stunning high scoring wins over Belfast Celtic (6-0) and Glentoran (5-0) at the Showgrounds (in which John Barr scored hat-tricks in both games) - Ballymena credibly again finished in sixth position in the Irish League.

The City Cup campaign saw Ballymena finish joint fourth with Derry City in an encouraging end to the season, which included a 3-2 win over winners Glentoran at the Oval. The success story of the season was undoubtedly the goals of local boy John Barr who finished with 32 goals for Ballymena in all competitions.

The Annual General Meeting of shareholders negatively centred around the financial concern which was facing the club with falling attendances at games and a lack of an active supporters club, which saw the club post a loss of almost £600 for the season. Despite the proposal of a reduction in the playing budget last year – the wages being paid were higher than ever! Chairman McClelland called on the Ballymena public to get behind the team like they did during the first season of the club.

⚽ *1932/1933* ⚽

Ahead of the 1932/33 season Ballymena were boosted by the return of fans' favourite Jamie Shiels after just one term in the League of Ireland with Dolphin, where he had finished as the Dublin club's top goalscorer. In addition to Shiels' return, amateur international James McClelland joined from Cliftonville alongside Scottish players - Daniel Patterson (Dolphin), James McPherson (Derry City) and William Paterson (Morton).

This new batch of Scottish players would be direct replacements for their highly paid yet underperforming fellow countrymen who were all subsequently released by the club in May 1932 (including Robert Stoddart and Andrew Haddow

Jamie Shiels. Courtesy of Ireland's Saturday Night

who had positively contributed 32 goals between them). The only survivor of the cull was Glaswegian goalkeeper James King who accepted a reduction in wages and remained as the club's trusted number one between the sticks.

There was a first for the club on the opening day of the season, as the 5-3 victory over Newry Town was the first time in five attempts that the Light Blues won their opening league game. Defeat to Glentoran four days later would typify the on-going struggle produce consistent results throughout the season. Looking to strengthen the attacking options there were two further new signings in Patrick Lee – a former team-mate of Shiels at Dolphin and Bangor's Alistair McElfatrick during the Autumn.

The Gold Cup semi-final replay against Linfield on 16th November coincided with the official opening of the new Parliament Buildings at the Stormont Estate by the Prince of Wales (later King Edward VII) and a public holiday in Belfast and most provincial towns including Ballymena. Following the agreement between the two clubs, the game was moved from Grosvenor Park to Windsor Park to accommodate the bumper holiday crowd, in excess of 22,000, that witnessed Linfield prevail over the Light Blues to reach the final, winning 2-1.

Arguably Ballymena's best performance of the season came the week before Christmas when struggling Ards were the unfortunate recipients of an 8-2 annihilation at the Showgrounds. Alistair McElfatrick scored five of the Braidmen's goals with Patrick Lee scoring a brace and Danny Patterson completing the rout. Patterson would eventually ask for his release before the season was even finished as he was unable to cope with the abuse from the terraces.

In January, the special affiliation that the Braidmen had built up with the Irish Cup competition was tainted with a 4-2 defeat to struggling Cliftonville in the first round. This was the first time the club had been eliminated at the first hurdle in their short history but even more galling for supporters who watched the team go four goals down before half-time at the Showgrounds. Quarter-final defeat to Ards in the County Antrim Shield was also to follow, as the season would end with an empty trophy cabinet at Warden Street.

Ballymena's inconsistent form meant the club's lowest league placing of eighth position. The team carried their poor form into the City Cup campaign which was also the worst to date. Despite a morale boosting seven goal win against Cliftonville other results proved disappointing and a tenth place finish was the best United could muster. In the final game of the competition (and also the season) the 4-1 defeat to Belfast Celtic sealed the City Cup for the west Belfast men.

At the end of the season, 39-year-old team captain Billy McCandless informed the directors that he would be retiring from football. With the best wishes of all involved at Ballymena he returned to Scotland to become manager of Scottish First Division side Dundee, where he spent five seasons at Dens Park. Hopes were briefly raised by the local press who prematurely announced the return of Hoody McCambridge as captain on loan from Cardiff City. The story stirred locals into a frenzy that their favourite Ireland international was returning to the Braid only for Bristol Rovers to scupper the deal at the final hour by making a permanent move for the forward in May 1933.

Ballymena team picture from the start of the 1933/34 season – the club's final year in senior football

⚽ *1933/1934* ⚽

Keen to improve on the club's poor showing during the past season the committee secured an impressive coup in luring brothers, Jackie and Stanley Mahood to the Showgrounds in July 1933. Left-winger Jackie, a four-time Irish League champion with Belfast Celtic and eight capped Ireland international, had failed to agree terms with Celtic despite the initial expectation that his signature for another year at Celtic Park would be a formality. He was reunited with his less decorated older brother Stanley an inside left who had been playing for Derry City, after leaving Belfast Celtic a few years before.

Jackie Mahood. Courtesy of Northern Ireland Football Greats

Irish international centre-half Gerry Morgan, formerly of Linfield and Nottingham Forest, was an adequate replacement for

McCandless as team captain when he arrived from Cork City in July. There was also a welcome return for defender Gordon McDairmid from Dundalk, still

revered for his performances during first two seasons of the Ballymena club. Other signings included Jock Wallace and John Williamson.

The now customary summer turnover of players meant prolific John Barr was allowed to leave along with virtually the entire forward line of McElfatrick, McClelland, McPherson and Lee. Defender William Paterson moved to reigning Irish League champions Belfast Celtic. A slow but steady start to the 1933/1934 Irish League campaign was boosted when centre-forward Frank Lucas joined from Glentoran in September and scored the goals that fired the team up the Irish League table during the first half of the season, scoring twice on his debut in the 4-2 win against Coleraine.

Frank Lucas. Courtesy of Ireland's Saturday Night

Jackie Mahood became only the third player to win a full international cap whilst at the club in mid-September, winning his ninth (and final) cap appearing on the wing against Scotland at Parkhead in Ireland's 2-1 win. Only five weeks later an impressive 2-1 home victory over his former club Belfast Celtic was marred when he suffered horrific leg break only 11 games into his season – which would permanently end the winger's career at the age of 35.

Results in the league did not wane as they continued their purple patch of form throughout the Autumn and into December. Ballymena went undefeated in ten consecutive games to lift the Sky Blues into second place in the table following a resounding 7-0 win at home to Newry Town in which Frank Lucas bagged five of the goals. The turning point of the campaign came in December when the streak came to end with a 4-2 defeat to leaders Linfield at home and in-form Frank Lucas became embroiled in an irreconcilable dispute with the club that resulted in his transfer back to Glentoran in January, Lucas had remarkably scored 17 goals in 18 games in his short time at the club and proved to be a major loss during the season half of the season.

Ballymena's Irish Cup trail lasted until the quarter-finals; following a comfortable 3-1 victory over Glenavon in the opening round but exited the competition with a disappointing 4-1 defeat away to Belfast Celtic. The form throughout 1934 had been poor, with only the goals of Shiels and talented teenage winger Charlie

McIlroy giving fans some excitement as Ballymena slipped from second to fifth by the season's end with only two wins from the final eight league fixtures.

Thumped 6-1 in the Shield by Linfield and already half-way through a mediocre City Cup campaign - few spectators in attendance at Clandeboye Park on 7th April, 1934 for the seemingly low key City Cup game between Ballymena and Bangor would be aware of the significance of this fixture in the history of Irish League and senior football in Ballymena.

Seven days after the Bangor game the *Ireland's Saturday Night* broke the shock news that the club had been suspended by the Irish Football Association. The story went back to a league committee meeting in January 1934 when Ballymena chairman Albert McClelland made a throwaway comment to his peers after the meeting that "something has to be done regarding payments to amateur players". These comments were reported to the IFA council by Irish League President and Linfield representative John Ferguson who

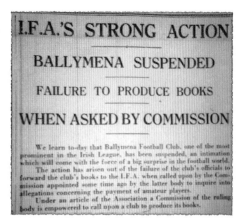

I.F.A.'S STRONG ACTION

BALLYMENA SUSPENDED

FAILURE TO PRODUCE BOOKS

WHEN ASKED BY COMMISSION

We learn to-day that Ballymena Football Club, one of the most prominent in the Irish League, has been suspended, an intimation which will come with the force of a big surprise in the football world.

The action has arisen out of the failure of the club's officials to forward the club's books to the I.F.A. when called upon by the Commission appointed some time ago by the latter body to inquire into allegations concerning the payment of amateur players.

Under an article of the Association a Commission of the ruling body is empowered to call upon a club to produce its books.

News breaks of the club's suspension first in the Ireland's Saturday Night on 14th April 1934

submitted the evidence to an IFA commission currently investigating the state of the game. The commission requested an explanation from McClelland for his comments in a meeting the following month. Although the Chairman declined to comment Ferguson alongside fellow Linfield colleagues William Tate and Fred McKee gave evidence which implicated not only McClelland but also Ballymena's secretary, Samuel Eagleson. The latter had allegedly admitted to the payment of amateur players at the club and subsequently the Irish FA requested to inspect the club's books.

Ballymena's remaining three City Cup games against Cliftonville, Belfast Celtic and Glentoran were all postponed and never played as the dispute rumbled on throughout April and May. There was now a stand-off between the IFA and the football club. The lack of progress caused great anxiety amongst the Ballymena townsfolk, many condemning the drastic approach taken by the governing body who refused to negotiate with the Ballymena directors. Eagleson noted that he and the club's directors had taken this action "with our eyes open" but shock reports suddenly began to surface that the club would be wound up. Belfast Celtic's secretary Bob Barr had stated "It would be a tragedy to lose a club with the standing of Ballymena".

By the end of May 1934 with the suspension still in force the Irish League took ownership of the registrations of all the club's professional players (James King, David Flannigan, Stanley Mahood, Jack Mahood, Gordon McDiarmid, John McNinch, James Shiels, Robert Stewart and John Williamson) as the club directors were given a final deadline of 9th June to submit the books or face a permanent suspension. The club officials didn't budge and the suspension was duly imposed on Ballymena Football & Athletic Club were subsequently out of football. The club was eventually voluntarily wound up two years later and shareholders received their 'first and only dividend' of 2s and 1d in the summer of 1936.

Out of the shadows there was some light for the football public of Ballymena as proposals for a new club to carry on the town's legacy in senior Irish football were already underway, but it was a disappointing and undignified end to the original Ballymena club after only six short years.

Chapter Two

A new United era cut short (1934-1940)

⚽ 1934/1935 ⚽

Rumours of a new club forming had been circulating since the end of May 1934, this was seen as to the only viable option with the future of Ballymena FC hanging in the balance and no visible signs of resolution.

Anxious to preserve senior football in the town Simon McCrory, William McNeice and T. Moore came together to submit an application for a new Ballymena club for entry into the Irish League at the League's Annual General Meeting on 20th June. The application centered on the six years' experience the applicants had in an advisory capacity to the original club, as well as the guaranteed backing of their shareholders and supporters along with an agreement with the County Antrim Agricultural Association for lease of the Showgrounds.

Crusaders and the new Ballymena club both applied for the vacant league space. There had been expectations that League of

PUBLIC NOTICES.

BALLYMENA UNITED F.C.

A MEETING

in connection with the above will be held

IN THE TOWN HALL
On MONDAY, 25th inst.
At 8 p.m.

ALL INTERESTED AND WISHING TO BECOME MEMBERS SHOULD ATTEND.

Notice of the public meeting for the new Ballymena United FC placed in the local newspapers

Ireland club Shelbourne would also submit an application as they attempted to break away to re-join the Irish League which they had previously been members of until 1921. However, despite much speculation the application was not forthcoming. Following a vote of member clubs, the new club was unanimously accepted into the League for the 1934/35 season.

The late journalist Dr. Malcolm Brodie wrote in a *Ballymena Observer* feature years later that on the night of the vote the Irish League Management Committee were not keen to reinstate the new Ballymena club under the same name as the suspended one. Whilst in the in the waiting room Tom Douglas, secretary of Cliftonville, suggested to McCrory and McNeice that they add the suffix of 'United' to the application as a suitable new name – and Ballymena United Football Club was born! Douglas, one of the sponsors of the new application, hailed from the Braid and had got the idea having previously played for the defunct junior team of the same name. It is safe to assume that the quick thinking of the Cliftonville secretary was crucial to the continuation of senior football in the town.

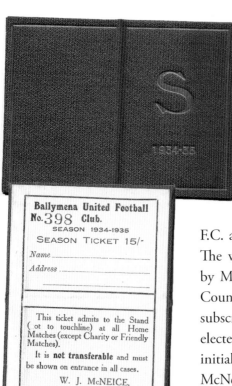

One of the first ever Ballymena United season tickets

A public meeting was advertised to invite potential members to the first meeting of Ballymena United F.C. at the Town Hall on Monday 25th June. The well attended meeting was presided over by Mr. David Henry, chairman of the Urban Council in which over £1,000 in membership subscriptions was pledged to the new club. Also elected into office were the key men behind the initial application with McCrory as Chairman, McNeice as Secretary and Mr. H. Shanks was appointed as treasurer. Members appointed a sub-committee consisting of McCrory, McNeice, Ernie Staunton, William Moore, John Gough (goalkeeper of the 1929 team) to secure players. Of the 22 members who made up the general football club committee, 15 had been members in the old club. Along with the same ground, equipment and even playing kit (graciously donated by Albert McClelland) the new club was identical to the old one with the only difference being the omission of McClelland himself and Samuel Eagleson who were indefinitely suspended from having any involvement in Irish Football.

Crucially for Ballymena United, the fans of the old club unanimously pledged their allegiance to the new club as a continuation of their previous affiliation. There was no difference in their eyes and is ultimately to this day one of the main factors that allow Ballymena United (as we now know it) to preserve the short yet rich history of the old Ballymena senior club as part of the full history of the club.

The Irish League gave Ballymena United officials a week's exclusivity to engage with all Ballymena FC's registered professionals. However with many of the players sceptical of United's chances for the new season, only four players were retained; James King, John Williamson, Jock Wallace and John McNinch. Edward McCormack and Charlie McIlroy joined the two prominent Belfast Clubs (Linfield and Celtic) before the club's situation was fully resolved. Jamie Shiels also joined Belfast Celtic, Robert Stewart went to Ards, Jamie Surgenor moved to Coleraine and Gordon McDiarmid joined Glentoran – now managed by former captain Davy Reid.

One of the first requests of the members was that a player-manager was appointed to lead the team. The new Ballymena United committee selected former Ireland international half-back Joe Miller from a group of 15 applicants. Born in Coleraine, Joe played for Middlesbrough, Hibernian and joined the club from Third Division side Bournemouth & Boscombe. Having to recruit a new batch of suitable players the summer saw a new influx of faces - Scottish junior international full-back Steve Mitchell from Coleraine, Eddie Mitchell

Eddie Mitchell

The first ever new look Ballymena United team in August 1934 before the 3-1 win against Coleraine at the Ballymena Showgrounds.
Back row: Jock Williamson, John McNinch, James King, Robert Campbell, William Pratt.
Front row: Eddie Mitchell, Steve Mitchell, John McGowan, Joe Miller, George Conlin, James Moir.

(Glentoran), John Agnew (Belfast Celtic) and Robert Wilkinson (Dundela). In keeping with the precedent set by the old club – an influx of Scottish players would make up the new look Light Blues - James Moir (Cowdenbeath), John McGowan (ex-Queen of the South & Portsmouth), George Conlin (Hamilton Academicals), Robert Campbell and William Pratt (both Third Lanark) would agree terms with the Braidmen.

The first game of the new Ballymena United club was played against Glentoran on 18th August, 1934 in front of a gate totalling £173 at the Oval. United came from behind to draw 1-1 through Robert Campbell's second half equaliser. The team for Ballymena United's first fixture included no less than seven Scottish players and lined up; King, McNinch, S. Mitchell, Williamson, Pratt, Miller, E. Mitchell, Campbell, McGowan, Conlin and Moir.

Four days later the team secured their first win with a 3-1 victory over derby rivals Coleraine with two goals from Eddie Mitchell and one from John Williamson. However it was to be a tough induction period for the club as a run of only one win from eight games throughout the Autumn left United lingering deep in the bottom half of the Irish League table with goalscoring being the main concern for player-manager Miller on the pitch.

In December a chance conversation between leading supporter Bob Reid and a fellow pigeon fancier from Lancashire recommended two brothers from Accrington Stanley who would come into the team and have an instant impact on a struggling season. Centre forward Richard Hargreaves scored on his debut against Glenavon and didn't stop scoring for the rest of the season. His brother Edgar played on the wing and impressed many with some industrious displays.

The biggest success of the season came in a competition which had provided such great memories for the old club as United reached the semi-finals of the Irish Cup in their first season. The newest club in the competition had ironically beaten two of the oldest in Cliftonville and Distillery in the opening rounds but failed to overcome Glentoran at Solitude, as Ballymena United lost 3-0 to the East Belfast side (who would go onto win the competition the following month). The team would also bow out at the semi-final stage in the County Antrim Shield as Miller's men put up an equally fruitless display against Linfield, losing 4-0 at Grosvenor Park.

Despite new signings Adam Buckley from Ballyclare Comrades and ex-England International Vincent Matthews from Shamrock Rovers, the Light Blues played out the end of season City Cup competition to minimal excitement. Home gates of £14 (Ards) and £24 (Glenavon) barely would have covered the expenses, but produced more encouraging results in comparison to the league campaign including four wins from the final five games of the series made up for a poor start typified by a heavy 7-1 defeat to cup winners Derry City - to finish ninth in the final standings.

Vincent Matthews

General feeling at the first Annual General Meeting was that members were pleased with the team's performance during the season given the circumstances faced by the directors and players. There was also a change of Chairman as the well-respected D. B. Elliott took up office after Simon McCrory confirmed that he did not wish to stand for re-election. It was revealed at the meeting that amidst financial pressures the players had accepted a pay-cut during the season but more positively regular fundraising efforts from the club's loyal supporters left the club with a deficit of only £10 after the first year in business.

Despite the satisfaction of the season past, the Chairman and Directors decided against renewing the contract of the player-manager. The club's first manager had failed to last a full year in the job; unfortunately this would be an early indication to followers as to the lifespan of a Ballymena United manager at the Showgrounds! All but three of the professionals would be released by the club - including the English Hargreaves brothers (Richard had finished top scorer with 24 goals) along with the remaining Scottish imports.

⚽ *1935/1936* ⚽

The summer of 1935 saw another large recruitment drive at the Showgrounds for United's second season. The marquee signing was English defender Fred Phoenix from top French top club Racing Club de Paris, who had just finished third in Ligue 1. With his considerable experience in both British and Continental

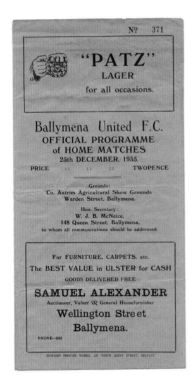

One of 1935/36 matchday programmes issued by the club

football, Phoenix was the natural choice as club captain, filling the void left by Joe Miller with a selection committee formed to take charge of team affairs.

Veteran Ballymena forward Johnny Dalrymple was appointed to the dual-role player-groundsman, after spending the last few seasons with local Intermediate side Summerfield. Elsewhere, Irish amateur international Alex Connell was astutely recruited from Glenavon, as was local teenager Albert Barr from Cliftonville and inside-forward William Jones from Shrewsbury Town. Regulars such as Robert Blair, John McNinch, Steve Mitchell, Adam Buckley and John Wallace made up the mainstay of the team throughout the season. There was also a constant revolving door of unknown amateurs appearing in the team with many lasting no more than a handful of games. Selectors used no less than 40 different players of which 27 were debutants during the 1935/36 season.

Team line-ups from Ballymena United v Linfield in December 1935

The season started with defeat to Belfast Celtic quickly followed by a heavy 5-1 loss to Newry Town as the Braidmen struggled for any early season consistency. A club record 8-1 defeat away to Portadown raised concerns over the capabilities of the team but they did bounce back with three straight league wins against Cliftonville, Ards and Coleraine to move up to eighth in the Irish League.

Ballymena United reached the semi-final of the early season Gold Cup following victories over Cliftonville (4-2) and Glentoran (3-2) in the first two rounds but came unstuck in the last four at Solitude when Distillery came from behind to beat the Light Blues 2-1. This would unfortunately be one of the few high profile games the team would be involved in throughout an otherwise miserable season.

In early 1936 the club exited both the Irish Cup and the County Antrim Shield at the first round stage with little fight; losing 3-1 to Portadown in the Cup in January and then a month later a 4-1 defeat away to Distillery in the Shield. Captain Pheonix's impact was limited and he left the club before Christmas - as from the Gold Cup semi-final in November onwards United went on an unenviable run of 15 games without a win (11 draws and 4 defeats) that lasted until February. Victory finally came in the final league game against Larne, but it was only enough to confirm an eleventh place finish which was the lowest league placing for the club or its predecessor.

Final 1935/36 Irish League table in the Ireland Saturday Night in February 1936

The City Cup eventually brought the season to a welcome close as the twelfth place finish similarly marked the lowest ever finish in the competition. Bizarrely, one rare positive in the City Cup came in late March when Linfield were soundly beaten 3-0 at the Showgrounds with goals from impressive local winger Johnny Mitchell and two for James Billingsley (signed in January from Cliftonville).

Following eight consecutive years of service to senior football in Ballymena, International full-back Jock McNinch became the first player to be granted a benefit (testimonial) by the club. The game against Linfield at the Showgrounds saw the two sides equally split eight goals, but unfortunately this was the last time supporters would see the McNinch in Ballymena colours. Following a record 316 appearances and 15 goals for both Ballymena FC and Ballymena United combined, Jock made the move west to Sligo Rovers. His stay in the League of Ireland lasted only a few months before he returned to the Irish League with neighbours Larne and after retiring from playing he would go on to become a referee and a linesman in senior football.

⚽ 1936/1937 ⚽

Looking to improve on a dismal season past, but still without a manager the club brought in Scottish forward Daniel McAllister from Huddersfield Town and Bangor winger William R. Moore. The most important of the close season signings was English defender Joseph Smallman – the Barnsley native proved to be an adequate replacement for McNinch at full-back.

Jimmy Surgenor – a reliable local player who had drifted between Summerfield and senior football for years was appointed player-manager of Sligo Rovers and quickly built his team around talented Braidmen. – Goalkeeper Robert Blair and Billy Miller transferred to the League of Ireland alongside established locals such as Pat O'Kane, Robert Gourley and Jock McNinch. Sligo's Ballymena contingent would win the Free State League for the first time in the club's history, while United continued to struggle closer to home in the Irish League.

True to form, Ballymena United lost their opening fixture to Newry Town with Daniel McAllister's goal proving to be only a consolation in the 3-1 home defeat. Local bragging rights were gained through a 1-0 win against Coleraine but that positivity would be fleeting as it would be the first of only two wins from the first 17 competitive fixtures. Defeat to Portadown on 24th October left the Light Blues propping up the table in last place and the team would not leave this position for the remaining 14 games of the Irish League season, reflecting how poor the 1936/37 season was for the team. Thankfully Ballymena United would not finish as many places down the league structure for a further 65 years!

Eager to solve the chronic goalscoring problem the committee coaxed legendary Glentoran forward Fred Roberts (who had once scored 96 goals for the Glens during 1930/31 season) to come out of retirement in December but his return only lasted for two games over Christmas, scoring one goal. Linfield Swifts' young forward James McDowell came into the side and performed admirably in the new year in a struggling team.

Fred Roberts

In the midst of eight consecutive league defeats throughout the winter, Ballymena United surprisingly hammered Ards in the Irish Cup first round in January winning 5-1 with a hat-trick for Coleraine based forward Daniel Fisher. Despite the apathy surrounding the team the cup run produced another shock victory. The 1-0 win over title-challenging Derry City at the Showgrounds in the quarter-finals set up a last four tie with Belfast Celtic. The West Belfast club were the dominant force in Irish League football at the time and the semi-final at Distillery's Grosvenor Park pitted top of the league against bottom but Ballymena forced a replay with a 1-1 draw thanks to William Moore. The Braidmen ran out of luck two days later though losing the second game by three clear goals without reply.

Form in the early stages of the City Cup had been excellent before the Irish Cup semi-final and the team looked like banishing the memories of the nightmare Irish League campaign. However the cup replay defeat spelt the end of United's season in more ways than one as the players were criticised for slacking off in the final weeks of the season, losing six of the final seven games in the competition to eventually finish eighth in the final table. A hugely forgettable and trophyless season was compounded with a 5-1 County Shield defeat to Glentoran in the first round.

⚽ *1937/1938* ⚽

With the finances as tight as ever the committee could make only make limited changes to the playing squad during the summer of 1937. Two local half-backs returned to mid-Antrim from the League of Ireland to join Ballymena United with John McCartney joining from Shelbourne and Pat O'Kane from Sligo Rovers arriving at the Showgrounds.

Unfortunately the poor results continued from where the previous season had disastrously left off as a miserable 9-1 defeat away to Derry City in the second game would surpass the unwanted record as the club's heaviest ever defeat. In fact the first eight games of the 1937/38 season failed to produce a single win which included defeat in the first round of the club's 'bogey' competition, the Gold Cup, going down 3-0 to Belfast Celtic.

Needing to halt the club's alarmingly poor start to the season, the club committee promoted full-back Steve Mitchell to the role of player-manager in late September.

Steve Mitchell. Courtesy of Coleraine FC

The well respected Scottish defender was now in his fourth season at the Showgrounds and his appointment instantly transformed the fortunes of the Light Blues. Mitchell started his tenure at his former club Coleraine on 25th September with a stunning 6-2 victory at the Ballymena Showgrounds (John Wallace scored a hat-trick with Dick Olphert hitting a further two goals and Jamie Surgenor rounding off the scoring).

The first of Mitchell's recruits was a fellow Scot by the name of Robert 'Bob' Sclater, a talented centre forward signed from Shelbourne and had previously played for Hibernian. Sclater was complimented by the acquisition of Ballymena born winger Robert Gourley, who joined the club following a short spell with Blackburn Rovers having previously played for Portadown and Sligo. The instant change in fortunes of the team was nothing short of remarkable.

Ballymena United followed up the Coleraine win with a merited draw at Windsor Park against Linfield the following week before going on a stunning run of form which produced 10 wins from 12 in the remainder of 1937, chalking up impressive wins against title challengers Glentoran and Derry City. The notoriously difficult Christmas period provided some of the most exciting football ever seen at the Showgrounds starting with a 7-2 win over Glenavon on Christmas day, and followed by wins against rivals Coleraine (6-3) and eventual champions Belfast Celtic (1-0).

Mitchell had recruited Broughshane goalkeeper Matt Redmond from Summerfield and only one more defeat followed in the final six remaining league fixtures. United, having climbed the league each week, finished fifth in February only eight points off Belfast Celtic in first place. Surely had Mitchell been appointed earlier in the season the club could have gone on to win their first Irish League Championship as Bob Sclater had already scored 32 goals in 18 league games and had quickly become the most feared forward in Ireland.

Expectations were high for the in-form Ballymena team going into the Irish Cup and a first round victory over Linfield in front of a phenomenal crowd at the Showgrounds only added to the excitement about the current team's potential. A record gate of £236 watched on as goals from Sclater, Moore and Gourley sealed a 3-2 win. The luck of the draw wasn't in United's favour as cup holders Belfast Celtic were the quarter-final opponents and it took two replays to force a result after two scoreless draws. The titanic battle between the two sides ended with a 1-0 victory for the Celts in the third game of the series – as the West Belfast team marched on to complete a league and Irish Cup double.

Surprisingly the City Cup produced a disappointing return for Ballymena United, who began the competition as favourites. The team lost their way in March with consecutive defeats to Bangor, Glenavon and Distillery killing off any chance of silverware and a seventh place finish was United's modest reward. Improved form in the County Antrim Shield saw the club reach the final of the competition for the first time, but the team couldn't recreate their Irish Cup heroics against Linfield, losing 3-2 at Grosvenor Park on 27th April.

Despite the disappointment, it was to be considered a good season for the Braidmen - the best since the formation of the new club. The goals of Bob Sclater were invaluable as he finished the 1937/38 season with 50 goals in all competitions (which included seven hat-tricks!). Sclater's return set a club record for goals in a single season that has never been beaten. The Scot's form also merited inclusion in the Irish League side alongside his manager for the game against the League of Ireland in March.

1938/1939

In his first full season as player-manager Steve Mitchell made few changes to a team widely expected to challenge for honours during the 1938/39 season. Two inside forwards were brought in to boost the attack, namely Glentoran's Richard Horner and Derry City's John Grant. The two summer signings were direct replacements for Patrick O'Kane and Robert Gourley who failed to agree terms with the club at the end of the previous campaign.

Straight out of the traps in August, Ballymena took full points from the first three games against Derry, Newry and Cliftonville scoring 13 goals to become early leaders in the Irish League championship. A surprise 7-0 defeat by Glenavon at Mourneview Park proved to be only a minor blip as the Braidmen went six games unbeaten through September to return to the top of the table following impressive victories over both Glentoran and Linfield. The club strengthened their panel during the autumn, signing winger John Pierson from Arsenal, defender Blair Vincent from Coleraine and Englishman William Dowall from Red Star Paris Olympique - however the latter only lasted a month before returning to professional football with Notts County.

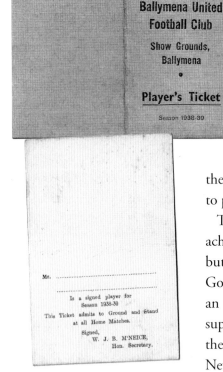

Ballymena United Football Club

Show Grounds, Ballymena

•

Player's Ticket

Season 1938-39

Mr. ....

....
Is a signed player for
Season 1938-39
This Ticket admits to Ground and Stand
at all Home Matches.
Signed,
W. J. B. M'NEICE,
Hon. Secretary.

1938/1939 Player issue season ticket

The Glenavon defeat aside, Ballymena United achieved an almost flawless start to the season but a heavy 9-3 defeat to Belfast Celtic in the Gold Cup first round marked the beginning of an unexpected period of inconsistency which supporters hadn't become accustomed to over the past 12 months. Losses to Portadown and Newry and another trouncing from Belfast Celtic (8-0) at home – as United slipped to third in the table.

In November the club was dealt a further blow when player-manager Mitchell was abruptly forced out of action with appendicitis and the club committee immediately took up management of the team with the assistance of senior players John McCartney and Bob Sclater. The popular Scottish defender sadly wouldn't recover from his illness and never returned to the field in a light blue shirt, but was an active supporter from the side-lines for the next two seasons.

Despite the loss of their leader, the team rallied and returned to form throughout December and the hectic Christmas period with Sclater finding his scoring boots again – notching up a superb double hat-trick in the 6-2 win against Ards that moved the Sky Blues back into second spot. The 4-0 win against Coleraine on Boxing Day was followed by further wins against Linfield and Glentoran to leave the North Antrim men breathing down the necks of runaway leaders Belfast Celtic, with three games remaining at the start of January 1939.

The outside chance in-form Ballymena United had of bringing a first Irish League title to the town were cruelly dismantled with a shock 7-2 defeat at Shamrock Park against Portadown which handed Belfast Celtic the title with two games to spare. There was some end of season cheer as United went to Celtic Park on the final day of league fixtures in late January with goals from Dick Olphert and Sclater securing the 2-1 win needed to confirm the runners-up spot in the table – the highest ever finish by a Ballymena side in the Gibson Cup chase.

John Grant's Irish League runners-up medal from the 1938/39 season.

Having reached three Irish Cup finals in the first three seasons of the old club – the expectant Ballymena public were not disappointed with the reformed club's run in the competition this season. Bob Sclater's solitary second half goal was enough to overcome Glentoran at the Showgrounds in the first round and the same player scored twice in a titanic quarter-final battle with cup holders Belfast Celtic which ended 3-1 in United's favour. Winger John Kirby – recently signed from Distillery - scored the third to secure a semi-final berth in front of a massive £221 gate at Warden Street.

Having missed out on a first Irish League Championship, attentions turned to the realistic promise of a first City Cup for the club. With five wins from the first six games, Ballymena United narrowly led the City Cup at the half-way stage in March but the goals suddenly dried up and four defeats in the final seven games (including five goal reverses against Belfast Celtic and Glentoran) saw the Sky Blues finish a

The match of the season; newspaper advertisement for the 1939 Irish Cup final'

disappointing sixth in the table. However, results in the City Cup were excused as a tight 3-2 Irish Cup semi-final win at the Oval against Portadown set up a first Irish Cup final appearance in eight years - the first time the new club had achieved this.

Regardless of the recent poor run of form Ballymena United went into the 1939 Irish Cup final as slight favourites against old cup final foes Linfield in April but it was a disappointing let down for the Ballymena supporters. A crowd of 17,500 at Solitude but the game was over as a contest nine minutes into the second half as Linfield scored their second goal. The Blues won the final 2-0 and it could have been at least half-a-dozen if not for the form of Redmond in the United goal who won all the plaudits for a tremendous display in an all-round disappointing performance.

The successful season allowed the club to clear all the outstanding debts; however there was a feeling of disappointment as players were presented with runners-up medals for both the Irish League and Irish Cup that their promising side had again finished without silverware for their efforts.

⚽ 1939/1940 ⚽

In 1939 Northern Ireland was not a pleasant place to be and with unemployment rising to over 21% the Irish League instructed players to take a 15% pay cut to aid the war effort in preparation for the inevitable conflict ahead of the 1939/40 season.

On the field, Ballymena United had strengthened the team with the acquisition of Scottish duo George Grant from Clapton Orient and David Summers from Greenock Morton alongside local players John Swann (from Partick Thistle) and Alex Shannon (Belfast Celtic). However the club also lost a number of their team that finished runners-up in both League and Cup with John Grant, John McDaid, Jock Wallace and J.P. Surgenor seeking pastures new and whilst John Kirby sealing a move to England with Bristol Rovers.

Ladies' Ballymena United season ticket for the 1939/1940 season

The new look Braid line-up, with five debutants, won their opening game of the season against Ards in the City Cup campaign which had now been moved to the beginning of the domestic season for the first time. This opening victory was as much as the supporters could savour in the opening months as, despite the high expectations on the team, they lost the next six consecutive games in the worst run of losses the team had ever put together which also included an early exit from the Gold Cup to Newry Town.

Poor form and results paled into insignificance though as on 3rd September 1939 Britain declared war on Germany and the Second World War officially began. On the mainland, all males aged 18-41 were conscripted for military duty and the English Football League ceased after only a handful of fixtures of the 1939/1940 season immediately splitting into regional war-time leagues. The Irish League continued until the end of the season as compulsory conscription was not enforced in Northern Ireland, and teams remained intact for the majority of the campaign.

Irish League football wasn't without its own difficulties though as within two weeks of the declaration the Road Transport Board had declared that all buses would be made unavailable with immediate effect. Coupled with a skeleton rail service operating throughout the province and a rationing of petrol, it made great difficulty for supporters travelling to games and gates subsequently plummeted. By the start of October, the Ballymena United committee asked the professionals in the team to take a reduction in pay which was widely accepted with the exception of defender David Summers who sought his release to return home to Scotland in an attempt to find work as a riveter.

Amidst all the distractions, Ballymena's City Cup series proved to be a disaster, as they failed to build on the opening win against Ards and won only three of their next 12 fixtures to finish firmly in the lower reaches of the final table. In December, the Braidmen boosted the start of their Irish League challenge with the return of two home-grown players Albert Barr from Manchester City and Billy McCready, the pair were also joined by Scotitsh inside-forward Alex Weir (formerly of Waterford and Glenavon).

The new arrivals improved the performances on the pitch as Ballymena United returned to goalscoring ways with big wins over Larne (5-1), Coleraine (6-1) and Newry Town (8-2) before the end of the year but too many dropped points throughout December meant that the club entered 1940 in a mid-table position in a highly competitive Irish League. Eleven wins from the next twelve games in all competitions at the turn of the year kick-started the season. Not only did the team quickly move into third position in the table but they also swiftly progressed in the Irish Cup with wins against Bangor and Dundela in the opening two rounds of the much coveted Irish Cup.

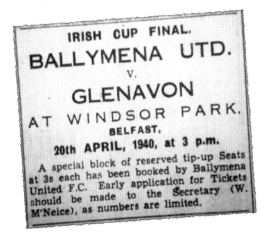

In arguably the game of the season, the Light Blues stunned the all-conquering Belfast Celtic in the semi-finals of the Irish Cup at Solitude, winning 2-0 with goals from Bob Sclater (who was enjoying another goal-laden season, eventually chalking up 44 goals) and George Grant.

On 20th April, 1940 Ballymena United faced Glenavon in the final of the Irish Cup in front of a paying crowd of £1,369 in receipts for the first all provincial Irish Cup Final at Windsor Park. The team lined-up as; Redmond, Vincent, Swann, Barr, McCartney, Rosbotham, Grant, Olphert, Sclater, Weir, Moore. The Braidmen put their cup heartbreak from the previous year behind them to beat the Lurgan Blues 2-0 with goals from William Moore and Bob Sclater either side of half-time. In a civic reception to celebrate the historic cup victory a rousing speech from Mayor William Shaw heartily congratulated the club on it's achievement; "These are the qualities which have kept our country in the forefront in the field of sport, and they are the qualities which will enable our fighting services to smash Hitler and his filthy gang!"

Sadly, this was to be one of the last times the majority of this talented team would play together competitively. The league season finished four days later with a comfortable 5-0 win against Ards at the Showgrounds with George Grant scoring and Bob Sclater fittingly scoring a hat-trick in what would unknowingly be his last game for the Sky Blues sealing a fourth place League finish. End of season friendlies against Dundalk and Ballyclare Comrades followed over the next month as the players parted for the summer break.

Little over a month after the Cup it was declared that the British Army would be seizing control of the Ballymena Showgrounds complex in a shock announcement which left Ballymena United officials little option but to request a temporary resignation from the Irish League until the conclusion of the war or at least until the ground situation could be resolved. The letter to the Irish FA is documented below.

IRISH CUP RETURNS TO BALLYMENA

GLENAVON DEFEATED BEFORE HUGE CROWD

VICTORS NEVER STRETCHED

GATE RECEIPTS TOTAL £1,369

By SPECTATOR

BALLYMENA UNITED 2, GLENAVON 0

1940 Irish Cup final headlines from the Ballymena Observer

IRISH FOOTBALL ASSOCIATION, LTD.

OFFICIAL PROGRAMME

IRISH CUP FINAL

BALLYMENA UNITED v. GLENAVON

At WINDSOR PARK

Saturday, 20th April, 1940

KICK-OFF - 3 p.m.

Price - - - Twopence

1940 Irish Cup final match programme

Ballymena United's Irish Cup winning team from 1940.
Back row: John Dalrymple (Trainer), Simon McCrory (Chairman), Albert Barr, Blair Vincent, Matthew Redmond, John Swann, James Rosbotham, Alex Weir, Alex Shannon.
Front row: Samuel Callendar (Treasurer), George Grant, Robert Olphert, Johnny McCartney, Bob Sclater, William Moore, William McNeice (Secretary).

> *31st July, 1940*
>
> *"I am instructed to inform you that owing to the fact that our grounds have be requisitioned for National purposes, it will not be possible for this club to commence competitive football on 17th August, 1940 and in consequence make application for your permission to withdraw from the competition in the meantime.*
>
> *"The position of the club was fully discussed at a special meeting of the members held on Wednesday 24th inst. and although every suggestion was considered it was not possible to overcome the difficulty, and resolution passed as follows; 'This club is unable at present to take part in Irish League football owing to the fact it has not suitable grounds.'*
>
> *"My committee hope you will appreciate that our withdrawal is due to the exercises of the times and for reasons which are completely beyond our control.*
>
> *"We hope when the crises of the moment is overcome as we are convinced it will be, the club will be allowed to return to league football and play its part in the furtherance of the game."*

Ballymena United proposal to retain a non-playing membership to the Irish League until situations were resolved was met with some objection, notably from Linfield but fortunately passed by the member clubs who agreed that Ballymena should be given dispensation to not compete in the Gold and City Cups and to review in November their circumstances before the start of the Irish League series. However, the review was never to take place as only a few weeks later the Irish League suspended all competitions and formed an eight team 'Northern Regional League' for the 1940/41 season which became the only competitive war-time senior football division in Northern Ireland.

Along with Ballymena United, five other clubs (Coleraine, Larne, Newry Town, Bangor and Ards) all dropped out of senior football following the introduction of the Regional League with some clubs retaining their senior status by playing under the name of their reserve team in the Intermediate League during the war. There had been speculation in November 1940 that Ballymena might return to senior football temporarily solely to defend their Irish Cup but because of the complications, it never materialised.

IRISH CUP HOLDERS OUT OF FOOTBALL.

BALLYMENA DECISION.

GROUND NOT AVAILABLE.

SUMMERFIELD CLUB'S OFFER.

Ballymena United Football Club, at a special meeting on Wednesday evening, decided that it was unable to participate in football at the present time owing to a suitable ground not being available. An amendment to adjourn the meeting for a week was defeated.

Mr. Simon M'Crory (chairman), who

The shock news announced in the Ballymena Observer

Unfortunately it's unclear what happened to the majority of the 1940 Irish Cup winning team after the end of that season. Unaware of how long the conflict would last, Ballymena retained the registrations of their professionals and many of the players throughout the Irish League joined the forces and played football for their assigned regiment and regularly informally guested for teams competing in the Regional League.

Known survivors of the Second World War include captain Johnny McCartney, goalkeeper Matt Redmond who guested for both Linfield and Derry City during the war years; defender John Fullerton whose son Jackie would go onto star on the field and on the television; Billy McCready and Albert Barr would both return to the club whilst Matt McPeake would earn a living as a well-respected scout in England.

Arguably the club's greatest ever goalscorer Bob Sclater settled in Ballymena with his new wife but had his football career cut short by a nasty head injury sustained playing football – he had scored a remarkable 136 goals in only 114 appearances during three seasons. Forward Alex Weir served his time in Ulster during the war but bizarrely went onto to become manager of the Iceland national team during qualification for the 1958 World Cup later in his career.

There were unfortunately three players that would never return home, paying the ultimate sacrifice during the war. Irish Cup winners George Grant and John Swann alongside reserve team player John Esler all sadly lost their lives fighting for their country.

Ballymena United remained in a state of suspended animation throughout the war, as the Northern Regional League would run for seven seasons from 1940/41 to 1946/1947 and would be exclusively won by either Belfast Celtic or Linfield. Football continued at intermediate level in the town as Summerfield continued at Flixton Park but failed to attract much additional support from floating United fans. The war would take its toll on most Irish League clubs none moreso than Glentoran, when their Oval grounds were bombed by German airforces attacking the nearby Harland & Wolff shipyard during the 'Belfast Blitz'.

Thankfully there would eventually light at the end of a very dark tunnel.

Chapter Three

Post war Showgrounds struggles (1946-1957)

⚽ *1946/1947* ⚽

By late 1945 and with the war won, Ballymena United were finally fit to resume activity and return back to the Irish League ahead of the 1946/47 Regional League season. After successfully regaining access to their Showgrounds base, friendlies with Belfast Celtic and Linfield were suggested but never fulfilled as the County Antrim Agricultural Association attempted to return the complex back to its original purpose with the benefit of a new pavilion and changing rooms which were completed by the football club through voluntary labour of members and supporters to the value of over £1,000.

In February 1946 successful admission to the Northern Regional League alongside neighbours Coleraine (who had been playing in the Intermediate League throughout the war) was granted. Billy Reid was appointed as the club's first non-playing manager in June and was immediately tasked with forming a new look team virtually from scratch to compete in the league. Reid had once been capped by Ireland and was a former Glentoran and Hearts centre-half who was also the brother of Davy and John Reid who had been the mainstay of the original Ballymena's Irish Cup winning team in 1929. Popular former player

Ballymena United's first post-war team line-out pictured at the Showgrounds at the beginning of the 1946/47 season

Billy McCready returned and was appointed as the club's trainer – a role which he would fill for the next four decades.

Matt Redmond, John Fullerton and Albert Barr all returned to the club without hesitation but Reid's team was naturally made up largely of new faces. Ireland international winger Norman Kernaghan arrived from Distillery and was quickly made captain. Kernaghan was joined by Aberdeen forward John Neilson, Michael Canning (Shelbourne), Jackie Robinson (ex-Birmingham City and Glentoran), John Collins (Hibernian) and former Preston North End half-back Frank Houghton was recruited on amateur terms after impressing for the Royal Ulster Rifles whilst based in Omagh during the war.

Ballymena United finally returned to competitive football after six years on 17th August 1946 winning 2-1 against Distillery in the opening fixture of the Gold Cup series at the revamped Ballymena Showgrounds with a debut brace for Scottish forward John Neilson. The face of the Showgrounds had also been changing with the unveiling of the new pavilion and changing rooms the week before by Councillor Patrick Murphy.

However, three days later, a formidable return to Celtic Park brought United back down to earth with a 5-1 defeat to eventual Gold Cup winners Belfast

Celtic. It was a roller-coaster start for the Sky Blues with supporters almost guaranteed goals as home wins against Coleraine (6-2) and Cliftonville (5-1) were sandwiched either side of a 6-0 reverse to reigning Regional League champions Linfield.

It was a positive start for the Braidmen in their return to football but after a 2-1 win against Derry City – a game in which the prolific Neilson's winning goal was his ninth in the opening six games – but a massive blow was dealt in September when manager Reid resigned from his role as manager of the club due to work commitments at the Queens' Island shipyard and the team was managed by the selection committee headed by Chairman Sam Callendar for the remainder of the season.

Results proved erratic during the course of the extended 14 game Gold Cup campaign but a credible fourth place finish (from eight teams) was a positive comeback going into the Regional League in November 1946. The league campaign started with three consecutive draws and then was followed by the club's heaviest ever defeat - losing 10-1 to Belfast Celtic at Celtic Park as the team struggled to readjust to life back in senior Irish football.

Ballymena bounced back immediately with wins against Distillery (3-2) and Derry City (2-0) but their Regional League campaign (which had the eight teams play each other a repetitive four times) took a familiar pattern over the course of the season as they failed to win any of the 12 games against the main three Belfast teams (Celtic, Linfield and Glentoran). They did manage two commendable draws against champions elect Belfast Celtic in December and in the penultimate game in April.

Into the New Year and the Irish Cup proved fortuitous for the Sky Blues after having received a 'bye' in from the first round, they comfortably dispatched struggling Cliftonville, 5-0 over two legs in the quarter-finals to set up an epic three game semi-final with Glentoran. The

Selection of Ballymena United matchday programmes from the 1946/47 season

BALLYMENA UNITED

Redmond

M'Ilroy   Canning

Houghton   Cardwell   Irvine

Sneddon   M'Inally   M'Dowell   Doherty   Feeney

REFEREE: SERGEANT MARTIN.

Shepherd   Nelson   M'Gibbon   Ayres   Stevens

Beasley   Watson   Taylor

Bacuzzi   Freeman

Hinton

FULHAM

Official match programme and line-ups from United's friendly with Fulham at the Showgrounds in May 1947

East Belfast Glens, who had relocated to Grovenor Park after the Oval was destroyed, beat United 2-1 at the third attempt following two 1-1 draws in April 1947 – they would eventually lose the final to Belfast Celtic.

Leading goalscorer Neilson went AWOL in January and returned to his native Scotland refusing to play for the club again. After months of dispute, he was eventually transferred to Clyde for £300. The selection committee went through a massive turnover of players throughout the season with 49 different names appearing on the teamsheet and the late season line-up becoming increasingly unrecognisable from Reid's early season eleven. William Clarke (Stockport County), John McInally (Cowdenbeath) and Walter Sneddon (Royal Air Force) all impressed in the second half of the season as the selectors were also forced to fully utilise the club's reserve team which had been admitted to the Intermediate League for the first time.

The limp ending to league proceedings which resulted in only the one win from the final nine games meant the goal-shy Braidmen surrendered a top half finish in their first season back and ended up fifth in the league table, but after six years without any football the club officials and supporters weren't too worried.

In May supporters were treated to an end of season friendly with London side Fulham (then of the old English Second Division) in which the Braidmen aided by a strengthened team which included Huddersfield Town's Irish international inside-left Peter Doherty won the game 3-1, with Doherty scoring twice. This was the first time that that a Football League club had visited the Showgrounds since Everton in 1930. Ballymena also competed against Coleraine for the hastily arranged North-East Challenge Cup which the Bannsiders won 7-4 over two legs; the competition was billed as the first of an annual traditional but never reappeared the following year.

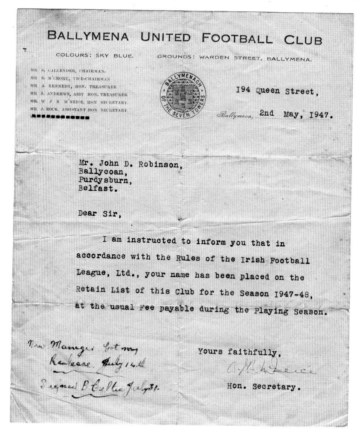

Letter from secretary William McNeice to John Robinson to have his services retained for the following season

⚽ 1947/1948 ⚽

Ahead of the 1947/48 the Irish League formally returned after a seven year hiatus and football in Northern Ireland welcomed back four clubs; Ards, Bangor, Glenavon and Portadown for the new season as normality was finally resumed. Only Larne and Newry Town would not return, choosing to stay in intermediate football, leaving a new look 12-team top division.

Ballymena United appointed a new manager in July 1947 in Bob McKay, the 46-year-old former Scotland international inside-right coming to the club with an impressive football pedigree having played for Newcastle United, Rangers and Sunderland as well as a short spell as Dundee United manager before the war.

Team picture from August 1947 before the opening game of the season against Bangor in the City Cup.
Back row: Bob McKay (Manager), James Jackson, Charles Archer, Frank Houghton, Matt Redmond, Charles Gavin, Syd McIlroy, William McCready (Trainer).
Front row: Alfred Kennedy (Treasurer), Norman Kernaghan, James McStay, Seamus D'Arcy, John McInally, William Spalding.

McKay brought an influx of Scots from his native Glasgow to the Braid to make up his new look team at considerable expense.

Forward William Spalding joined from Aberdeen along with James Jackson (Clydebank), Charles Gavin (Arbroath), Charles Archer (Shettlestown Violet). These new faces complimented the retained professionals from the previous campaign; Redmond, McIlroy, Kernaghan, McInally and Houghton. It was a blank slate for McKay as many of last season's players had already gone with Albert Currie and Jackie Robinson both joining Belfast Celtic and Michael Canning moving to Distillery.

The Sky Blues started the new season with no less than six Scottish players on show in their opening City Cup game against Bangor at the Showgrounds – as McKay's men chalked up half a dozen goals in a pulsating 6-4 victory over the Seasiders with another new Scotch signing James McStay (previously with West Brom) scoring a hat-trick on his debut.

Wins against Cliftonville (City Cup) and Glenavon (Gold Cup) meant United opened the season with three wins and were unbeaten throughout August. A dip in form throughout a miserable September produced four defeats and two draws from their six games ruling the team out of contention for City Cup glory and progression in the Gold Cup also. It wasn't until mid-October that the Ballymena United supporters saw their team win again with a stunning 6-2 win over Glenavon at the Showgrounds, the highlight of the City Cup campaign as United finished mid-table.

The Irish League season started in early November with yet another win against Glenavon (this time at Mourneview Park) with the visiting Braidmen winning 2-1 with goals from John McInally and William Spalding. The Sky Blues only lost one of their opening seven games and quickly established themselves as viable challengers in the three horse race for the Gibson Cup alongside Belfast Celtic and Linfield.

One player who attracted major interest at the turn of the year was wing-half Frank Houghton. The English defender had been a key player for the Sky Blues over the past 18 months but he joined Newcastle United of the English Second Division for a club record £5,000 hours after playing his last game for the club in the Irish Cup first round defeat to Linfield in January 1948. The cup game proved a double windfall for Chairman Simon McCrory as the visit of the Belfast Blues attracted a club record gate to the Ballymena Showgrounds with more than 10,000 spectators watching on as United narrowly lost 4-3 to Linfield.

Jimmy D'Arcy

The loss of Houghton knocked the team's form as the next six league games failed to produce a win with Ballymena dropped as low as fifth in the table and falling out of contention for the championship. Another player leaving the club for England was centre-forward Seamus D'Arcy who made the switch to Charlton Athletic of the First Division also for £5,000 in March after 19 goals in just 30 games. Also known as 'Jimmy', D'Arcy joined from his native Newry Town in the summer having spent the war years playing in the League of Ireland and went onto to win caps for his country and had productive spells at both Chelsea and Brentford. McKay moved quickly to use the money to

Eric Trevorrow signs for Ballymena United in April 1948 in front of club officials. Courtesy of Ballymena Observer

Secretary William McNeice's County Antrim Shield winners medal from 1948

sign forward Thomas McCormack from Glentoran as his replacement for a club record £1,000 fee.

McCormack made an immediate impact scoring twice against Coleraine on his debut to spark a late rally in the final league games. Leading scorer Norman Kernaghan scored a hat-trick against champions Belfast Celtic in the final game of the league season to win 4-3 as Ballymena leap-frogged Glentoran and Distillery to deservedly finish the campaign third in the league table.

For the first time, Ballymena United entered the Inter-City Cup (a cross border competition founded in 1942) and the first time that the club would face League of Ireland opponents in a competitive environment but due to travel restrictions the Braidmen had to play their 'home' games at Cliftonville's Solitude ground in North Belfast. A fine 4-1 first leg win against Shelbourne in the first round was enough to see United through to the quarter-finals as a 1-0 defeat at Tolka Park in the second leg was enough to confirm a last eight clash against Shamrock Rovers. The Dublin side proved too strong for McKay's team winning 8-3 on aggregate after a 4-1 defeat at Glenmalure Park and a 4-2 scoreline at Solitude.

As part of the transfers of Houghton and D'Arcy friendlies at the Ballymena Showgrounds were arranged between Newcastle United and Charlton in May. Supporters were spoilt for football choice as Luton Town were also visitors to the Braid alongside Scottish club Airdrieonians. The Newcastle game (which ended 3-2 to the Tyneside club) marked an

impressive first appearance of a 20-year-old Glaswegian full-back Eric Trevorrow signed from Parkhead Juniors – the first of many, many sterling performances by the Scottish defender, who signed professional terms soon after.

The exhibition games proved to be the perfect warm up for the County Antrim Shield final against Linfield in May which Ballymena had comfortably reached after wins against Bangor and Ards. John McDonald a virtually unknown forward signed from Ballymoney United in January had impressed in the Inter-City Cup games and scored twice in the Shield final as the Sky Blues won their first ever County Antrim Shield beating Linfield 2-1 at Celtic Park to sign off the season in style. This was also the first time the competition had been won by a team from outside of Belfast a point not missed by Chairman Simon McCrory at the club's AGM, where Treasurer Alfred Kennedy also noted an impressive £6,000 credit in the club's end of year accounts – the biggest profit made by the club to date.

Team picture taken at Celtic Park in March 1949 before the club's final ever game against Belfast Celtic.
Back row: Alfred Kennedy (Treasurer), Michael McWilliams, Eric Trevorrow, Sean McCann, John McIlreavey, Harry Murphy, James Jackson, Billy McCready (Trainer), J. Watt (Vice-Chairman).
Front row: Bob McKay (Manager), Norman Kernaghan, Thomas Williamson, Patrick Cronin, Paddy Corr, John McDonald, William McNeice (Secretary).

⚽ 1948/1949 ⚽

Much was expected of McKay's second season at the Showgrounds as he kept faith in the majority of his County Antrim Shield winning team. In came goalkeeper Sean McCann from Belfast Celtic, forward Tommy Williamson from Portadown and Scottish defender Harry Murphy (a good friend of Eric Trevorrow) joined from Parkhead Juniors to replace the departed Charles Gavin who was released after a dispute with the manager. Murphy was also the son of former Ballymena forward Jamie Murphy who had been a firm favourite in the 1930s at the Showgrounds.

A disappointing City Cup campaign began the season with only one win from the opening five games and the Gold Cup quest ended just as quickly after a quarter-final replay defeat to Glenavon. Ballymena bounced back with a win against Glentoran at the Showgrounds which sparked a mini-revival winning the next two games against Distillery and Coleraine but the team eventually finished seventh in the City Cup table.

Irish League started well in late November with a fine 5-2 win against Coleraine as John McDonald continued on his impressive end of season form with a brace against the Bannsiders (McDonald would eventually finish as the club's leading goalscorer with 18 goals by the end of the campaign). The erratic start to the league campaign had supporters wondering which team was going to show up as there was no consistency to the early league results, which included a dismal Christmas day 5-0 defeat to Belfast Celtic at the Showgrounds.

By the start of the New Year the club was hit hard by injuries to key players and naturally struggled for any consistency as they were knocked out of the Irish Cup in the first round by Coleraine and also suffered an 8-0 defeat to Ards at Castlereagh Park. The team did have a positive February as two goals from a young Paddy Corr sealed a 2-1 win over Derry City to move the club into fourth in the Irish League table. Unfortunately it was all downhill from there on as only one win from the final eight league games after the Derry win meant McKay's men finished a disappointing ninth in the Irish League table.

The defence of the County Antrim Shield also lasted only one game. Following a bye through to the quarter-finals the trip to Glentoran resulted in defeat by a solitary goal. Having seen the Shield leave Belfast for the first time a year before, there was another first in 1949 as Linfield Swifts won the competition to become the first reserve side to lift the trophy.

At the end of April the club's AGM proved to be a fiery affair, as manager Bob McKay blamed the team's failings on the injuries of his players but also fervently complained about the interference regarding team selection from the committee. As the result of a unanimous vote he was subsequently not offered a new contract and freed to leave the club. The club also felt the strain of their unsuccessful season after making a substantial £2,200 loss for the year.

The season drew to a close with a benefit match for long serving goalkeeper Matt Redmond. The Broughshane goalkeeper's made his debut with the club 12

Match programme and ticket from Matt Redmond's Benefit match in May 1949'

years previously, clocking up 211 appearances for his hometown team (which would have been a lot more but for the intervention of the war). An Irish League Select defeated the Sky Blues at the Showgrounds on the 1st May in a game in which Redmond couldn't even attend let alone participate due to a bout of flu. He would already have played his last game for the club and was transferred to Larne the following season. Managerless United officially finished the season with a dismal 4-0 home defeat to League of Ireland champions Drumcondra in the first round of the Inter-City Cup.

Away from the Showgrounds, Belfast Celtic withdrew their membership from the Irish League at the end of the 1948/49 season after an infamous Boxing Day brawl between Linfield supporters and Celtic players in which Jimmy Jones suffered a broken leg and was only saved from further injury by United goalkeeper Sean McCann (a former team-mate) in the stands. Celtic's final football was a successful tour of America in the summer and despite lingering hopes that a resolution would be found at boardroom level, the club never returned to Irish football.

In the close season the club was dealt the terrible news when record-signing Tom McCormack passed away after a long illness, the forward had not played for the club since September 1948.

⚽ 1949/1950 ⚽

Following the unfortunate demise of Belfast Celtic at the end of the previous season, Ballymena United were the main beneficiaries after their farewell tour of the United States as in August the management committee appointed Celtic's Billy McMillan as player-manager to replace McKay in August 1949. McMillan had won international caps for both Northern Ireland and Eire during the war years and had won every honour the Irish League had to offer and he brought his former team-mates Joe Douglas and Reggie Simpson to the club with the press dubbing the new look Sky Blues as 'Ballymena Celtic' before the start of the 1949/50 campaign.

Irish League handbook issued to clubs for 1949/50 season

The new look side involved an almost complete overhaul from the previous season with eight debutants lining out for the opening game of the season against Distillery at Grosvenor Park, which started the City Cup series with a 2-2 draw. Only Trevorrow, Irvine, and Corr would be familiar faces to the travelling supporters that evening. Harry Murphy had been transferred to Falkirk, Norman Kernaghan had been released and other notable departures included Syd McIlroy (Larne), William Spalding (Bristol City) and James Jackson (Third Lanark).

One defeat from their opening eight games was an encouraging start at the Braid as the group stage of newly established Ulster Cup competition was conquered flawlessly with three wins from three games. Australian forward Daniel Lavery joined from Glentoran, whilst goalkeeper Liam Flannigan established himself as first choice goalkeeper after his transfer from Glasgow Celtic.

Early season form unfortunately deserted McMillan's Ballymena for the remainder of 1949 onwards beginning with defeat in the quarter-final of the Gold Cup to Distillery in September as the team only managed three victories between then and the end of the calendar year. The City Cup had ended in November with a seventh place finish as the hopeful introduction of forwards John Doris and David Kavanagh (Dundela) couldn't produce the goals required.

The Braidmen sank to the bottom of the Irish League table on Boxing Day following a 6-1 defeat to Linfield at Windsor Park, however they only propped up the other eleven teams for a day as 24 hours later they secured their first win of the Irish League season with a 4-1 victory against Coleraine – two goals from Paddy Corr, and one apiece for Daniel Lavery and David Kavanagh rejuvenating sky blue spirits. Defender Harry Murphy also returned to the club less than six months after being freed by the club – he rejoined from Falkirk and would be an ever-present for the second half of the season, providing a steadying influence on a leaky back line.

Despite the morale boosting win against the Bannsiders, 1950 began in a similar vein, with no league victories in January and a early Irish Cup exit to Bangor – losing 2-1 to the Seasiders at Clandeboye Park in the first round of the cup. The County Down side would also knock United out of the County Antrim Shield at the same stage by the same scoreline in April.

The Ulster Cup resumed at the semi-final stage on 19th April, seven months after United had topped their group, a fantastic 2-1 victory over league leaders Glentoran at Windsor Park set up a first Ulster Cup final for the club a week later against neighbours Larne, now playing in the Intermediate League. Grosvenor Park was the venue for the final which the Invermen (who had former Ballymena favourite Matt Redmond in goals) won 2-1 to claim the first ever senior trophy.

Ballymena United finished out the season two days later with a 5-1 defeat to Derry City at the Brandywell to end a forgettable season – finishing eighth from 12, avoiding league re-election by only two points. Outgoing Chairman John Watt stated at the AGM in May, "We had hoped that Billy McMillan would instil some of the Celtic spirit into the team, but the performance of the team has not been good". Unsurprisingly McMillen wasn't retained by the committee and was replaced by 33-year-old former captain Norman Kernaghan who was appointed as manager in May 1950.

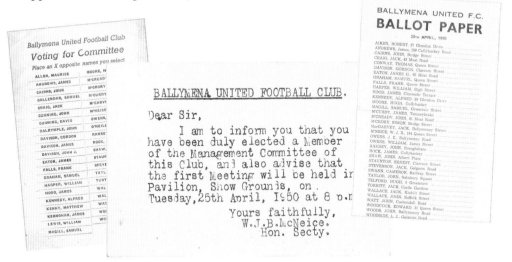

Ballot papers for 1950 Ballymena United management committee election

Ballymena United team picture from April 1951 before the Irish Cup semi-final against Portadown
Back row: William McCready (Trainer), Harry Murphy, James Rodgers, George Gray, Joe Douglas, J. McCready.
Front row: Vincent Morrison, William Anderson, Robert Ewart, Joe Barr, Eric Trevorrow, Gerry O'Hara, Jack Currie.

⚽ 1950/1951 ⚽

Kernaghan took to overhauling the playing staff over the summer of 1950 with Paddy Corr (Coleraine), Reggie Simpson (Crusaders) and Davy Kavanagh and Liam Flannigan making way for Vincent Morrison and George Bell (both Crusaders), Joe Barr (Linfield) Walter Long to name but a few. Kernaghan also introduced a local young left-winger and farmer Jack Currie into the first team from the Reserves.

There were seven new faces for the Ulster Cup season opener against Intermediate League side Ulsterville, which United started with a comfortable 4-0 victory. Progression to the knock-out stages of the Ulster Cup was undone by defeat to Coleraine in the third and final group game in September. A Gold Cup semi-final was assured early in the season but a 4-1 capitulation to Linfield at the Oval saw the end to any hopes of

Norman Kernaghan. Courtesy of Northern Ireland Football Greats

Ballymena captain Harry Murphy is presented with a lucky shoehorse before the 1951 County Antrim Shield final against Distillery at Solitude. Courtesy of Ballymena Observer

early season silverware for the new manager.

The City Cup preceded the Irish League and inconsistency was the theme of Ballymena's results throughout the eleven game campaign, chalking up a win one week and losing the next, but finishing a respectable fifth place going into the serious matter of the league. The 6-2 thrashing of Ards in the penultimate City Cup game (a game with six different United goalscorers) gave fans hope for a promising Autumn in North Antrim.

1951 started with an impressive win over title-challengers Linfield at the Showgrounds in mid-January, Jack Currie scoring a last minute winner to seal a 3-2 victory. That was as good as it was to get in the league though as the second half of the Irish League was a catastrophe, as the team went on a run of eleven league games without a win and eventually slipped down the league standings to 10th position. Kernaghan has attempted in vain to add new quality to his team with goalkeeper Jim Rodgers, inside forward Gerry O'Hara (ex Portadown and Fulham), half-back George Gray and forward R. Ewart (both Distillery) all being recruited amongst others in the new year, but it wasn't working for the former Ireland international and he tendered his resignation in March 1951.

The only solace for the suffering Braid followers was an extended run in the Irish Cup competition. The morale boosting first round victory over rivals Coleraine at home and progress past a quarter-final replay against Cliftonville meant a semi-final with Portadown in Belfast, which the Light Blues overcame thanks to goals from Anderson and Ewart to send the team through with a 2-1 win.

The league strugglers had made their way to their first Irish Cup final since 1940 against a Glentoran team that had romped home to the Gibson Cup; the team was Jim Rodgers, Eric Trevorrow, Joseph Barr, Gray, Harry Murphy, Douglas, Morrison, Anderson, Ewart, O'Hara. Currie. Glentoran comfortably won a one-sided final 3-1, farmer Jack Currie getting a mere consolation for the Sky Blues.

United bounced back from their Irish Cup final defeat to reach a second final of the season squaring up to Cliftonville in the final at Windsor Park on 16th

May, but despite taking the league through Joe Douglas and a second half goal from Jack Currie (his 12th of the season to finish top goalscorer) the match ended scoreless to force a replay. However, with only a few days left in the football calendar for the 1950/1951 season, it was decided that the replay would be held over until the start of the next season.

⚽ *1951/1952* ⚽

Chairman Sam Callender and his committee decided against appointing a replacement manager over the summer following Kernaghan's departure but undertook some astute recruitment themselves with teenage forward Billy Cubitt – a Harryville lad who joined from Larne. full-back Ernie Johnston also made the move from Inver Park and another Larne native James Mullan returned home from a successful spell at English side Barrow, completing the trio of signings with East Antrim connections. John Mitten (younger brother of the infamous 'Bogota

Team picture from March 1952 at Grosvenor Park before 2-2 draw with Distillery.
Back row: Samuel Callendar (Chairman), William Cubitt, Gerry Fegan, Ossie Bailie, Sam Mitten, Harry Murphy, William McCready (Trainer).
Front row: William McNeice (Secretary), Ernie Johnston, Eric Trevorrow, Joseph Barr, John Mitten, William Quinn, James Lyness.

Bandit' Charlie Mitten) also joined the Sky Blues after a spell at Middlesbrough. Brother Charlie, formerly of Manchester United fame, was currently plying his trade in Colombia to avoid the restrictions of the £12 maximum weekly wage amidst much controversy.

The majority of the Irish Cup final team stayed in place with the exceptions of Gray, O'Hara and Ewart who were all released at the end of the season. Jackie McIlreavey also left to go back to his native Coleraine during the close season.

Centre-forward James Mullen made arguably one of the best debuts ever seen in a United shirt scoring all four goals in the 4-1 City Cup victory against Distillery on the opening game of the season. Two days later the team completed some

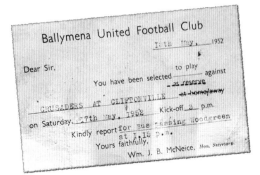

unfinished business from the previous campaign – with the County Antrim Shield final against Cliftonville at Windsor Park which had been held over. Ballymena fielded five changes from the original game in May (four of whom weren't even at the club for the first game!) and convincingly won the game 3-0 with two early goals from Billy Cubitt and Jack Currie inside ten minutes, the latter added a third early in the second half to bring the Shield back to Ballymena for the second time.

Festival of Britain shield

In 1951 the government led a campaign known as the Festival of Britain aimed at promoting good feeling in post-war Britain. The Irish League organised a one-off Festival of Britain Cup for all clubs in place of the traditional Ulster Cup to mark the celebrations. Starting in August, United contested an extremely tight three team group which also included Coleraine and Derry City. The group was tied between United and the Bannsiders after four games meaning a group play-off was required to settle the semi-finalists, given the already crowded autumn schedule with no access to floodlights – the competition was set aside until the following spring.

Despite the aforementioned win against Distillery, the City Cup was a disappointment as the Sky Blues only won two more games in the eleven game series (against Crusaders and Coleraine) to finish ninth from twelve teams in the final cup table. The winning goal in the Crues game was scored by Sam Mitten another brother of John who had been recommended to the club in September by his sibling after playing centre-forward in the Chesire League.

The Irish League started in disastrous form in November as a 5-0 defeat to Portadown at Shamrock Park in the first game sent Ballymena straight to the bottom of the table. Local all-round sportsman Ossie Bailie was quickly brought in to fill the troublesome goalkeeping berth after the Portadown massacre with United erratic as always in the Irish League, the team proved hard to beat in the first half of the season but were drawing too many games to make headway up the standings as they drew six out of nine games during the winter months

Ballymena began the comeback trail to the Irish Cup final and took the long route to the final – needing two replays against Distillery in the first round and another replay to progress past Cliftonville in the quarters. Luck ran out in the Windsor Park semi-final against Ards as the afternoon was compounded by Eric Trevorrow's unfortunate own goal saw the County Down side run out 3-1 winners, with Jimmy Lyness' goal proving only a consolation in the second half. Summer signing Lyness had quietly gone about his business all year and would finish as the club's top scorer with 21 goals at the end of the season.

Throughout 1952 United's resilient league form saw them sneak slowly up the table with notable wins over Glentoran and a struggling Linfield side. Only two defeats in the second half of the season (one of which was against champions Glenavon) and boosted by the goals of the English Mitten brothers meant that United finished the season fifth in the table come April.

The defence of the County Antrim Shield, which the club had won at the start of the current season, lasted only until a quarter-final replay with Glentoran but there was more success with the resumption of the Festival cup. United won the delayed play-off against Coleraine (3-2) and progressed to the final against Crusaders at Solitude after defeating Glentoran 1-0 in the semi-final thanks to Lyness' early strike. The Sky Blues were to end the 1951/52 season as they had started with a 3-0 win against a North Belfast club to earn the silverware. Lyness, who had thrived in the competition, scored twice in the final with ex-Linfield & Weymouth guest forward Harry Walsh scoring the third on his debut appearance.

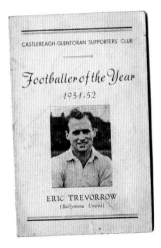

Dinner menu from Eric Trevorrow's Ulster Player of the Year presentation dinner in 1952

Jimmy Kelly

There was one final individual honour that came the way of a Ballymena United player as following yet another sterling season, defender Eric Trevorrow was awarded the Ulster Footballer of the Year award from the Castlereagh Glentoran Supporters' Club. This was only the second season the award had been presented, and the likeable Scot was a worthy winner in the eyes of supporters and peers from across the Irish League.

⚽ 1952/1953 ⚽

The committee tried in vain to appoint a new player manager during the summer months of 1952, meeting a number of candidates but, baulking at the proposed £1,000 transfer fee for their unnamed first choice, the team selection was again managed by a five man sub-committee of Sam Callender, William McNeice, William Ward, Sam Graham and Alfie Kennedy. Their main pre-season recruits included defenders Jimmy Simpson and Dessie Brown (both Crusaders) and centre forward James Baker (Ayr United) as well as veteran winger Jimmy Kelly who had previously starred for Derry City and Ireland.

Treasurer William Ward (supported by his committee) implemented a revolutionary new bonus scheme for professional players in the 1952/53 season based on the team's league position and results and it certainly motivated the players who won the first three Ulster Cup games with James Baker scoring a hat-trick on his debut in the opening game of the season against Derry City. Though despite a promising start in the competition – the Ulster Cup eventually proved a write-off as the Braidmen plummeted into the doldrums with six defeats in the next seven games of the group stage.

More goals were required and the astute signing of Scottish inside-left Charlie McMullan was a catalyst in the team's Autumn revival as they mounted a late challenge in the City Cup competition with four consecutive wins to move from mid-table to second place, right on the heels of runaway leaders Glentoran. But defeat in the final game against Coleraine cost the United team a set of runners-up medals, finishing in third place behind Glentoran and Linfield.

Undeterred by the City Cup disappointment, the Sky Blues raced to the top of the Irish League in December with maximum points from the first four games following wins against Portadown, Ards, Cliftonville and Distillery. Former Belfast Celtic forward Paddy Bonnar signed from Aldershot for £300 and took the place of the transfer-listed Sam Mittten who moved to Portadown in January. Bonnar scored on his debut in the 5-3 win over Crusaders at the Showgrounds with the team established as surprising front-runners in first place in the Irish League at the half-way point.

It wasn't all smooth sailing for Ballymena as they were forced out of the Irish Cup after two replays in the first round to Coleraine. The pressure was too much for club captain Eric Trevorrow who voluntarily relinquished his responsibility to focus on his own performances, recommending that close friend Harry Murphy was the ideal candidate to now captain the team. Murphy's leadership started with United going back to the top of the league after an impressive 4-0 win over interim league leaders Glenavon which sparked a run of form that saw the team go ten consecutive games without defeat and maintain on top as supporters soon dared to dream that the league championship was finally going to come to rest in the town for the first time.

Optimism was sky high at Easter with United still holding their place two points clear at the top of the table but defeat to Glentoran at the Showgrounds allowed the East Belfast side to draw level on points with United with only three games to go in the Gibson Cup race. Confidence completely drained from the players in the final month of the campaign as defeat to Coleraine in the penultimate game on the same afternoon that Glentoran beat Derry City meant that the Glens were crowned Irish League champions at the Brandywell. Defeat to Linfield in the final game meant a disappointing third place finish for Ballymena, who also exited both the Gold Cup and County Antrim Shield to Ards at the quarter-final stage.

Match programme from Eric Trevorrow Benefit against Huddersfield Town in April 1953

The season finished in May with a benefit match for Eric Trevorrow against Huddersfield Town at the Showgrounds. Supporters were treated to a specially strengthened Ballymena United line-up which drew 4-4 with the Yorkshire club (who had just been promoted to the First Division) with Glenavon's Jimmy Jones scoring a hat-trick during his guest appearance in a sky blue shirt.

⚽ 1953/1954 ⚽

Members had stressed at the last AGM that a manager would be essential for the progression of the team and it was Glaswegian Samuel Picken who was appointed as the new player manager of Ballymena United in August 1953 (the first manager in two and a half years). Having been out of football for a year, Picken had previously played inside-forward before the war for Partick Thistle and had since had spells

Chairman Sam Graham and trainer Billy McCready discuss summer transfers. Courtesy of Ballymena Observer

with Airdrieonians and Cowdenbeath and was getting his first taste of both management and Irish football.

Before Picken had arrived there had already been changes to Ballymena United's title challenging team as Billy Cubitt was surprisingly allowed to join Distillery and top goalscorer Jimmy Baker was free to team up with Ards. Forwards Jimmy Lyness and John Mitten were both released, the latter eventually spending time in prison for forgery and fraud.

Monaghan based centre-forward Liam Coll was recruited from Sligo Rovers to lead from the front and got on the scoresheet as the Braidmen steam-rolled Derry City with an inspiring 6-0 start to the season at home in the Ulster Cup. The impressive result lulled supporters into false expectations of their team in the early weeks of the season as United struggled for any form in a relentless Ulster Cup and City Cup fixture list which forced the club to play 15 matches in little over six weeks.

Seven defeats in a row had rocked confidence in the Showgrounds camp and Picken blooded endless new players to try and stop the rot. Eventually the team regrouped following an enforced international break and bounced back with a fine 3-0 win at Seaview against Crusaders with short-term signing Frank Moody (from Sligo Rovers) scoring twice. The manager proclaimed that his players could now 'hold their heads high again as they walked through the town' after the City Cup victory. United finished the competition in ninth place and could only enviously watch on as Coleraine's 4-1 win at Warden Street in the final game of the series clinched a first City Cup trophy for the Bannsiders.

Manager Walter Rickett welcomes John Thomson to the club. Courtesy of Ballymena Observer

Picken recruited William McClure (Yeovil Town) and Noel Young (Derry City) and both players proved integral to a remarkable start to the Irish League in November. A plethoria of goals from McClure and Coll in particular sent Ballymena to the top of the Irish League at Christmas after six wins from seven games which included a stunning 5-1 home win over Coleraine which was described by the *Ballymena Observer* as the 'Greatest display in years'.

United had maintained a narrow one point lead over second placed Linfield at the half-way point of the Gibson Cup race and had been linked with signing of legendary Celtic and Manchester United winger Jimmy Delaney, who eventually opted to join Derry City. Ironically failure to capture the Scotland international cost the Sky Blues as Delaney scored the only goal in the Irish Cup first round tie at the Brandywell to give Ballymena United an early exit from the competition. Bizarrely Ballymena United Reserves progressed further in the Irish Cup than the first team during the 1953/54 season. The second string had qualified for the cup for the first time after losing in the final of the Intermediate Cup on Christmas Eve and had beaten Ballyclare Comrades in their first round tie before gallantly losing 2-0 to Linfield at Windsor Park in the quarter-final.

Things immediately started to go wrong after the cup defeat as a shock 4-0 defeat to Distillery knocked the team off the top of the table. The team picked up only one win from the next five league games and dropped as low as fifth in the table but with a late rally of wins over Ards and Coleraine – the sky blues eventually secured fourth place - disappointingly a full nine points behind one-time rivals Linfield.

There was further disappointment in the final of the County Antrim Shield which the team had reached via the most difficult route possible – beating both Linfield and Glentoran (who finished the top two clubs in the Irish League table) in the quarter and semi-final matches. Mid-table Distillery were the opponents at Solitude in a lack-lustre game which was dubbed the worst final in years as Jim Wilson's goal was enough to seal a 1-0 win for the Whites and ruin any hopes of silverware for the Braidmen. Sam Picken was a peripheral figure in the team throughout the season making only 14 appearances, but had started in the final – the manager had been backed by the committee and members to continue to build a capable team for next season but he wouldn't necessarily be there to see that ambition through.

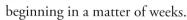

⚽ *1954/1955* ⚽

With preparations already underway for the new season it was a shock when player-manager Samuel Picken went to the club to request a release from the club to return to his family in Glasgow. Chairman Samuel Graham reluctantly sanctioned the request and the search began for a new manager with advertisements immediately placed in cross-channels papers in July for the start of the new season beginning in a matter of weeks.

United searched high and low for a suitable boss and applicants even included a Hungarian international player but it was only a week before the start of the new season that they found their man. 37-year-old winger Walter Rickett arrived in August from Halifax Town having had a sterling career with both Sheffield United and Wednesday winning England 'B' international honours with the latter, as well as playing in the 1948 FA Cup final for Blackpool in their 4-2 defeat to Manchester United.

Newry born John Fearon was recruited from Dundalk alongside Glentoran's Scottish goalkeeper James Clarke who had been brought in to replace the injured

John McCann as two of Rickett's five debutants in the first game of the 1954/55 season in which a comfortable 4-0 win against Cliftonville at the Showgrounds would be a misleading indicator for supporters as to the team's capabilities.

Scottish defender Harry Murphy celebrated seven years at the Braid with a benefit match with a twist as Ireland took on Scotland at the Showgrounds with the teams made up of players from the Irish League. The Irishmen won the entertaining game 4-0 in early September. Results had been very poor throughout a miserable Ulster Cup campaign as five straight defeats forced the chairman to publicly ask for supporters' forbearance during this period as Rickett moved to boost his forward line with Robert Burke (from Burnley) and John Thomson (from Ards) both joining the club.

The player-manager quickly found his feet on the pitch with some impressive City Cup performances and alongside the goals of Thomson the team foraged to the top three of the table – the highlight of which was Rickett's late winner in the 3-2 win at Windsor Park against Linfield. United eventually finished fifth in the City Cup but also lost out to Glenavon in the semi-finals of the Gold Cup at the Oval – the Lurgan Blues completed an early season cup double winning both the City Cup and the Gold Cup competitions.

Ballymena's ill-fated Irish League quest started with four consecutive defeats to leave the club propping up the other eleven teams at the turn of the year. Centre-forward Liam Coll (who had struggled to replicate his form from last season) was transferred to Second Division Doncaster Rovers in a swap deal for Eire international Kit Lawlor. Noel Young who had proved to be one of the few shining lights in United's midfield would also move to Doncaster in the New Year.

With Thomson now AWOL in Scotland, defeat in the first round of the Irish Cup against Crusaders at the Showgrounds was not unexpected but the revenge of a 3-1 win at Seaview the following week finally moved the Sky Blues off the top of the league table. It proved only temporary as defeat to fellow strugglers Cliftonville at Solitude proved the catalyst for a worrying end to the competitive season as it would be 10 games and two months before team would taste victory again (ironically against the Reds in the quarter-final of the County Antrim Shield).

Off the field spiralling debts of £934 provoked an emergency meeting of members to try and financially stablise the club and in a noble move fans' favourite John Fearon handed his wages back to help the club. The looming re-election was

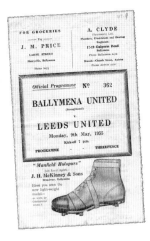

confirmed with the 3-0 defeat to Coleraine with two games to spare and last place was confirmed with a 3-1 defeat to Bangor – to finish off what was undoubtedly the club's worst ever season to date. Despite finishing bottom of the Irish League - the tag of the 'worst team in Ireland' was thankfully avoided with a 5-2 friendly win against Dundalk who had finished bottom of the League of Ireland.

The fans did have some end of season interest (aside from a County Antrim Shield semi-final defeat to Crusaders) as the famous Leeds United visited the Showgrounds as part of a short tour of Ireland accompanied by their star Welsh international John Charles who would soon go on to break the British transfer record with his move to Juventus. The Yorkshire men's fitness eventually told against their part-time opponents winning 6-2. The Braidmen had caused a scare leading twice early in the game with goals from Kit Lawlor and John Fearon.

Lawlor finished as top scorer in a dismal season with 12 goals in 22 games as the club's AGM was described by attendees as having the atmosphere of a wake. Chairman Sam Graham was re-elected as Chairman and reiterated that a lot of hard work would be required to get the club back on its feet, starting with a clear-out of the underperforming players. There was also no place for player-manager Walter Rickett as the club committee decided that it was an expense they could do without as the Englishman was released on good terms on 30th May, 1955.

⚽ 1955/1956 ⚽

With no manager and no money and coming off a worst ever league finish it was a fairly bleak summer of 1955 for Ballymena United as they continued to lose key players. With former manager Rickett staying in Ireland with a move to Dundalk, he was joined in the League of Ireland by Kit Lawlor who wanted to return closer to his Dublin home and was released to join Drumcondra. John Fearon's time at the Showgrounds also came to an end when he moved to Portadown.

Worryingly there was no influx of replacements for the departing senior players, only Linfield's half-back Don McMillan came in alongside Billy Cubitt who made a welcome return to the club after two seasons at Distillery - the Harryville man had guested for the team in the Leeds United game last season. The selection committee were heavily reliant on amateur players throughout the season as the Secretary boldly declared that the club had the 'best amateur talent ever', highlighting in particular speedy Larne born winger Harry Baxter promoted from the Reserves.

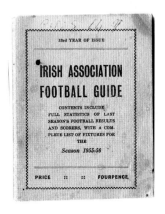

It was another poor start of the season which killed off any of the limited early optimism as Ballymena finished bottom of the Ulster Cup group with four defeats from the five games. Defeat in the first round of the Gold Cup to eventual winners Linfield by three goals at the Showgrounds was yet another early cup exit for the beleaguered Braidmen.

In the City Cup a win against Portadown at Shamrock Park was followed a week later with a superb 3-2 win against Glentoran with a last minute winner for the Sky Blues in what was undoubtedly the highlight of a miserable first half of the season. United finished up ninth in the City Cup competition and had looked to sign off the series with a win against second-placed Coleraine at home and despite leading 2-0, the Bannsiders fought back to score three goals to go joint top of the cup table with Glenavon and force a deciding play-off test match against the Lurgan Blues.

Rumours resurfaced regarding a potential move for Derry City's Jimmy Delaney (now living in Cushendall) ahead of the start of the Irish League campaign but proved too expensive a commodity with the club keen not to fall back into debt,

Delaney opted for a move to Cork Athletic and United instead signed forward Frank Haslett from Crusaders who despite scoring on his debut against Glenavon could not fight the tide of one of the worst runs of form seen at the Showgrounds as United lost seven of their opening eight league games to be alarmingly rooted to the bottom of the table come the start of 1956.

Remarkably United moved out of the league's basement with a stunning 4-1 win over Glentoran in January – a game in which the impressive Frank Haslett scored twice (he would finish as joint top scorer on nine goals alongside Davy McCartney and John Thomson). Though the East Belfast Glens sought their revenge in the Irish Cup a few weeks later at the Oval winning 4-0 in the first round of the competition.

Club officials made the declaration that they wanted to sign a player coach as the selection committee found it hard to scout potential players whilst working full time jobs and were also boosted by the news that the club had once again found secure financial footing and now proclaimed to be only one of two Irish League clubs that were debt free. Solvent but still bottom of the league Ballymena produced one of the shocks of the season in February as they travelled to Windsor Park and beat runaway league leaders Linfield 2-1 with John Thomson scoring a late winner from the penalty spot – this was the only game the Blues lost all season en route to the Irish League Championship.

Ballymena again finished bottom despite three wins from last four games they were again forced to apply for re-election alongside Cliftonville but members and officials remained cautiously optimistic at the end of the season with the announcement that over £1,100 of debts had now been wiped from the accounts and there were now no excuses for lack of success at Warden Street.

⚽ 1956/1957 ⚽

Team building began in earnest in the summer of 1956 and despite not attracting a player-coach or manager as desired the committee recruited a raft of new professionals to replace the underperformers of the previous two seasons. Irish international goalkeeper Ted Hinton joined from Bangor, the 34-year-old had played regularly for Millwall and Fulham and was infamous for playing with his false teeth stored in the net for safe keeping during games. Thomas Walker from Ards and Arthur 'Mousey' Brady from Crusaders both joined the ranks with

The new all seated wooden stand at the Showgrounds opened during the 1956/57 season

undoubtedly the most influential summer capture – Jimmy McGhee a Scottish goal poacher from Greenock Morton who had previously been on the books of Kilmarnock and Darlington.

The new faces were integrated into a team that still included stalwarts such as Trevorrow, Murphy, Cubitt and Brown and it was a positive start to the season as Billy Cubitt's 85th minute equaliser against reigning champions Linfield stole a point in a 1-1 draw in the opening game. Linfield reportedly brought upwards of 50 busloads of supporters to the game which also marked the opening of the new covered grandstand which would be affectionately known in later years as the 'O'Kane Chicken Stand' after a long running sponsorship deal emblazoned on the wooden structure.

Form in the Ulster Cup was inconsistent but still a vast improvement on last season thanks mainly to the goals of McGhee who scored eight goals in his nine games in the competition (including a hat-trick against Coleraine) as the Sky Blues chalked up wins against Glenavon, Ards, Glentoran, Cliftonville and the Bannsiders. The team finished fifth from twelve in the Ulster Cup table but were hit with blows to both their veteran Scottish defenders. Eric Trevorrow cruelly breaking an ankle in the Coleraine game and Harry Murphy unceremoniously left the club after nine seasons due to a falling out with selectors and mutually agreeing his release from the club in October.

The Irish League campaign started in the autumn with a trio of defeats before a convincing 6-1 win against Portadown in which Davy McCartney scored four goals. The game against the County Armagh men was one of the few bright spots in yet another terrible campaign as it marked the only win from the first ten games in which only the abysmal form of Cliftonville kept them off the bottom of the league. United even managed to increase the slender gap over the Solitude men with a hard fought 4-3 win over the Reds the week before Christmas.

1957 continued in frustratingly poor form as it wasn't until March that the team won another game, going ten agonising fixtures failing to give supporters any cheer including another Irish Cup first round defeat to Portadown – this was the fifth season in succession that the team had failed to progress past the first hurdle of the famous old trophy. The only shining light of this period was the emergence of talented winger Tommy Stewart, promoted from the reserve team, the Belfast youngster scored six goals in his first six games in the team.

Only one more league win followed (against Crusaders) as United finished eleventh in the Irish League table and a third consecutive re-election loomed. It was the club's poorest ever points total but the paltry nine points from 22 games was still three points more than the struggling amateurs of Cliftonville. Supporters were understandably livid with the team's performances and a vote of no confidence was called upon the club's management committee as the Pioneer supporters' club unsuccessfully attempted to gain control of the club.

Ballymena United finished the season with an equally difficult City Cup campaign (finishing tenth) but some overdue cheer was provided in the County Antrim Shield with a fine 1-0 win over Linfield in the quarter-final with Tommy Stewart scoring yet again. Stewart also scored in the 3-2 defeat to Distillery in the semi-final of the Shield, chalking up a remarkable 19 goals in 25 games and earning Amateur international recognition and was only bettered in the goal charts by the impressive Jimmy McGhee who scored 22 goals in the struggling side.

Despite successfully gaining re-admittance to the Irish League for the 1957/58 season, something had to change at the Showgrounds.

Chapter Four

McCrae, Trevorrow and Twentyman (1957-1970)

✪ *1957/1958* ✪

Dissatisfied with the ignominy of a club of Ballymena United's stature having to apply for league re-election, the commitee overhauled the playing staff with notable captures including Glentoran goalie Harry Bond, Larne's half-back Tommy Lowry and Distillery's Billy Twinem, brought into compliment the few established professionals that avoided the summer cull; Trevorrow, Brown, Cubitt and McGhee. Some of the notable summer departures included Tommy Stewart to Linfield and Arthur 'Mousey' Brady to Crusaders and no new deals for Ted Hinton and John Walker.

Harry Bond

After a dismal start to the competitive season with one win from eight games come September the United committee appointed their first manager in three seasons when they hired 37-year-old Scottish inside-forward Alec McCrae from Falkirk as player-boss. Little did the club's long suffering supporters realise that the former Hearts and Middlesbrough veteran would go on to lead arguably one of the greatest Ballymena United sides to glory during the 1957/58 season.

It didn't start smoothly though, as a dismal City Cup defeat to amateurs Cliftonville in McCrae's first game was followed four days later exiting the Gold Cup at the quarter-final stage to Ards. The City Cup was used by McCrae as an experiment as he continued to tinker with his new team and started to bring new faces over from his native Scotland – Glaswegian John Egan was one of the first to arrive and was followed by William Forsyth, a former Falkirk team-mate of the manager.

When the Irish League started in November McCrae's influence on and off the pitch started to show with a shock 3-1 victory over Linfield with the player-manager scoring twice. With the festive football

Alec McCrae

season quickly approaching, a 17-year-old winger by the name of Eddie Russell was brought into the first-team for a league game against Cliftonville on 21st December, Ballymena won the game comfortably 4-0 and the young Larne man kept his place in the side for the rest of the season and beyond.

Following a stunning 5-1 Boxing Day win against Glentoran, United went into the New Year in second place in the league but despite hopes of a title challenge quickly ended a few weeks

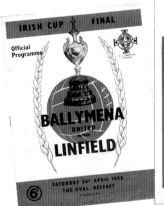

1958 Irish Cup final programme

Action from the 1958 Irish Cup final
Courtesy of Ballymena Observer

later when Linfield inflicted the same scoreline on the Braidmen. Attentions quickly turned to the Irish Cup in February, starting with a 5-0 victory over Dundela of the 'B' Division in the first round and was followed by a tough quarter-final against league leaders Ards at the Showgrounds which the home side won 3-1 with goals from Jimmy McGhee (two) and Tommy Lowry. The resulting semi-final showdown with Derry City proved never to be in doubt with a dominant Ballymena side comfortably progressing to the final for the first time in seven years with a three goal win. Lowry and McGhee again found the net alongside John Egan this time.

The 26th April 1958 will always be regarded as one of the great Ballymena United performances in the Irish Cup against Linfield with the famous ex-England and Newcastle United forward Jackie Milburn leading the

Ballymena United players with the Irish Cup in the Oval dressing room.
Courtesy of Ballymena Observer

Signed dinner menu from celebration dinner for winning the 1958 Irish Cup.

The famous 1958 Irish Cup winning team picture containing only ten players circulated in large numbers to joyous supporters.
Inset: David Holden (Committee), James Andrews (Treasurer), Eddie Johnston.
Back row: J. McCready (Assistant Trainer), William Cubitt, Thomas Lowry, Harry Bond, Eric Trevorrow, Des Brown, William McCready (Trainer).
Front row: Samuel Graham (Chairman), William Forsyth, Jimmy McGhee, Alec McCrae (Manager), John Egan, Eddie Russell, William McNeice (Secretary).

opposition line. Supporters of a certain vintage could always rhyme off the eleven men without breaking breath, whilst those that didn't have the pleasure were often reminded – Bond, Trevorrow, Johnston – Brown, Lowry, Cubitt – Egan, Forsyth - McGhee, McCrae and Russell.

24,000 fans packed in to the Oval grounds in East Belfast for the game, a cup final crowd which has to-date never been surpassed in attendance. Two early goals did do the damage, stunning the Windsor Blues – the first from deadly marksman Jimmy McGhee early in the game and the second was with 25 minutes on the clock when Eddie Russell doubled the lead with what proved to be the final goal of the game.

Delirious supporters invaded the Oval pitch at the final whistle, jubilant after seeing the Sky Blues win the Irish Cup for the first time since 1940. The trophy eventually had to be presented to McCrae and his team in the changing room and later upon their return to the town they paraded the cup through the town from the back of a coal lorry with the streets of the town lined with supporters welcoming back their victorious team.

The remaining domestic matches were almost an anti-climax, but the Cup winners wrapped up their Irish League campaign with back-to-back games against title chasing Glenavon – the first game at the Showgrounds two days after the final went the way of County Antrim men, winning 3-2 with goals from McGhee, Stewart and Egan. This effectively handed the Gibson Cup to Ards for the first time in their history with a game to spare. The season ended with a surprise defeat to Distillery in the semi-final of the County Antrim Shield, but that couldn't take the shine of a memorable season which also ended with a third place league finish for McCrae's heroes.

Chairman Sam Graham declared the campaign as Ballymena's most successful season since 1928/29, with Tommy Lowry being awarded the members' Player of the Year award and cup final goalscorer Jimmy McGhee was again leading goalscorer with 34 goals in 38 games! In a season of notable debuts – McCrae gave a debut to 16-year-old defender Arthur Stewart – son of Robert Stewart from the old Ballymena side of the 1930s.

The season was signed off with a benefit game for defender Dessie Brown to mark the Belfast man's six seasons of service to the club, as the Showgrounds hosted a fixture against an assembled All Star XI and a strengthened United team. The All Stars won the game 5-2 which included two goals for Charlie Mitten, the infamous former Manchester United player whose brothers Sam and John had played for the club alongside Brown. This season also marked the formation of the Seven Towers Ballymena United Supporters' Club, which would go on to become one of the longest serving clubs in Irish League football. The Seven Towers celebrated 50 years of service to the parent club in 2008.

⚽ 1958/1959 ⚽

Expectations had risen dramatically by the summer of 1958, as to whether McCrae could finally lead the Braidmen to the promised land of an Irish League Championship. There was little change to the panel during the close season – William Walsh was Ballymena United's only summer arrival in August, the former Falkirk forward having just completed national service in his native Scotland.

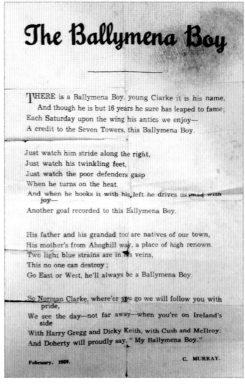

The Ballymena Boy

THERE is a Ballymena Boy, young Clarke it is his name,
  And though he is but 16 years he sure has leaped to fame;
Each Saturday upon the wing his antics we enjoy—
A credit to the Seven Towers, this Ballymena Boy.

Just watch him stride along the right,
Just watch his twinkling feet,
Just watch the poor defenders gasp
When he turns on the heat.
And when he hooks it with his left he drives us mad with
    joy—
Another goal recorded to this Ballymena Boy.

His father and his grandad too are natives of our town,
His mother's from Aghoghill way, a place of high renown.
Two light blue strains are in his veins,
This no one can destroy;
Go East or West, he'll always be a Ballymena Boy.

So Norman Clarke, where'er you go we will follow you with
    pride,
We see the day—not far away—when you're on Ireland's
    side
With Harry Gregg and Dicky Keith, with Cush and McIlroy:
And Doherty will proudly say, " My Ballymena Boy."

February, 1959.   C. MURRAY.

A poem in celebration of young starlet Norman Clarke written by Mr. C Murray

Outgoing was cup winner John Egan who was released on the eve of the new season, returning home to Scotland to join Stranraer.

United started erratically in the Ulster Cup opening with a 5-3 defeat to Crusaders but bounced back a few days later with victory over struggling Glentoran. Never one to shy away from giving talented young players a chance in his team, McCrae unearthed another teenage gem when he blooded 16-year-old winger Norman Clarke from Harryville Amateurs in the defeat to Cliftonville in August. A multi-talented sportsman, Clarke would go onto note in his autobiography 'The Ballymena Boy' that he would often play rugby in the morning for Ballymena Academy and then senior football in the afternoon.

Despite a poor showing in the City Cup series which ended with four straight defeats and an eighth place finish, the team made an impressive start to the Irish League Championship at the Showgrounds with Linfield being turned over 2-1 with goals from Eddie Russell and Willy Forsyth; this was followed the next week with another two points against Bangor at the Gold Coast.

Despite six wins from the opening nine league games the Sky Blues were firmly in mid-table and well out of the race for the Gibson Cup. Inconsistency plagued McCrae's men in the league as they failed to win more than two consecutive league fixtures throughout the season.

In late March, Jackie Milburn and Linfield sought to avenge their Irish Cup defeat from the previous year, in the semi-final. Having beaten an understrength United 5-0 a week before in the league, critics felt the Belfast team underestimated Ballymena as Eddie Russell's stunning winning goal came just after half-time to seal a 2-1 win and a place in the cup final again. Buoyed by the cup success confidence was high and going six games unbeaten during the Championship run-in pushed the Braidmen into the top three.

Come the 25th April 1959, the Sky Blues were led out into their second consecutive Irish Cup final by McCrae in a rematch of the 1940 showpiece with the Braidmen up against Glenavon at Windsor Park. There were only two changes to the eleven from the final twelve months previously – Norman Clarke and William Walsh the only new faces in place of Egan and Forsyth. The final proved to be a tame affair for the 20,000 fans (with a gate of £2,700) as Jimmy Jones' equaliser 12 minutes from time cancelled out Tommy Lowry's strike just before the hour mark and forced a replay between the two sides.

Having finished the league campaign with defeat to Cliftonville, United dropped out of the top three in the table between the final and the replay. Eleven days after the first attempt, 17,000 supporters gathered back at Windsor for the Cup Final replay, with McCrae naming an unchanged team. Unfortunately for the County Antrim men Tommy Lowry's missed penalty after a quarter of an hour proved decisive as goals from McVeigh and Magee meant that the Irish Cup went back to Lurgan.

1959 Irish Cup final programmes for the original tie and replay

Alec McCrae before 1959 IC final. Courtesy of Ballymena Observer

Harry Bond smothers a dangerous ball from a corner against Glenavon in the Irish Cup final. Courtesy of Ballymena Observer

Another trophy disappointment was the County Antrim Shield as United faltered to Linfield in a semi-final replay, losing by three goals without reply.

Speculation around the future United's top young stars had been an unwanted distraction throughout the season; Eddie Johnston looked odds on to join Middlesbrough in January but the move didn't materialise, Newcastle United took a keen interest in Lowry. The majority of cross-channel attention focused around teenage sensation Norman Clarke who had admirers in Arsenal, Wolves and Leeds to name a few but signed a new contract with United after the Irish Cup semi-final with his parents wanting him to remain in school, locally. Clarke's stock rose with the call-up to the Irish Amateur International team, alongside Russell and Johnston who also won caps throughout the campaign.

At the end of season AGM in May, there was no change in the boardroom for the second consecutive season. The treasurer revealed that the club's expenditure was the highest ever of £9,000 for the year, but the club still managed a credit balance of £42. Goalkeeper Harry Bond was voted as the club's player of the year by members and it was also announced that player-manager Alec McCrae had been awarded a new two year contract off the back of the success of the last two seasons.

Long serving trainer Billy McCready was given full international honours as trainer, in unfortunate circumstances following the untimely death of 'Uncle' Gerry Morgan. The popular Irish team trainer had previously captained the old Ballymena team in 1934 and had been a key background figure in the Northern Ireland coaching staff, enjoying much success in the World Cup in Sweden a year earlier.

⚽ 1959/1960 ⚽

Local forward Hubert Barr returned to the club during the 1959 close season; the school teacher had enjoyed a short spell with the club as a youngster but spent the last few seasons establishing himself as a talented Irish League goalscorer with rivals Coleraine. Barr was joined by a double signing from League of Ireland side Bohemians – forward Vincent Maguire (an Eire 'B' international) and defender Jimmy Lowe.

Eddie Russell had travelled to England to discuss a transfer to First Division Blackpool during the summer, but the Amateur International eventually decided

BALLYMENA   *Presented with "THE ROVER"*

Collectable 1959/60 team picture issued as a postcard in the Rover football magazine.
Back row: Billy Cubitt, Arthur Stewart, Alec McCrae (Manager), Harry Bond, Eddie Russell, Eddie Johnston, Vincent Maguire.
Front Row: James Lowe, Tommy Lowry, Hubert Barr, Norman Clarke

to stay with the Sky Blues. Despite keeping the talented winger, the club were dealt a major blow when Jimmy McGhee was forced to retire when he badly injured his back falling off a roof whilst working as a labourer. McGhee had been the top goalscorer at Warden Street for the past three seasons and won many admirers as with 77 goals. Only Jamie Shiels and Bob Sclater had scored more goals at the Showgrounds.

Ballymena started the season well – narrowly missing out on qualification to the Ulster Cup final after losing the opening game of the season to Crusaders but remaining undefeated in the remaining four fixtures to finish second the group. There was a similar story in the City Cup as after an opening defeat away to Distillery. The Sky Blues won the next six games on the trot including wins against the Belfast 'Big Two' (of Linfield and Glentoran) at home which put United in serious contention of silverware in the competition.

On 21st October 1959 in-form Ballymena travelled to the Lowlands of Scotland for a hastily arranged friendly against Falkirk at Brockville Park – this was the first time Ballymena United had played outside the island of Ireland. Alec McCrae had organised the venture with his former employers and would score United's

The travelling Ballymena United party en route to the friendly away to Falkirk. Courtesy of Ballymena Observer

only goal in a 4-1 defeat. *The Ballymena Observer* reported that after the game McCrae had been offered the vacant post of player-manager at Falkirk which he turned down.

The fixture also acted as a shop window for half-back Tommy Lowry who secured a £4,000 transfer to the Scottish Second Division club almost a week later, following United's Gold Cup semi-final draw against Linfield at Grosvenor Park. The transfer stirred friction between the committee and McCrae over the next few weeks so much so that the manager was absent for the 3-0 defeat to Bangor in November. There were fears that he wouldn't be returning to the Braid and although the situation was sorted before the next game, it would only be a temporary resolution.

In November, Hubert Barr's impressive early form (scoring 11 goals in his first 12 games) earned a call-up from Peter Doherty to the Northern Ireland 'B' team for a friendly against France at Windsor Park and it was the Ballymena man who scored the home side's only goal in a 1-1 draw. To date, Hubert remains the only Ballymena United player to represent Northern Ireland at this level.

With the uncertainty regarding McCrae's future at the Showgrounds and the loss of a key player in Lowry the team's form dipped – winning only one game from eleven from when Tommy left until the New Year and completely capitulating on a promising City Cup opportunity. Languishing in the bottom reaches of the Irish League table in early 1960 and despite starting the year with morale boosting wins against Crusaders and Glentoran, McCrae took charge of his last game away to Bangor on 16th January, having accepted the vacant manager's post at struggling Scottish First Division side Stirling Albion. He had informed the club his principal reason for leaving was 'to settle in Scotland with his wife'. Chairman Sam Graham reluctantly accepted McCrae's decision as the club 'didn't want to stand in his way'. By March, McCrae had become manager of Falkirk and returned to the Braid for an end-of-season friendly with Lowry in tow, which Ballymena comfortably won 3-0.

Rudderless Ballymena, now being managed by the club's committee throughout the early part of the year – floundered in the league and exited the Irish Cup at the hands of Distillery in the quarter-final losing 5-3. There had been much speculation surrounding the vacant post at the Showgrounds. Aberdeen's Jock Mitchell and Partick Thistle's Billy Simpson were touted as possible successors to McCrae. One name that was documented early on was that of Englishman Geoff Twentyman, recommended to Ballymena officials by former player Matt McPeake – now living on Merseyside and acting as a scout for Sheffield Wednesday.

On 29th March 1960, Twentyman arrived on Irish shores and completed the paperwork to become the new player-manager of Ballymena United for a fee of £2,000. The 30-year-old centre-half had carved out a career in professional football with his hometown club Carlisle United and then Liverpool. Legendary manager Bill Shankly had brought Twentyman into the team as a youngster at Carlisle and was appointed as manager at Anfield in December 1959. Shankly apparently begged Geoff to stay at Anfield to join his revolution starting with getting the team out of the English Second Division.

Geoff's move to the Braid with only seven games remaining in the season left little scope for impact during the 1959/1960 season. Despite defeat in his debut to Glentoran and a disappointing County Antrim Shield exit to Glentoran Seconds (an ignominious honour of being the first Ballymena United team to be defeated by the reserve team), the remaining Irish League fixtures provided a hearty return with four wins and a draw from the final five games which boosted the Sky Blues into a respectable fifth place in the standings.

⚽ *1960/1961* ⚽

Twentyman embarked his first full season in 1960 with the majority of McCrae's squad re-signed. The only major summer signing during the close season was

forward Peter Mitchell, a Dubliner from League of Ireland side Transport. Mitchell scored twice on his debut against Crusaders and another brace seven days later against Cliftonville but his impact in the team was limited and he would return to Shamrock Rovers later in the season.

Ballymena United match programme from the 1960/61 season

Mitchell would act as cover in the early season games for star forward Hubert Barr who had prestigiously been selected to the Great Britain squad for the 1960 Olympic Games in Rome. Barr left for Italy on 23rd August with the travelling party that included only two other Ulstermen in the all-amateur squad of players. Unfortunately Hubert would have to watch from the bench in all of the games as Great Britain failed to qualify from the first round group stage that included hosts Italy, Brazil and China. The 1960 games would be the last time that GB entered a men's football team until the London games in 2012.

United stormed out of the blocks in the 1960/61 campaign and topped their Ulster Cup group with four wins from five games to reach the final for the first time since 1950 with a game to spare; it would be the middle of September before the high-flying Sky Blues would taste defeat. In October 1961, Ballymena faced Glenavon in the final of the Ulster Cup with the Sky Blues (playing in their unfamiliar white change strip) getting revenge for the Irish Cup final disappointment two years previously. United convincingly won 3-1 with Hubert Barr scoring a brace and an own goal from Glenavon's McKinstry bringing the Ulster Cup to North Antrim for the first time. The large crowd at Grosvenor Park hailed the impact of their English player-manager, with many staying behind after the game to hail their leader with the newly claimed trophy won in one of United's greatest performances.

Fresh from the early season silverware Twentyman's men pushed on in the final stages of the City Cup series, and chalked up some impressive victories, notably

United manager Geoff Twentyman is presented with the Ulster Cup in the dressing room at Grosvenor Park after the 3-1 win against Glenavon.

against Linfield (4-2), Cliftonville (W 6-0) and Coleraine (W 5-2). Chasing the Ulster Cup finalists Glenavon in the race for the City Cup ended with two games to go, the Lurgan Blues drew 3-3 at the Showgrounds to kill off the Ballymena hopes of a second trophy in as many months. Twentyman had to be content with a second place finish in the final standings.

The Irish League started well for the in-form Braidmen and they quickly set themselves out as one of the front runners for the Championship. In December the player-manager was dealt a blow when winger Eddie Russell damaged ligaments and he would miss the remainder of the season, having to seek surgery on his injured knee. The club failed to find a suitable replacement but had a credible Christmas period of results which included wins against Glentoran and Distillery. On New Years' Eve, Ballymena United lost their first home game since March (an impressive 15 consecutive games) to Coleraine, 3-1.

1961 started with another defeat this time to Portadown, but this was followed by three victories against Linfield, Cliftonville and Bangor moving the Sky Blues up to third in the Irish League table. The 2-1 victory over the league leaders from Windsor Park proved the most impressive with Norman Clarke's early goal being followed by free scoring Hubert Barr's winner, this had onlookers quietly suggesting Ballymena as potential title-challengers at the start of February.

Ballymena United's 1961 Ulser Cup winning team pictured at the Showgrounds.

The title crusade was over quickly however, following a draw against second-placed Ards and a shock 5-1 defeat to Distillery. So too was the quest for the Irish Cup, as 'B' Division Ballyclare Comrades became the first Intermediate side to defeat the Braidmen in the cup. The reigning Steel and Sons Cup holders humiliated their senior counterparts 3-1 at Dixon Park in a game which was described as one of the biggest cup upsets of that period.

Linfield Swifts were the unfortunate recipients of United's cup backlash with an 8-2 thrashing days later in the County Antrim Shield first round – a game in which Hubert Barr scored a post-war record five goals in one game. Ballymena would eventually reach the semi-finals of the competition but limped out to an early Trevor Thompson goal as Glentoran won 1-0 to progress to the final in May. Unsurprisingly Barr again ended the season as leading goal-scorer with 34 goals and stalwart defender Billy Cubitt won the club's player of the year award.

The league season finished strongly with another victory against Linfield, this time at Windsor Park – the first time Ballymena completed a league 'double' over the Blues since the 1938/39 season. A 6-0 win over Irish Cup winners Glenavon at the Showgrounds on the final day of the season sealed a fifth place finish for the third year in succession. All was not rosy in the United camp as long serving defender Eric Trevorrow threatened to leave the club after losing his place in the team and whilst the situation was eventually resolved, local winger John Smyth couldn't be convinced to stay as he left for Glentoran in April citing the abuse form the terraces as the reason for his departure.

During the AGM in May, Chairman Sam Graham announced that next season the team would be made up mostly from professionals but less than two weeks later the club was stunned with the sudden departures of three key players; Hubert Barr (to Linfield), Eddie Johnston (to Glenavon) and Arthur Stewart (to Glentoran). All three players had been asked to re-sign. Secretary William McNeice took to the local press to insist that Ballymena had tried to keep the trio of amateurs but insinuated that they had been lured away by rival clubs. Barr and Stewart would eventually become full Northern Ireland internationals and make moves to professional football in England with Coventry City and Derby County, respectively – without a penny coming Ballymena's way.

⚽ 1961/1962 ⚽

Replacing the goals of Hubert Barr was an especially tricky issue for the manager. Cyril Greenfield (Walsall), Jim Emery (Barrow) and fellow Carlisle native Brian Tickell (Gateshead)formed a new look forward line during the early stages of the season – but only scored 14 goals between them with none of the trio making more than a dozen appearances for United. Whilst the forward line had changed the reliable stalwarts returned as the mainstay of the team in Bond, Trevorrow and Cubitt with much also expected of the maturing young local talent of John 'Smudger' Smith, Roy Dobbin, Eddie Russell, and Norman Clarke.

The defence of the Ulster Cup didn't go beyond the group stage after a stuttering start – only the one win from the five group games and also a first round exit in the Gold Cup to Glentoran at the Oval. Ballymena United's attempt in the City Cup was as a disaster, which had started promisingly with the 5-2 win over Ards in the first game but then led into November with five consecutive defeats. The *Observer* led with the headline 'The feast after the famine' after Ballymena bounced back with an 8-1 mauling of Cliftonville – Galgorm man Jimmy Small bagged a hat-trick in that game, the first goals of a season in which he would finish as leading marksman.

Rumours were circulating the town in November that Geoff Twentyman would be moving on having put his Ballymena house up for sale. These rumours were quickly quashed as results looked be improving with another impressive high scoring win, this time a seven goal salvo against Derry City and a more moderate 2-0 win over Bangor The City Cup wrapped up in the late autumn with an eighth place finish going into the Irish League, starting promisingly with a 2-1 win over Glentoran

Christmas Day 1961 marked a first for the club as Ballymena United Reserves reached the final of the prestigious Steel and Sons Cup, facing up against 'B' Division front-runners Carrick Rangers captained by former United defender Dessie Brown. The first game ended in a 2-2 draw in front of a festive 10,000 crowd packed into Solitude, but Rangers eventually overcame the club's young second string by a single goal in the replay at Grosvenor Park.

Ballymena United went into 1962 as joint leaders in the hunt for the Gibson Cup but off the pitch speculation had been rife all season that Norman Clarke would finally make the move to professional football in England after being courted by Football League clubs since making his debut four seasons ago. Wolves and Brighton had been linked with the 19-year-old winger, but come February it was the North East calling and a £6,000 fee was agreed with Second Division Sunderland. The Amateur international made the switch with expectations of

his potential sky high. He finished with 144 games and 33 goals in Ballymena colours and would be widely regarded as the most exciting young footballer produced in the town of Ballymena, Clarke's final game was a 2-0 victory over Ards at the Showgrounds on 10th February.

Geoff Twentyman accompanies winger Norman Clarke as he makes the move to Sunderland in January 1962. Courtesy of Norman Clarke autobiography

Scouse born Stanley Woodall (signed from Welsh club Pwllheli) filled the space in a reshuffled forward line following Clarke's departure. To the surprise of supporters and the on looking media, Ballymena pushed on in their pursuit of a first Irish League title, going top of the table in February and whilst dropping unnecessary points due to a number of drawn games, they stayed in first position through until March in a four horse race closely followed by Portadown, Ards and Linfield. The Irish Cup played little part in the Braidmen's thoughts this season, losing in the first round to Crusaders at Warden Street.

Whilst Twentyman's team were top of the league at the business end of the league season, they faced the misfortune of the most difficult run-in, facing all three of their aforementioned rivals in the final five games. It unfortunately proved too much for the Sky Blues as they failed to win any of the three games and were knocked off their perch with a 6-1 thrashing from Linfield with two games to go. Confidence was knocked out of a team that just couldn't go the distance and the local papers accepted that this wouldn't be the year that Ballymena United would claim an historic first championship.

Portadown defeated Ballymena in what was effectively the race for second place on the final day of the season, with the Armagh side winning 3-1 to condemn the club to a third place finish. It was a disappointing end to a season that promised so much as Linfield won the league title by just two points. The sub-plot of the final day drama at Shamrock Park was the 559th and final appearance of Eric Trevorrow in a Ballymena shirt after 14 years outstanding service. Twentyman afforded the Scottish defender the captaincy for his farewell appearance as he retired at the age of 36. Eric would be awarded the club's player of the year award at the AGM the following week, with Chairman Sam Graham boldly stating that 'No player has ever given better service to a club than Eric has to Ballymena'.

Losing the league title race to Linfield was almost inevitable in hindsight. It was their year, the most successful year that any Irish League club ever had, winning all seven of the trophies entered during the 1961/62 season. Hubert Barr scored a remarkable 48 goals in his first (and only) season in South Belfast before his move to England for £8,000.

⚽ *1962/1963* ⚽

Despite the success of a squad that ran the league championship to the final weeks of the season past, Ballymena United's team that took the Seaview field on the opening fixture of the 1962/63 season had no less than seven new faces on show.

Long-serving Harry Bond unable to agree terms on a new deal had left the club. Glenavon defender Gerry Kearney was brought in to replace Trevorrow in the back line and Twentyman brought two new forwards to the club with Billy Keenan (Distillery) and Jack McDowell (Glentoran); McDowell was the son of Linfield's successful Scottish manager Isaac McDowell. The two new forwards would be vying to fill the void left by the committee's surprise decision to sell last season's top marksman Jimmy Small to Ards. It was a decision which prompted a number of angry letters aired in the local press written by supporters, outraged by the treatment of the Galgorm centre-forward and distressed at how many local players the club had lost in the last few years to Irish League rivals.

It was an poor start for the Sky Blues in the Ulster Cup, finishing fourth in their qualifying group of six teams and winning only once in the aforementioned opening game against Crusaders. This led into a more productive City Cup campaign which, although inconsistent, provided a few wins and a fifth place finish going into the league season.

In September Twentyman had outlined that he would be implementing a welcome policy of promoting young local talent in his team this season though at this point the details of the club's precarious financial position was not clear to supporters. Despite the struggles with results in the early part of the season, it transpired that Geoff had turned down a coaching role with Norwich City. The offer had been rejected by the 32-year-old as it would have meant retiring from playing.

William McNeice (Secretary), Geoff Twentyman (Player-Manager), Sam Graham (Chairman) and Billy McCready (Trainer) discuss player selection during pre-season in 1962. Courtesy of Ballymena Observer

The player-manager added some more new faces to the team throughout the autumn, Manchester United's 'B' International Jim Shiels came in and became first choice full-back. 19-year-old Ballymoney goalkeeper Monty McKinney quickly became the number one goalkeeper, promising Scottish midfielder Brian Callan joined from Portadown and inside-forward Bobby Burke returned home after a spell with Burnley.

In the Gold Cup, a very understrength team was shown up by Derry City with the Candystripes putting five past a beleaguered Ballymena side. By the turn of the year results had improved and Ballymena were currently third in the Irish League table –the defeat on Christmas day to Crusaders would be the only black mark in the opening eight league games. In fact, from the Gold Cup semi-final defeat onwards the team would only lose two of the next 18 games in all competitions (to Crusaders as mentioned, and Distillery). The goals of top scorer Ken Halliday (signed from Banbridge Town) paved the way but too many draws were hampering the team's progress up the table.

Impressive Irish Cup home wins over Portadown (4-1) in the first round and Glentoran (3-1) in the quarter-final (the latter a much needed highest attendance for the season) meant an Irish Cup semi-final against in-form Distillery. It was to be a disappointing afternoon for the Braidmen as the Whites ran out comfortable 3-1 winners with Bobby Burke getting Ballymena's late consolation goal.

The iconic cover of the Social Club Gazette matchday programme which was published from 1961 until 1972.

The number of drawn fixtures ultimately cost the Braidmen a higher league finish than the fifth place they found themselves in – Ballymena drew half of their games (11 from 22) which was more than any other team and only lost four games throughout the series, the same as Champions Distillery.

With rumours and speculation rife throughout the season the financial reality of Ballymena's woes became clear at the AGM in May when club treasurer Bob Read unveiled a debt of £1,095. He noted that all clubs in the Irish League had noted a decline in attendances. The committee felt the boom in people watching television was a major contributory factor. Ironically it was also noted a few weeks before that Ballymena had voted strongly against a proposal for changing the football calendar to facilitate 'summer football' –fifty years on the same arguments are being heard throughout local football!

Forced financial restrictions meant that Geoff Twentyman was asked to run the team on £80 per week, a challenge that he felt that was impossible to do to reach the ambitions of the club's committee and supporters. He asked for his contract to be mutually terminated in May 1963. Stating that he was very sorry to be leaving Ballymena – the *Ballymena Observer* paid Geoff the compliment of being regarded as 'one of the club's greatest centre-halves'. Geoff would return to his native Carlisle United to rejoin the club he started his career with for one season before going on to manage Hartlepool United.

In 1967, Bill Shankly brought Twentyman back to Anfield to become chief scout at Liverpool. It was there that Geoff developed a reputation for unearthing some of Britain's best young talent as he recommended names such as Kevin Keegan, Alan Hansen, John Toshack and Phil Neal who would go onto win countless honours in England and Europe. It was reported there were no less than six of Twentyman's recommendations in Liverpool's first European Cup winning team of 1977. He would leave England in 1986 and join Graeme Souness in Glasgow to take up the role of chief scout of Glasgow Rangers.

⚽ 1963/1964 ⚽

Managerless Ballymena United faced a tough summer in 1963 in which a period of austerity was enforced as the committee attempted to recruit a capable team. Brian Callan was the first to be released to free up wages and expenses that had been used to fly him over from Scotland every week. For the third consecutive season – Ballymena lost their top goalscorer as Ken Halliday went to Workington in the English Fourth Division.

Last season's player of the year John 'Smudger' Smith was promoted to team captain. The versatile Liverpool born player, who by then had won both Amateur and Inter-League honours, had become a firm fans favourite since making his debut 1960 and settling in the town after marrying a local girl.

The opening game was a disaster for Ballymena United as they went down by an embarrassing double figure score - with the *Ballymena Weekly Telegraph* describing the 10-1 defeat to Crusaders in the Ulster Cup as a 'massacre'. The score matched United's record defeat to Belfast Celtic in November 1946 in the Northern Regional League. Whilst the team bounced back with a win against Cliftonville and a draw against Derry City these results would only paper over the cracks by the time the City Cup campaign approached in September.

Seven straight defeats in the City Cup had set alarm bells racing with the Braidmen rooted to the bottom of the table. An article in one of the Belfast papers on 25th October 1963 questioned whether there would even be a senior

Ballymena United players pictured in August 1963 before the Ulster Cup win over Cliftonville at the Showgrounds.

football team in Ballymena next season according to Secretary William McNeice. Supporters were also in uproar as unsettled captain Smith was quickly sold to Distillery for a cut-price £900 without a suitable replacement lined up.

In late November, with immediate action required a delegation from Ballymena United travelled to Wigan to speak to Tranmere Rovers' 34-year-old Dave Hickson about becoming player manager at the Showgrounds. Hickson had made his name as one of the only players ever to play to play for all three Merseyside clubs (Everton, Liverpool and Tranmere) and the centre-forward would agree to make the move to Irish football for the rest of the 1963/64 season.

Hickson's impact was immediate and an impressive 4-1 victory in the final City Cup game against Bangor gave the club hope that the season could possibly be salvaged with the Irish League starting the following week. Whilst the team grew in confidence, they were devoid of any luck on the field – winning only one of the first half-dozen league games before the turn of the year. After a poor festive period of one point from three games (a thrilling 5-5 draw with Derry City) the Sky Blues started 1964 in tenth place, hovering just above the re-election places.

Dave Hickson's 1964 employment permit to work in Northern Ireland. Courtesy of the Hickson family

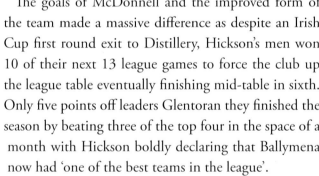

In January, Hickson was forced to deal with his main striker's decision to emigrate to South Africa. Jack McDowell – who had scored 19 goals (and would still finish the season as leading goalscorer) – was leaving with his wife to play for Bloemfontein FC. This gave a window of opportunity to a young Belfast based forward called Mal McDonnell, who had played a handful of games earlier in the season before being loaned out to Ballymoney United. Mal instantly make his mark in the team scoring 16 goals in 18 games in the second half of the season.

Mal McDonnell. Courtesy of Ballymena Observer

The goals of McDonnell and the improved form of the team made a massive difference as despite an Irish Cup first round exit to Distillery, Hickson's men won 10 of their next 13 league games to force the club up the league table eventually finishing mid-table in sixth. Only five points off leaders Glentoran they finished the season by beating three of the top four in the space of a month with Hickson boldly declaring that Ballymena now had 'one of the best teams in the league'.

Members unanimously decided to retain the services of player-manager at the end of year meeting. The club had turned over a profit of £221 for the season – achieved by successful reduction of wages by a third coupled with the transfer of Smith and the sale of Geoff Twentyman's old house! Tough tackling defender Dave Cloughley was voted as the stand out player of the year. The policeman was signed from Glentoran and captained the Northern Ireland Amateur International side on three occasions throughout the season.

Memorandum of Ballymena United Football Club

An Agreement

made this 5th day of May, 1964

between BALLYMENA UNITED FOOTBALL CLUB, whose Grounds are situate in Ballymena, in the County of Antrim, hereinafter called the Club of the one part, and David Hickson. (hereinafter called "the Player") of the other part.

1. The Club hereby agrees to engage the Player from the 15th day of August, 1964, until the 30th day of April, 1965 (both inclusive), for the purpose of Playing Football with the Club.

2. The Player hereby agrees to serve the Club for the purpose and period aforesaid, and not to engage himself to play football for any other person or Club during the said period.

3. In consideration of such service the Club hereby agrees to pay to the Player the sum of Twentyfive Pounds, per Week. from 15th August, 1964 until 30th April, 1965, except in Charity Matches, the amount paid to be pro rata to amount received from Charities Committee.

Provided always that the Player shall play in all Club Matches when required, and shall keep himself sober and in good playing form, and attend regularly to training and generally observe training instructions and do all that is deemed necessary to fit himself as an efficient football player.

....

....

4. Should any accident occur to the Player or he be in any way injured whilst at practice or play so as to incapacitate him from playing, the above sum shall continue to be paid; but should he be unable to play to the satisfaction of the Committee of the Club, through any cause other than the above named, payment will be withheld.

When unable to play through accident or injury a Doctor's Certificate m u s t be produced to that effect, and forwarded to the Secretary of the Club without delay.

As witness, the hands of the said Parties.

Name and Address of Witness:

Samuel Graham

172 Clonavon Bmena.

For and on behalf of Ballymena United Football Club:

William JB McNeice

Secretary.

Daniel Hickson

Player's Signature.

Ballymena Observer

Manager Dave Hickson's contract extension signed in May 1964. Courtesy of the Hickson family

Ballymena United before their 1964/65 season opener against Coleraine at Warden Street.
Back Row (left to right): Billy McCready (Trainer), David Russell, Roy Dobbin, Armstrong Beckett, Hugh Buchanan, Eddie Russell, Robin McCabe.
Front Row (left to right): Billy Cubitt, Tom Smyth, Arthur Thomas, Dave Hickson (Player-Manager), Gerry Kearney, Mal McDonnell.

⚽ *1964/1965* ⚽

Ballymena Observer, Thursday, August 13, 1964 **9**

MISADVENTURE VERDICT AT INQUEST ON BALLYMENA UNITED F.C. CHAIRMAN

CARBON MONOXIDE POISONING WAS CAUSE OF DEATH

A VERDICT of death through misadventure due to inhalation of carbon monoxide, a constituent of coal gas, was returned by the jury at the inquest on Mr. Samuel Graham, chairman of Ballymena United F.C., in the Courthouse last week.

On 30th July 1964 a dark cloud was cast over the club with the death of Chairman Samuel Graham. The 56-year-old had been on the United committee since 1935 and suffered carbon monoxide poisoning in his Queen Street home. A minute's silence was held before the pre-season friendly with First Division Stoke City in his honour, with Vice-Chairman Jimmy Rock taking over as acting chair until further notice. United lost the game by six goals without reply against a Stoke side with Northern Ireland star Jimmy McIlroy playing a starring role for the Potters in the well-attended exhibition match.

There was little summer transfer movement; Hickson brought in an unknown English forward named Arthur Thomas from Ellesmere Port who would take to the Irish League like a duck to water – scoring 14 goals before the end of September to lead the Irish League goal charts. His goals would prove invaluable as the mercurial Mal McDonnell would miss almost two months of football after he was internally suspended for playing prohibited Sunday football in Belfast.

A disappointing start to the 1964/65 season meant exits in the Ulster Cup and Gold Cup in September. Hopes of the City Cup also disappeared quickly as inconsistency turned to a negative consistency. The Sky Blues would lose seven straight games throughout the early autumn, before bouncing back with a 7-2 win against Cliftonville at Solitude with a hat-trick from Thomas.

Chairman David McKeown. Courtesy of Ballymena Observer

A special meeting of members was called in early October to appoint a new Chairman. Acting chair Jim Rock couldn't accept the role due to work commitments and local building contractor David McKeown was elected to succeed the late Samuel Graham. McKeown wasted no time as the newly appointed leader of the football club –in his first season he supplied a new kit for the first team, fixed the press box as well as completely re-fitting the club rooms and dressing rooms.

Despite a strong finish to the City Cup (eventually finishing eighth) and a solid start to the Irish League campaign with two wins and two defeats in the first four games, Hickson was sacked by the club at a meeting on 22nd December 1964. Faith had been lost in the Englishman who had developed a fiery temper having been sent off no less than twice in the past year and was jeered by his own supporters in the defeat to Portadown a few days earlier.

Rumours had circulated in the press as to the next Showgrounds boss with England international Peter Broadbert and ex-Celtic star Bobby Evans names touted in the local papers. In late January, 29-year-old George Smith – a school-teacher from Scotland who had been out the game for 12 months through illness but previously with Dundee United – was appointed the new player manager of the club. He became the youngest ever manager in the Ballymena's history. United paid £1,000 to Dundee United for his services and he immediately moved to the town with his wife into a house built by chairman McKeown.

The managerial upheaval didn't do any favours for the club who had started 1965 in third place in the table, and it would not be until mid-February until the Braidmen would get their first win of the new calendar year. There was also an inglorious exit in the Irish Cup with a 3-1 derby defeat to Coleraine at home, with interim captain George Taggart scoring United's only goal. But despite this, the Sky Blues made a late push up the league table which all started with a stunning late winner from player manager Smith against Linfield, as Ballymena won 3-2 at Warden Street.

George Smith. Courtesy of Ballymena Observer

Smith's men kept battling away and four league wins from four in March moved the club into third in the table and also within touching distance of leaders Derry City. Unfortunately Easter defeats to both Glentoran and Linfield took away any building momentum, with Ballymena United having to settle for a sixth place finish for the 1964/65 league season. United's final chance of silverware for the season was the County Antrim Shield and after an agonising 270 minutes in a semi-final saga of two replays in the semi-final against Larne, a late penalty from the Intermediate side was enough to kill of Ballymena's season at Solitude.

Thomas would be a unanimous choice for the player of the year award at the end of season meeting of members, scoring 40 goals in his first season in Irish football. This season also marked the retirement of a true United stalwart as Billy Cubitt ended his 12 year association with the club after 485 appearances and 13 goals. Billy would go down in history as one of the longest serving Ballymena United players. The Harryville defender was granted a benefit game against a strengthened Harryville Amateurs team at the start of the following season.

⚽ *1965/1966* ⚽

George Smith had spent the summer of 1965 trying to add quality re-signing John 'Smudger' Smith from Distillery, Portadown's Robin Burke, Glentoran defender Tommy Brannigan and local winger Tommy 'Tucker' Aiken (from Glentoran II). The domestic season started earlier than ever on 7th August and

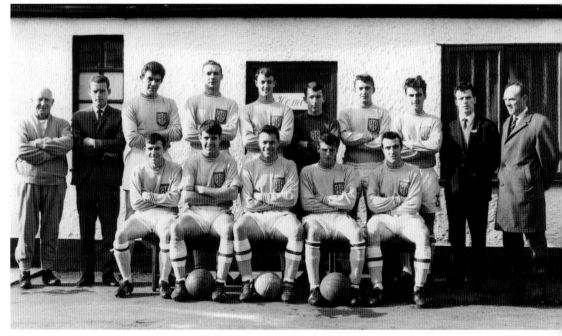

Ballymena United's 1965/66 team picture taken at the Showgrounds.
Back row: Billy McCready (Trainer), Robin Burke, David Cloughley, Unknown, Roy Dobbin, Sean Walsh, Eddie Russell, Tony Smith, John Eric Smith, David McKeown (Chairman).
Front row: Thomas Aiken, Arthur Thomas, George Smith (Player-Manager), Thomas Brannigan, Mal McDonnell.

was altered to include an 11 game Ulster Cup series before the Irish League season running between September and February. The City Cup tournament would now complete the campaign.

United started well with some impressive free-scoring Ulster Cup results, the best of which was a 7-3 hammering of Ards at home to move the club into second place at the half-way point of the competition. Results fell away though with too many draws eventually meaning a mid-table finish. Frustratingly the draws continued into the early stages of the Irish League. Smith's United always carried a goal threat and chalked up the club's record home victory on 18th September against perennial strugglers Cliftonville – winning 8-0 with goals from Arthur Thomas (3), Mal McDonnell (2), John Smith (2) and Tommy Brannigan.

A double blow was to hit the club at the start of November as press speculation that Derry City were rumoured to be interested in United talisman Arthur Thomas. This sparked a scramble for the Birkenhead schoolteacher's signature as Glentoran and Linfield made enquiries for the player previously thought to be off limits to other clubs. Linfield won the race and signed the forward who had scored 57 goals in 56 games for only £2,000, a decision that infuriated Ballymena supporters. The second blow came during the same week when player-manager George Smith was immediately forced to retire from football after being diagnosed with a previously undetected heart defect.

The sale of Thomas coupled with the inconsistent results meant the natives were restless and answers were sought of the club's committee who had been accused of carrying too many 'pensioners' at board room level. Members held a meeting in December and both committee and manager were given a vote of confidence by members – although Vice-Chairman Jim Rock resigned, sarcastically citing the negative influence of too many 'football experts' amongst the club membership.

There was a late surge in the league following eight weeks undefeated, with Ballymena four points off first place with four games to go, three of which against the teams above them in the standings. The hype would be quashed as quickly as it arose with a drab goalless draw against Linfield at the Showgrounds, a game which attracted a crowd of almost 10,000 in the biggest gate seen in Mid-Antrim since the Boxing Day fixture against the same opponents in 1948. Smith's side followed this up with an uninspiring 5-1 reverse to Derry City to kill off hopes of even a runners-up place. A single David Cairns goal brought a win against Glenavon on the final day of the Irish League season in February to secure a fourth place finish – the highest finish in four years.

Ballymena pinned their hopes on the Irish Cup and progressed via a replay in the first round against Derry City – only a week after the 5-1 thrashing in the league by the same team. Speculation had been that 19 year old winger 'Tucker' Aiken had been poised to seal a transfer to Bury for £4,000 but he scuppered the deal by informing the English club that he would only move when United were out of the Irish Cup. The gesture was well received in Ballymena, but despite the Sky Blues eventually falling to Coleraine in the quarter-final in a tie that required two replays, Bury backed out of the deal and signed someone else. United took some solace in clearing over £1,000 in their share of gates from the three massive attendances against the Bannsiders.

Having finished fourth and with enthusiasm for the team described as being at 'high pitch', Ballymena United qualified for the inaugural (yet short-lived) 'Top Four Trophy' – a competition where the top four teams in the Irish League table played off against each other. Ballymena drew with champions Linfield to force a replay in the semi-final, the Sky Blues lost 1-0 two weeks later.

The City Cup didn't provide supporters with much end of season cheer either as Ballymena finished eighth but there was some comfort in a first County Antrim

Shield final in 12 years. A comfortable 4-0 win for Linfield at Solitude finished the season on a bum note. George Smith had signed a new one-year contract as manager in February after the successful end to the league but come the AGM in May questions were being asked of the Scot with Smith claiming that his team 'never got over the defeat to Coleraine in the cup'.

Eddie Russell receives a clock from supporter Robert Montgomery as a farewell gift before leaving for Canada, with player-manager George Smith looking on. Courtesy of Ballymena Observer

Eddie Russell dealt the club a shock when he announced in April that he would be immigrating to Canada at the end of the season. After an impressive 333 appearances (and 76 goals) a benefit match at the end of the season had been proposed for his nine years of loyal service, the game could not be arranged due to the availability of the Showgrounds complex and Russell's leaving date. Added to this sought-after wing-half Tommy Brannigan, who also won the club's player of the year award, had also planned to immigrate away from Northern Ireland to Australia but he shelved those plans amidst interest from a host of Football League clubs. Brannigan's form during the 1965/66 season was acknowledged when he was selected as a reserve for the Northern Ireland full international team in May for a friendly against West Germany.

⚽ *1966/1967* ⚽

Trusted with improving on their top four finish manager George Smith outlined his desire to become the first Ballymena manager to take the club into European competition and strengthened his panel with Chris Broad from Carrick Rangers and Duncan MacColl (the latest in a long line of Scottish forwards) arriving from Barnsley. Ballymena United started well with a 5-0 Ulster Cup win against Cliftonville.

A first for the club was the introduction of substitutes in the Irish League and the first sub used by the club was against Ards in August 1966. David Cairns replaced Samuel Craig after 57 minutes, the change reaped instant rewards as Cairns scored a 23 minute hat-trick to set the club on their way to a 4-2

Ballymena United's 1966/67 team picture taken before the Ulster Cup defeat to Coleraine in August 1966.
Back row: George Smith (Manager), John Walker, Roy Dobbin, Sean Walsh, John Eric Smith, Tony Smith, David McKeown (Chairman).
Front row: Allen Stewart, Duncan MacColl, David Cairns, David Cloughley, Tom Aiken, Thomas Stewart, Thomas Brannigan, Billy McCready (Trainer).

victory. Ballymena eventually finished fifth in the Ulster Cup table after a solid, yet unspectacular start to the season. The Braidmen started their Irish League without a win in their first six fixtures, and were suffering at the bottom of the table. They were dumped out of the Gold Cup with a 7-3 reverse to Glentoran in the quarter-final at the Oval at the end of October.

Struggling United were boosted by Norman Clarke's returned to the club in the autumn. The 24-year-old winger had been cruelly forced out of action for almost two years with a cruciate knee injury. He had signed off with a benefit match at Roker Park in September against Charlton Athletic and returned home for a second shot at part-time football. Clarke's second debut was in the 4-1 win over Portadown. The win against Portadown wasn't enough to save George Smith, who was duly sacked on 31st October. The Scot hadn't appeared on the pitch all season much to the frustration of the committee who felt they needed a manager to be playing to justify his wages. Smith left his

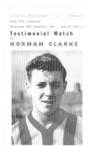

Match programme from Norman Clarke's Sunderland testimonial in September 1966

Ballymena teaching post soon after and returned to Stirling where he would eventually become a local television pundit for Scottish football.

United moved quickly to try and appoint a new player manager, with Hibernian's Pat Quinn strongly touted for the job in the local press but the £10,000 asking price from the Easter Road club quickly put cold water on any potential deal. In the interim it was Norman Clarke who took the reigns as player-coach for six weeks, taking the club into the New Year. Despite a rejuvenation on the pitch he resigned from his role to focus solely on playing – citing the additional workload from his recent enrolment at Stranmillis College as the main factor. The club appointed a selection committee consisting of David McKeown (Chairman), Billy Swann (Vice-chair) and Jim Rock to manage the selection and preparation of the team for the remainder of the season.

Clarke had steadied the ship during the winter and United started to play some tasty football, winning 7-3 against Crusaders and 5-1 against Bangor. Despite defeats against the Belfast 'Big Two' of Linfield and Glentoran over Christmas the Sky Blues finished 1966 in a respectable fifth place in the league. The goals of Mal McDonnell had been crucial to the upturn in fortunes but a broken shinbone on Christmas Eve against Linfield would end the talismanic forward's season prematurely. He would still finish as the club's leading goalscorer with 26 goals in just 24 games!

Hopes were almost completely pinned on the Irish Cup following the completion of the Irish League campaign which ended with an underwhelming 7th place finish. The first round trip to Distillery in February was to be equally as disappointing, losing 3-0 to the Whites. By this stage supporters had already given up and encouraged building for next season as fruitless City Cup and County Antrim Shield attempts failed to produce any silverware.

Chairman David McKeown had been campaigning for the club to appoint then Shelbourne manager Gibby McKenzie who had been looking a return to Northern Ireland. Without the backing of his fellow committee and members no official approach was made to the former Portadown boss. The club noted a loss of £1,400 for the financial year and were also struck with a number of discontented players; Club captain Dave Cloughley and talented winger 'Tucker' Aiken handed in transfer requests and Norman Clarke voiced his dissatisfaction in that he 'wasn't enjoying his football'.

⚽ *1967/1968* ⚽

Frank Treacey (St. Mirren) and Ray Patterson (Killsythe Rangers) were the committee's two main summer signings. Club captain Dave Cloughley who had sought a transfer late in the previous season, moved to Glenavon with former fans' favourite and Irish Cup winner Tommy Lowry brought back as a replacement (but the former Falkirk player would only make a handful of appearances after moving from Glenavon). One of those appearances was a memorable 11 goal thriller in the opening game of the season against Crusaders, which Ballymena edged by a single goal to win 6-5. Whilst the club started the season with an indifferent Ulster Cup series (finishing 7th from 12) one player who started the

season on fire was Mal McDonnell who scored 13 goals in the 11 games of the competition after a return from injury.

Still seeking a permanent player manager since the departure of George Smith almost a year before, a surprise written application from former manager Dave Hickson (who since leaving the club three years ago had spells with Fleetwood Town and Ellesmere Port) was successful. Amidst some scepticism from the press and supporters he was re-appointed by the committee as player-manager on 7th September, 1967. Hickson's second debut ended in a dismal 6-1 defeat to Glentoran at the Oval – this had actually been an improvement on their last outing, having lost 8-1 to Glenavon in the Gold Cup four days earlier.

Results didn't drastically improve as hoped with Hickson back in charge, seven defeats from eight games in the early stages of the Irish League had the Sky Blues were quickly languishing at the bottom end of the league table. Hickson unearthed the club's first European player during this transition period. Danish wing-half Eskild Strasiak was drafted in for four games but couldn't agree terms and quickly returned home to Odense Boldklub, future European opponents of the club. Another departure was talented winger Tommy Aiken finally sealing his move to England with Doncaster Rovers.

By Christmas, the committee's patience had run out with Hickson with supporters now staying away in their droves from the Showgrounds and the

Englishman was sacked for the second time the week before Christmas 1967, the Englishman wasn't long out of the game before reappearing in the vacant manager's position at Bangor for a very short spell.

In January 1968, Ballymena United opened their new purpose build 'social centre' on Slemish Drive beside the Showgrounds, at a cost of £20,000. The Social Club opening (mirroring similar new buildings across Irish League) was extremely popular from the offset and had attracted almost 1,000 members by the summer and it would be a major source of new revenue for the parent club over the next few years.

Late that same month, Ballymena United appointed the latest in a long line of player-managers tasked with changing the fortunes of the club, Scottish international defender Alex Parker. The 32-year-old former Falkirk and Everton full-back was capped 15 times by the Scots and also appeared at the 1958 World Cup – the first player to appear for the club who played in the World's greatest football competition.

Alex Parker

Parker arrived with three league games remaining for United but made little impact as the club finished seventh and also exited the Irish Cup to Crusaders in the first round at Seaview. With the sudden loss of form of Mal McDonnell, Glaswegian Mick McGowan was signed from Dumbarton. The new forward only managed two goals in ten games as the Sky Blues finished the season poorly with a mediocre City Cup campaign and a surprise exit to Larne in the County Antrim Shield.

There had been speculation driven by the Ballymena United committee and local press that a new purpose built football stadium should be part of a new town planning commission for the benefit of the football club. The debate would rumble on for a few years with virtually no tangible progress. Some good news for Parker and United was the return of fans' favourite Eddie Russell from Canada. The Larne winger had enjoyed a successful spell with Lachine Rangers in Quebec but returned home to Northern Ireland with his family after only two years away.

⚽ *1968/1969* ⚽

Parker made some shrewd business in the summer unearthing a host of unknown players who would go on to be established Irish League stars – centre-half Roy Coyle came from Ballyclare Comrades, defender Bobby Averell from Coleraine and Dundela's leading goalscorer Jimmy Martin all joined the ranks at the Showgrounds – but all started slowly as United struggled early on. There was also an opportunity for a local winger Jackie Fullerton who had previously starred with Larne.

It was barely mid-September by the time the notoriously fickle Ballymena public were calling for the head of the manager. The team had endured a wretched start to the season, having to wait 11 games until the club recorded their first win of the campaign a 5-2 win against Cliftonville, this saved Parker's men from finishing bottom of the Ulster Cup table.

Not satisfied with the erratic performances of regular goalkeeper Sean Walsh, a 16-year-old Jim Platt was given the opportunity between the sticks. Parker's faith was repaid with some dazzling performances by the Ballymoney youngster who instantly started attracting the attention of professional scouts. The manager had previously outlined his desire to give young players a chance in the first-team and it was beginning to pay dividends. There was no place though for former player of the year Tommy Brannigan whose alarming drop in form meant he was sold to Distillery.

Results went from the ridiculous to the sublime during October as the Irish League season got underway. The Braidmen secured six consecutive wins – the highlight of which was undoubtedly a 6-1 mauling of Coleraine at the Ballycastle Road with Mal McDonnell helping himself to four goals to move Ballymena United into fourth place in the league. Gary Erwin was also in free scoring form which attracted the attention of Geoff Twentyman who was now acting as a scout for Liverpool, Erwin would eventually finish the season as joint leading scorer with Jim Martin on 19 goals.

Results fell away with five defeats from six games going into the winter as Mal McDonnell moved down South to Dublin side St. Patrick's Athletic for £2,000 in December. His final goal in his final game against Glenavon, his 137th in United colours, would make him the leading goalscorer in the club's history and a record that still remains to this day.

In December Parker recruited Wales international (and fellow 1958 World Cup veteran) Mel Hopkins from Brighton & Hove Albion on a short-term contract to limited effect. It was a mid-table season for Ballymena Unitedby the end of the league season in January the team hadn't moved from seventh position for over half of the campaign.

The Irish Cup campaign was late starting at the end of February as United progressed to the quarter-finals after a first round win over Carrick Rangers but were subsequently beaten by Distillery in the last eight at the Showgrounds. Free scoring United's goals dried up during the City Cup as the club failed to make any progress in the competition to end the season with a whimper with only three wins from the eleven games.

⚽ 1969/1970 ⚽

Parker brought in a host of new attacking options during the summer of 1969. 22-year-old forward Vic Fleming who had been Portadown's player of the year last term, alongside Carlisle United's Jim O'Rourke and Jim Herron from Glentoran in a swap deal with defender Roy Coyle. Despite the influx of forwards, goals were shy in an unusually busy pre-season which included heavy defeats to Peterborough United, Mansfield Town and Drumcondra.

It prepared the Sky Blues for a decent start to the season in the Ulster Cup; sitting top of the table after six games following wins against Cliftonville, Distillery, Ards and Crusaders. They fell away in the second half of the campaign with four defeats on the bounce to eventually finish third in the placings. The City Cup was without success but United reached the semi-finals of the Gold Cup – losing 3-1 to Coleraine at the Oval. Despite the inconsistent form Parker had kept full faith in the youngsters including teenage goalkeeper Jim Platt and blooding other youngsters such as Billy Richardson and Quinton McFall. Platt had attracted the interest of Rangers and Aberdeen and had also been for pre-season training at Liverpool during the summer.

Jim Herron's early season goals quickly dried up and he was sold to Bangor, another player out the door was Jackie Fullerton to Glenavon after suffering at the hands of the terrace 'boo-boys'. United lost six of their opening eight Irish League games and were only prevented from propping up the league table by the equally poor Cliftonville - pressure was starting to grow on the manager from the notoriously impatient United faithful.

On 8th December 1969, Alex Parker was sacked as Ballymena United manager with the *Ballymena Times* overdramatically describing the club as at the 'lowest ebb in their history'. Whilst the role as Showgrounds chief was widely accepted as a poisoned chalice, many understood that Parker didn't have much luck during his two years at the club. The Scot was fixed up with a playing contract at Dublin side Drumcondra before Christmas and also went onto have a short managerial spell at Southport. Back in Ballymena the manager's position was filled swiftly by a familiar face, that of the legendary Scot Alec McCrae who had guided the club to the Irish Cup in 1958.

Returning manager: Alec McCrae

The move didn't produce miracles in the Irish League championship as although the new manager started with an encouraging draw against Crusaders and a win against Glenavon it would only paper over the cracks of United's struggling outfit as the team only won two games in the second half of the league season. They successfully moved out of the re-election positions but still finished a disappointing tenth in the league – the club's lowest finish in 13 years.

McCrae was to guide the Braidmen back to an Irish Cup final against all likelihood – having been dealt the toughest draw in the first round against runaway league leaders Glentoran who had already plundered over 100 goals by the time the two sides met at the Oval in January. The Sky Blues conquered the East Belfast side through two Jim Martin goals in the second half. Crusaders were disposed of in the quarter-finals. There was derby delight for the club in the semi-final as Brian Nicholl, a youngster plucked from local league obscurity set United on their way to a first Irish Cup final in 11 years with a 2-0 win against Coleraine at Windsor Park in March.

Despite the vocal objections of both United and final opponents Linfield the IFA made an unpopular decision to host the showpiece final at Solitude, home of Cliftonville, on 4th April 1970. The restricted capacity of the North Belfast venue opposed to the preferred venue of the Oval would be rumoured to cost United over £800 in gate receipts. The restricted crowd of 15,000 (5,000 of which were backing the Sky Blues) would watch on as despite an early opener from Vic Fleming, Ballymena would be outclassed and outdone by two Phil Scott goals for the Windsor Park men for their 30th Irish Cup victory – manager McCrae even admitted post-match that, 'The best team won'.

Teenage sensation Jim Platt had already sealed his dream move to professional football, agreeing a deal with Second Division Middlesbrough eventually worth £10,000 to the Sky Blues but had negotiated to stay until the Irish Cup final before his move to the North East. Platt would go on to make almost 500 appearances for 'Boro in over

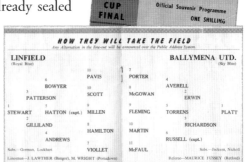

a decade of service and would also be understudy to Pat Jennings in the Northern Ireland squad and part of the legendary 1982 & 1986 World Cup squads.

United's season wasn't over though as three weeks after the final, the Sky Blues started their quest to be All-Ireland Cup winners in their first entry into the Blaxnit sponsored competition. An away first round tie against Sligo Rovers was the first cross-border tie the club had faced since the Inter-City Cup in 1949. Despite the big crowd (which went against the norm in a poorly supported competition) the trip to Connaught was fruitless as United's season ended with a 3-0 defeat to their League of Ireland opponents – another season without a trophy at the Braid.

Chapter Five

Never a dull moment (1970-1979)

⚽ 1970/1971 ⚽

With McCrae back at the helm and a near miss in the Irish Cup, United had started the seventies with quiet optimism that the club had turned the corner and moved on from a decade of managerial changes and underachievement. This optimism was in stark contrast to the changing political backdrop in Northern Ireland with growing civil unrest having already had a detrimental effect on local football attendances - the 1970/71 season saw a 33,000 drop in numbers across the league season from the previous year.

Arthur Stewart
Courtesy of Ballymena Times

Ballymena produced two summer transfer coups as months of negotiations after Derby County defender Arthur Stewart returned home in August 1970 – the local defender had fallen out of favour with manager Brian Clough and also turned down an offer from Cork Hibernians to re-join the Sky Blues after ten years. The reliable and steady Stewart was joined by a maverick Scottish winger called Sammy Frickelton who joined from Welsh side Rhyl but had previously played with his native Falkirk. Few could have expected the impact Frickelton would have on the club!

It was a slow start for the Sky Blues as they crammed five Ulster Cup games into the first two weeks of the season, winning unconvincingly against Cliftonville by a single Ray Starrett goal in the opening game. A series of draws forced the club back into the transfer market with Scottish forward Stan Vincent, Tommy Gowdy and John Platt (brother of goalkeeper, Jim) all coming into the side and rewarding McCrae with a 2-1 win against Glentoran at home. Whilst winning the Ulster Cup was already mathematically impossible, a stunning five goal performance against eventual cup winners Linfield inspired by Frickelton and sealed by a Jim Martin hat-trick was the highlight of the early season fixtures.

Sammy Frickelton
Courtesy of Ballymena Times

Footballing mercurial Frickelton was an instant hit with supporters with his trademark goal celebration of removing his shirt to reveal a large tattoo of King William of Orange upon his chest, prompting the infamous chant of "Sammy show us your chest!" from the terraces. The volatile Scot also had quickly fallen foul of the officials as he found himself suspended for the whole month of October and United's form suffered as a consequence. Captain Eddie Russell had also missed three months of the season through injury as Ballymena played out a poor City Cup attempt and after three replays in the Gold Cup against Cliftonville and exited the competition in the first round.

McCrae brought Alec Donald to the club in January from Derry City; the industrious Scot who had previous Football League experience with Port Vale was joined by returning winger Tommy Aiken from Welsh club Bangor City, after a disappointing spell at Doncaster Rovers. With United floating in mid-table, attentions turned to the Irish Cup and another surprise first round victory against Glentoran thanks to Jim Martin's goal meant a highly anticipated quarter-final derby away to Coleraine. It proved to be the biggest let down of the season as Ballymena lost 2-0 without a fight.

The league run-in was focused on United's ambitions of securing a place in the lucrative Texaco Cup for next season. The new cup sponsored by the American petroleum giant who had recently bought into the local market was a competition aimed at clubs who hadn't qualified for European competition in England, Scotland, Northern Ireland and the Republic of Ireland. The success of Derry City in the first year of the competition had also outlined the major potential financial benefits to a participating Irish League club. Ballymena, needing to secure a top five finish (a position they had held since the turn of the year) confirmed their place on the penultimate game of the season beating Glenavon 4-2 with two goals from Donald and one apiece for Russell and Vincent. The club finished the season with a 3-1 defeat in the semi-final of the County Antrim Shield to Crusaders at the Oval.

At the end of the season 76-year-old William McNeice stepped down as club secretary – a position he had held since 1934. McNeice was a popular figure at the club and across the Irish League and highly respected for his bank of knowledge. He was elected to the new honorary position of President of the football club at the AGM with Jimmy Coulter being elected to fill the vacant office of secretary.

In the summer of 1971, the County Antrim Agricultural Association bought out their lease of the Showgrounds facility from the Adair Estate for £12,000 and took ownership of the ground. Despite concerns from the football club (who had still reserved hope of a purpose built football stadium within the town) assurances were given that they could continue as anchor tenants as normal.

⚽ 1971/1972 ⚽

Although McCrae kept faith with his team for the following campaign, Sammy Frickelton had petulantly claimed at the end of last season that he wouldn't be back at the club after an internal suspension for violating training rules but managed to put his differences to one side and returned for pre-season despite interest from both East Fife and Linfield.

Ballymena United hosted a unique fixture in August 1971 when Israeli side Beitar Tel Aviv became the first club United played from outside the United Kingdom and Ireland. The match was to be billed as part of the ill-fated 'Ulster 71' festival aimed at promoting 50 years of the state of Northern Ireland, not the ideal campaign to be hosting within the backdrop of a county in turmoil. The government backed United with £500 to cover the cost of the fixture which Ballymena lost 3-1 with Jim Martin getting the home consolation goal against the travelling side. United's pre-season preparations

also included an overdue benefit testimonial for long-serving Eddie Russell (now starting his 13th season at the club) against Finn Harps at the Showgrounds which the Sky Blues comfortably won 4-0.

The opening weeks of the season were filled with incident which set the tone for the rest of a rollercoaster season as following the impressive 3-1 win against Coleraine in the Ulster Cup which started the season, United followed this with three consecutive defeats in the same competition. The last of the trio of losses was a dismal 7-0 defeat to Portadown at Shamrock Park which prompted the shock resignation of manager Alec McCrae on 30th August. The 49-year-old had been considering his position for a while, but seemingly the perilous financial position and the restriction in player transfers was the deciding factor as he stepped down as manager of the club for the second time - Arthur Stewart was quickly (and somewhat reluctantly) installed as player-manager of the club for the rest of the season.

Stewart began his leadership of the team with a 2-1 win against Cliftonville in the Ulster Cup but the next controversy wasn't far around the corner for the Braidmen. On 11th September, Ballymena travelled to the Brandywell for a game against Derry City, which would unwittingly play a major part in the history of the Irish League. During the game, the Ballymena United team bus was hijacked by local masked youths and set alight in the troubled Bogside area of the city. While no-one was harmed, barring a local priest who attempted to stop the crime, the event would be the catalyst for the Irish League's decision with the security forces that the safety of players or spectators could no longer be guaranteed at the Brandywell – forcing Derry City to play all their 'home' games at the Coleraine Showgrounds 30 miles away.

Front page of the Ballymena Observer on 16th September 1971

Despite the scare Stewart revitalised a United team that would finish runners-up to Linfield in the Ulster Cup and embark on their Texaco Cup quest with a two legged tie against Waterford United. It was the Irish League side who won the first round tie 6-5 on aggregate after an impressive 3-2 win at the Showgrounds and a six goal draw at Kilcohan Park – a game in which United sported their new look tangerine away strip. The quarter-final first leg against Shamrock Rovers was one of the biggest games at the Showgrounds in years. The game drew a crowd in excess of 8,000 fans and supporters didn't go home disappointed as the team produced one of the all-time great performances to win 4-1 with two goals from Jim Martin and one each for Bobby Averell and Sammy Frickelton. The second leg was a formality as in-form United drew 1-1 at Tolka Park to progress to the lucrative semi-finals with Jim Martin scoring United's goal – setting an individual club record as this was the 12th consecutive game he had found the net.

Ballymena United went into the semi-final against Scottish club Airdrie in unbelievable form having just come out of setting a club record 16 game unbeaten streak but were shocked to learn that Airdrie would refuse to travel to the province due to the ongoing political unrest. After much debate and protest the first leg of the semi-final was 'neutrally' played at Stranraer's Stair Park in late November with over 1,000 supporters making the short journey across the Irish Sea. The team lost 3-0 killing off hopes of a dream final. Despite also losing the second leg 4-3 at Airdrie two weeks later and restoring some

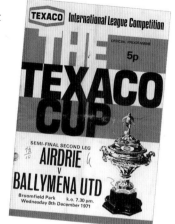

pride – the money spinning Texaco Cup journey had come to an end. The Scots eventually lost out to English First Division champions elect Derby County over two legs in the final of the competition.

Between the two legs of the Texaco semi-final, Ballymena United had given the supporters some cheer on 4th December by winning the City Cup for the first time in the club's history and marking the first silverware in 11 years at the Showgrounds! The tense Windsor Park final against Ards was won by a single Bobby Averell goal ten minutes from time. Unfortunately while many onlookers thought this was on the beginnings of a special season for the Sky Blues, few would have envisaged that it had already peaked.

Naturally, expectations were sky high for the start of the Irish League but an inconsistent start was followed by an alarming slump in form through January and February as four consecutive defeats left the Braidmen languishing down

Ballymena United players celebrate winning the City Cup for the first time, after beating Ards 1-0 in the final. Courtesy of Ballymena Observer

in ninth position. The Irish Cup was short-lived following a lifeless 1-0 first round defeat to Crusaders at Seaview but it was shortly after this the major problems at the club began to unravel before the eyes of manager Arthur Stewart. City Cup hero Averell announced that he was emigrating to Canada to keep his family safe from the 'troubles' and played his last match in March before jetting off to Toronto. Shortly after Averell's announcement leading goalscorer Jimmy Martin would be next to leave making the shock decision to quit football at the end of the 1971/72 season on religious grounds. The Belfast lay preacher who would set a post-war record of 44 goals that season stated 'I want to devote more time to the study of God's work'.

Temperamental forward Sammy Frickelton had seemingly reached the end of his continual ongoing feuds with the club in March when a bid was accepted from Glentoran (now managed by Alec McCrae) but at the final hour the deal was called off following McCrae's sudden resignation as manager at the Oval. United's final months of the season were visibly unsettled and inconsistent as despite a morale boosting win 2-1 win over Linfield, the Sky Blues finished the season a disappointing seventh and faltered in the quarter-finals and semi-finals of the Gold Cup and County Antrim Shield, respectively.

At the end of the season, despite the slump in form during the second half of the year, Chairman David McKeown expressed his satisfaction in one of the club's most successful seasons having won the City Cup and been Ulster Cup runners-up. The club had also managed to become financially sound for the first time in the best part of a decade off the back of the Texaco Cup run, clearing all the historic debts and made a substantial £1,000 profit in the process.

⚽ *1972/1973* ⚽

The summer of 1972 allowed for an upgrade to the Showgrounds facility. The 'Clock' terrace on the Slemish side of the ground became a covered facility for supporters for the first time thanks the help of voluntary labour from those connected to the club. One aspect staying the same at an ever changing Showgrounds was Sammy Frickelton who was staying at the Braid – but sadly not through his own choice. The Scot had been arrested by local police in the village of Martinstown and charged with possession of a firearm which would land Sammy in custody for almost a year.

Few changes were made to the team during the close season as only Englishman Thomas Dixon joined from Carlisle United and Sammy Scott from Cliftonville – both making a limited impact on the club and neither lasted further than the following summer. Striker Gary Erwin returned for another crack at senior football whilst Quinton McFall turned professional after being subject to a rejected £5,000 bid from Airdrie after the winger's impressive performances during the Texaco Cup games last season.

Jim Davidson, signed from Dundela in February, was now tasked with replacing the 44 goals of the departed Jim Martin. The Belfast-based forward got off to a good start with the first goal of the season against Cliftonville in the new

Clock stand at Showgrounds. Courtesy of Ballymena Times

Carlsberg Cup (a-pre-season competition) which only lasted two rounds for the Sky Blues as after progressing past the Solitude Reds, Ballymena were abruptly dumped out 6-0 by Ards.

Undeterred, Ballymena started their regular season well in the Ulster Cup and after only the one defeat from eight games, they found themselves top of the table with only three games remaining but scuppered hopes of winning the competition with two defeats against Linfield and Bangor. This allowed rivals Coleraine to

sneak in and win the cup. This was followed by a swift and forgettable exit from the group stage of the City Cup by November.

Off the pitch, the Irish League was coming to terms with the withdrawal of Derry City on 13th October 1972. A vote had been cast between all clubs regarding allowing the Candystripes to return to their Brandywell home for the first time since the Ballymena bus incident in September 1971. Ballymena United voted in favour of a return but current landlords Coleraine abstained crucially meaning that Derry lost the vote and subsequently felt there was no other option but to withdraw from Irish League football rather than suffer continual losses whilst playing games at the Ballycastle Road. This would lead to a 13 year wilderness period for the club before eventually joining the League of Ireland in 1985 – the vacant place freed for the 1972/73 season was filled at short notice by Larne.

Sammy Frickelton's last game of the season came on 30th December in the 4-2 defeat to Coleraine and he started his stretch in prison in early January – striker Paul Kirk from Glentoran was recruited as a replacement for the detained Scot. The manager was boosted with the unexpected return of Bobby Averell from Canada. The sturdy Magherafelt defender had been playing with Toronto Metros and had recently kept arguably the world's greatest ever player, Pele, at bay during an exhibition match against Santos as part of the Brazilian club's North American tour.

There was a second first round Irish Cup exit in two years when the Sky Blues succumbed to Glenavon after a replay. There was a cup 'first' for the Braidmen in April, as Ballymena bowed out of the County Antrim Shield at the quarter-final stage after a thrilling 5-5 draw with Glentoran. It was a game in which the club experienced their first penalty shootout. United cruelly lost the shoot-out 5-3 in which reserve team goalkeeper Andrew Kirkpatrick made only his second senior appearance. A trio of early cup exits was compounded with a 5-1 loss to Portadown in the Gold Cup at the end of the season.

Ninth place was the final return for the team's inconsistent endeavours through the Irish League season as Sammy McAuley was voted player of the year after a superb first season in senior football joining from Harryville Amateurs. He also had enticed his cousin and former team-mate at the Amateurs John Sloan to join the club. Seventeen-year-old Sloan made his debut in a low-key 2-2 draw against Larne in April. Another player under the microscope was Paul Kirk who had attracted a great deal of interest from English clubs and spent two weeks on trial at First Division Aston Villa but the Midlands club did not come back to meet the £10,000 valuation attached to the young striker.

In a first for the Irish League, the girls of Ballymena United set up the first all-female supporter's club in the Irish League. The 'Bluebirds' had originated out of Ballymena's only supporters club at the time, the Seven Towers, who had refused to accept the fairer sex as members.

⚽ 1973/1974 ⚽

During the summer of 1973, new club president David McCarthy died in a car crash only weeks after being elected to both the NI Assembly for North Antrim and the club presidency. McCarthy had taken up the honorary position following the death of William McNeice during the season past and had hoped to bring some political influence to the club's efforts for a new stadium within the town.

Arthur Stewart kept together the core of his squad from the previous season (including sought after Paul Kirk) with 22-year-old goalkeeper Robert Brown the only new face in the team after first-choice goalkeeper Monty McKinney picked up an early season injury. United would start the season without the imprisoned Sammy Frickelton (until November) and Bobby Averell was not due back from a summer spell in Canada until September. Stewart therefore put faith in young local players confidently proclaiming 'we have some of the best young talent in the country'. Ballymena started the season in the Ulster Cup with seven

Ballymena United's team pictured in August 1973 before a 3-0 win against Cliftonville in the Ulster Cup
Back row: Len McCall; Dessie Orr; Quinton McFall; Monty McKinney; Brian Todd; George Blair; Billy McCready (Trainer).Front row: Jeff Blair; Jimmy Young; Tommy Gowdy; Arthur Stewart (Manager); Sammy McAuley; Jimmy Brown.

Ballymena based players in the starting eleven and a comfortable 3-0 win against Cliftonville repaid Stewart's confidence.

That confidence from the Cliftonville game was unfounded as United lost the next four Ulster Cup games to be ruled out of trophy contention early on. Stewart was particularly annoyed with the performance in the 4-0 defeat to Distillery. Results improved with a late rally in the competition which included an impressive 2-0 win over reigning champions Crusaders, with United eventually finishing fifth. Their good form also took the Braidmen to the semi-finals of the Gold Cup, ending with a penalty shoot-out defeat to Bangor.

The penalty defeat to the Seasiders would be the only defeat in 12 games as in-form United started the City Cup group stage in fine form with wins against Cliftonville, Larne and Crusaders and a draw against Glentoran. They looked certain of a place in the final until Coleraine's Johnny McCurdy's long range goal in the last second of the crunch final group game meant that United lost 2-1 to the Bannsiders and sickeningly missed out on the City Cup final.

With the league season starting in good form for the club an added boost of Sammy Frickelton's return to action after 11 months on Boxing Day and the remarkable 3-2 victory over Linfield. Bobby Brown horrifically suffered fractured skull at home to Crusaders a few weeks later and was taken to Royal Victoria Hospital. A metal plate in his head was required and Bobby McKenzie from Ballyclare Comrades was brought in for the remainder of the season. At the other end of the pitch United were going through a lean spell in front of goal – not aided by leading scorer Paul Kirk going on trials with Sunderland and Reading as the big forward was determined to go full-time despite his club manager desperately wanting him to settle in Ballymena.

In February, Ballymena inflicted another defeat on Linfield in the first round of the Irish Cup with Alec Donald's 89th minute winner at Windsor Park. This was the fourth win in five attempts during 1973/74 as the Sky Blues remained undefeated against their South Belfast opponents all season. In the league United had cemented their place in the top four throughout the season, but too many dropped points and finishing the campaign with four games without a win meant that a respectable fourth place would be Ballymena's reward.

The performance of the season was undoubtedly saved for the Irish Cup quarter-final as United ran riot over reigning league champions Crusaders with a remarkable 7-1 win at Warden Street in which Paul Kirk (twice), Des Orr, Brian Todd, Quinton McFall, Gary Erwin and Eddie Russell all got on the scoresheet. The semi-final proved a more difficult obstacle against neighbours Larne as three games couldn't split the two sides at Seaview. Penalties eventually decided the coveted Irish Cup final place. Sammy McAuley's winning strike sealed a 4-3 shoot-out win for the men in blue, but leading goalscorer Paul Kirk's red-card meant he would cruelly miss the showpiece final.

For the Irish Cup final at Windsor Park on 27th April, the manager made the controversial last minute decision to replace the suspended Kirk with teenager John Sloan, leaving 23-goal striker Brian Todd on the bench against Ards. The Harryville youngster justified Stewart's faith by scoring United's equaliser in the final. The Sky Blues however lacked attacking ideas in the final – losing 2-1 to the County Down side. It was a defeat that hit Sammy Frickelton harder than most, he felt that the team had got it wrong on the day and the game would be the last the fans would see of their Scottish idol in a sky blue shirt. He was transferred home to junior side Bo'ness United during the summer.

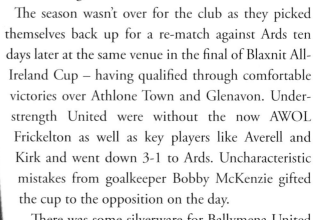

The season wasn't over for the club as they picked themselves back up for a re-match against Ards ten days later at the same venue in the final of Blaxnit All-Ireland Cup – having qualified through comfortable victories over Athlone Town and Glenavon. Under-strength United were without the now AWOL Frickelton as well as key players like Averell and Kirk and went down 3-1 to Ards. Uncharacteristic mistakes from goalkeeper Bobby McKenzie gifted the cup to the opposition on the day.

There was some silverware for Ballymena United though as player-manager Arthur Stewart was named as Ulster Footballer of the Year –the first time a Ballymena United player had won the coveted award since Eric Trevorrow in 1952. Stewart had been closely linked with the Glentoran job at the end of the season after George Eastham departed but committed his future to the club at the AGM declaring; 'We have a nucleus of a good side, capable of winning any domestic competition'.

⚽ 1974/1975 ⚽

Picking up the pieces after the disappointing end to the previous season wasn't easy for Arthur Stewart. Frickelton had already left and there was discontent amongst the ranks, with Paul Kirk still actively trying to force a move away from the club. Cup final goalkeeper Bobby McKenzie moved to Ards and out of favour Brian Todd was freed to join Larne. The only new face to the squad was Derry based winger Eamon McLaughlin who joined from Athlone Town.

The Sky Blues started the season well with a comfortable 4-1 Ulster Cup win against Cliftonville but it was an uninspiring campaign in the competition with United finishing mid-table. Paul Kirk had started the season rejuvenated with 5 goals in 9 games and was selected as the football writer's player of the month for

September. No sooner had he received this award than the club were forced to suspend the Belfast striker after he went on a self-imposed strike citing that he was fed up travelling. Despite having been courted by top English clubs for the past 18 months, Kirk was sold to Crusaders for an undisclosed fee.

Kirk's last goal in Ballymena colours had come in a 2-0 Gold Cup quarter-final win against Linfield which would be the first steps en-route to a first final appearance in the competition since 1931/32. Rivals Coleraine were clinically dispatched in the semi-final with an impressive 5-1 win at Warden Street, setting up a Gold Cup final at Windsor Park against Glentoran on 13th November. Attendance was restricted to an unusually small 2,000 – but those in attendance witnessed what Chairman David McKeown claimed to be 'one of the greatest goals scored at Windsor' when Quinton McFall's winner sealed a first Gold Cup for the Braidmen –Ballymena United won 3-2 with Jimmy Brown and Dessie Orr getting the other two goals. Spare a thought though for Gary Erwin (who finished the season as top marksman with 18 goals)

Quinton McFall
Courtesy of Ballymena Times

who couldn't join the midweek celebrations as he was checked in for nightshift at the Michelin tyre factory by 11pm!

Despite expectations rising regarding the capabilities of United's talented team – the City Cup was a bust and it took until the Christmas holiday period for a slow-burning Irish League campaign to start when three wins from four games set off 1975 in a positive note. It wasn't until January that Stewart landed a replacement for Kirk. Linfield's Barry Brown re-joined the club after protracted transfer negotiations and scored on his second debut after only 23 minutes against Distillery. Despite the additional firepower. United crashed out of the Irish Cup at the first hurdle to Glentoran who inflicted some revenge with a 6-3 defeat of the Sky Blues at the Oval.

With the Irish Cup out of the way, Ballymena started to find some league form going seven games without defeat, they began to push for the European and Texaco Cup places with impressive wins during the spring over Coleraine, Portadown and Crusaders and a record equalling 8-0 thrashing of Glenavon at the Showgrounds (in which Barry Brown grabbed a hat-trick). United would finish in fourth place and secure a place in the Texaco Cup. Had it not been for

The 1974/75 Gold Cup winning team pictured alongside the club's management committee pictured in December 1974.
Back row: (All Committee Members) Ken Barr; Jim Jones; Tom Cubitt; Ken Hood (Treasurer); Alan O'Loan; Maurice Millar; George Marcus; Jimmy Coulter (Secretary); Jim Rock; Sammy Magill.
Middle Row: Gary Erwin; Eamon McLaughlin; Bobby Averell; Robert Brown; Quinton McFall; Sammy McAuley; David McKeown (Chairman).
Front row: Gerry Convery, Tommy Gowdy, Jim Brown, Arthur Stewart (Player-Manager), John Sloan, Dessie Orr, Billy McCready (Trainer).

late season defeats to Glentoran and champions Linfield a first shot at European football would have been a distinct possibility. Texaco Cup qualification didn't even become a consolation as the cup (now a solely All-Ireland affair) was pulled during the summer of 1975, now financially unsustainable.

Eddie Russell finally brought the curtain down on his illustrious Ballymena United career at the end of the season. He had only managed two senior appearances in his 16th and final season at the club, spending the year mentoring and working with the club's young reserve team. Those two appearances remarkably brought the Larne man level with Eric Trevorrow's club appearance record of 557 games – a record which looks unlikely ever to be broken. Eddie would keep his association with the club as Arthur Stewart would quickly appoint him as his assistant manager, the first person to fill this role at the football club.

⚽ 1975/1976 ⚽

Ulster had been a no-go area for football visiting teams throughout the seventies, in fact no national teams had visited Belfast since the former Soviet Union in 1971

Northern Ireland played most of their 'home' international games in England. In April 1975 Yugoslavia broke the embargo and international football returned to Windsor Park. This was enough to convince new Nottingham Forest manager Brian Clough to become one of the first mainland club sides to return to the province in August, participating in a short tour with games against Coleraine and Ballymena United, The result against the full-timers was a formality as Forest (with five players who would go onto win the European Cup four years later) won 3-0 at the Showgrounds.

Stewart finally managed to tempt forward Jimmy Martin out of his three year religious exile to don the sky blue shirt again. The only other major transfer of pre-season was Portadown defender Davy Malcolmson who was the reigning player of the year at Shamrock Park. Unfortunately his appearances were limited throughout the season by a recurring back injury.

It was another slow start to the season in the Ulster Cup as United scraped to a disappointing tenth place finish, but it was in the Gold Cup where United and particularly Jimmy Martin found their goal-scoring boots. Like the old London bus analogy – you wait 43

Jimmy Martin
Courtesy of Ballymena Times

years for one and two come along in a row, as Ballymena United swept all in front of them to reach the Gold Cup final again, beating Portadown (4-2), Distillery (6-0) and Glenavon (4-1) in the semi-final. Jimmy Martin scored eight goals (including two hat-tricks) in three games to announce his return to Irish League football!

The Gold Cup final was a re-run of the 1931 final as fierce rivals Coleraine met the Sky Blues at the Ballymena Showgrounds on 13th November. United had the fortune of playing every round of the competition at home. The final was the biggest gate in Irish football so far that season as the Bannsiders raced into an early two goal lead after half an hour but despite Barry Brown pulling a goal back the Gold Cup was heading back to Coleraine as they held out for a 2-1 win.

Teenage goalkeeper George Dunlop was drafted in to replace the injured Robert Brown for the start of the league series. The former Manchester City apprentice was plucked from Glentoran's second team and his composed performances meant that he remained as number one for the duration of the season. It was a reasonable start to the Gibson Cup trail as despite starting with a loss to Glentoran at the Showgrounds, the Sky Blues lost only once again until mid-January. They also managed some revenge against Coleraine before Christmas with a superb 5-1 victory at Warden Street.

In the Irish Cup, the first round draw threw up what looked like a straight forward tie against 'B' Division Carrick Rangers but the Taylors Avenue side had other ideas, causing the shock of the round winning 3-2 at the Showgrounds in January. With former Ballymena midfielder Jimmy Brown at the helm as player manager Rangers went onto the create possibly the greatest underdog story in Irish football history by winning the Irish Cup in 1976, beating Linfield in the memorable final.

Defeat in the Irish Cup was the catalyst for the end of 34-year-old Stewart's tenure as United manager. The 4-2 defeat to Coleraine in early March (a game in which Arthur scored both of Ballymena's goals) was his last game as Ballymena United's longest serving manager. The sacking of the popular Stewart by the committee from his £3,000 per year post provoked accusations of back-stabbing at

The Ballymena Observer's sympathetic headline confirming Arthur Stewart's departure in March 1976.

boardroom level by the local papers. Chairman David McKeown explained that the committee's decision was 'one vote short of being unanimous'. Stewart's release from both his managerial and playing contract allowed him to spend a short spell with Distillery before he spent the summer playing soccer in New Jersey,

Assistant manager Eddie Russell was swiftly appointed as the new boss of the struggling Sky Blues for the remainder of the season. Despite only winning two of his seven league games, the club managed to scrap together a top half finish in the league. The new manager surprisingly engineered a triumphant end to a poor season by winning the County Antrim Shield in the final weeks of the season. After comfortable early round wins over Dundela, Chimney Corner and a semi-final win over Linfield, the Braidmen convincingly won their third provincial shield at Inver Park against Arthur Stewart's Distillery – two goals from Barry Brown and one apiece for Jim Martin and Kenny Russell marked a 4-0 win to sign off the season on a high note.

John Sloan was voted as the club's player of the year after an outstanding season in the United engine room but dealt the club a blow when he informed the manager he would be stepping back from his commitment to football to focus on his religious studies much like Jim Martin four years before him. As a compromise it had been agreed with Eddie Russell and his newly appointed assistant Alex McKee that he would train independently of the squad and be available for Saturday matches for the following season.

Ballymena United's 1976 County Antrim Shield winning team.

Goalscorer Kenny Russell's 1976 County Antrim Shield winners' medal

⚽ 1976/1977 ⚽

The 1976/77 season will be remembered (and quickly forgotten by all involved!) as the worst season in the club's history on and off the field. Eddie Russell entered the season optimistic form off the back of the Shield win in May, and added defensive cover to his side in talented full-back Don Johnston from Ards and Terry Moore from Athlone Town. Both of whom disappointingly made limited impact on the team during the year.

It was the worst ever start to a season by the team, as the team lost eight of the opening nine games. With results on the pitch at a low ebb, the club were stunned in September when a mystery blaze at the Showgrounds devastatingly ripped through the grandstand, club rooms and spread to the adjoining social

Ballymena United's team pictured in August 1976 before the defeat to Coleraine in the Ulster Cup
Back row: Alec McKee (Assistant Manager); Billy McCready (trainer); Billy Barr; Barry Brown; George Dunlop; Eamon McLaughlin; Alec Donald; Eddie Russell (Manager).
Front Row: Dessie Orr; Tommy Gowdy; Jim Martin; Bobby Averell; Sammy McAuley; Terry Moore; John Sloan.

club causing an estimated £300,000 worth of damage. The fire brought the club to its knees with a disaster fund set up to aid the survival of the club with club treasurer Ken Hood calling on local businesses to show their support – the club even contacted Watford's famous chairman Sir Elton John with a view to making a contribution to the fund for the financially crippled football club.

United, now forced to play games on the training pitch in the shadow of the Showgrounds main arena, finished rock bottom of the Ulster Cup with two points from eleven games. The Gold Cup, shockingly, was even worse as the Braidmen lost all five of their group games. Questions were being asked of the future of the Ballymena United manger with calls from the sidelines for his resignation ahead of the start of the Irish League campaign.

It took until 27th November for the team to register their first win of the season after 18 games. It was Ards who succumbed to the league's basement side as Ards' John Flannigan deflected a Terry Kingon shot past his own goalkeeper for a 1-0 win. Kingon had been signed only days before from Portadown for

Aerial view of the Ballymena Showgrounds after the devasting fire which destroyed the main stand and social club

£2,750 and his inspired debut performance gave the small band of remaining Ballymena supporters some much needed cheer.

It would be short-lived joy for the Sky Blues as the team didn't win again until the New Year, making it one victory in 23 attempts and Eddie Russell couldn't see 1976 end quick enough. He was also troubled by constant player discontent with transfer requests from his key (albeit underperforming) players George Dunlop, Barry Brown and Jim Martin causing disharmony amongst a fragile squad. The latter two had scored 52 goals between them the season before, but would eventually score a combined total of eight strikes during 1976/77.

English clubs were lining up for the services of the talented goalkeeper Dunlop, with Everton, Queens' Park Rangers and Tottenham Hotspur all rumoured to be interested and a bid from Brighton & Hove Albion of £5,000 was rejected out of hand by the United board. Off-form striker Jim Martin was also interesting clubs closer to home and he sealed a £2,500 transfer to Linfield a week before Ballymena were unceremoniously dumped out the Irish Cup, 4-1 by Distillery.

Only two league wins followed after the cup exit and almost inevitably in April Eddie Russell was sacked as manager of the football club with his assistant Alec McKee taking over as caretaker boss for the final few games. McKee could only watch on in horror as Ballymena's defence of their County Antrim Shield lasted only ninety minutes against Ards' second string in an embarrassing end to a dismal season at Castlereagh Park.

The end of season annual meeting unsurprisingly painted a grim financial picture for the club with a loss of £3,500 for the year and £16,000 owed to creditors, Treasurer Ken Hood called on supporters to help pull the club out of this latest financial disaster.

1977 also marked the beginning of the stock car racing lease at the new Ballymena raceway which opened surrounding the main pitch at the Showgrounds.

⚽ 1977/1978 ⚽

Billy Johnston was appointed as manager and took over a club in turmoil during the summer of 1977 – with a host of players still adamant they wouldn't be part of the club's plans for the new season. Having formerly managed Crusaders to the Irish League little over a year before, the 34-year-old selected ahead of applicants Jimmy Brown and Alec McKee by the club's committee in May to try and restore pride back to North Antrim.

His first move was to bring the experienced Drew Cooke in from his former club Crusaders and make him club captain. Tommy Gowdy was surprisingly released to join Distillery, unsettled winger Quinton McFall was sold to Glentoran after nine years at the club. Goalkeeper George Dunlop would eventually move to Linfield in October after his self-imposed strike forced the move. With virtually no money to sign new players during the close season he picked up midfielders Ronnie Butcher (from Coleraine) and Jim Nelson (from Dungannon Swifts) as well 21-year-old Ronnie McCullough in a swap deal with Bangor that saw Dessie Orr go to Clandeboye Park.

Off the field arguably the biggest signing of the summer was the charismatic Freddie McFaul who was appointed the club's first ever commercial manager on the recommendation of Billy Johnston. The former Coleraine secretary was already a well-known figure in local football and quickly set about the task of saving the Sky Blues from financial ruin – securing a highly lucrative £3,000

Ballymena United's first ever shirt sponsorship with Phillips Datsun is unveiled at the Showgrounds in October 1977 before the Gold Cup game against Glentoran.
Back row: David McKeown (Chairman); Sammy McAuley; Alec Donald; Robert Brown; Ronnie McCullough; Tom Sloan; Ronnie Butcher; Terry Kingon; Freddie McFaul (Commercial Manager).
Front Row: Billy McCready (Trainer); Alan Simpson; Barry Brown; Drew Cooke; Jim Nelson; Billy McAvoy; Billy Johnston (Manager).

shirt sponsorship deal with Phillips Datsun (a Belfast based car dealership) which was the only such deal in the Irish League that season. McFaul would also raise a further £8,000 in an innovative high profile promotion to raffle a car supplied by the new sponsors.

With the renewed optimism of financial security the Sky Blues started the season with signs of progression although still forced to play on the training pitch at the Showgrounds as work on the main arena pitch overran into the autumn. Goals from Drew Cooke and David Kenny kicked off the Ulster Cup with a 2-0 win over Distillery as while inconsistent in the results, it was a far cry from last season's misery as Johnston's team finished 7th in the final standings.

On 22nd November 1977, Ballymena United finally returned to their home pitch (which the *Ballymena Guardian* boldly claimed to be as good as Wembley!) for the opening Hennessey Gold Cup game against Glentoran. Former

Manchester United and Scotland forward Denis Law was paraded about before the 3,500 crowd to mark the return to the Showgrounds. It was however the high-profile capture of Ards legend Billy McAvoy, signed only 24 hours before the homecoming, who stole the limelight with two goals in the 2-1 win against the Glens.

United were rocked by captain Cooke's dislocated ankle two weeks later, this would rule him out for the rest of the season. Thankfully the emergence of talented Harryville teenager Tom Sloan in the United midfield was an early season boost to Johnston, but even moreso was the manager's persuasion to coax his older brother John out of the footballing wilderness. The Sloan brothers were the first brothers to play together in the United first team since the Mitten siblings in the early 1950s.

On the pitch there was no end to the agony of the start of the Irish League as Ballymena United lost their opening seven games in succession and finished the year firmly rooted to the bottom of the table. It took until mid-January for the under-performing Billy McAvoy to finally fire United to a win, scoring the only goal against Bangor at the Showgrounds. The former Ards striker saved his next match-winner for his former club in the Irish Cup quarter-final. Despite the league woes the club progressed to the semi-finals of the Irish Cup having comfortably defeated Amateur League side Downpatrick Rec. in the first round of the competition.

Johnston was paired against his former employers from North Belfast in a semi-final saga that lasted three games at Windsor Park. It took two replays and

penalties to decide who would progress to the final, but after three 1-1 draws, it was Ballymena who conquered the Crusaders on penalties and set up an Irish Cup final showdown with Irish League champions, Linfield. The semi-final victory would also book United's passage into Europe for the first time in the club's history as Linfield had already qualified for the European Cup through winning the league. The Braidmen would debut in the European Cup Winners' Cup next season regardless of the final day outcome.

Come cup final day Linfield proved just too strong, as in front of a 12,000 crowd at the Oval the Blues ran out comfortable 3-1 winner as Jackie McClean's goal for Ballymena proved to be little more than a consolation strike. Ironically Linfield's second goal came from teenage defender John Garrett from Ballymena. Incidentally Ballymena's sky blue shirts were forbidden from promoting their shirt sponsors at the say so of the BBC and reverted to a traditional plain number for the final.

The Irish Cup final had been a welcome distraction from the other domestic failures of the team who were forced to apply for re-election to the league for the first time since 1957. They suffered yet another County Antrim Shield exit to lower league opposition, this time to neighbours Chimney Corner of the 'B' Division. On an individual level, Tom Sloan was acknowledged by the football writers as the league's Young Player of the Year for 1978 and was invited on Tottenham Hotspur's post-season tour of Norway.

⚽ 1978/1979 ⚽

The transfer saga of the summer of 1978 was that of Tom Sloan's move to professional football. Interest from Tottenham had waned following his trial following the Norway tour and it was former European Cup winners Manchester United that eventually lured the Harryville lad to Old Trafford in August for an initial fee of £25,000 this would eventually rise to a cool £32,500 after Sloan made 10 appearances for the Red Devils.

Johnston, boosted by his new transfer kitty, signed Ballymena-based schoolteacher Sammy McQuiston from Glenavon and beat rivals Coleraine to the signature of the highly rated young winger Gerry Mullan from Limavady United. Midfielder Brian Jess joined from Distillery but it was farewell to one of the club's longest serving players as the injuries caught up with veteran defender Bobby Averell. He retired after 328 appearances for the clubs in his two spells and ten seasons with United.

Newly promoted to the new position of General Manager, Freddie McFaul travelled to UEFA headquarters in Zurich in July for the Cup Winners' Cup first round draw. United drew the Belgian cup winners KSK Beveren, a team made up of mostly part-time players from outside Antwerp. They would go on to be surprise winners of the Belgian First Division for the first time in their history that season. Going into the first leg in Antwerp in excellent form, United

BALLYMENA UNITED

The club's only ever Panini sticker from the Euro Football 1979 collection

lost 3-0 in front of a crowd of 13,000. They would lose to the same scoreline back at the Showgrounds in the second leg, losing 6-0 on aggregate for the first foray into European competition.

The new experience in the Cup Winners' Cup unfortunately negatively affected performances in the Ulster Cup as the team threw away a three point lead, dropping points against Portadown and Cliftonville. Johnston's men still led the table going into the penultimate game against Glentoran, this attracted a big gate to Warden Street, but despite opening the scoring through Gerry

The European Cup Winners Cup

BALLYMENA UNITED
v Beveren

1978-9
OFFICIAL PROGRAMME

Mullan, the East Belfast men eventually won 2-1 and the cup hopes were over for the Sky Blues. Defeat to Crusaders in the final game meant that the team also missed out on runners-up medals, eventually finishing third.

Recently sacked Coleraine manager Ivan Murray was signed solely as a player for £2,000 but it was two unknown teenagers who started making waves at the club – Tony McCall and Nigel Worthington – the latter even forced former player of the year Sammy McAuley out of the team for the majority of the season at full-back.

The team finished a respectable second place in a tough Gold Cup group and took that form into the opening game of the Irish League against Portadown and John Sloan's late winner sealed a 1-0 win. The following week Glentoran were left stunned at the Showgrounds, when they were on the receiving end of a 5-1 hammering. McQuiston and Mullan both scored twice with captain Ronnie McCullough scoring the other. Many onlookers now thought that United could be an outside challenger for the Gibson Cup, but that idea was short-lived after a dismal Christmas period that would cost manager Billy Johnston his job in early January 1979.

Reserve Team manager Alex McKee was initially the preferred choice as manager but inexplicably turned the job down allowing former Glenavon manager Alan Campbell to take the job on a gentleman's agreement with the club, refusing a written contract of employment. His first game in February came in the middle of another terrible run of league form for the Sky Blues who were in the middle of a sixteen game streak without a win since the five goal salvo against Glentoran.

That form would last until mid-April and the team would only be prevented from propping up the table by a Distillery side experiencing an even worse season.

Sammy McQuiston's double against Crusaders in the Irish Cup without reply did provide supporters with some light relief for United's supporters but a replay defeat to Portadown in the quarter-final meant it was business as usual for struggling Ballymena. A late rally of results at Easter which included a 2-0 win at home to Coleraine in which McQuiston would bag another brace (eventually finishing as leading goalscorer with 18 strikes) the

Sammy McQuiston
Courtesy of Ballymena Times

club would still finish in 11th place and was embarrassingly forced to apply for re-election for the second year running.

Thankfully though, the patience of the Ballymena public was soon to be rewarded with the start of an unforgettable era of football at the Showgrounds.

Chapter Six

The glory years (1979-1989)

⚽ *1979/1980* ⚽

A feature article that appeared in the local media in late 1979 was a piece outlining how football had safely survived and even grown in popularity during the devastating Troubles of the 1970s. In Northern Ireland it was now fully expected to flourish in the following decade, as over 50,000 supporters across the league had returned to the terraces to cheer on their Irish League teams.

Sick of the mediocrity that the last few seasons had served up Chairman McKeown (assisted by Freddie McFaul's continued fundraising and increased social club income) handed Alan Campbell the largest playing budget ever afforded to a Ballymena United manager to build a worthy championship team at the Showgrounds. Campbell wasted little time adding quality to the core of his panel; Birmingham-born defender Graham Fox was the first arrival from Sligo Rovers. Goalkeeper Brian White and Drogheda United's Brendan Tully (nephew of Celtic legend, Charlie Tully) also joined in the summer alongside record marquee signing of £9,000 striker Paul Malone from Glenavon.

Paul Malone. Courtesy of Ballymena Times

Relations with the Agricultural Association plummeted at an all-time low during the close season with the pitch destroyed by show jumping at the annual Ballymena Show in May leaving the football club homeless yet again until late-October. Embarrassingly for the club the pre-season friendlies against Carlisle United and Southampton originally scheduled to be held in the town had to be hastily moved to the Coleraine Showgrounds and similar fixtures against Luton Town and Dumbarton were postponed.

The bookmakers' 50/1 shots for the Irish League started the Ulster Cup in fine form with wins against Portadown, Glentoran and Distillery which fired the Sky Blues to the top of the cup table after the opening three games. Too many draws throughout the eleven games would eventually cost the team a higher position in the final Ulster Cup standings, as the Sky Blues finished third; a commendable achievement given that Campbell's new look side had been forced to play all eleven games away from home.

21-year-old Crusaders full-back George Beattie was the latest recruit to Campbell's ever evolving and improving team ahead of the Gold Cup games in which United finally returned home to the Showgrounds. Ballymena Council's recreation officer Des Allen had made the announcement that United's homecoming would be against Coleraine on 27th October and the Sky Blues didn't disappoint in front of a huge crowd, winning 4-2 with goals from Malone, Fox, McQuiston and captain Davy Jackson. This game also marked the first edition of the new 'Light Blue Leader' programme which became a staple of the matchday experience for home fans throughout the 1980s. Ballymena would comfortably win all five Gold Cup group games to sail through to the final against Linfield the following month.

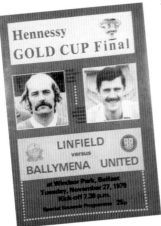

The Gold Cup final, controversially played at Windsor Park at the request of competition sponsors Hennessey, proved to be a step too far for high-flying Ballymena United. Sammy McQuiston had equalised after Linfield had taken an early lead, but Warren Feeney's winner broke the visitors' hearts in front of the assembled 7,500 crowd. Far from despondent after the 2-1 defeat, Alan Campbell confidently declared that his side would 'bounce back' from the disappointment.

Following the final disappointment Campbell's side fell to unwelcome defeats at Glentoran and Cliftonville but marked a sign of intent with an 8-0 win against Distillery at the Showgrounds with John Sloan and Paul Malone both bagging hat-tricks. They followed this result up two weeks later with a remarkable five goal demolition of league leaders Linfield at Warden Street, another hat-trick from Malone signalling to the rest of the league that Campbell's men were now genuine challengers for the title!

In December 1979, a dark cloud was cast over the football club when 43-year-old General Manager, Freddie McFaul was tragically killed in a car crash outside Limavady. Both the club and the town were in mourning as Ballymena United lost arguably one of the most influential figures in the history of the club who had brought thousands of pounds of revenue to the Sky Blues. Social Club chairman Sammy Magill was appointed to the unenvious position of McFaul's successor as General Manager.

General Manager Freddie McFaul who passed away in December 1979.

Ballymena started 1980 in fine form, with impressive wins over Larne, Bangor, Portadown and a five goal salvo against Coleraine which Paul Malone bagged his third hat-trick in four league games (finishing the season with 28 goals as leading scorer). The stunning form of key players Sloan, Gerry Mullan, McQuiston had moved the Sky Blues up the table and on to a stunning 15 game unbeaten run which left the Braidmen within only two points of one time runaway leaders Linfield and expectations that a title push was suddenly on going into the final two months of the campaign.

In the Irish Cup, Ballymena had to navigate through a replay against struggling Bangor (now managed by Billy Johnston) in the first round and eventually progressed after a 2-0 win at Clandeboye Park. Another stiff test against Portadown in the quarter-final was overcome to set up the country's two in-form teams in the semi-final against Linfield at the Oval. With both teams potentially still going for a league and cup double – it was the experienced South Belfast men (managed by former United defender Roy Coyle) who won 1-0 thanks to Peter Dornan's header just after half-time. Linfield also went on to beat Crusaders in the final a month later.

Despite an unexpected blip in the team's league form during the Easter period in which another defeat to Linfield at Windsor killed off hopes of a first Gibson

Cup and effectively handed the league championship to the Blues, the Sky Blues confirmed their position as runners-up on the final day of the season. They finished above Glentoran to qualify for UEFA Cup for the first time. Whilst a first Irish League title again evaded Ballymena this was the highest league finish achieved since the 1938/39 season and also the first time European qualification was achieved on merit.

Campbell's men finished the campaign with the County Antrim Shield competition and despite stumbling through the first two rounds against lower-league opposition by beating Glentoran II and Barn United they successfully progressed to the final with a 3-0 semi-final win against Larne. The Shield final against Crusaders proved a scoreless and uninspiring affair at the Oval, but Ballymena prevailed on penalties winning 3-1 to claim the historic trophy for the fourth time in the history of the club this marked the start of a 'golden era' of success for Ballymena United Football Club.

Individual honours would be awarded to talented Northern Ireland youth international Tony McCall (courted by Tottenham and Queens Park Rangers throughout the season) who was named Ulster Young Player of the Year. Central defender Ronnie McCullough was again named as the club members' player of the year after the successful season. The Carrickfergus hard-man had been due to immigrate to Canada but postponed the move in order to give European football

The new grandstand at the Warden Street side of the ground with perimiter fence.

a shot with his team-mates in the Autumn.

The fans had flocked back to the Ballymena Showgrounds during the 1979/80 season and by the summer they would have some of the best facilities in the Irish League at their disposal with the completion of the modern new 1,300 seated grandstand at a cost of £250,000. Unfortunately a garish new perimeter fence would be erected as part of new UEFA regulations for clubs qualifying for European competition at a cost of £11,000 to the football club. Also born out of the new found fanbase was the formation of a new supporter's club in the town – the Paradise club was formed by fans from Magee's Clothing factory on Paradise Avenue in Harryville mid-way through the season.

⚽ *1980/1981* ⚽

There was an early start to the 1980/81 season for Ballymena United in late-July against League of Ireland side Shamrock Rovers (now managed by former Leeds favourite Johnny Giles) in the first round of the short-lived Tyler Cup, the latest in a long line of unsustainable attempts at creating a competitive All-Ireland competition. Ballymena's involvement was short-lived with a disappointing 2-0 defeat in a game that marked the opening of the new grandstand for at the Showgrounds.

In an unusual summer at Warden Street there had been virtually no transfer movement at the club as only club captain Davy Jackson had retired after being told he wouldn't be featuring in the manager's plans. Three weeks after the Tyler Cup the domestic started with impressive early Ulster Cup wins against Portadown (5-2) and Distillery (5-0) but on 29th August manager Alan Campbell was unfortunately involved in a car crash on the Sydenham bypass on route to

Ballymena United players and officials pictured in October 1981 after winning the Ulster Cup to accompany the County Antrim Shield on the sideboard.

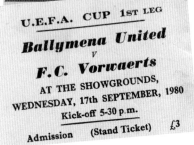

a game against Ards at Castlereagh Park. Campbell broke both his legs the accident and would be incapacitated for the majority of the season as he had to get his legs reset over a dozen times. In his absence assistant manager Ivan Murray took over responsibility for day-to-day team affairs for the remainder of the season.

Campbell's incapacitation couldn't have come at a worse time for the club, going into the European games against East German outfit FC Vorwaerts. Secretary Jimmy Coulter had attended the UEFA Cup draw in July and pronounced the draw as 'the worst we could have hoped for' – missing out on potential games against the likes of Manchester United, Juventus and Barcelona. Despite Coulter's reservations, the team produced one of the finest performances in the club's history in the first leg at the Showgrounds, winning in European competition for the first time. Vorwaerts took an early lead through Frank Geyer but Ballymena's first ever euro goals came in the second half through Sammy McQuiston and John Sloan to seal a memorable 2-1 in front of 5,000 jubilant fans.

Hopes were high going into the second leg two weeks later behind the iron curtain but two early home goals undid all the good work from the first leg as the Sky Blues eventually lost 3-0 on the night and 4-2 on aggregate. Vorwaerts were matched with West German neighbours VfB Stuttgart in the second round, losing 7-2 on aggregate in the competition. Bobby Robson's Ipswich Town side went on to win the competition.

Undeterred by the European exit, Ballymena returned to domestic action with a bang sealing the Ulster Cup at Clandeboye Park against Bangor in style with a 5-1 win. Davy Neill, Gerry Mullan, Sloan, McQuiston and Paul Malone all got on the score-sheet in front of a large travelling support. This was only the second time the club had won the Ulster Cup, exactly 20 years since Geoff Twentyman inspired the first victory.

Gerry Mullan's early season form earned him the Football Writers' player of the month award for September and a place in the Northern Ireland squad which quickly alerted interest from a number of top English clubs. Gerry soon sealed a huge £40,000 transfer to Everton in October 1980. He unfortunately failed to make an impact on Merseyside despite breaking through into Northern Ireland's squad just in time for the 1982 FIFA World Cup in Spain. With the money burning a hole in the club coffers United were on the hunt for the best local talent making unsuccessful bids for Dessie Dickson (Coleraine) and Jim Cleary (Portadown). The club eventually broke the bank with a record signing for an Irish League club as midfielder Peter McCusker joined from Cliftonville for a hefty £11,000 fee. Goalkeeper Denis Matthews also joined from Glentoran £4,000, replacing Brian White as the first choice custodian.

Club caption Graham Fox and record signing Peter McCusker with the Ulster Cup.

An unexpected Ulster Cup hangover had stifled the Gold Cup hopes with mid-table finish in the group stages going into the start of the Irish League championship in November. The league started well for the Sky Blues with four wins from five games but a poor Christmas period which produced no wins from four festive games. Defeat to title rivals Linfield at Windsor Park left the Braidmen trailing behind the Belfast 'Big Two' in third place at the start of the New Year.

Still optimistic of silverware, United progressed past a tough first round tie in January against rivals Coleraine at the Ballycastle Road in January. The following quarter-final against Cliftonville was all about one man – Paul Malone. The in-form striker was rated as 50/50 ahead of the Solitude clash but was risked by Campbell and rewarded Murray with a marvellous hat-trick in only eight second-half minutes as Ballymena won 4-1 to progress to a semi-final with unbeaten league leaders, Glentoran at Windsor Park. At the first attempt, the Sky Blues trailed by two goals before David Neill and Nigel Worthington's late strikes forced a replay; three days later United dominated and won 2-0 with two goals from Paul Malone to send his side into the Bass Irish Cup final to face Glenavon.

In the Irish League Glentoran were the team of the season as they finished the 22 game league series unbeaten, with Linfield close behind in second. Ballymena seemingly with one eye on the Irish Cup had to settle for third place as they dropped points with defeats to Glenavon, Crusaders and Bangor in the final half-dozen fixtures to concede any lingering hope of sneaking their way into contention they eventually finished nine points off the pace.

There was an Irish Cup final first on 25th April, 1981 – when the game was postponed due to freak weather as heavy rain flooded the Windsor pitch! The game was rescheduled for a week later as the Braidmen clinched their first Irish Cup in 23 years to add the Ulster Cup already in the trophy cabinet at the Showgrounds. It was Sammy McQuiston's goal in the 88th minute that proved to be the winner in a lack-lustre final. Manager Alan Campbell had also appeared back in the dugout for the first time since August and received hero's welcome from the United faithful.

Manager Alan Campbell celebrates winning the Irish Cup in the Windsor Park dressing room along with his players.

Teenage defender Nigel Worthington was selected as the Ulster Young Footballer of the Year and was transferred to Notts County (who had just been promoted to the top flight of English football) for a deal that would net the club £70,000 – a record Irish League export at the time. The deal would have been worth another £10,000 had Nigel won an international cap at Meadow Lane but the full-back's rapid progression hindered another windfall as he was transferred to Sheffield Wednesday three years later, he won the first of 66 full international caps. Spells at Leeds United and Stoke City would continue an impressive professional career throughout the nineties and Worthington progressed into management, earning a spell as manager of Northern Ireland in 2007 which lasted four years.

The financial boost of the Worthington transfer was on top of a £2,400 profit announced at the Annual General Meeting as Chairman David McKeown declared the season as 'something special'. It would go onto be widely regarded as the football club's most successful ever season. Leading goalscorer Paul Malone was voted as the club's player of the season after another fantastic goalscoring campaign at the Showgrounds.

⚽ 1981/1982 ⚽

The Irish Cup winners revelled in the success and Campbell (now back in full control following his recovery from injury) was afforded a huge transfer kitty (by club standards). £3,000 was spent on Cliftonville's Frankie Moffett, also incoming were 34-year-old Tony O'Doherty from Dundalk and Coleraine's Seamus McDowell in a swap deal with the unhappy Pat Mullan (brother of Gerry) who had submitted a transfer request after being left out of the Irish Cup final squad in May. Brian White was freed to join the RUC team and Alec Donald retired from senior football after 11 seasons at the club to focus on coaching the youth team.

Defending the Ulster Cup in the first two months of the season with virtually the same improved squad wasn't straight forward as the performances were unrecognisable from that which supporters had become accustomed to. United started the series (and season) with defeat at Linfield at Windsor Park – the first of seven defeats in the competition as the trophy was tamely surrendered, Ballymena United finishing ninth in the final Ulster Cup table.

Ballymena United's team pictured before the Roma game in September 1981.
Back row: Alec Donald; Armstrong Beckett; Alexander Elliott, Ronnie McCullough, Frank Moffatt, Denis Matthews, Davy Neill, Paul Malone, ?, Ivan Murray (Assistant manager).
Middle row: Alan Campbell (Manager), Peter McCusker, John Sloan, Seamus McDowell, Graham Fox, George Beattie, Tony O'Doherty, Billy McCready (Trainer).
Front row: Brian Hutchinson, Davy Smyth, Tony McCall, Tommy Huston.

The dismal run of results was not ideal preparation for the daunting task of the Cup Winners' Cup first round tie against Italian giants AS Roma. In July the draw against the Italian Cup winners (who had also finished runners-up in Serie A) brought widespread approval from the officials at Ballymena for their third venture into European football, given the stature of the Italians in respective comparison to previous opponents Beveren and Vorwaerts. The Rome club boasted a number of players who had starred in the summer's World Cup tournament including Brazilian Falcao and captain Bruno Conti. Serie A's leading scorer Roberto Pruzzo and Carlo Ancelotti (who would go on to become one of Europe's greatest managers) would also line out for the Giallorossi.

The midweek first leg was hosted at the Ballymena Showgrounds with an early 4pm kick-off due to a stock car meeting arranged for that evening. The result was always going to be a formality given the quality of the opponents and, after holding the Romans until well into the second half, goals from Odoacre Chierico

Roberto Pruzzo gets the better of Ballymena United in the Olympic Stadium. Courtesy of www.almanaccogiallorosso.it

and Ancelotii sealed a 2-0 win. Two weeks later 50,000 fans (including two dozen from Northern Ireland) gathered at the Olympic stadium and watched on as Roma made light work of their part-time opponents winning 4-0 on the evening and 6-0 on aggregate. Alan Campbell claimed the result to be a moral victory for his team, Roma would go out of the competition in the next round to Porto.

By the start of the Gold Cup group stage, under pressure Campbell had already seen enough of all three of his new players as he put McDowell, Moffatt and O'Doherty on the transfer list alongside underperforming record signing Peter McCusker. Money was spend attempting to fix the team's woes with the recruitment of Crewe Alexandra's forward Michael Guy and Ray McGuigan from Glenavon.

This kick-started the season as Campbell's men cruised to the final of the competition unbeaten through a tough group. The Gold Cup final against Linfield in December again controversially at Windsor Park, started well for Ballymena with Paul Malone's opening goal but Martin McGaughey's equaliser 15 minutes from time was enough to spur the Blues onto a 5-4 victory on penalties. United's veteran Sammy McAuley had the misfortune of missing the deciding penalty kick for United.

Captain Graham Fox had immigrated to Australia by the beginning of the Irish League season which didn't help shot-shy United who took until Boxing Day to record the first goals and win of the league season beating Coleraine 4-2 with transfer listed winger McCusker getting a surprise hat-trick.

The defence of the Irish Cup was equally as unsuccessful as the Ulster Cup, with a humiliating defeat to Distillery in the first round. The defeat and the subsequent vitriol from the terraces was enough to convince Campbell to call it a day, resigning on 2nd February and ignoring pleas from his committee to stay on. United's most successful manager revealed that the threat of physical violence from disgruntled supporters at New Grosvenor Park was the breaking point – labelling a section of the support as 'animals'. 28-year-old striker Paul Malone quickly threw his hat into the ring for the vacant post but it was caretaker manager Ivan Murray who was the natural choice as successor.

Murray's first game against Glentoran at the Oval was a disappointing 3-1 defeat for fifth place United going into the second half of the league campaign. An improved 1-1 draw with league leaders Linfield in his second game gave fans some hope but with only one win from Murray's first eight league games any European hopes quickly disappeared, the new manager describing his players as a 'disgrace'. Off the field things were equally as troublesome for Murray as new club captain Paul Malone and David Neill both requested transfers away from the club.

Disappointingly Ballymena United eventually finished the year in the bottom half of the table in seventh, one of the few highlights being Ipswich Town loanee Ronnie Burns' late goal in the 1-0 win over Glentoran at the Showgrounds. This handed the Gibson Cup to their arch-rivals Linfield with only a couple of games to play. The Sky Blues finished the 1981/82 season with defeat in the semi-final of the County Antrim Shield to Distillery.

Denis Matthews swept the board for the Player of the Year awards, establishing himself as one of the latest top quality goalkeepers to play for the club. Coincidentally two ex-Ballymena stoppers made it all the way to the summer's World Cup finals in Spain. Jim Platt and George Dunlop went as backup to Pat Jennings as Northern Ireland impressively progressed to the quarter-final stage of the competition. The uncapped John Sloan was included in Billy Bingham's provisional 40 man squad for the tournament but failed to make the cut down to 22 players ahead of the tournament.

Closer to home failure on the pitch and Campbell's frivolous spending had created a financial crisis by the end of the season. A loss of over £5,000 for the financial year, coupled with £17,000 of debt owed to the bank and creditors was declared. David McKeown's 18 years as United's longest serving chairman came to an end in June. Following a frustrating season as he was voted out by members at the AGM with Brian Millar taking over in his place and quickly calling for support as the club faced a perilous financial position going into the next season.

⚽ *1982/1983* ⚽

Ivan Murray's first summer in charge was a quiet one as the only low key summer signing was defender Liam Harbinson from Finn Harps. Local young talent such as Brian Crockard, Stephen Penney and Roy 'Wings' Smyth were blooded into the first team. Many of Campbell's underperformers headed towards the exit with Seamus McDowell, Frankie Moffatt and Tony O'Doherty all being freed to leave the club.

In pre-season Lawrie McMenemy's Southampton returned to Northern Ireland to play United at the Showgrounds. The Saints won 4-2 in front of a 2,000 crowd with Kevin Keegan, fresh from the 1982 World Cup, the star attraction for the Ballymena pubic. This appearance was one of his last in a Southampton shirt as the England international surprisingly moved to Newcastle United two weeks later.

The new season started reasonably well in the Gold Cup with Ballymena finishing second in their group behind eventual winners Glentoran. In late September an offer of an exhibition game against Scottish Premier League club Motherwell and a guest appearance from Northern Ireland legend and former European Footballer of the Year George Best was too good an opportunity for the club to turn down. 2,500 fans turned out to see the ex-Manchester United winger don a sky blue shirt as the home side impressed in a 2-1 win with Best and John Sloan scoring the goals.

Southampton's Kevin Keegan receives a souvenir from Ballymena mayor Sandy Spence

Ballymena United's team pictured before the Roma game in September 1981.
Back row: Ivan Murray (Manager), Paul Malone, Denis Matthews, Brian Crockard, Michael Guy, John Sloan, Peter McCusker, Brian Millar (Chairman).
Front row: Brian Huston, Sammy McQuiston, Ray McGuigan, Tony McCall, George Beattie, Stephen Penney.

George Best and a young mascot before the friendly with Motherwell

Victory against Motherwell boosted Murray's men to a decent finish in the Ulster Cup with five goal victories over Cliftonville and Bangor leading to fourth place in the final cup table. Murray also recruited Glentoran defender Robert McCreery to add some experience to his young side with unsettled Davy Neill going the opposite direction in a swap deal. Ipswich midfielder Ronnie Burns who had previously enjoyed a short loan spell returned to the club on a permanent transfer in October.

United and Ards shared eight goals in a pulsating start to the Irish League season in November but results were typically inconsistent from the off. Murray's men signed off on a disappointing 1982 with a festive away victory over rivals

Coleraine – winning 4-2 with goals from Michael Guy, Stephen Penney and two from Sammy McQuiston.

The renewed optimism that 1983 brought disappeared almost instantly as Murray dropped goalkeeper Dennis Matthews for the crunch Irish Cup first round tie at the Oval against Glentoran. United lost 4-0, a result which would mark the beginning of the end for Ivan Murray's short reign as Ballymena United manager. Another four goal defeat, this time away to Ards, was the final straw for the notoriously trigger happy Management Committee and Murray was fired on Friday 11th February after only a year at the helm.

Alec Donald took caretaker charge of the team and picked up two wins against Bangor and Glenavon to temporarily move the Sky Blues into third in the table. Despite hopes of a late push for European qualification, the tough Scottish taskmaster failed to win any of his remaining six games and United quickly fell out of contention by the end of March. The supporters voted with their feet as the team dropped from third into the bottom half of the league table within a month.

Alec Donald. Courtesy of Ballymena Times

Speculation had been rife as to Murray's successor in the hottest seat in Irish football – the *Ballymena Observer* reported over 17 applicants which included former crowd favourite Sammy Frickelton. Paul Malone also expressed a serious interest in becoming the club's player manager but with three games of the season remaining the club appointed 35-year-old schoolteacher Ian Russell as their latest manager with Donald as his assistant. Russell had spent three years at Crusaders and coincidentally resigned his Seaview post 72 hours after Murray's dismissal. He was well aware of the task ahead and the impatience of his new employers and he joked at one of his first supporters' club engagements that he would need asbestos pants for the Ballymena hot seat.

The new boss played out the final three games of the season with minimal success, Ballymena disappointingly finished eighth in the table and the building work started for next season. Off-the-field Sammy Magill stood down as commercial manager and also from the committee having failed to replicate the work of

Freddie McFaul. Another committee member not standing for re-election at the AGM was long-serving Jimmy Rock after a remarkable 47 years of unbroken service to Ballymena United.

⚽ *1983/1984* ⚽

Boosted by a cash windfall to the tune of £40,000 sourced from the latest instalment of the Nigel Worthington transfer (having reached 30 games for Notts County) and the £10,000 share of the IFA's profits after reaching the World Cup manager Ian Russell went on a heavy summer spending spree rebuilding his team ahead of the new season.

Graham Fox returned to the club as captain after winning an FAI Cup medal with Sligo Rovers and was joined by Cliftonville midfielder Ciaran McCurry. McCurry proved to be another expensive flop at £6,000, lasting only until January before being sold to Portadown. Defender Alan Harrison's transfer from Glentoran caused so much dispute that it was referred to an Irish League tribunal to decide the transfer fee. The resulting decision shocked the Braidmen as they were ordered to pay a vastly inflated £18,500 for the defender's services – a record transfer fee between two Irish League clubs and one that Ballymena United could ill-afford.

The biggest coup of 1983 was Russell's sensational acquisition of Jim Platt from Middlesbrough on a five year contract for an undisclosed fee. Platt was still Northern Ireland's second choice goalkeeper behind Pat Jennings and he

Jim Platt. Courtesy of Northern Ireland Football Greats

returned to his former club after 13 years on Teeside with ambitions of playing European football for the first time. Dennis Matthews quickly found himself surplus to requirements and moved to Ards and he was joined by former record signing Peter McCusker who had been on loan at Castlereagh Park since March. Ray McGuigan moved to Sligo, Tony McCall left before the start of the season to take up a college scholarship in South Carolina and Irish Cup hero Sammy McQuiston left the club to go into semi-retirement having become disillusioned with senior football.

Ballymena United started the season racing out of the blocks with McCurry taking only five minutes to make himself a hero. He scored the only goal at the Coleraine Showgrounds in the first game of the Gold Cup. An unbeaten start throughout August had raised hopes of qualification from the group stage of the competition but three defeats in the final three games meant that United would finish second in the seven team group table.

Defeat to Linfield in the first game of the Ulster Cup had already put pressure on Ian Russell and his expensively assembled squad. His players only managed one win from seven games in the competition, this came against newly promoted Carrick Rangers – who had been elected to senior football alongside Newry Town (as part of the new 14 team Irish League). The manager lambasted his players in the press and, as the cracks were beginning to show, from the side-lines the outcome was very predictable.

Ian Russell was sacked in late November after a 1-0 league defeat to Carrick at Taylor's Avenue, his tenure lasted only eight months. Once again Alec Donald was put in temporary charge of the team. Another individual leaving the Showgrounds was talented midfielder Stephen Penney who sealed a £25,000 transfer to FA Cup finalists Brighton and Hove Albion – a deal which some supporters felt undervalued the youngster who would go on to establish himself at Brighton and become a full Northern Ireland international..

By December the club punged into further chaos as Chairman Brian Millar inexplicably resigned from office citing 'personal reasons'. At a special meeting 31-year-old Cullybackey businessman Leonard Wiseman was elected as the youngest Chairman in the club's history unanimously outvoting experienced treasurer Ken Hood in a members vote. One of Wiseman's first moves was to shrewdly appoint experienced goalkeeper Jim Platt as the new manager. Platt took control of the team two days before Ballymena's New Years' Eve victory over Larne which moved the club into sixth position going into 1984.

Platt sensationally tried to land former international team-mate George Best on a month's contract but the four-figure appearance fee per game proved prohibitive. Best incidentally joined 'B' Division Tobermore

Chairman Leonard Wiseman

United for the Irish Cup first round tie against the Sky Blues at Fortwilliam Park. The former Manchester United star's appearance sparked massive interest but had little influence in a game which the Sky Blues comfortably won 7-0 as they started off their Irish Cup crusade. One player who wasn't going to be part of Platt's plans was striker Paul Malone who had been forced out of the team by Sion Mills' teenage sensation Johnny Speak, signed from Limavady United.

Malone came back to score the winner in the tricky second round game against Dundela but was demoted to the bench for the game of the season against Linfield in the cup quarter-final. 5,000 fans crammed into the Showgrounds for the visit of the reigning champions and Johnny Speak instantly became

Defender George Beattie celebrates winning the 1984 Irish Cup final with jubilant United fans. Courtesy of Ballymena Guardian

hot property as he scored the winning goal in a 2-1 victory. Speak repeated the feat with another late winner in the low-key semi-final against Cliftonville at the Oval to send the Sky Blues to the cup final with another 2-1 win.

In April player-manager Jim Platt became the club's first player in 51 years to win a full international cap when he deputised for Pat Jennings at Wembley as Northern Ireland lost 1-0 to Bobby Robson's England in the British Championship fixture. Closer to home, Ballymena finished the Irish League season strongly despite an inconsistent season and eventually finished sixth only three points behind Cliftonville in third place.

Platt recruited English forward Michael Ring from Brighton for the Irish Cup final at the expense of a young Kenny Shiels but it turned out to be one of the most one-sided Irish Cup finals in years against rank outsiders Carrick Rangers at Windsor Park. Captain Graham Fox settled his team-mates' nerves with a superb goal after only eight minutes and Brian Crockard bundled home a second goal just after half-time. The game was over as a contest when Rangers' keeper Tom Coburn conceded a penalty and was forced off injured after clashing with United's Jeff Wright. Former Ballymena player Geoff Blair went into goal but his first task was to pick Alan Harrison's penalty out of the back of the net.

Ballymena United's victorious players parade the Irish Cup through the town in 1984.

Johnny Speak capped off a wonderful debut season with the fourth goal whilst Carrick's Roy Fellowes scored a late consolation with virtually the last kick of the game.

With plans already afoot for the new season Jim Platt sensationally left the Irish Cup Winners to become player manager of Coleraine, much to the shock of supporters and officials. Paul Malone made a quieter exit from the Showgrounds after failing to even make the squad for the cup final – he joined neighbours Larne as their player manager after 115 goals in 194 games during his five seasons at Warden Street. Recipient of the Ulster Young Footballer of the Year award, Johnny Speak, was surprisingly allowed to join Dundalk for £5,000.

⚽ 1984/1985 ⚽

Before the dust had even settled from Platt's shock departure, the managerial post at Warden Street had already been filled as the Ballymena United committee surprisingly brought Alan Campbell back to the club for a second spell. Despite the abrupt end to his previous reign in February 1982, the club's most successful boss had retained a strong relationship with some members of the committee who sanctioned his return. The appointment however divided opinion amongst Ballymena supporters.

Campbell's first move to fill the massive vacancy in the forward line left by the departures of Malone, Speak and Michael Ring (who had ended his short stay at the club to join Hull City) by signing his own son, Alan Campbell Junior, from Distillery. Talented young midfielders Owen Daly (Limavady United) and the fiery Colin O'Neill (Larne) were recruited to freshen up the team. Glentoran's relentless pursuit of record signing Alan Harrison was unsuccessful but it unsettled the big central defender.

Ballymena's pre-season preparations stood up to the test of Second Division side Brighton & Hove Albion in a friendly as part of the Stephen Penney transfer. Rab McCreery's unfortunate second half own goal decided the game in the visitors favour but the spirited display from the Braidmen won plaudits from the Englishmen.

The opening game of the season ironically saw the Sky Blues welcome derby rivals Coleraine and Jim Platt back to Warden Street in the Gold Cup. The bad feeling between the two clubs continued off the pitch as United failed to budge on immediately releasing Platt's playing registration to his new employers. This left Platt resigned to the dugout as he oversaw his new team grind out a 2-1 victory. Three days later it was Paul Malone's turn to get one over on his former team as his new Larne team won 3-1 against Ballymena at Inver Park. Alan Campbell's difficult start to his second spell in charge continued throughout the Gold Cup, the team won only one of the seven group games and they failed to qualify for the knock-out stages of the competition.

The poor form wasn't ideal for another European adventure in September. The club had been handed their first real winnable draw in their fourth European tie in the Cup Winners' Cup first round against Hamrun Spartans of Malta. Campbell described the 1-0 first leg defeat at the Showgrounds as one of the 'worst ever' as Ray Xuereb's 19th minute goal made history as the first Maltese side to win a competitive European match. Campbell Jnr missed a penalty in the second half. The second leg a week later in the Maltese national stadium attracted 15,000 spectators who were stunned to silence by George Beattie's early goal after 8 minutes which levelled the tie. But United's great start wilted away in soaring Mediterranean temperatures as Xuereb scored twice either side of half-time to win the game and the tie 3-1 on aggregate amidst scenes of delirium from the Maltese faithful and disgust for United officials. Hamrun Spartans lost to Dynamo Moscow from the Soviet Union in the second round of the competition.

Undeterred by the European failures, the Sky Blues quickly bounced back with four consecutive Ulster Cup wins to qualify for the semi-finals of the competition. Former United striker Paul Malone inflicted semi-final defeat again on United with his new Larne side for the second time with a 3-1 win at Windsor Park in November. The Inver men would eventually lose to Linfield in the final.

Despite the outspoken Alan Campbell completely writing off his team's chances of winning the Irish League, Ballymena were the early pacesetters winning five of the opening seven games. Campbell Jnr repaid his father's faith by scoring the goals that sent the Sky Blues to the top of the table in early December. Keen to maintain their title push, Campbell splashed out £6,000 on Carrick Rangers' Stevie Conville with the aid of funding from supporters clubs. The diminutive midfielder made an instant impact scoring twice in the 3-1 win against Glenavon and also a late equaliser during the Boxing Day derby against Coleraine which kept the Braidmen in the title hunt.

Johnny Speak

Suspensions to key players were the killer for Campbell in the early stages of 1985. Discipline cost the club vital points and they drifted further and further away from the chasing pack in the league. Campbell was strongly linked with the vacant Glentoran job after Ronnie McFall was sacked but pledged his immediate future to United. He made another big signing in January as he brought Johnny Speak back from a disappointing spell with Dundalk for £7,000. Dubbed the 'prodigal son' in the local media, Speak would endure a tough season in front of goal suffering a lean second half of the season on his return to the Irish League.

The Irish Cup proved to be a welcome distraction from a faltering league campaign as comfortable early victories over Amateur League sides Michelin and Killyleagh YC preceded a tougher quarter-final clash with Ards that was settled by a last-minute John Sloan goal. The resulting semi-final against Linfield proved a massive anti-climax as Ballymena went down to a 3-0 defeat at the Oval against Roy Coyle's men.

Beset by further injuries and suspensions, Ballymena disappointingly only recorded three league wins during the second half of the calendar year and finished a once promising season in eighth place. This was enough for manager Alan Campbell, he resigned for the second time, describing his regret at ever returning to the Ballymena Showgrounds as the past season was a 'nightmare' for him and his family. He took particular grievance with the treatment of his son by sections of the Ballymena United supporters. Chairman Leonard Wiseman was talked out of resigning his position by friends and supporters in what was a turbulent end to a disappointing season at the Braid. Once again summer had the committee searching for yet another new manager tasked with changing the fortunes of the club.

⚽ *1985/1986* ⚽

The club moved quickly to fill yet another managerial vacancy at Warden Street in May 1985, with former Carrick Rangers boss Jimmy Brown, a former player with the Sky Blues a decade previously. Brown had been sacked from Taylors Avenue and had agreed in principal to become boss of 'B' Division side Harland and Wolff Welders before United came calling with an offer the Belfast man couldn't refuse.

Jimmy Brown

Brown brought trusted faces from Carrick with defender Roy Fellows and goalkeeper Ricky Adair joining prolific strikers David McAlinden (Cliftonville) and David Dugan (Ards) they had been purchased to replace the outgoing Alan Campbell Junior (last season's leading scorer) who left for Distillery as quickly as his father had left the club. Michael Guy's dispute with the club from the previous season continued and the Londonderry striker went AWOL after failing to report back for pre-season and would not kick a ball in anger all season.

Ballymena United pictured during pre-season in August 1985.

Club captain Graham Fox dealt the club a blow by announcing his premature retirement only two games into the season. Brown moved quickly to appoint Alan Harrison as his new captain. The Braidmen had started the new season in uninspiring form losing to Newry Town and Portadown coupled with a scoreless draw against Dundela of the 'B' Division in the three Ulster Cup group games, United failed to qualify for the next round.

The 13-game Gold Cup series which followed provided very few positives, barring a 5-1 mauling of Crusaders (who would go on to win the competition) with goals from John Sloan (2), Colin O'Neill (2) and David Dugan. The County Antrim Shield would give United supporters something to cheer with a comfortable route straight through to the final in late October after wins against Larne, Distillery II's and then Dundela in the semi-final. Despite entering the club's first Shield final since 1980 against Distillery as favourites, a disappointing performance resulted in a 3-1 defeat

Colin O'Neill

for Ballymena United. Johnny Speak scored the only goal as consolation for United against the Whites.

Brown wielded the axe after the Shield debacle and another five goal Gold Cup win followed, this time against Portadown. United finished a disappointing 11th in the cup standings but had been buoyed by the performances of maverick central midfielder Colin O'Neill who was attracting strong cross channel interest from clubs such as Everton and Chelsea.

Goalkeeping proved a problem position this season with the former Cliftonville and Carrick manager using no less than five different custodians over the course of the season. Out-of-form captain Alan Harrison found himself on the sidelines in December and responded by submitting a transfer request. Despite a seemingly amicable resolution pre-Christmas with the manager, the club's record signing was not to be seen again in a Sky Blue shirt.

On New Year's Day, the club was dealt the sad news of the death of long serving board member and current President Jimmy Rock who passed away after a short illness. On the pitch Ballymena United started 1986 with a 1-0 defeat to Glentoran at the Showgrounds. The Irish Cup run that promised to salvage something from the season only lasted two rounds, a 5-1 first round victory over Institute, in which the Drumahoe side's flying winger David 'Dibby' Dougherty moved to the Braid immediately after the game, set up a quarter-final derby clash away to Jim Platt's Coleraine – United lost 2-1.

During the aforementioned Irish Cup win over Institute, John Sloan reacted angrily to being substituted by the manager and became the latest player to ask for a transfer away from the club. Sloan reluctantly settled his differences with Brown to keep his place in the team but it would be his last season in a Ballymena shirt. Graham Fox also returned to training, following a decision to back-track on his early retirement, to play in the final games of the season.

Despite an inconsistent season for the club, Chairman Leonard Wiseman, who had called for more stability at the club upon his appointment, offered Brown a new two-year extension to his deal at the club. The Sky Blues scraped a top half finish, as despite losing their final two games they confirmed their credible seventh place. Johnny Speak finished top goalscorer for the Sky Blues with 18 goals in all competitions.

⚽ *1986/1987* ⚽

Tragedy struck the club during the summer of 1986, with the sudden death of Brian Crockard on 22nd June. Affectionately known as 'Crow', Brian had unknowingly dived into the shallow end of a swimming pool whilst on holiday in Spain. Given his popularity amongst players and supporters, the club moved to fittingly re-name the player's lounge at the Showgrounds as the 'Crockard Room'. The name is in active use to this day in memory of a potential United great whose career was cut far too short.

Brian Crockard. Courtesy of Ballymena Guardian

The manager's other two main summer signings both hailed from the North coast as centre-half Brian Donnelly and striker Billy Pyper both joined the club alongside Stephen McKee from Linfield. Long serving midfielder John Sloan after 478 appearances and 85 goals – moved to Coleraine for a nominal fee. Former captain Alan Harrison was also sold to the North West, joining Derry City in the League of Ireland for £7,000.

Jimmy Brown's biggest summer coup was bringing Linfield defender John Garrett to the Showgrounds to replace the void left by Brian Crockard's passing. Brought up in the nearby Rectory Estate and a United season ticket holder in his youth, John had been surprisingly released by Roy Coyle after over 300 appearances for the Windsor Park side. Unfortunately his homecoming season was to be marred by injury in October as a recurring knee injury sidelined Garrett for the majority of the season.

Michael Smyth in action against Linfield. Courtesy of Ballymena Times

United's season started well as the early season Ulster Cup group stage was a formality and a 3-0 win against Crusaders in the quarter-final set up a last four clash with Linfield at the Oval. Some questionable refereeing decisions cost Ballymena a place in the final in the opinion of the manager, as despite an encouraging performance, Linfield won the game 2-1. This was the second time that Roy Coyle's side had put the Sky Blues out of a competition, having already won the County Antrim Shield quarter-final at Windsor Park in August.

Brown's men bounced back four days later when they ended a winless run against Jim Platt's Coleraine side. Striker Billy Pyper came off the bench on his senior debut at Warden Street with only nine minutes remaining to score the winner against his hometown club. The win was one of the few moments of cheer in an inconsistent start to the season at the Showgrounds, Ballymena languished in the bottom third of the table and low on confidence after a dismal 7-2 defeat to Glentoran at the Oval.

Colin O'Neill's winner against Portadown in late November sparked a mini-revival as United only lost one game from six throughout December to finish 1986 in ninth place. The mercurial O'Neill's winner at Shamrock Park was his last goal in United colours as after looking set for a break into English football with

Johnny Speak. Courtesy of Ballymena Times

Millwall, the deal was scuppered at the last minute. Instead he ironically moved to Portadown in a deal reportedly worth £9,500. O'Neill eventually got his chance across the water with Motherwell a year later, winning three caps for Northern Ireland and the Scottish Cup in 1991.

The departure did not deter Ballymena as Jimmy Brown led the club to a remarkable surge up the Irish League table (and also earn a new contract in the process). Six wins and only one defeat in the final nine games of the league season meant Ballymena finished sixth and even mounted a late charge for European football but defeat to Newry Town in the final game in February cost the Braidmen a fourth place finish. Irish Cup hopes were also cruelly dashed a week later with the 2-0 defeat to Paul Malone's Larne in the first round with Michael Guy scoring for the Inver Park men after recently returning to football from a two year exile.

United's season was effectively over. A dismal showing in the Gold Cup group stage and another heavy cup defeat to Linfield in the inaugural season of the new League Cup ended a mediocre season for the Sky Blues, Johnny Speak returned to form as leading goalscorer and the ever-dependable Stevie Conville was voted as the members' and players' player of the year for 1986/87.

The lack of progress was enough for Chairman Leonard Wiseman who resigned in April 1987 and was replaced by the vice-chair Gordon McIlrath despite competition from Treasurer Ken Hood for the post. In June, Don Stirling began his long association in office as he became only the fifth secretary of the club when he took over from Ken Barr who also stepped down citing the growing commitments involved with the post.

⚽ *1987/1988* ⚽

With funds cut for the playing budget Brown blasted the 'greedy' nature of Irish League players during the summer. Ronnie Burns moved to Portadown with Jeff Wright heading to rivals Coleraine and Stephen McKee was forced to move closer to home with Bangor due to difficulties travelling. Hard-up United were forced to put faith in 20-year-old goalkeeper Damian Grant who had returned home from Port Vale and Ards' Ricky Simpson, Brown also promoted Stephen 'Goosey' Young into the first team panel during pre-season, the industrious young midfielder from Galgorm had joined from Ballymoney United in March.

Ballymena started the season dreadfully losing five games in a row throughout August and September and quickly exited the Ulster Cup at the group stage. It was enough for manager Jimmy Brown who surprisingly resigned after the 4-1 loss to Larne at Inver Park with assistant Alan Fraser in tow. Whilst the parting was amicable, Brown expressed his disappointment in being unable to utilise more of the £30,000 raised through the sale of players. £9,500 of this was secured only a week before when Brown begrudgingly sold star striker Johnny Speak to newly promoted Derry City. 22-year-old Speak would finish as the leading goalscorer in the League of Ireland for the Candystripes during the 1987/88 season.

Reserve team manager Alec McKee was installed as manager and he appointed the experienced John Garrett as his number two (becoming the first local manager in 12 years since Arthur Stewart). The reliable Stevie Conville was made as

Ballymena United's team pictured in January 1988 after unveiling a new sponsorship deal with McBurney Transport.
Back row: Jim Scott, Michael Nicholl, John Garrett, Billy Pyper, Norman McBurney (Main Sponsor), Damien Grant, Brian Donnelly, Joss Arbuthnot (Trainer), George Kernohan.
Front row: Derek Donaghy, Ian Hamilton, David Dougherty, Robert Carson, Steve Conville, Richard Simpson.

McKee's captain and a 1-0 win against Ards in the Gold at the Showgrounds was the perfect start for the new regime, Billy Pyper scored the game's only goal.

New manager Alec McKee

A resurgence in the team's performances followed with four wins in the next five games, this included progression to the final of the County Antrim Shield. Despite being massive underdogs in the semi-final against Glentoran at the Oval, captain Conville inspired the Sky Blues to a well-deserved 1-0 victory. One dejected Glentoran player is noted in the next *Light Blue Leader* programme as saying 'Alex McKee must have put something in their tea. I haven't seen a Ballymena team battle like that in years.' The final at the same venue in late November nearly didn't go ahead against Newry Town due to bomb alerts in Belfast. A restricted attendance of 1,000 watched on as United's early lead (gained through David Dougherty) was cancelled out by two Newry goals either side of half-time and the border men secured their first senior trophy.

McKee's honeymoon had ended by Christmas with exits in the Gold Cup, League Cup and the Floodlit Cup, United competed in <u>eight</u> competitions during the 1987/88 season, and were floating in mid-table at Christmas. There was some festive joy for supporters as Goosey Young scored twice in stunning 3-2 win against Glentoran at the Showgrounds. The club also secured a lucrative £5,000 shirt sponsorship deal with local haulage firm McBurney Transport in January 1988 through committee member Norman McBurney. Few could have envisaged the role the McBurney family would have in the club for the next quarter of a century and that this would go onto be one of the longest shirt sponsorship deals in European football history.

Early in the New Year goalkeeper Damien Grant inoccously broke his ankle during training just as he was starting to find his feet in the Irish League. Philip McGaughey (brother of Linfield legend Martin McGaughey) was brought in for the remainder of the season. McKee also recruited Cliftonville striker Michael McDonald to help solve the team's goalscoring problem but only produced four goals in 18 games in a disappointing season for the forward. McDonald's soon to be born nephew would eventually surpass his sporting talents – golfer Rory McIlroy.

There was a first for the club in March in the routine end-of-season Irish League game against Ards. The Showgrounds hosted its first game under floodlights thanks to the £90,000 grant aided installation. United eventually finished the league season with McKee's resolute yet unspectacular team finishing mid-table in seventh.

Ballymena United's main silverware hopes remained in the Irish Cup until the latter stages of the season as wins against Dunmurry Rec. and Distillery meant a semi-final showdown with Glenavon in East Belfast. McKee described the 2-0 defeat to the Lurgan Blues as the worst performance of the season as they disappointed fans by freezing on the big occasion. Another golden chance of silverware which the club failed to capture was in the final of the one-off County Antrim Centenary Chalice (a competition to mark 100 years of the County

Antrim FA). The Braidmen conceded four goals in the first half against Glentoran and never recovered, eventually losing 4-2.

⚽ *1988/1989* ⚽

McKee started his first full season in charge of the Braidmen with majority of his panel retained from the previous season. He included three major summer signings in Larne striker Paul Hardy, Draperstown based winger John McKee joining from Portadown and Coleraine's Dermot Doherty (a nephew of former Northern Ireland manager, Peter). The latter would not be seen in a United shirt until November after being injured against Partick Thistle in a pre-season friendly.

Injuries would be the scourge of Ballymena United's early season ambitions. On the eve of the season, the manager bizarrely found all three of his goalkeepers (Damien Grant, Joe McErlean and Sean Moore) injured and was forced to bring UUJ's Paul Brown in to cover for the opening games of the season. First-choice Damien Grant fortunately returned in August, earlier than expected from the broken ankle, and would be a virtual ever present for the remainder of the season. Central defender Brian Donnelly was also crocked at Dixon Park in first game of the 1988/89 season and lost his place to 22-year-old Broughshane farmer John Heron. Heron would flourish in the heart of the Ballymena defence after spending a few seasons on the periphery of the first team.

Two opening defeats to Ballyclare Comrades and Coleraine killed off any hopes of progression in the Ulster Cup in the first of the cup competitions that preceded the Irish League. September's seven game Gold Cup series started with a lot more promise with a 2-0 away win against Coleraine thanks to goals from John McKee and Welsh forward Alun Wood. It was back down to earth the following week with a 4-1 defeat to eventual Gold Cup winners, Linfield at the Showgrounds and a dismal 2-0 reverse against Larne seven days after.

McKee's side avoided defeat in their remaining four matches, but with one win and three draws they squandered a decent chance of a semi-final spot and eventually finished fourth from seven. The League Cup provided little additional joy as after a cagey 2-0 win against Armagh City, United were dumped out by Cliftonville in the quarter-final stages. The Sky Blues were already out of three cup competitions before Halloween!

The highly rated Doherty finally made his debut as United started their Smirnoff Irish League campaign with a tight 1-0 defeat to Linfield. The Sky Blues got off the mark with a 2-0 win in the league in the next game against Coleraine which would see the debut of an unknown 21-year-old nimble winger Dessie Loughery signed from Intermediate League side Roe Valley the previous week. This coincided with an unbeaten spell throughout November (albeit via three draws and the Coleraine win), but promising shoots were emerging from Ballymena's lack-lustre start to the campaign. Paul Hardy was starting to score goals and local teenager Lindsay Curry shot to prominence from November onwards having returned home from a two-year apprenticeship at Manchester City.

In December, club captain Stevie Conville dealt the club a blow by refusing the offer a new contract and as a result was transferred to Glenavon amidst a flurry of interest from other clubs in the league. McKee boldly instilled 22-year-old Michael Smyth as Conville's replacement as captain. Meanwhile on the field, the draw specialists finished 1988 without a win since the Coleraine game but with a steady resilience that brought six draws from their next eight games.

1989 started with three league wins against Newry, Portadown and Ards. This quickly shot the Sky Blues up the league table but it was the Irish Cup that would give the team most of their success during the new year. United's hard-working outfit manouvered through the opening three rounds past Distillery, Ballyclare Comrades (via a replay) and Crusaders to progress to the semi-finals of the Irish Cup.

Many onlookers barely gave United a prayer of a chance in the semi-final against champions elect Linfield at the Oval. Goalkeeper Damien Grant produced an endless string of heroic saves that kept United in the tie during the first game which ended 1-1. The teams returned to East Belfast a few days later where Doherty and Hardy were to become the heroes firing the unfancied Sky Blues into their third Irish Cup final in eight years.

With McKee's Irish League hopes having deteriorated after only two wins since January – Ballymena finished an uninspiring league season in ninth place only

Semi-final hero Paul Hardy celebrates the memorable replay victory over Linfield

Action from the 1989 Irish Cup semi-final

a point ahead of Irish Cup final opponents, Larne. The Oval was the setting for the battle of the County Antrim neighbours but the sun-drenched East Belfast venue played host to a dismal Irish Cup final with Paul Hardy's 73rd minute back-heel deceiving Vince Magee and trickling over the line for the only goal of the game. The famous trophy returned to Ballymena for the sixth time and opened up the doors to European football once again.

United finished the season by falling to Glentoran at Seaview in the semi-final of the Country Antrim Shield by two goals without reply. Irish Cup goalscorer Paul Hardy (ironically from Larne) finished as leading goalscorer with 21 goals in his first season at the Showgrounds. Outstanding teenage winger Lindsay Curry was awarded the Ulster Young Football of the Year, the fifth player from the club to win the award.

Away from the glamour of the Irish Cup victory, a young man from Carnlough was starting out on his football career in England. Highly rated reserve team defender Brendan Rodgers joined Reading on an apprenticeship. Rodgers failed to break into the Royals' first team and having been forced to retired with a knee injury at 20 he turned to coaching and quickly moved through the youth ranks under

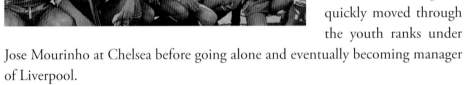

Jose Mourinho at Chelsea before going alone and eventually becoming manager of Liverpool.

Chapter Seven

Relegation, twice (1989-2001)

⚽ *1989/1990* ⚽

The summer of 1989 posed the question, could the Irish Cup winners push on and challenge for the Gibson Cup for the first time?

There was very little transfer activity the following summer, with the entire cup winning team committing for another campaign at Warden Street. The only

Ballymena United line-up pictured in September 1989 before Gold Cup defeat to Linfield.
Back row: Alec McKee (Manager), David Smyth, John Heron, Joe McErlean, Paul Hardy, John Garrett, Stephen Young, Willy Cully (Physio), Joss Arbuthnott (Physio), Billy McCready (Trainer).
Front row: Paul Gribben, John McKee, Ian Hamilton, Michael Smyth, Des Loughery, Kevin O'Neill, Lindsay Curry.

question mark was over mercurial teenager Lindsay Curry who was being courted by Linfield but eventually re-signed. Both of McKee's only major summer signings came from beaten Irish Cup final opponents, Larne. Davy Smyth returned to the club eight years after winning an Irish Cup winners medal as a 17-year-old for a fee of £7,500 (set by an Irish League tribunial) and was joined by 32-year-old striker Tom Sloan – not to be confused with the midfielder sold to Manchester United ten years previously by the club.

Secretary Don Stirling flew out to UEFA headquarters in Geneva during July for the draw for the European Cup Winners' Cup first round which could have set the Sky Blues up for a tie against the likes of Celtic, Sampdoria or Barcelona. The draw pitted Ballymena United against Belgian giants RSC Anderlecht in September. The 20 times Belgian champions had previously won the competition twice in their history alongside the UEFA Cup and Super Cup.

Domestically the season couldn't have started much worse for the Sky Blues as they failed to win a single game throughout August and September losing seven of their opening nine games. First disappointment was the Ulster Cup competition which opened the season and with three consecutive group stage defeats, United finished bottom of their group and were quickly eliminated. Elimination followed in the same stage of the Gold Cup, not ideal preparations for the European games against Anderlecht.

Ballymena United fans made themselves heard in the Belgian capital despite the result. Courtesy of Ivan Russell

The Braidmen travelled to the Belgian capital with trepidation, winger John McKee describing the game in the *Ballymena Guardian* as "lambs for the slaughter". A crowd of around 7,000 spectators (including 40 or so travelling supporters) gathered at the Vanden Stock stadium and watched the Ulster part-timers take on a side who were almost all International footballers. The Anderlect team in the first leg would eventually collectively amass almost 500 caps during their careers! It proved to be an uphill challenge from the start for the Sky Blues, they would go down by six goals without reply in Brussels. Goals came from Kari Ukkonen, Arnor Gudjohnsen (father of future Barcelona and Chelsea striker Eidur) and two apiece for Marc Van der Linden and Luc Nilis. Despite it being the club's heaviest defeat in European competition the home crowd gave Alex McKee's side a standing ovation.

Two weeks later the Belgian cup winners visited the Ballymena Showgrounds for the formality of the second leg of the first round tie. United were further set back after first choice goalkeeper Damien Grant was ruled out injured from the first game and Antrim based reserve goalkeeper Joe McErlean was drafted in, but he couldn't prevent Anderlecht from chalking up four goals without reply to confirm the club's worst aggregate result in European competition, losing 10-0 over the two legs.

Life post-Europe didn't get any easier for McKee's struggling side as they suffered the embarrassment of being knocked out of the first round of the League Cup in extra-time to Brantwood at Skegoneill Avenue – unfortunately this wouldn't even rank as the worst cup exit this season. Disheartened by performances, McKee offered his

A disappointed Joe McErlean couldn't prevent the Anderlecht onslaught. Courtesy of Ballymena Times

resignation to the club but was talked out of leaving by his assistant John Garrett, Garrett himself did stand down as McKee's right hand man in November citing he had 'lost the respect of the players', but remained as a player Likewise young captain Michael Smyth also stood down from his role to be replaced by popular Broughshane farmer John Heron for the remainder of the season.

Despite having already exiting four separate cup competitions, Ballymena's league form throughout the winter was very impressive losing only once in November and December to challenge at the top end of the league table, with excellent wins against rivals Glenavon (3-1) and Linfield (2-1).

The defence of the Irish Cup was swift as Ballymena United were eliminated at the first hurdle by 'B' Division side Dungannon Swifts after a replay. After drawing 1-1 in the first game, the Tyrone side humbled the Sky Blues after extra time in the replay to compound a miserable season of cup competitions for United.

Lacking goals in the side, McKee looked to Scotland in February to bring in young Motherwell forward Neil Candlish on loan for the rest of the season. He made a positive impact and scored the first goal in undoubtedly the game of the season beating champions Linfield 5-1 at the Showgrounds. A stunning victory which included goals for Billy Pyper (two), Lindsay Curry and Ian Hamilton.

In late March, with only six games to go Ballymena United hosted leaders Portadown at Warden Street and took a two goal lead after just 17 minutes with goals from John McKee and Thomas Sloan but eventually lost 3-2. That was the turning point for the Sky Blues who won only one of the final six games to eventually finish fifth in the table. A disappointment in the eyes of supporters but the club's highest league finish in nine seasons. Portadown would finish the season top of the pile for their first ever Irish League championship.

Lindsay Curry finished the club's top goalscorer for a Ballymena United team that only managed 49 goals in their 41 games. Veteran John Garrett was voted as the Players' Player of the Year. Whilst Ballymena United's season ended disappointingly, it was also the same for our new found Belgian friends as they reached the final of the European Cup Winners' Cup narrowly losing to two extra time goals from Sampdoria's Gianluca Vialli in Gothenburg.

⚽ *1990/1991* ⚽

1990 saw very little summer transfer activity, there were no incoming deals. Lindsay Curry was again courted by Linfield all summer and eventually moved to Windsor Park in October. Ricky Simpson returned from a spell in New Zealand to rejoin the club

BALLYMENA UNITED F. C.

Season Ticket

SEASON 1990-1991

The first competition of the 1990/91 season was the Ulster Cup in which brought two defeats in the first two games against Crusaders away and Portadown at home to leave Ballymena United perilously close to an early elimination at the group stage. In need of a high scoring win against Larne in the final group game, United won 5-0. Dessie Loughrey's 84th minute goal was enough to tip the goal difference in United's favour and a second place finish to set up a quarter-final against Glenavon. McKee's side were comfortably disposed of by four goals without reply at Mourneview Park.

Following on the Gold Cup produced a similar return as a stumble through the group stage into second place was rewarded with a quarter-final away to Portadown. The 3-1 defeat sent Sky Blues crashing out of the competition in early October. Thankfully the opening to the Irish League had started well for United, with two wins and a draw from the first three games.

In October McKee looked to the Amateur League in search of goals, recruiting Sammy Smyth from Islandmagee and securing the return of Neil Candlish from Motherwell on a permanent basis. It wasn't enough to prevent Ballymena's free-fall down the league table after only winning one more league fixture before Christmas, slumping down as far as twelfth in the table. Smyth did give his new club some festive cheer, scoring the winning goal in the Boxing Day derby against Coleraine at the Ballycastle Road.

Another Irish Cup fifth round defeat in inauspicious circumstances came in January after a

Neil Candlish. Courtesy of Ballymena Times

3-2 defeat to Omagh Town at St. Julian's Road, the Tyrone club's first season after getting elected to the Irish League. Manager Alex McKee offered his resignation for the second time in two seasons after the defeat.

Ballymena United were beginning to make a habit of cup defeats to lower-league opposition and a first round defeat in the County Antrim Shield at home to 'B' Division side R.U.C. (the team from the Royal Ulster Constabulary – the then police force in Northern Ireland). This was another addition to the list of the club's most embarrassing defeats.

A late flurry of results with six wins from the last eight meaningless league games, pushed Ballymena up into a more respectable placing in the league standings, finishing eighth to secure a top-half finish. Limavady winger Dessie Loughery started to come of age in his third season, finishing as leading goalscorer and winning the player of the year award. In April 1991, McKee resigned from his post as manager after four seasons in charge after his relationship with the club's committee began to deteriorate. Ballymena United initially struggled to fill the vacancy for a new player-manager even with the assistance of the Scottish FA.

⚽ 1991/1992 ⚽

Jim Hagan was the only applicant for the post giving the committee little option but to go with the 35-year-old Larne man. Albeit without any managerial experience, Hagan had been widely regarded as the best local player never to be capped by his country having had success with Coventry and Birmingham alongside winning the La Liga 'Overseas Player of the Year' award in 1988 whilst

Jim Hagan

at Celta Vigo ahead of Gary Lineker, who was playing for Barcelona at the time. The central defender also boasted spells in America and Hong Kong but had spent the previous campaign in Sweden with ILK Oddevold.

Hagan, who also doubled as the club's new commercial manager, made no summer signings but promoted reserve team manager Shay Hamill to the role of his assistant. The pair laid down strict new methods and disciplines at the Showgrounds ahead of the 1991/92 season. There was also major progression off the field as the club formed strong links with Leonard Wiseman's successful Cullybackey Blues youth club as the club attempted to harness the best young talent in the town.

The hardest job of the summer was keeping hold of the sought-after full-back Michael Smyth who signed a new contract with the promise of a testimonial to fend off interest from Glentoran. In other departures winger John McKee dropped down to junior football with Draperstown Celtic (who paid a £2,000 fee for him), Sammy Smyth also dropped down to Islandmagee and Thomas Sloan retired. New faces may have been needed though as the Braidmen lost the first game of the season to away struggling rivals Coleraine.

Despite the Coleraine setback, Hagan's men started the season in fine form starting with a 2-0 win against champions Portadown in the Ulster Cup. This kicked-off a fine run of seven wins from eight games throughout August and September. Unfortunately the only blip was the Ulster Cup quarter-final which was lost on penalties to Crusaders. The goals of the dynamic 'Tartan Terror' Candlish and Dessie Loughery made for fantastic viewing from the terraces as United comfortably progressed to the semi-final of the Gold Cup and went into the Irish League campaign high on confidence.

The football club was in mourning in September though with the death of the popular Billy McCready after a short illness. The former player, trainer and groundsman had given half a century of service to Ballymena United Football Club and only a few months previously had been presented with a merit award by the Football Writers for his outstanding service to Irish Football.

The good start to the season prompted Glenavon to test United's resolve with a £10,000 bid for captain John Heron which was rejected for being way off the valuation placed on the Broughshane defender's head. The Irish League season started with disappointing draws against Larne and Carrick and didn't get much better throughout the autumn, losing in the semi-final of the Gold

Billy McCready

Cup to Glentoran at Seaview but again winning against high-flying Portadown in October with Candlish again bagging a brace.

United's inconsistent form meant that they would spend the whole league season in the bottom half of the table. Fans were continually frustrated by glimpses of the team's ability to perform as they comfortably beat Glentoran at the Showgrounds but then lost 6-1 to Ards at Castlereagh Park a few weeks later and also made early exits from both the County Antrim Shield and Floodlit Cup. Hagan recruited Motherwell forward Ross Tannock on loan (on Candlish's recommendation) but despite two goals on his debut against Ballyclare, his loan wasn't extended beyond the New Year.

Needing to revitalise his struggling squad the manager brought in Robert Craig from Glentoran for £10,000, Timmy Connolly from local morning team Dynamo Star and veteran midfielder Harry McConkey from Ballyclare Comrades. The latter scored the winning goal on New Year's Day against Crusaders as the club aimed for a better 1992 but that victory was the only one from 13 league games as the Sky Blues dropped alarmingly into the bottom two in the table following a 4-0 defeat to Glentoran at the Oval. Matters weren't helped by the influential Dessie Loughery being ruled out for the rest of the season in January after a rough challenge from Alfie Stewart in the 6-0 defeat to Portadown.

The Irish Cup was a lot more successful and glossed over the league failings

with a comfortable route the semi-final with wins against Dundela, Omagh Town and Oxford United Stars. The semi-final against Glenavon in April turned into a nightmare for Jim Hagan when he gifted the Lurgan Blues two of their goals in the convincing 3-0 win over the beleaguered Ballymena men at Windsor Park. Victorious Glenavon went onto the win the Irish Cup with a 2-1 win against Linfield in May.

Ballymena limply finished their dull league season off in tenth position but the club had already started building for next season with the welcome yet unexpected return of Johnny Speak from Derry City £15,000 in late April. Speak had been a key figure in Derry's City's team both domestically and their European adventures and had almost secured a £50,000 move to Spanish second division side UE Figueres. He returned to a hero's reception at the Showgrounds for his third spell in United colours.

⚽ 1992/1993 ⚽

Boosted by the signings of Speak and long term target Mark Carlisle from Chimney Corner, Jim Hagan had challenged his side to break into the top four in the Irish League but by the end of pre-season the manager had become disillusioned with the attitude of players. Midfielder Darryn Magill (from Queen's Park Rangers) was the only other summer arrival as Jim Scott left for Coleraine whilst Brian Donnelly and Ricky Simpson also left the club as the cup winning squad started to break up.

Much like the previous summer, all eyes were on defender Michael Smyth who had just won the members' player of the year and had a £40,000 price tag placed on his head on to fend off both Glentoran and Portadown. But after appearing for the Irish League side against Everton at the start of his tenth (and proposed testimonial) season he agreed a £25,000 move to Glentoran. Another player in high demand was Neil Candlish who almost moved to Portadown for £33,000 only for the deal to fall through when the Ports failed to finance the deal. The former Motherwell man eventually signed a new deal with United.

Early season form was a mystery as United failed to get out of their Ulster Cup group after being drubbed 6-0 by Ards in the final group game. They progressed in the following Gold Cup, defeating Larne and Carrick in the group stages and then Distillery in the quarter-final. This set up a semi-final clash with Cliftonville at Windsor Park. Cliftonville had surprisingly recruited former West Ham and Celtic wildchild striker Frank McAvennie for this one game. The Scottish player's influence told against United as the Reds won 2-1 to progress to the final of the competition.

Johnny Speak. Courtesy of Ballymena Times

With United having a good start to the league series Hagan's next signing was arguably the best of his tenure when he took a chance on Raith Rovers' midfielder Phil Burn who had just finished a short loan spell at Glenavon. It was the form of Burn and the goals of Johnny Speak that took the club to their first final in four years as wins against Omagh Town, Distillery and Crusaders led to a place in the Floodlit Cup finale with Portadown in December.

On the night the team failed to do themselves justice as Portadown ran out 3-1 winners at the national stadium. Neil Candlish's second half goal proved only a consolation for the Braidmen.

Chairman Ken Hood described the United fans as 'patient and passionate' after the Floodlit Cup failure but patience was running out with some supporters after more erratic displays over the Christmas period. With only one win from nine league games (which was the bragging rights in the Boxing Day derby against Coleraine) tensions flared on New Years' Day against Bangor when a protest against manager Jim Hagan took place after the game,

Winless in 1993, United faced an unenviable challenge away at Mourneview Park in the fifth round of the Irish Cup. United produced a stunning display against the holders Glenavon, Neil Candlish's hat-trick sealed a memorable 3-0 win which reignited the Sky Blues' season. The Braidmen repeated the feat a week later in the league winning 2-0 in Lurgan and Candlish scoring both goals – a player that Glenavon boss Alan Fraser had said wouldn't even have got into his team!

Hagan spent £9,000 on Derry City's Gregory Kearney to beef up the midfield but he was sent-off the following round of the Irish Cup at Cliftonville in a bad-tempered encounter. The Reds won the sixth round tie 2-0 and both Kearney and team-mate Timmy Connnolly were sent off with strong criticism from both the manager and Chairman Ken Hood regarding their conduct as Ballymena

Jim Hagan with his head in his hands during the Floodlit Cup final defeat against Portadown. Courtesy of Ballymena Times

United exited the cup with only nine men on the field.

The Irish Cup exit effectively was the end of the club's season as Bangor dumped Hagan's men out of the Floodlit Cup in the quarter-finals in March and league results meant that it was increasingly unlikely the club would even finish in the top half of the league table. That month the Ballymena

Showgrounds was the centre of a media frenzy as popular British rock group Electric Light Orchestra (ELO) announced a reformation comeback gig at the Warden Street venue. This was quickly overruled by the notoriously God fearing Ballymena DUP lead council with Cllr. Roy Gillespie infamously quoting that 'Rock music stands for the Devil, drugs and debauchery!'.

Back on the pitch United played out a largely disappointing season with only one win from the final eight games to finish tenth in the Irish League. In the penultimate home game of the season visiting Glentoran won 8-2. The game was remembered for the quick intervention of physio Alan Kennedy who saved Glens' winger Justin McBride's life after he had swallowed his own tongue after an accidental clash of heads with Phil Burn. Elsewhere John Garrett (who had been injured for the past two season) went on loan to Carrick Rangers to try and salvage his career but eventually retired at the end of the season.

Much of the speculation at the end of the 1992/93 season was regarding the future of under-pressure Hagan but it was the Chairman who was the one ousted by the club's members. Ken Hood's two years at the helm came to an end when vice-chairman and main sponsor Norman McBurney was sensationally voted in as the new chair of the committee with Gordon McIlrath taking the number two role.

⚽ 1993/1994 ⚽

The biggest news in Irish football in 1993 was the introduction of promotion and relegation of senior football after many years of campaigning. The proposal from Cliftonville which was finally accepted by the majority (but not all clubs) was that from the 1995/96 onwards the Irish League's current 16 teams would split into two new 8-team divisions (the 'Premier' and 'First') with the competing teams decided by the accumulative league positions over both the 1993/94 and 1994/95 seasons. United voted in favour of the restructuring but all clubs became very aware of the financial implications of potentially being cast adrift into the unknown wilderness of the First Division.

Neil Candlish's tedious ongoing transfer saga had finally come to a welcome end with £27,000 changing hands with Glentoran for the Scottish forward in June. Ambitious to retain the club's top flight status, Hagan was permitted to finance deals for two vastly experienced new Scottish players to boost his team's chances

Davy McCabe. Courtesy of Ballymena Times

of survival, 31-year-old striker Davy McCabe arrived from Morton having previous goalscoring history with Airdrie, Motherwell and Kimarnock, he was joined by Partick Thistle central midfielder Sammy Johnston who had almost 300 professional games in Scotland under his belt.

Johnston marked his debut with a goal in the Sky Blues' first game back at the Brandywell since 1971 and the bus burning incident during a pre-season friendly. Jim Hagan was fully aware of the huge pressure on him and his players to succeed this season and further strengthened his panel with the signing of Fintan McConville from Glenavon for £12,500. Leaving during the summer were fringe players Ian Hamilton, Seamus Duffy and Darryn Magill.

Late goals from Dermot Doherty and Des Loughery saved an opening day Ulster Cup fixture against Newry Town but it was an underwhelming start to the season in the Ulster and Gold Cups. United and their expensive new Scottish imports managed only two wins from the opening six group stage games combined – it was enough in the Ulster Cup though as qualification to the quarter-finals was assured. Progression was halted by Linfield with a 1-0 defeat at Windsor Park.

The all-important Irish League season started well with a McCabe hat-trick in the 5-2 win over Carrick Rangers but Hagan (who had already admitted to be disillusioned with his players after a 5-1 Gold Cup defeat to Portadown) came to the end of the line after a 3-2 defeat to Ballyclare Comrades the following week. Regarded as one of the nicest men in local football, Hagan's departure was unsurprisingly amicable but he admitted that he felt on trial from the hierarchy of the club during every match.

Eager to appoint a new manager Chariman Norman McBurney and his committee interviewed two candidates – former Glentoran manager Tommy Jackson and recently departed Derry City boss Roy Coyle. The club chose Jackson who had a fine football pedigree with 35 international caps, a lengthly spell in professional football in England as well as a wealth of experience in management both sides of the border. With a degree of hindsight the club might have appointed differently as Coyle eventually became the most successful manager in Irish League history at Glentoran adding to his impressive list of honours amassed at Linfield, Ards and Derry.

'Jacko' was promised funds to rebuild his team and got off to a superb start with a 3-2 win against his former club Glentoran on 9th October at the Showgrounds. Goals came from Phil Burn, Johnny Speak and Jason Gilmore. The jubilant scenes at the final whistle were ironically the end of the honeymoon period for the manager as United lost their next five games in succession and would only win one more game in the rest of the calendar year as supporters' morale dropped to depths of despair.

Tommy Jackson. Courtesy of Ballymena Times'

Beset by goalkeeping problems, Jackson brought Glentoran's Dean Smyth to the club for £6,000 but a steady debut clean sheet against Crusaders aside, the new number one couldn't prevent the constant stream of goals being scored against Ballymena. The manager described his players as 'imposters' following an embarrassing 5-2 defeat against Coleraine in the eagerly anticipated Christmas fixture. An overhaul was quickly required as with the largely unimpressive Johnston already released – forwards McCabe and Hardy were also transfer listed with Omagh Town's Barry McCreadie deemed a more cost effective and reliable option to save United's season.

It wasn't long until the fans started to turn on the manager after the 3-0 defeat to Ards at home (it was the 12th defeat in Jackson's 16 games in charge). Discontent only continued to intensify a few weeks later with another three goal defeat this time to lowly Carrick Rangers in the Irish Cup fifth round. Ironically Kenny Shiels' side contained a number of ex-United players including ex-manager Jim Hagan. Jackson's response was to transfer-list six of his first team panel including the ineffective Gregory Kearney, Dermot Doherty and Robert Craig.

On the face of it things could not possibly have got worse for the club who were currently 14th in the league table, but a pathetic League Cup first round to Tobermore United on penalties surpassed all even the bleakest of outlooks. Managed by former United cup winner Jim Scott, Tobermore had been rooted to the bottom of the 'B' Division and managed to hold take their senior opponents to spot-kicks after a goalless 120 minutes, Ballymena man Lawrence Robinson scored the winning penalty after Roy Davidson had missed for United. Tommy

Jackson declared the defeat as easily his worst experience in football management to date.

The aftermath of the Tobermore debacle did slowly spark some renewed spirit on the field as five wins from the final league games moved the club into the still ultimately disappointing final position of 11th. The club were quick to write this season off as a disaster but with the final position having a huge bearing on the impending league split the club made formative calls to extend the new Premier Division to ten teams this fell on deaf ears at league level.

After months of consultation meetings and preparation, the club announced itself as a private limited company in May 1994 ending almost 60 years of committee lead membership. The new limited status was pushed by Chariman McBurney in order to make the club more financially sustainable and to leverage new revenues to assist with the vital promotion push of the 1994/95 season; Norman McBurney was voted as Chair of the new seven man Board of Directors as a majority shareholder alongside other major stakeholders Gordon McIlrath and David Blair, other inaugural directors of the new company included Robert Cupples, Maurice Smyth, Bertie Gault and Ian Hunter.

⚽ *1994/1995* ⚽

The new Board of Directors and the management committee were under no illusions as to the massive task in hand going into the 1994/95 season. The team needed to finish in the top four positions to be certain of a place in the new Irish League Premier Division for the following season.

Funding was made readily available to manager Tommy Jackson who splashed out £12,500 on Trevor McMullan from Coleraine and also lured Lindsay Curry back to the club from Larne in a swap deal for Stephen Young. There was also a failed club record bid for Portadown's Scottish forward Sandy Fraser but the next best solution was found when Fraser's old Shamrock Park strike partner Stevie Cowan was snapped up from Scottish junior club Linlithgow. Cowan had

Ballymena United players pictured during the unsuccessful 1994/1995 season. Courtesy of Ballymena Times

plundered 130 goals in 145 games for Ronnie McFall's title winning sides and was the star striker Jackson felt could fire the Braidmen to safety.

Barry McCreadie moved back to join his brother Roy at Omagh Town and Gregory Kearney joined Finn Harps in a summer upheaval at Warden Street.

Jackson went back to his old club to recruit winger Jim McCloskey and added more firepower with young Lifford based striker Barry Patton from Omagh Town in preparation for one of the most important seasons in the club's history. Middlesbrough based defender Tony Hall was also a late addition to the panel signing on loan from Berwick Rangers on the eve of the new season.

Supporters and officials believed that Jackson now had a squad capable of competing in the Irish League but it was a slow start with no wins in the opening three Ulster Cup group games (including a 5-0 defeat by Glenavon) which prompted the manager encourage fans to have patience as his new look team attempted to gel. September Gold Cup wins against Omagh

Tony Hall. Courtesy of Ballymena Times

Town and Bangor took the pressure off the manager as Johnny Speak scored winners in both games to progress to the quarter-final.

The Irish League season started with a disappointing draw against Carrick and a late win against Ballyclare Comrades but then took a turn for the worse with defeats to both Ards and Glentoran at the start of October. Cowan had proved a massive disappointment in front of goal with only the single strike on the opening day against Larne to his name – he was quickly deemed surplus to requirements and shipped out to Cliftonville before Halloween. The same couldn't be said for Englishman Tony 'Nobby' Hall who won seven supporters' man-of-the-match awards in his first 13 games to prove a massive hit at the Showgrounds and he would quickly be offered a permanent contract.

Manchester United manager Alex Ferguson was a VIP guest at the Showgrounds as he ran the eye over both Coleraine and United on a scouting missing during the Gold Cup quarter-final on 11th October. Paul Carlyle's fluke goal sealed a 1-0 win for the Bannsiders and also sealed the fate of manager Tommy Jackson who was sacked after the game almost exactly one year after his appointment. Despite the funding afforded to him, Tommy left with the unenviable tag of having one of the worst win records of any Ballymena United manager and the board acted quickly in a last ditch attempt to salvage the season.

Reserve team manager Gary Erwin (remembered fondly as a popular player in the 1970's for United) was appointed in a caretaker capacity until the New Year with Alec Donald appointed as his assistant. 'Chunky' Erwin had previously managed Larne and taken the unfashionable Inver Park side to fourth place in the league a few years before. He had been back at the Showgrounds as manager of the second string since March. Gary came in with an optimistic view that Ballymena United could beat the drop and with the help of a hastily arranged loan signing of Kilmarnock forward Danny Crainie the Sky Blues sensationally defeated Linfield 2-1 at the Showgrounds in his first game in charge, the new Scottish talent superbly grabbing the winning goal.

Unfortunately ex-Celtic striker Crainie's debut was cut short and he wouldn't reappear until December but his performance was enough to convince the club to offer a two year contract. Results from then on were still inconsistent before hitting an unwelcome slump in November as United lost four games from five and exited both the Floodlit Cup and the County Antrim Shield in the first round. This prompted Erwin to shockingly transfer list ALL of his professionals and quickly release the short-term signings such as Mark O'Neill, Gary Powell,

Matty Brooks, Mark Farrington and Adam King – all players that were panic signings by the new manager based on having been previously with professional clubs but none of whom will go down as having a memorable stay in County Antrim.

The fight for promotion was suddenly back on in December with an impressive three consecutive wins against Bangor, Portadown and Newry Town. The Newry game in particular gave renewed hope of a climb to safety with a stunning record-equalling 8-0 win against the border side. It was a bizarre game in which United goalkeeper Damien Grant was voted man of the match and the lights going out after 87 minutes but the result being allowed to stand. Club captain John Heron saved a point on Boxing Day against Coleraine in the 1-1 as the Sky Blues looked to 1995 with a great degree of optimism.

Typically that optimism was quickly quashed as Ballymena started the New Year with no wins from their first five league games throughout January. The club's top flight status was hanging by a thread with the team occupying the lowly 13th position. The Irish Cup was equally as disappointing for supporters as Omagh Town took the club to a replay in the fifth round tie and the Tyrone men left the Showgrounds with a 1-0 win at the second attempt to progress in the competition. The League Cup was little better with a second round exit to fellow strugglers Ballyclare Comrades at Warden Street.

After the Ballyclare defeat manager Gary Erwin admitted defeat and the club's directors were once again advertising for a new manager willing to take on the First Division. Erwin stayed on for a couple of weeks as the search was underway but within two weeks former Glenavon manager Alan Fraser was brought back to the Showgrounds as the new gaffer with Eric Bowyer as his assistant. Fraser had previously been the Reserve team manager under Jimmy Brown and had been surprisingly sacked in November from his position at Mourneview Park.

Gary Erwin. Courtesy of Ballymena Times

There was no magic wand and no miracle, Fraser failed to win any of the remaining eight games and Ballymena were mathematically relegated on 25th March with a 2-1 defeat away to Distillery with five games to spare. The following week champions elect Crusaders came to the Ballymena Showgrounds in huge numbers and sealed their third Irish League championship with a comfortable 2-0 win with early goals from Stephen Baxter and Glenn Hunter.

With only pride left to play for, United travelled to the Ballycastle Road on the final matchday. The fate of their bitter derby rivals was in their hands as Coleraine were battling with Bangor for the final spot in the new Premier Division for the next season. In a truly farcical situation Bangor had to lose against Ards to stay up (in a ridiculous scenario that would need a book in itself to explain) but a Coleraine win would see them survive. In a drab encounter teenage defender Paul Muir confirmed Coleraine's relegation with an injury time goal-line clearance from Stuart McClean's header much to the delight of the visiting fans and the astonishment of the home ones.

Ballymena United eventually finished eleventh in the two year assessment that produced some of the most disappointing football seen in years. It was now a massive rebuilding exercise ahead for Fraser in the unknown wilderness of the new First Division.

⚽ 1995/1996 ⚽

Ballymena United manager Alan Fraser was handed a massive war chest in the 1995 close season with one objective – an instant return to the top division.

Alan Fraser. Courtesy of Ballymena Times

United would be playing the 1995/96 season in the inaugural First Division season alongside Ballyclare, Carrick Rangers, Coleraine, Distillery, Larne, Newry Town and Omagh Town.

Major surgery was conducted with many of the club's underperforming senior professionals moving on. Trevor McMullan was sold to Crusaders whilst Johnny Speak returned to the League of Ireland with Finn Harps. The popular mainland duo of Danny Crainie and Tony Hall were two of the first to be transfer-listed by Fraser and eventually sealed moves to Ross County and Waterford Untied, respectively.

Crusaders full-back Stephen Stewart was the first arrival and was soon followed by a trio of promising Linfield fringe players

Jason Allen, Nigel Boyd and John McConnell. The latter was appointed as the new club captain in place of long serving John Heron who was frozen out of the manager's plans. Up front £10,000 was spent on Larne talisman Tom 'Tucker' McCourt and a further £8,500 on Scottish forward Mark McWalter from Coleraine. Goalkeeper Robbie Beck and veteran Scottish midfielder Ally Mauchlen were also both recruited from Fraser's former club Glenavon.

With the heavy spending United were made early favourites for promotion with the bookies and were an unrecognisable outfit with seven debutants in the first game of the new season. Mark McWalter's debut goal sealed a 1-0 League Cup win over Chimney Corner at Allen Park. The former Arbroath and St. Mirren striker missed the next six weeks of the season after fracturing his skull in an accident at home! Ballymena stayed in the League Cup for only three days, losing in the second round to Portadown and then failing to qualify from either the Ulster Cup or Gold Cup group stages in September. Arguably the new faces required some time to settle into a rhythm but the players were blasted as a 'laughing stock' after the dismal 4-0 defeat to Ards at the Showgrounds.

The league season started in late September with a home win over Carrick Rangers and the Sky Blues shot to the top of the table with seven points from the opening three games. Despite a blip with a 1-0 defeat to Distillery, the Braidmen didn't lose another league game during the rest of the calendar year but drew far too many games and weren't scoring enough goals. McWalter and McCourt in particular failed to live up to their billing as United struggled to keep up with early pacesetters Coleraine and Distillery.

Ballymena United's Reserves managed to bring some overdue silverware back to Warden Street when Jimmy Young's men won the prestigious Steel and Sons Cup for the first time in the club's history. There was a replay required with Amateur League side Dromara Village as Stephen Lynch scored a late winner to seal the 2-1 win at Seaview.

Fraser had splashed out £15,000 on classy Portadown midfielder Peter Murray before Christmas to take the collective season spending over £50,000 and the new signing had confidently declared that United could catch Coleraine in the title race. Murray's prediction was the 'kiss of death' as United went six games in succession without a win in the league as the Bannsiders had already started off a 20 game unbeaten sequence. The 1-0 defeat away to Newry Town in January had even left manager Alan Fraser contemplating resigning from the increasingly impossible task of changing the fortunes of the club.

Ballymena United Reserves celebrate winning the Steel and Sons Cup for the first time in December 1995. Courtesy of Ballymena Times

By February, McCourt had gone AWOL and Coleraine were on the brink of the league title. The inevitable was duly confirmed on 28th February with seven games remaining as Kenny Shiels' men brushed their derby rivals aside with a 4-0 win to claim the First Division title in style – at that stage of the campaign Coleraine had opened up a remarkable 26 gap on the Sky Blues. The irony wasn't lost on the home faithful who had watched United relegate their side 10 months earlier and now had condemned their neighbours to at least another season in the much maligned First Division.

Peter Murray. Courtesy of Ballymena Times

Come the Irish quarter-finals United had nothing to lose against Glentoran having progressed past Chimney Corner and Armagh City. United took the game to their Premier Division opponents in the replay, following a scoreless draw four days earlier, racing into an early 2-0 lead with goals from West Ham loanee Chris Moors and Fintan McConville after half an hour. Winger Dessie Loughery was torturing the Glens and had it not been for a hamstring injury, the game may have turned out differently. Young Englishman Glen Little scored hat-trick to send the East Belfast men back on track to winning the Irish Cup with a 4-2 win at the Showgrounds.

With the pressure off, Alan Fraser's men hit form and finished the season with seven consecutive wins to secure second place in the table, they signed off the 1995/96 campaign with a pulsating 4-3 win against champions Coleraine in April but despite the moral victory the gap still remained 18 points between the two sides. With Bangor relegated from the Premier Division and the Irish League confirming that both divisions would be increasing to ten teams ahead of the 1997/98 season, there was a quiet confidence that Alan Fraser's men were now ready to step up to the main table again.

⚽ 1996/1997 ⚽

There was a change in the club's hierarchy during the summer as accountant Edwin McLaughlin took over as Chairman from Norman McBurney. Club accountant McLaughlin had only joined the company as a director the previous season and ended the outgoing Chairman's three year tenure. Norman stated that it was almost a conflict of interests being the club's main sponsor and also the Chairman.

Fraser released his mainland trio of Mark McWalter, Ally Mauchlen and Phil Burn as he looked to build a panel of locally based players for the promotion push. Former captain John Heron was finally freed from his exile to join Distillery for £3,000 and midfielders Lindsay Curry and Fintan McConville started the season transfer listed and were quickly moved on. There was no major influx of signings this summer only hard-man midfielder Ian Bustard signed from Larne, Dundalk native John Smyth from Glenavon and striker Ciaran Feehan formerly of Cliftonville being added to a strong yet settled promotion chasing squad.

The bookies had once again placed the favourites tag on the Braidmen who started their season with a surprise 1-0 defeat to Dungannon Swifts in the League Cup first round only a week after beating the Stangmore Park side 5-1 in a pre-season friendly at the same venue. The Sky Blues also exited the new knock-out formatted Ulster Cup in the first round to Crusaders over two legs, but performed well against the Premier Division challengers in both games.

Wins against Bangor and Larne in the group stage of the Gold Cup allowed United to build some momentum as they qualified for the quarter-finals with a

Ballymena United pictured before the Irish Cup fifth round defeat to Bangor in January 1997.
Back row: Jason Gilmore, John Smyth, Declan McGreevy, Paul Muir, Robbie Beck, Phillip Knell, Jason Allen, Stephen Stewart.
Front row: Ian Bustard, Des Loughery, John McConnell, Nigel Boyd, Barry Patton, Ciaran Feehan.
Courtesy of Ballymena Times

game to spare. This set up a shock last-eight win over reigning Premier Division champions Portadown at home on penalties after a scoreless draw. The 2-0 semi-final defeat to Linfield at the Oval was a step too far for the steadily improving Sky Blues.

United hit the ground running at the start of the First Division campaign in September with seven wins from the first eight league games to soar straight to the top of the table. The goalscoring problems that Fraser had toiled over were now a distant memory as his team were hitting the headlines and were twice voted as the Football Writers' Team of the Month. Rejuvenated winger Dessie Loughery (now in his testimonial season) also bagged two Player of the Month awards for himself.

In November, the club were invited to enter their first cross-border competition since the ill-fated Tyler Cup in 1980, they faced a two legged first round tie in the new Irish News Cup against League of Ireland Premier Division outfit Sligo Rovers. United lost both legs of the tie, eventually going down 5-2 on aggregate. By the New Year the impressive run of results continued with 12 wins from 14 at the half-way stage of the campaign as United extended lead over nearest challengers Bangor and Omagh. It looked look increasingly likely that they would seal one of the two promotion spots.

Fraser splashed out £6,000 on Linfield's attacking midfielder Phillip Knell ahead of the Irish Cup fifth round but the blonde dynamo could not save the in-form Sky Blues from a surprise 3-0 defeat to fellow First Division side Bangor at Clandeboye Park. Progress in the County Antrim Shield was much more successful as opening round wins against Carrick Rangers and Chimney Corner (in which Dessie Loughery scored the goal of the season) set up a sensational semi-final with Portadown. Nigel Boyd's late equaliser was followed up by Ciaran Feehan's 'Golden Goal' in the 106th minute to win the match and progress to the final.

Kitman Bertnel Thompson appointed in November 1996 pictured in the Showgrounds dressing room. Courtesy of Ballymena Times

The Shield final (the club's first since 1988) against Cliftonville at Windsor Park grabbed the headlines for all the wrong reasons. On 4th February with United dominating play in the scoreless game, referee Alan Snoddy abandoned proceedings in the second half after bottles were thrown onto the pitch from the Cliftonville supporters. The match was replayed three weeks later (with a restricted 2,000 attendance) and after 120 minutes of play penalties were cruelly used to separate the two sides. Peter Murray's final spot kick was saved and the Shield was heading to Solitude after a 5-4 shootout win.

Fraser's Sky Blues did finish the season with silverware on the sideboard as they clinched the First Division title with five games to spare in March. Ciaran Feehan's second half goal against Distillery at Ballyskeagh sparked scenes of delirium on the terraces as the Braidmen confirmed the club's first league championship and a return to the top flight of Northern Irish football for the 1997/98 season. The trophy was presented to captain John McConnell three days later against Newry Town at the Showgrounds as Ballymena United finished 15 points clear of second placed Omagh Town. Omagh were also promoted into the new ten team Premier Division.

Such a memorable season ended with a well-deserved testimonial for winger Dessie Loughery who had finished his nine season as joint leading goalscorer with Ciaran Feehan (both on 16 goals). Rivals Coleraine, who narrowly missed out on the Premier Division title, were a suitable opponent for Loughery's showpiece which Ballymena won 5-1 with Peter Murray capping off a great season with a hat-trick.

Ciaran Feehan celebrates at Distillery after sealing the First Division title. Courtesy of Ballymena Times

Ballymena United are provided with a guard of honour by Newry Town players. Courtesy of Ballymena Times

Chairman Edwin McLaughlin and the First Division trophy. Courtesy of Ballymena Times

1996/1997 First Division champions. Courtesy of Ballymena Times

⚽ *1997/1998* ⚽

Manager Alan Fraser kept faith in his First Division title winning squad ahead of the club's first assault on the Premier Division. The only major departure of star striker Ciaran Feehan (who had immigrated to Australia) was a blow but he was swiftly replaced by Dublin forward PJ O'Connell from Bangor. This was followed by a 'homecoming' for Scottish maestro Neil Candlish who re-joined the Sky Blues from Portadown. Local midfielder Jason 'Deano' Gilmore was the only other departure of note, choosing to start in Division One with Larne.

United kicked-off their season with a comfortable 4-1 victory over Dundela at Wilgar Park in the opening round of the League Cup with Barry Patton scoring a hat-trick – few could have envisaged the impact the Lifford based striker would have in his fourth season at the Showgrounds. Progress in the same competition continued with victory over Newry Town on penalties and then came to an abrupt end with a 6-1 defeat to Glenavon in the quarter-finals.

With only one home game from the opening ten fixtures (due to a combination of ground maintenance and poor Irish League fixture planning), Ballymena United started the Premier League campaign in fine form with three wins from the opening four games. A 1-0 win against Coleraine had the Braidmen as surprising leaders of the pack in the early weeks of the season. September provided a stiff reality check though as the team lost five games in succession during a relentless schedule and bombed out of the Gold Cup at the group stage.

An upsurge in form throughout October seen wins against Ards, Coleraine and Cliftonville pushed United back up the table and they were rewarded for their endeavours with the 'Team of the Month' accolade from the writers, the same month in which Alan Fraser won the managerial award. November followed up with a further draw against Linfield and a 2-1 win at the Oval against Glentoran with goals from Patton and Peter Murray.

Back-to-back games against the title challenging North Belfast sides Cliftonville and Crusaders sent Ballymena United fans into dreamland in December as firstly a 4-0 win against the Solitude Reds (a <u>third</u> win in the league against Marty Quinn's men) and then a miraculous 4-3 win against the reigning Irish League champions at Seaview in which Neil Candlish scored a stunning late goal to send the Sky Blues to the top of the Premier League. Many onlookers suddenly began to believe in a Christmas miracle that the Gibson Cup could be coming to the Showgrounds for the first time in the history of club.

Barry Patton. Courtesy of Ballymena Times

7,000 fans crammed into the Ballymena Showgrounds for the Boxing Day derby against Coleraine, the biggest crowd seen at the Warden Street venue in years. United drew 2-2 with goals from Philip Knell and Barry Patton. In form Patton was attracting strong interest from League of Ireland champions Derry City after plundering 20 goals in the first half of the season. Much to Derry manager Felix Healy's disappointment Barry signed a new three year contract to stay at the Braid but unfortunately as soon as the ink was dry the goals began to dry up with only six more goals during the rest of the season.

With Patton's immediate future secure in January, the management committee broke the bank to secure a high-calibre strike partner to take United to the next level. A club record £20,000 was invested in the services of Crusaders' record goalscorer Glenn Hunter (allegedly against the initial wishes of manager Alan Fraser). Despite a brace on his full debut against Coleraine, the goals didn't immediately flow for Hunter and United as hoped as the Lisburn based striker failed to settle into his new surroundings.

The heightened pressure at the start of 1998 took its toll on the players as no wins

Record signing Glenn Hunter. Courtesy of Ballymena Times

from the next seven league games slowly edged Ballymena out of contention for the Gibson Cup. January also marked a first round exit in the Irish Cup to eventual winners Glentoran via a replay. Some of the other minor cup competitions did provide some respite from the faltering league campaign as United reached the semi-finals of the Floodlit Cup (losing to Cliftonville at Windsor Park) and the final of the maligned Irish News Cup. Having chalked up a remarkable 11-2 aggregate victory over Kenny Shiels' Coleraine in the semi-final United succumbed to unfancied Omagh Town over two legs in the final.

Ballymena's title challenge was now a distant memory with only four league wins since New Years' Day but they did manage to secure a commendable top five finish on goal difference on the final day of the season with a 2-0 win against already relegated Ards thanks to goals from Paul Muir and Dessie Loughery. Barry Patton inevitably finished as top scorer (with 26 goals in all competitions) and also won the Player of the Year award. Manager Alan Fraser was left contemplating his position following United's capitulation only to be talked out of resigning by Chairman Edwin McLaughlin.

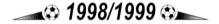

⚽ *1998/1999* ⚽

Having spent the early part of the summer talking the manager out of resigning his post, Chairman Edwin McLaughlin and Vice-Chairman both stepped down from their roles during the close season. McLaughlin was eventually talked out of the idea and stayed on but McIlrath stood by his surprise decision. Former Larne boss Shay Hamill returned to the club as Reserve team manager following the departure of Jimmy Young.

There was an urge for Alan Fraser to push the club on but Ballymena United experienced a quiet summer of transfer dealings at the Showgrounds. The golden pot of money had started to dry up with the only signatures being that of local boy Darren Parker joining from Glentoran and Keith Percy an experienced midfielder from Loughgall. Veteran defender Stephen Stewart joined Bangor as the only major departure. Outside of the spotlight teenage youth team defender Chris Baird was also transferred to English Premier League side Southampton for £5,000 – the Rasharkin native would go on to establish himself in English football and win over half a century of international caps for Northern Ireland.

United opened their season with a 1-0 victory against Glenavon at the Showgrounds, record signing Glenn Hunter getting the only goal. The day was overshadowed by the Omagh bomb that went off shortly after kick-off, killing 29 innocent people in the County Tyrone town centre. Fraser's team was built on a strong and experienced defence and conceding only one goal in their opening five games (which included a 1-0 win against Irish League champions, Cliftonville) they quickly moved towards the top of the league table in early September.

Chris Baird

Having struggled to hold down regular places veterans Peter Murray and Neil Candlish both returned to their former clubs; Cliftonville and Portadown. The team's home form was key as Ballymena lost only one of the opening 11 games at the Showgrounds, this meant that the Sky Blues sat proudly in fourth place following a 1-0 victory over Linfield and a 1-1 draw with early league pacesetters Glentoran. United also had topped their Gold Cup group comfortably, but bowed out of the competition in the quarter-finals at Portadown in late November.

It was the quarter-final stage of the County Antrim Shield as well in which United exited in December. There was some winter relief as Dessie Loughery's first half goal proved the winner in the 1-0 Boxing Day win over Coleraine. Inconsistency had been the Sky Blues' biggest enemy during the first half of the

Ballymena United's team pictured during the 1998/1999 season.
Back row: Mark Carlisle, Jason Allen, PJ O'Connell, Robbie Beck, Paul Muir, Declan McGreevy, John McDowell.
Front row: Phillip Knell, Neil Candlish, Barry Patton, Ian Bustard, Peter Murray, Nigel Boyd, Stephen Stewart.
Courtesy of Ballymena Times

season but they remained fourth at the turn of the year, still well in the hunt for European qualification for the first time in ten years.

1999 started poorly for the Sky Blues as they lost in the first round of the League Cup to Linfield and had to wait until mid-February for their first league victory of the calendar year. They had saved their best performance of the season until now as they convincingly defeated title chasing Linfield 4-2 at the Showgrounds to end the Belfast Blues' title challenge – the highlight being long-serving full-back Mark Carlisle's stunning long range volley (only Carlisle's second goal in almost 300 appearances!).

With Europe out of the equation given the erratic league form attention was focused on the Irish Cup. Progression through the first three rounds was assured with wins against three First Division sides; Larne, Ballyclare Comrades and Distillery, to set up a semi-final against Portadown at the Oval in April (the club's first Irish Cup semi-final since 1992). It was a miserable afternoon for Ballymena United's supporters as a lack-lustre performance against Ronnie McFall's side ended in 2-0 defeat.

To compound the misery of not reaching the Irish Cup final, Portadown's opponents for the showpiece decider, Cliftonville, were thrown out of the competition a week before the final for fielding the ineligible Simon Gribben in their semi-final victory over Linfield. The trophy, prize-money and European qualification was handed to Portadown without a ball being kicked. Whilst no-one in football wants to win trophies by administrative blunders the monetary benefits to financially struggling Ballymena United would have been hugely desirable.

The league season ended with Glentoran being crowned Irish League champions at the Showgrounds with a 6-3 victory on the final day. The Glentoran defeat was also Alan Fraser's last game after four years as Ballymena United's manager. He was sacked hours after the final whistle with United finishing in an underwhelming sixth position in the league table and reserve team manager Shay Hamill was appointed as caretaker manager for the final game of the season.

The Glentoran game was also the last for fans favourite Dessie Loughery. The Limavady winger had made the shock revelation earlier in April that this season would be his last with the Sky Blues as he wanted to finish his playing career closer to home due to travelling. Unimpressed caretaker boss Shay Hamill accused Loughery of showboating during his final appearance at the Showgrounds against the Glens and put him on the bench for the Irish News Cup final at Finn Harps.

Manager Alan Fraser (left) and Chairman Edwin McLaughlin (right) parted ways in April 1999. Courtesy of Ballymena Times

For the second consecutive season Ballymena United had found themselves in the final of the cross-border competition for clubs in the North West of Ireland. They travelled to Ballybofey to face the Donegal side, which included former United striker Johnny Speak, with an young and experimental side and Loughery named on the bench, much to his disapproval. He subsequently left the ground and didn't play competitively for Ballymena United again. Finn Harps won the low key final 2-0 in what was the last year of the poorly supported competition.

⚽ *1999/2000* ⚽

In May 1999, the Ballymena United committee moved swiftly to appoint former Glenavon and Bangor manager Nigel Best who had won Irish Cups with both clubs in the last decade. The 49-year-old schoolteacher beat off competition from inexperienced Stephen McBride for the United hotseat and appointed Kieran Harding as his assistant manager. Former midfielder Joe McCall was also appointed Reserve team manager in place of Shay Hamill who had served as caretaker first-team manager.

Best had to deal with some enforced departures early in his tenure as experienced goalkeeper Robbie Beck retired and Ian Bustard moved to Carrick Rangers whilst Dessie Loughery unceremoniously ended his 11-year association at the club after the Irish News Cup final disagreement. He joined bitter rivals Coleraine much to the disappointment of Ballymena supporters. Young goalkeeping starlet Richard McKinney made a move to professional football on the eve of the new season with Manchester City (then playing in England's third tier) for £15,000 and potential future add-ons.

With limited resources at the new manager's disposal Dublin goalkeeper Dermot O'Neill signed from his former club Glenavon and was entrusted as the club's new number one. Also incoming at Warden Street were young talents

Richard McKinney. Courtesy of Ballymena Times

Gareth Fulton from Portadown and Barry Tumilty from Newry Town alongside midfielder John Gregg (son of former Manchester United goalkeeper, Harry) from Coleraine.

The Premier League season opened with a drab scoreless draw against Best's former employers, Glenavon. Draws would be the tone of the 1999/2000 season for Ballymena United as they would go onto set a record for the highest number of draws in an Irish League season. The Glenavon stalemate was to be the first of SEVEN draws in the opening ten league games of which the Sky Blues failed to win any. The team struggled for goals and although being hard to beat, the lack of goals meant a regular place in the bottom two by September.

Finally the first win of the season came at the start of October in the first round of the Gold Cup with a 3-2 victory against Crusaders with goals coming from Glenn Hunter, Scott Drummond and John Gregg. That win visibly boosted confidence at the Showgrounds with back-to-back league wins against fellow strugglers Lisburn Distillery (4-3) and Cliftonville (2-1). Glenn Hunter scored a hat-trick in the Distillery game and his goals were to be vital for the Sky Blues over the course of the season as he started to convince supporters he was worth his hefty transfer fee.

In November 1999, Ballymena Borough Council unveiled their ambitious plans for the future of the Ballymena Showgrounds with funding being sourced externally for the redevelopment of the main arena including a new grandstand on the terraced side of the ground. In other changes at the club long serving defender Paul Muir was moved out to Crusaders but Nigel Boyd (who had looked certain of a summer move to Linfield) returned to the United team alongside veteran 'hard-man' Ray McGuiness signed from Limavady United.

Pressure had quickly mounted on the manager as Ballymena went 12 games without a win throughout November and December. They were cut adrift alongside Distillery at the bottom of the Premier League as the eagerly anticipated new millennium approached. By this stage Ballymena were already out of both the Gold Cup and County Antrim Shield following defeats to Linfield and Bangor.

Ballymena United entered the new century of the back of four consecutive stalemates but got back to winning ways with a 2-0 victory over Glenavon in early January thanks to goals from Middlesbrough loanee Andrew Swalwell and Glenn Hunter, only the team's third win in 23 games!

Nigel Best. Courtesy of Ballymena Times

The Irish Cup, under cup specialist Nigel Best, was welcome distraction from the constant struggle of the league campaign. Early round victories against County Armagh sides Loughgall and Bessbrook United lead to a mouth-watering quarter-final against Coleraine at the Ballycastle Road Showgrounds. Ballymena narrowly lost the last eight clash by a single goal in front of a large travelling support to end any hopes of silverware at Warden Street, having earlier been removed from the League Cup thanks to Portadown.

Attentions quickly returned to the Irish League as Ballymena's top-flight future was in the balance with no wins since New Year's Day. Losing six of the next eight fixtures (almost exclusively by the odd goal in each game) sent the Braidmen to the bottom of the ten team table. With the bottom placed team being automatically relegated to the First Division and the ninth place team facing a play-off against the runners-up from the second tier, United claimed a huge three points at the end of March with a 2-1 win over Lisburn Distillery.

The win was undone two weeks later as the Whites won the reverse fixture by the same scoreline to leave Nigel Best's side all but confined to at least a play-off place. Within a couple of days the team had embarked on the start of a great escape that Steve McQueen would have been proud of. Goals from Hunter (who else?!) and Phillip Knell earned a priceless 2-1 win against Glentoran at the Showgrounds. A draw with Cliftonville set up the final day drama with a three-team battle to avoid the bottom places. United started the afternoon bottom of the table but amazingly finished 4.45pm on the 28th April in eighth position after the 2-0 win over Portadown at Shamrock Park – retaining the club's Premier Division status on goal difference ahead of Cliftonville.

Talisman Glenn Hunter was acknowledged as having kept the club up with his 23 goals (accounting for over half of the team's total goals during the season) and received every single vote in the Player's Player of the Year poll.

Ballymena United players celebrate surviving relegation to the First Division at Shamrock Park in April 2000.
Back row: Barry Tumilty, Jason Allen, Mark Carlisle, Glenn Hunter, Darren Parker, Scott Drummond, Barry Patton.
Front row: Phillip Knell, Nigel Boyd, Gerry Flynn, John McConnell, Terry Tennyson, Andrew Swalwell.

⚽ *2000/2001* ⚽

Having survived relegation by the skin of their teeth manager Nigel Best faced a tortuous summer of 2000 trying in vain to put together a team with his wages budget halved from the previous season. The first blow of many was dealt when club captain John McConnell and influential midfielder Philip Knell both rejected new reduced deals to join former boss Alan Fraser at First Division promotion hopefuls Bangor.

Goalkeeper Dermot O'Neill retired, whilst Darren Parker and Barry Patton were freed on the eve of the new season to join Ards and Omagh Town. Extreme cost-cutting measures took over the club with no replacements immediately sought. The only incoming transfer was untested striker Michael Dillon who had finished as leading goalscorer in the Ballymena Intermediate League for Limavady based side Drummond United. Midfielder Kieran Loughran who had been on loan from Crystal Palace signed a permanent deal at his hometown club.

Off the field the club was also in disarray, Treasurer Robert Cupples was appointed Chairman of the football club in August 2000 with barely a committee in place. He replaced Edwin McLaughlin, who had stepped down at the end of the previous season. Secretary Don Stirling also stood down after 14 years and was replaced by experienced civil servant Billy Bell, in the start of a major upheaval in the club's hierarchy.

Despite an impressive pre-season showing against Shamrock Rovers, the local pundits widely tipped Best's young and inexperienced side for the drop. Two draws in the opening league games against Cliftonville and Glentoran (in which United scored last minute equalisers in both) were followed by a stunning 2-0 win away to Coleraine. Scott Drummond scored twice at the Ballycastle Road with Michael Dillon producing an electrifying performance against the title-challenging Bannsiders to fire unfancied United up into second in the table.

United's season was soon dealt a hammer blow when newly appointed captain Glenn Hunter announced that he would be taking a five month sabbatical from football totrain to become a firefighter. Best strengthened his midfield with Northern Ireland Under-21 midfielder Gerard Lyttle from Peterborough United and New Zealand international Blair Scoullar, the latter on the recommendation of John Gregg.

Ballymena United pictured in August 2000 before the season opener with Cliftonville at the Showgrounds.
Back row: Mark Carlisle, John McDowell, Paul Callaghan, Gerry Flynn, Barry Tumilty.
Front row: Michael Dillon, Terry Tennyson, John Gregg, Glenn Hunter, David Calderwood, Nigel Boyd.
Courtesy of Ballymena Times

The early season form did not last as throughout September and October the Braidmen managed only one win from nine games and were also knocked out of the Gold Cup by First Division side Dungannon Swifts in the first round. Although early November saw a 3-2 win against bottom club Crusaders at Seaview (which gave some much needed breathing space between the clubs) there were continued growing concerns over Nigel Best's uninspiring defensive style of football.

A succession of heavily league defeats to Omagh Town (4-0), Linfield (5-1) and finally Newry Town (5-2) called time on Best's 18 month reign as manager. He was sacked, along with assistant Kieran Harding, after the Newry game in early December, with Chairman Robert Cupples citing 'the club needed a fresh start'. Bizarrely the committee appointed the club's physiotherapist George Magill as caretaker manager with sidelined captain Glenn Hunter as his assistant, both having had zero managerial experience prior to the appointment!

With the club in chaos, Magill admirably managed a draw against Portadown and a 2-1 win against Cliftonville in a game which included Tony Anderson scoring from the half-way line for Ballymena United and Tommy McCallion controversially scoring through the side netting for Cliftonville. There also was defeat in the County Antrim Shield quarter-final to Linfield during December.

Three defeats over the festive period against Glentoran, Coleraine and Glenavon came before the appointment of a new manager in January 2001. Moyola Park manager and former United player Kenny Shiels was the early front runner. Despite concerns from hardened supporters over his previous managerial history with rivals Coleraine – he was the man tasked with saving the Sky Blues from relegation by the United committee. The Magherafelt based manager promoted Joe McCall from Reserve team manager to be his assistant in the dugout.

It was a dream start for Shiels' tenure as a 2-1 win at home to Omagh Town. Goals from Nigel Boyd and Kieran Loughran gave the club renewed hope that league survival was still possible. That misplaced hope lasted all of three days as United suffered a crushing defeat to bottom-placed Crusaders at the Showgrounds, as the North Belfast side closed the gap at the bottom of league table, with Ballymena United currently in ninth position.

Midfielder Barry Tumilty scored a last minute equaliser at Windsor Park against league leaders Linfield and talisman Glenn Hunter returned to action to see the Sky

Chairman Robert Cupples pictured with new manager Kenny Shiels in January 2001. Courtesy of Ballymena Times

Blues through the first hurdle of the Irish Cup against Lurgan Celtic with two goals in a 4-2 win. Shiels quickly attempted to build his own side for the relegation run-in. He unceremoniously disposed of no less than half a dozen of Best's signings, Kiwi Scoullar and his fellow countryman Aaron Burgess were released alongside Ricky Culbertson, Terry Tennyson and leading goalscorer Scott Drummond.

The replacements began with versatile defender Shea Campbell who was bought from Dungannon Swifts for a bargain £800 and veteran goalkeeper Tim Dalton was instilled as Shiels' number one after joining from Portadown. Linfield teenager David McAlinden was thrown into the Braid defence and three Southern players - Glen Brien (Bray Wanderers), John O'Loughlin (Limavady United) and Brian Morrisroe (Dundalk).

The change in personnel didn't help the beleaguered Sky Blues as they lost eight of their next nine games in all competitions and were now rock bottom of the Irish League. Exits in the Irish Cup to Glenavon and League Cup to First

Division leaders Ards left Shiels' men with the sole focus of league survival. The Irish League and the rest of sport in Northern Ireland was brought to a virtual stand-still in March when an outbreak of foot and mouth disease in farm animals led to widespread cancellations in sporting activity preventing any competitive football for over two weeks. This gave Ballymena a chance to regroup with only seven games to go but upon resumption a devastating 3-1 midweek defeat at Seaview to Crusaders virtually compounded the lifeless Sky Blues to spending the next season in the second-tier.

What followed in the next five games, with the pressure seemingly off a United side who had been written off at all quarters, was a staggering resurgence. Three wins (and three clean sheets!) against Glenavon, Omagh Town and Newry Town and a 1-1 home draw against Linfield at the Showgrounds, on the night they confidently expected to be crowned Irish League champions, gave Ballymena a chance going into the final game of the season.

The old football cliché that 'The pain you can take, it's the hope that kills you' couldn't be more appropriate on the 28th April 2001, as many supporters dared to believe the great escape was going surpass the final day heroics of the season previous. Ballymena United were at home to Portadown in a reverse of the same scenario 12 months before and Crusaders had champions Linfield and a two

point lead over the Braidmen. Despite the best efforts of Shiels' men a 3-3 draw with Portadown was not enough to lift them off bottom spot as with Linfield beating the Crues – the Sky Blues were down by a single point.

Relegation to the First Division for the second time in five years was confirmed. The devastated players left the pitch, many never to be seen in a Ballymena shirt again as grown men shed a tear on the terraces whilst standing to applaud the efforts of the players.

Jason Allen comes to terms with the club's relegation to the First Division in April 2001. Courtesy of Ballymena Times

Chapter Eight

The long wait for success (2001-2015)

⚽ *2001/2002* ⚽

Relegation in 2001 proved a watershed moment for the club and a chance to rebuild from the ground up both on and off the pitch. Despite reduced gates, sponsorship and prize money in the First Division, the new look committee lead by Chairman Robert Cupples set about reducing the club's debt attributed to a decade of overspending by their predecessors. By the summer work was also already well underway on the impressive new home grandstand but wouldn't be ready for use during the season.

It was a clean slate for manager Kenny Shiels as an exodus of senior players meant he began pre-season with only eight retained players with any senior experience. Gerry Flynn (Coleraine), Gerard Lyttle (Newry Town), Barry Tumilty (Portadown) and Jason Allen (Crusaders) were amongst those who chose to stay in the Premier Division and were to be replaced by a group of youngsters and virtual unknowns.

Mark McNicholl and Trevor McLernon signed from Shiels' former club, Moyola Park with Mark McMenemy (Coagh United) and Adam Hamilton (Crusaders) just a few of the host of low-key arrivals at Warden Street. They joined veteran defender Paul Byrne (Glenavon's record appearance holder) who had stepped down from his role as player-manager at Ballyclare Comrades to add a bit of experience to Kenny's kids. Unfortunately a broken arm in pre-season delayed Byrne's involvement until December.

Tommy Wright. Courtesy of Ballymena Times

The marquee signing of the summer was undoubtedly the surprise coup of former Northern Ireland international goalkeeper Tommy Wright. Following the 37-year-old's release from Bolton Wanderers, Wright returned home and Ballymena were rumoured in the local press to have persuaded the former Newcastle United and Nottingham Forest stopper with a third of their playing budget to join the assault on first time promotion. Shiels also appointed 23-year-old Harryville defender John McDowell as club captain for the season.

It started well for the new-look Braidmen as a large travelling support made their way on the opening Friday evening of the league season to witness a comfortable 2-0 victory away to Carrick Rangers. Growing optimism following the opening win that promotion would be a formality quickly diminished as United failed to win any of their next six games, including defeats to both Institute and Limavady United in the first ever league meetings between the sides.

Ballymena United's early season prediction of being the favourites for promotion was quickly being reassessed with Shiels' young side struggling to cope with the physicality of First Division football. Distillery took an early lead in the Championship race and would be the team to beat all season, buoyed by protracted transfer of United's Glenn Hunter in September. Following a contractual dispute – he ironically made his Distillery debut in at home in a 4-0 victory over United. The travelling fans were incensed with Hunter's press comments months earlier which claimed he would not sign for another First Division club.

It was clear more experience was required in Shiels' team and robust ex-Crusaders striker Peter Withnell was an instant hit. Ex-Leeds United defender Paul Beesley proved to be a cumbersome, expensive luxury and lasted only a handful of games. The gamble on goalkeeper Tommy Wright also had failed to pay off as he was forced to retire from football with a chronic knee injury after just seven appearances. Introducing the former Down GAA forward Withnell alongside a young Shea Campbell (who had been transformed from full-back to striker) began to work well, as United managed good form to lose only one of their seven games throughout October and November. The midfield was also bolstered in the autumn with the signings of Lee Patrick from Crusaders and Tyrone GAA 'All-Star' Stephen O'Neill,.

Peter Withnell. Courtesy of Ballymena Times

The restructuring of the League Cup allowed the manager to blood his young starlets in against Premier Division opponents during the four group games. Despite a 5-0 thrashing against rivals Coleraine, the kids showed up well but failed to qualify for the quarter-finals. Trevor McLernon did manage an impressive winner from the half-way line in the 2-1 victory of Premier Division high-flyers Omagh Town. Progression in the County Antrim Shield proved a lot more comfortable with home wins against Dunmurry YM and Ards to earn a first Shield semi-final appearance since 1997.

Shiels' uncanny knack of sourcing obscure players was again proven in November, when United unveiled the signing of 21-year-old Liberia international forward Leon Browne on a two-year contract. The young African lodged with Chairman Robert Cupples in his Kells home but failed to make an impact at Warden Street as he struggled to cope with the physicality and climate and was quickly released. Browne's only moment of glory was a very late equaliser against promotion rivals Institute at Drumahoe in early December; a game which sparked controversy when John Ferry disallowed two Ballymena United goals in injury time.

Leon Browne. Courtesy of Ballymena Times

The weather wiped out all the holiday fixtures but United's threadbare squad (now littered with teenagers) continued to grind out results as they a earned a superb last-minute victory over Limavady United and also fought back from 3-1 down to draw 4-4 with Larne in a pulsating game at the Showgrounds. Arguably the most memorable game of the season was saved for the Irish Cup. Following a scoreless draw away against Omagh Town in the fifth round they came back to the Showgrounds and carved out a superb 2-1 victory with goals from Nigel Boyd and Lee Patrick with only ten men for 87 minutes after Withnell had been dismissed early on.

Ballymena's season virtually fell to pieces in the immediate aftermath of the Omagh win. They were unceremoniously dumped out of the County Antrim Shield after a 4-0 semi-final defeat against Linfield The following week an equally inexperienced team went out of the Irish Cup to Glenavon, leaving Shiels' side to fight it out for promotion in the final months of the season.

Defeats to promotion rivals Institute and Dungannon Swifts in March and back-to-back draws with bottom side Ballyclare Comrades mathematically ended the Sky Blues' chances of a return to the top-flight. The season petered out with insignificance as on the final day of the season, following a 1-1 draw away to Bangor (a landmark 400th game for full-back Mark Carlisle). Neighbours Larne managed a remarkable 7-1 victory over Limavady United to leap-frog the Sky Blues in the league standings. This condemned Kenny Shiels' side to fifth place out of ten and their worst ever league finish – an unspectacular 15th from 20 teams in the two divisions.

Lisburn Distillery with Glenn Hunter eventually stumbled across the finishing line to win the First Division title. Institute pushed them all the way but the Londonderry side's second place finish was enough to guarantee promotion and top-flight football for the first time in their history. For underachieving Ballymena, Peter Withnell finished top scorer and was the winner of many of the supporters' major player of the year accolades.

One shining light from the 2001/2002 season was the Thirds' run to the final of the prestigious Harry Cavan Youth Cup. Kenny Whitbread's side agonisingly lost on penalties to Ballinamallard United III at Stangmore Park. Many of this squad either had already senior experience or would go on to play for the first team at the Showgrounds.

The new stand at the Ballymena Showgrounds packed to capacity for the Bolton Wanderers friendly in September 2002.
Courtesy of Ballymena Times

⚽ 2002/2003 ⚽

Ahead of the 2002/03 season the Irish League had decided after eight years that it was going to revert back to square one with the return of a 16 team league - with four promotion places available to the eight teams competing in the First Division. The consequence for the bottom four clubs who failed to achieve promotion would be the loss of their senior status and thus intermediate football in the new league structure – something which Ballymena United couldn't dare imagine for fear of financial ruin.

Having now acclimatised to the surroundings, Shiels sourced players with top flight experience for his Ballymena United side who were again billed as favourites for the First Division title. Defender Alfie Stewart was appointed club captain after joining from Moyola Park and popular midfielder Trevor McMullan returned to the club for a third spell. The veteran duo were joined by new faces in Joe Gray (Coleraine), Paul Millar (Ards) and Paul Evans (Newry) whilst brothers Oran and Gareth Kearney proved astute signings from Moyola Park and Ballymoney United.

Work had now been completed on the impressive 2,000 capacity grandstand at a cost of £3million. The new structure included corporate facilities, over a dozen changing rooms and home to the new office and board room which had previously been housed in the O'Kane Stand. The home supporters would now reside exclusively in the new stand with visiting fans being granted the freedom of the old Warden Street stand despite the scarce visitor numbers across the First Division clubs.

The old Ulster Cup returned for the First Division clubs as a warm-up for the league season due to the limited number of league games scheduled. Ballymena United started their season with a uninspiring 1-1 draw at home to Carrick Rangers. The Sky Blues bounced back with high scoring victories over Ballyclare Comrades (6-0), Bangor (5-1), Armagh City (4-1). Hopes of a first Ulster Cup since 1980/81 were dashed with in the final round of fixtures when Limavady United stunned the Sky Blues with a shock 3-0 win, handing the first trophy of the new season to Dungannon Swifts.

In September English Premiership side Bolton Wanderers drew a capacity

crowd of 4,000 to the Showgrounds for the grand opening of the new stand. Spirited Ballymena gave their full-time guests a tough game but lost 2-0 to Sam Allardyce's side. The game also marked the lucrative agreement signed between Ballymena United Youth Academy and the Lancashire club to develop young footballers. Shiels also revealed in the local press that he had bizarrely been rebuffed in his enquiries with the representatives of ex-England international Paul Gascoigne to appear in the fixture.

The goals continued to flow for the Sky Blues in the League Cup with five and seven goal wins against Institute and Limavady and a long overdue 3-1 win over Coleraine sealed progression past the group stage. The Sky Blues were already into a fine rhythm and cruised by Crusaders in the quarter-final to set up a semi-final against Premier Division leaders Glentoran at the Oval. It proved to be one of the most entertaining games seen in years as the Ballymena went toe-to-toe with the East Belfast side, coming from 3-1 down to level thanks to goals from Shea Campbell and John O'Loughlin. They were denied by two late goals (both of which were questionably offside) as Glentoran progressed to the final against Linfield as 5-3 winners.

The league campaign had so far proved a formality for a Ballymena side brimming with confidence and they quickly sailed to the top of the division. United's spirit was epitomised when the Sky Blues came from behind against Larne to win 3-2, with Shea Campbell's winning scissor kick proving to be one of the goals of the season. Ballymena had won 10 of their opening 12 games (including a 5-2 victory over second place Dunngannon)

Shea Campbell. Courtesy of Ballymena Times

and it wasn't until late December they tasted league defeat with consecutive home defeats to Bangor and Limavady United.

All the talk on the terraces was around the mercurial Shea Campbell who by Christmas had plundered 25 goals. His partnership with the equally free-scoring Peter Withnell had made him the hottest young property in the Irish League and was attracting interest from England and Scotland. Portsmouth (then Champions-elect of the English First Division) were the first to make a move in early October but to keep the young Armagh man's feet on the ground Shiels misinformed the local press they were looking at defender Gareth Kearney! A week long trial with Iain Dowie's Oldham Athletic was arranged and with a host of Irish League teams waiting in the wings, it looked like the end of Campbell's stay at Ballymena with his contract due to expire in mid-January.

The Irish Cup fifth round game against Portadown would have been a fitting swansong for the striker as he headed a late equaliser in his last game to earn the Sky Blues a replay against the reigning league champions. Campbell surprised everyone by signing a new two year deal with the Braidmen ahead of the cup replay a few days later. The increased media attention drew one of the largest home crowds seen at the Showgrounds in years to witness a rampant Portadown win 6-0 and progress to the next round.

Ballymena's league form since Christmas had been erratic but Shiels successfully guided his men to the final of the County Antrim Shield on 4th March 2003. Progression had been fairly comfortable for United as they defeated Ballymoney United, Lisburn Distillery and then Chimney Corner in the semi-final to set up a final showdown with Glentoran. Roy Coyle's men had home advantage but a large, vocal travelling support could only watch on as Glentoran edged closer towards a 'clean sweep' of trophies with a clinical 3-0 victory over United with goals from Darren Armour, Andy Smith and Scott Young.

Promotion back to the top flight was finally assured later that month following a 2-0 victory over second-placed Dungannon Swifts with goals from Shea Campbell and Oran Kearney. The latter had also enjoyed an impressive first season in senior football scoring 16 goals from central midfield. The Sky Blues now had one hand on the First Division title with only five games to go.

The title race turned on its head two weeks later as Ballymena travelled to Stangmore Park on a Friday night to face the Swifts knowing that a win would put them on the brink of being crowned champions. With Ballymena leading 2-1, the home side had their goalkeeper sent off and from the resulting penalty Peter Withnell saw his shot saved by defender Johnny Montgomery. This proved the catalyst for a remarkable comeback from Joe McAree's side as they fought back to win the match 3-2.

With confidence visibly shattered following the Dungannon game, Shiels' side picked up only one point from their remaining three league fixtures and handed the championship to the County Tyrone side who at one stage during the season were 12 points behind the Sky Blues. A season that had promised so much for the club ended with three runners-up medals, but comfort had to be taken from promotion being assured and senior status retained for the 2003/04 season.

The end of season awards both at club and league levels were dominated unsurprisingly by young Shea Campbell, who finished the season on 38 goals. His form was rewarded with a call-up to the Northern Ireland Under-21 squad and he earned his only cap against Spain (who included Fernando Torres and Pepe Reina) in a European Qualifier in June 2003. Campbell became only the second Ballymena United player to represent the club at this level, the other being Tom Sloan in 1978.

⚽ *2003/2004* ⚽

With promotion now achieved United manager Kenny Shiels started his fourth season tasked with not only surviving but competing at the top end of the new Irish Premier League having faired so well against top-tier opponents during

Ballymena United players and official ahead of the 2003/2004 Irish Premier League season.
Back row: (All committee) John Taggart, Noel Millar (Treasurer), Bill Parkinson, John Murray, Nigel McIlrath, John Blair, Maurice Smyth (Vice-Chairman),
Billy Bell, John Maxwell, Brian Thompson, Kenny Whitbread (Company Secretary).
Middle row: Shea Campbell, Jamie Marks, Nigel Boyd, John O'Loughlin, Paul Burnside, Dwayne Nelson, Robert Robinson, Gareth Kearney, Garth Scates,
Kevin Ramsey, Paul Byrne.
Front row: Paul Evans, Kevin Duff, Oran Kearney, Trevor McLernon, Kenny Shiels (Manager), John McDowell, Joe McCall (Assistant manager), Joe Gray,
Conor Gregg, Ciaran Donaghy, Albert Watson.

the previous season. Unfortunately it was clear from the start his players were suffering from a hangover of the poor finish to their First Division campaign.

Three players recently released by Linfield were captured early on in the summer; Jamie Marks, Garth Scates and Justin McBride. They added both Premier Division and trophy winning experience to the Braidmen. Shiels' other major capture was the astute signature of Lancaster City defender Ciaran Donaghy (son of former Northern Ireland international, Mal).

Justin McBride

The manager put faith in the majority of his squad from last season, with the exception of the older statesmen who moved on to make way for the new arrivals. Fans' favourites Peter Withnell and Trevor McMullan moving to Larne and Armagh City, whilst club captain Alfie Stewart retired from football after a successful Irish League career spanning over two decades.

Bolton Wanderers returned to the Showgrounds during pre-season and despite debutant Garth Scates' stunning 35-yard drive which gave United the lead, the home side wilted in the July sun and eventually lost 7-1 to their Lancashire opponents packed with international quality. Ballymena did fair better a week later during Mark Carlisle's testimonial game against Scottish Premier League side Hearts. Shea Campbell produced an inspired performance and the two goals which defeated the Edinburgh side 2-1 (there was even a cameo appearance for Carlisle's former team-mate Dessie Loughery in the game). The game was Mark's last for the club as he mutually ended his 11-year association with the club after 436 games, moving on to Armagh City.

The domestic season started poorly for Kenny Shiels in the group stage of the League Cup as Ballymena United finished rock bottom of the group with Portadown, Institute and Glenavon after five defeats from six games. The only victory in six games came at Mourneview Park thanks to a solitary Oran Kearney goal.

The new Irish Premier League season started with the short trip to neighbours Larne. The rivalry between the clubs had become more ferocious during the time in the First Division. Oran Kearney continued his goalscoring exploits from the previous season and scored twice to give the Sky Blues a 2-1 win on the opening weekend of the season. The derby win was only a fleeting moment of joy for Ballymena as they struggled early on in their return to the top division going seven league games without a win. The introduction of teenage striker Kevin Ramsey from Celtic failed to make much difference to a toothless United attack with Shea Campbell struggling for fitness and form early in the season.

A 3-0 defeat to Limavady United in November, in what was their first win

Nigel Jemson. Courtesy of Ballymena Times

all season under new boss (and former Ballymena goalkeeper) Tommy Wright, increased the slowly rising pressure on Kenny Shiels in the United dugout. In an attempt to revive United's season, the club made the high-profile signing of former Nottingham Forest forward Nigel Jemson. The Englishman had been playing for Shrewsbury Town during the previous season and famously scored twice to knock Everton out of the FA Cup only eight months before.

Boosted by the arrival of Jemson and the return to fitness of Justin McBride, the Sky Blues finally won again on 15th November, defeating Glenavon 4-0 at the Showgrounds – a game which also marked the first of the club's successful corporate hospitality lunches which would prove to be a great success over the next ten years. With Jemson leading the line, United hit form in the league in the run up to Boxing Day winning the four of the next five games with victories over Ards, Newry Town, Portadown and Institute.

The return of the traditional Boxing Day fixture with Coleraine after a two year absence caught the public's imagination but the visit to the Ballycastle Road turned into a Christmas nightmare for Ballymena. Sean Armstrong scored a hat-trick in the 4-0 win for Marty Quinn's Bannsiders. Only a last-minute Jamie Marks equaliser saved United from double festive defeat against Larne on New Years' Day, the former Linfield midfielder scored a remarkable overhead kick to salvage a 1-1 draw.

The Irish Cup draw proved unkind again, as United faced a daunting January trip to the Oval to take on league champions Glentoran. Despite taking an early lead, the Braidmen lost 4-2 and made an early exit from the cup. The team had progressed further in the Shield with a third semi-final appearance in three seasons following victories over Dunmurry YM and Crusaders in the first two rounds. Resurgent Ards were the opponents in the semi-final at Seaview but it was the County Down side that progressed after a lack-lustre game which was compounded when Nigel Jemson received a red card late on and United lost 1-0.

Northern Ireland Under-21 defender Gordon Simms came on loan from Derry City in the January transfer window and immediately shored up the centre of the United defence with some exceptional performances. Ballymena improved during the final stages of the Premier League season, notably holding Champions-elect Linfield to a scoreless draw at the Showgrounds in a game that wouldn't have gone ahead but for a colossal effort on behalf of fans and even players shovelling snow off the pitch.

The Sky Blues finished the campaign strongly, losing only one of their final ten league games to finish sixth in their first season back in the top division. The season finished in style with a comfortable 3-1 victory over Irish Cup finalists Coleraine on the final day of the season. Although Campbell had failed to replicate his previous form he finished as leading scorer with 14 goals. This tally included a hat-trick against Omagh Town in which Jemson and the impetuous Campbell bizarrely came to blows on the pitch over penalty taking duties.

In a late season twist, confusion reigned over European qualification places. The Irish FA under UEFA governance had introduced a European club licencing requirement for the 2004/05 season which determined that clubs competing in European competition needed a specific licence. As one of only five teams to be granted the new licence, Ballymena qualified for the UEFA Intertoto Cup as the highest placed eligible team ahead of Lisburn Distillery (fourth) and Coleraine (fifth).

Following a fairly short legal proceeding against the decision led by Distillery, Ballymena were confirmed as the Northern Ireland representatives for the UEFA Intertoto Cup but were given only a matter of weeks to prepare for the first round fixtures at the end of June. There was now a growing belief around the club that the Sky Blues were on the brink of being a competitive force in the Irish League again.

⚽ 2004/2005 ⚽

The management committee had now cleared the club of their long standing debt since taking office in 2000 and invested heavily in new players to help push the Sky Blues onto the next level. Big summer signings included retaining impressive loanee Gordon Simms on a permanent deal from Derry City and also prizing former Northern Ireland international Rory Hamill from financially struggling rivals Coleraine.

Gordon Simms and Rory Hamill put pen to paper with Ballymena United in May 2004. Courtesy of Ballymena Times

Kenny Shiels also recruited experienced Glentoran duo Gary Smyth and Tim McCann, who had both been surprisingly released by Roy Coyle after a disappointing season in East Belfast. Smyth was immediately appointed club captain and was joined by Ballyclare Comrades' winger Eddie Hill and young goalkeeper William McFrederick from Fulham ahead of the Intertoto Cup games.

Nigel Jemson was not afforded a new contract at the Braid and returned to non-league football with Ilkeston Town. Veteran Paul Byrne retired from playing to become manager of Ballymoney United and long serving defender John McDowell joined Armagh City after falling out of favour with Shiels – he was joined in the Orchard County by dead-ball specialist Trevor McLernon. Popular midfielder John O'Loughlin was offloaded to Cliftonville to make room for Tim McCann, despite an impressive past season for the Letterkenny man.

The European adventure provided a logistical nightmare, as the Sky Blues were drawn against Odense BK of Denmark in the first round of the UEFA Intertoto Cup. On 20th June 2004, the 100 strong crowd of United supporters, who had travelled to the birthplace of Hans Christian Anderson, witnessed their own modern day fairytale with Ballymena's makeshift side drew 0-0 with their professional opponents. This was

Courtesy of Ballymena Times

Ballymena's first result away from home in Europe and also the first time the club had played a match on a Sunday. United fans dared to dream a week later with the return leg at the Showgrounds with a prize of a trip top Spanish side Villarreal awaiting the victors in the second round. The Danish side ruthlessly punished their Northern Irish opponents in the second leg scoring seven goals without reply ending Ballymena's European odyssey.

Back Row (left to right): Gordon Simms, Albert Watson, Shea Campbell, Trevor McNicholl (Goalkeeping coach), Ruari McClean, Oran Kearney, Rory Hamill.
Middle Row (left to right): Bertnal Thompson (Team attendant), Tim McCann, Nigel Boyd, Jamie Marks, Robert Robinson, Garth Scates, Ciaran Donaghy, Stephen McGarrigle (Physiotherapist).
Front Row (left to right): Pat Jordan (Coach), Eddie Hill, Gareth McLaughlin, Kenny Shiels (Manager), Gary Smyth, Joe McCall (Assistant manager), Justin McBride, Joe Gray, Sammy McVicker (Coach).

It was a two month wait until the domestic season started. The campaign kicked off with the League Cup and a trip to Lisburn Distillery who they had battled in the court room only a few months ago. The game finished 2-2 with a debut goal for Rory Hamill. The following week Larne visited the Showgrounds and stunned Ballymena with a 3-1 win. This provided an early season wake up call for Shiels as the team rallied in the remaining games to qualify from the group stage only to fall to Glentoran in the quarter-final.

The new Irish Premier League season kicked off for Ballymena with opponents for the historic first top-flight league game for Loughgall who had been promoted as First Division champions. There was jubilation at Lakeview Park as Ally Wilson scored the landmark first league goal for the Villagers as they won 1-0. The league form thankfully picked up throughout October 2004 as consecutive wins against Dungannon Swifts and Newry City with defender Gordon Simms scoring last minute winners in both games.

Ballymena sent a message to the rest of the league when they went to Windsor Park and ended champions Linfield's 33-game unbeaten streak. Teenage winger

Dominic Melly grabbed the only goal in a 1-0 win. This was the first Ballymena United victory at the international venue for 15 years! It was to go from the sublime to the ridiculous for the club though as only three days after beating Linfield, they were dumped out of the County Antrim Shield in the first round by Amateur League side Kilmore Rec.. Andy Waterworth's solitary goal condemned Kenny Shiels' team to arguably the worst result in the club's history.

United struggled for any form following the Kilmore Rec. game and won only once again until the New Year, the number of games drawn ending the speculative challenge for the league title. Goalscoring was problematic for United, this made Shiels' decision to let Shea Campbell leave on loan to his native Armagh City in the First Division even more bizarre. Shiels was rumoured to have had a personal dispute with the striker he had valued at £100,000 only two years before. The goals returned for Shea at Holm Park but the forgotten man was still freed to join Linfield in January.

The return of the Boxing Day derby to the Showgrounds was witnessed by a capacity all ticket crowd. Ballymena squandered a two goal lead against Coleraine to draw 2-2. The manager sought reinforcements with Campbell gone and Tim McCann the victim of a season-ending cruciate knee ligament injury, in came former Rangers striker Darren Fitzgerald from financially stricken Ards, winger Gareth Mullan from Derry City and English forward Matthew Nolan on loan from Peterborough United.

Results improved dramatically from February onwards. Ballymena went ten games unbeaten in all competitions to make a late surge for the European qualification positions. With notable victories over rivals Portadown and Lisburn Distillery during the Spring of 2005 the team climbed to fourth in the table. Fitzgerald had began to hit form with five goals in eleven games but his season was cruelly cut short when he too suffered a cruciate knee injury against his former club Ards in March.

The Irish Cup was favourable to the Sky Blues as home wins over Coagh United, Harland and Wolff Welders and a revenge victory over Kilmore

Gareth Mullan evades a Larne defender's challenge during the Irish Cup semi-final. Courtesy of Ballymena Times

Rec. set up a clash with Larne at the Oval in a repeat of the 1989 Irish Cup final. United were billed as clear favourites but a dubious penalty scored by Larne's Mark Dickson and a world class display of goalkeeping by former United custodian Alex Spackman (a goalkeeper Shiels had released after taking over as Ballymena manager) gave the Inver Park side a famous victory and a place in the showpiece final against Portadown.

Ballymena United stumbled through the remaining final games of the Premier League campaign, disappointingly finishing eighth and failing in their bid for European qualification. This was the final straw for the management committee who decided not to renew Kenny Shiels' contract and sacked the manager after four and a half years at the club. Shiels would reappear as manager of Larne a few seasons later and would eventually go onto forge an impressive career on the mainland as Director of Youth football at Tranmere Rovers before leading Kilmarnock to victory over Celtic in the final of the Scottish League Cup in 2011.

⚽ 2005/2006 ⚽

In one of the worst kept secrets in Irish League football, former goalkeeper Tommy Wright returned to the Showgrounds as manager for the 2005/06 season. Wright had successfully transformed unfashionable Limavady United

Tommy Wright. Courtesy of Presseye

in just 18 months and led them to fifth place in the Premier League. Former Sunderland and Linfield midfielder Jim Grattan was appointed as his assistant with Jeff Montgomery and David Dorrian joining from Limavady in a complete overhaul of staff at Warden Street.

Wright moved quickly to also mould a new-look side for the new season with Gary Haveron (Coleraine), Craig McClean (Ballyclare Comrades), Vincent Sweeney (Limavady United), Aidan Watson (Ards), Stuart King and Gregg Shannon (both Linfield) all joining the club in a busy transfer window.

Back Row (left to right): David Dorrian (Reserve Team Manager), Paul McDowell, Tim McCann, Jamie Marks, Gregg Shannon, Gareth Mullan, William McFrederick, Nigel Boyd, Garth Scates, Darren Fitzgerald.
Middle Row (left to right): Bertnel Thompson (Team Attendant), Dean Youle, Vincent Sweeney, Gordon Simms, Gary Haveron, Ciaran Donaghy, Albert Watson, Stuart King.
Front Row (left to right): Jeff Montgomery (Coach), Eddie Hill, Rory Hamill, Tommy Wright (Manager), Gary Smyth, Jim Grattan (Assistant Manager), Aidan Watson, Craig McClean, Michael Lavery (Sports Therapist)

Midfielder Oran Kearney who had been relentless courted by David Jeffrey joined Linfield when his contract expired.He had been persuaded to stay last season by Kenny Shiels (who was now his father-in-law). Goalkeeper Robert Robinson left for Newry – disappointed with the treatment of Shiels, whilst Justin McBride, Jamie Marks, Gareth Mullan, Joe Gray and Eddie Hill were all deemed surplus to requirements by the new manager.

The opening game of the Wright's tenure ended in defeat to Portadown in the first game of the League Cup group stage and followed a week later with a 2-1 home defeat to Newry City (who had now changed their name from 'Town' following city status being granted in Newry). There were two wins against newly promoted Glenavon but it wasn't enough as the Braidmen were knocked out of the competition after failing to qualify beyond the group.

Wright recruited ex-Wolves teenager Johnny Steele from America on a short-term deal and he scored the winning goal against his hometown club Larne in the first game of the new Premier League season in September. Steele returned to America after only six games and worked his way up the soccer leagues, surprisingly remerging in the MLS in 2012. He eventually signed for New York

Red Bulls playing alongside Thierry Henry and Tim Cahill and finally winning full international recognition under Michael O'Neill.

Ballymena continued the start of the league season with three defeats to Newry, Cliftonville and Loughgall and it was a month before the team won again. The impressive Vincent Sweeney scored the winner against Armagh City at Holm Park to release some pressure on Wright's under fire side. The form throughout the autumn months was very erratic as a win one weekend would often be followed

Kevin Kelbie

by defeat the next. The manager brought in defender Stephen Collier and former Liverpool midfielder Phil Charnock to boost the squad but neither made any lasting impression.

In December, the Sky Blues grabbed a superb last minute victory over Glentoran at the Oval when 20-year-old Kevin Kelbie came off the bench to announce himself to supporters. The Scottish forward had been signed from Glentoran in August but struggled initially at the club with an undiagnosed case of diabetes curtailing his performances. From December onwards the former Alloa player didn't stop scoring!

Sweeney was the matchwinners on Boxing Day against Coleraine at the Ballycastle Road as the 1-0 win started off a superb nine game unbeaten sequence of results into the New Year. This moved United into fourth place in the table by the start of February and secured a place in the County Antrim Shield Final. The quest started with a comfortable win in the 'Battle of Ballymena' against

Wakehurst and wins against Cliftonville and Larne allowed Tommy Wright's in-form team to progress to the decider against David Jeffery's Linfield.

Brimming with confidence on a miserable evening at Seaview, United took the lead in the first through Kevin Kelbie before his goal was cancelled out by Oran Kearney's equaliser. The in-form Scot almost won the game late on as his effort cruelly hit the bar but the typically ruthless Linfield went straight down to the other end of the pitch and Glenn Ferguson's 84th minute winner broke Ballymena hearts. Securing the Shield with a 2-1 victory was the first step in the Blues' winning all available trophies during the 2005/06 season.

Former Limavady United striker Paul Brown joined in January from Sligo Rovers and winger Gerard Rowe from Shelbourne on loan but Ballymena crashed out of the Irish Cup to Lisburn Distillery after a replay. The team hit a poor run of form which failed to produce any wins throughout February and March and the club fell out of any contention for European qualification through the league.

United finally won again in April after nine games without a victory, a single goal was enough to conquer Coleraine at the Warden Street Showgrounds. Tommy Wright completed his first season as manager by finishing seventh (behind Newry on goal difference) after a 1-0 win against Institute. Kevin Kelbie's injury time goal relegated the Drumahoe based side on the final day of the season. It was the 16th goal of the Scot's debut campaign as he finished as the leading marksman.

Other young players at the club were also getting deserved acknowledgment as both Aidan Watson and Craig McClean were shortlisted for the Writers' Young Player of the Year award, this eventually went to Glentoran's Philip Simpson. There were also call ups to the Northern Ireland Under-21 squad for William McFrederick and Albert Watson.

⚽ *2006/2007* ⚽

Following a solid first season for Tommy Wright as Ballymena United manager, the second season began with the optimism that the Sky Blues could be on the verge of the breaking into the top echelons of the Irish League. Wright continued to tweak his team with seasoned winger Mark Picking arrive from Linfield, Darren Murphy from Dungannon Swifts and goalkeeper Paul Murphy from Portadown. Northern Ireland Under-21 full back Aaron Callaghan and former player Lee Patrick also both arrived from Wright's old side Limavady United.

Wright authorised the departures of Vincent Sweeney (Limavady United), Rory Hamill (Dungannon Swifts) and Ciaran Donaghy (Donegal Celtic) but was dealt a major blow when club captain Gary Smyth was offered a surprise return to former club Glentoran. 21-year-old defender Albert Watson was given the responsibility on his young shoulders of becoming the new club captain of Ballymena United.

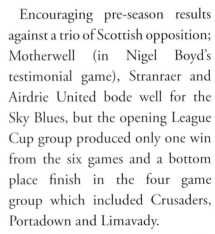

New United captain Albert Watson holds off Manchester City's Joey Barton at the Showgrounds. Courtesy of Presseye

Encouraging pre-season results against a trio of Scottish opposition; Motherwell (in Nigel Boyd's testimonial game), Stranraer and Airdrie United bode well for the Sky Blues, but the opening League Cup group produced only one win from the six games and a bottom place finish in the four game group which included Crusaders, Portadown and Limavady.

The highlight of the season came in late August with the visit of English Premiership side Manchester City for a belated glamour friendly as part of the transfer which took goalkeeper Richard McKinney to England in August 1999. Manager Tommy Wright was pivotal in securing the fixture with his former club managed by former Nottingham Forest team-mate Stuart Pearce. The 5,000 capacity crowd at the Showgrounds were treated to an impressive home performance against the likes of Joe Hart, Georgious Samaras and Joey Barton. United had levelled through Gary Haveron but goals from Antoine Sibierski, Bernardo Corradi and Danny Mills gave City a 3-1 victory.

September's home league opener against Glenavon produced three points the hard way as Ballymena came from two goals down to win 4-2. However one win from their next ten games in all competitions during October and November left pressure starting to mount on Wright's underachieving side. A humiliating 3-1 defeat to Dundela in the first round of the County Antrim Shield, the competition that Ballymena came within a crossbar of winning only nine months earlier, proved particularly hard to stomach.

Striker Kevin Kelbie had struggled to recreate the form of the his first season and Paul Brown had also failed to settle and broke his elbow falling on the stock car track at the Showgrounds early in the season. Come December, struggling United got back on track with back-to-back victories – the first a 1-0 win away to

Larne and then against newly promoted Donegal Celtic (in the first competitive game between the sides) by the same scoreline. A first goal in 18 months came against Donegal Celtic for Darren Fitzgerald who missed all of 2005/06 with his cruciate injury.

Boxing Day bragging rights went to Coleraine after a pulsating 3-2 defeat at Warden Street, but a week later a stunning win against Glentoran at the same venue with the same scoreline provided the club with a much more encouraging start to 2007. Gary Haveron's free-kick brought a welcome return to form for Kelbie against his former club.

January's transfer window allowed some much-needed squad strengthening – Gavin Melaugh (Donegal Celtic), Stephen Lowry (Limavady United) and Simon Kelly (Dundalk) all joined the club but failed to halt the chronic inconsistencies of the league campaign. They did aid progression

Kevin Kelbie celebrates his winning goal against Glentoran in January 2007. Courtesy of Presseye

to the quarter-finals of the Irish Cup after victories against Harland & Wolff Welders and Comber Rec. in the opening rounds. Reigning cup holders Linfield left it very late at the Showgrounds with Ballymena native Stephen Douglas' equaliser cancelling out Gavin Melaugh's opener in a tense cup tie to force a replay.

Controversy followed shortly after when Linfield manager David Jeffery refused to play the quarter-final replay the following week as originally scheduled, citing a fixture backlog from their Setanta All-Ireland cup commitments. After much debate the replay was played nearly a month later, with Linfield winning an exhilarating game 4-2 (Ballymena had led for a short period) to claim a place in the cup semi-finals.

Ballymena United's season ended without any fanfare as a low-key ninth place finish in the Irish League, this was a disappointing return for Tommy Wright and his players. There was greater success with the second string as David Dorrian's

Ballymena United Reserves after winning the club's first Reserve League title in May 2007.
Back row: Johnny Flynn, Randal Reid, Daley Carnduff, Gary Baird, Sean O'Neill, Aaron Holland, Aaron Stewart, Gary Haveron, Stephen Lowry.
Front row: Aaron Callaghan, Matthew Boyd, Chris Getty, Lee Colligan, David Cushley, Nigel Boyd, Glenn Dorrian.

impressive Reserve team won the Irish Reserve League championship for the first time. The side produced future Irish League regulars such as Sean O'Neill, Lee Colligan, Aaron Stewart, David Cushley and Johnny Flynn.

⚽ 2007/2008 ⚽

The summer of 2007 was a quiet one for Tommy Wright's Ballymena United as he entered his third season in charge and looking to improve on their disappointing league finish. There had been little surgery conducted on the same panel of players only defender Thomas Wray arrived from Irish Cup finalists Dungannon Swifts and Donegal based striker Davitt Walsh joined on loan from Bohemians. Veteran Darren Murphy left the club after only one season to return to Dungannon Swifts as reserve team manager.

Domestically the season started in miserable fashion for the Sky Blues, they suffered a 5-1 opening day League Cup defeat away at Linfield. United recovered

Ballymena United pictured in July 2007 before a pre-season friendly against Portstewart
Back row: Thomas Wray, Simon Kelly, Paul Murphy, Kevin Kelbie, Gary Haveron, Craig McClean.
Front row: Mark Picking, Darren Fitzgerald, Aidan Watson, Stuart King, Albert Watson.

the following week with a 3-1 away victory against Glenavon but results in the opening weeks of the season were erratic. A record equalling 8-0 win in the first round of the County Antrim Shield against Amateur League side Orangefield OB would give Ballymena United some light relief.

Glenavon were defeated again at Mourneview Park - this time in the opening fixture of the 2007/08 Irish Premier League campaign. This was the calm before the storm as a dismal run of results saw the Braidmen lose their next six consecutive games. This included exiting the League Cup at the first hurdle and the County Antrim Shield after defeat to Crusaders in the semi-final. Pressure was starting to mount on the manager with results continuing to falter but the introduction of 18-year-old West Belfast defender Johnny Flynn (promoted from

Johnny Flynn. Courtesy of Presseye

David Dorrian's reserve side) would prove to be the unlikely catalyst in the team's resurgence.

The club's fortunes changed almost instantly as the Sky Blues were unbeatable for the rest of the calendar year. After goals from Kevin Kelbie and Davitt Walsh secured an overdue 2-1 victory over Portadown in late October, the team went on a stunning 14-game unbeaten run that lasted until the end of January (the longest unbeaten sequence since Alan Campbell's class of 1979/80). Flynn's emergence coupled with the drive of Gavin Melaugh in midfield and the goals of the revitalised Kevin Kelbie fired United up the league table and won boss Tommy Wright the 'Manager of the Month' award for December. The club sat comfortably in fourth place at the turn of the year.

2008 started with the emerging belief that Ballymena United could possibly be potential title challengers following a stunning 4-2 victory over Glentoran at the Oval on New Years' Day. Typically for Ballymena United, that optimism only lasted a matter of days as English Championship club Norwich City approached Tommy Wright with an offer to return to full-time football as Glenn Roeder's goalkeeping coach at Carrow Road. An eleventh hour decision to stay at Warden Street by Wright included a new contract and additional transfer funds, a decision which was met with widespread approval by United supporters.

Given the team's recent success, the January transfer window prompted moves for Ballymena's key performers – defender Aaron Callaghan was lured to his native Derry City and Flynn (by now arguably the hottest property in Irish Football) moved to Blackburn Rovers for an initial fee of around £40,000 after fierce competition from Manchester City for the teenager's signature. Captain Albert Watson also rejected Linfield's strong advances and signed an improved deal at the club.

The loss of two key players and the Norwich City saga had clearly unsettled the team, Wright made hasty transfers bringing Davitt Walsh in permanently and Glentoran striker Michael Ward – the pair would only manage one goal between them in the second half of the season. Defeat in the Irish Cup fifth round replay to Newry City on penalties dealt a further blow to the team's confidence and the four consecutive league defeats that followed ended any lingering hope of any title challenge as Ballymena also fell out of the top four league positions.

On 22nd March, a routine league game against Lisburn Distillery provided controversy that would go so viral that it would appear in newspapers from Los Angeles to Sydney! The highly-charged game saw the Whites equalise in the tenth minute of injury time against nine-man Ballymena United. The controversy surrounding the 2-2 draw boiled over with altercations between managers Tommy Wright and Paul Kirk at the final whistle. It then spilled on the terraces and supporters encroached on the playing arena. Bizarrely a leg of lamb being found amongst the debris which provided the novelty press hook for the ugly scenes that followed the fixture.

Tommy Wright and Jim Grattan. Courtesy of Presseye

One win from the final six games of the Irish Premier League season resulted in a commendable but underwhelming sixth place finish for Ballymena. The morning of the final league fixture away to Newry City, Manager Tommy Wright announced his resignation from the club citing his 'disillusionment with Irish League football'. He would take up the goalkeeping coach role at Norwich City less than a month after leaving the Showgrounds. The final game of the Wright era ended with a 2-2 draw at the Newry Showgrounds with teenager Paul McNeill scoring the last goal under his leadership.

The club moved swiftly to appoint Wright's assistant Jim Grattan as the new manager and he was due to be unveiled at a supporter's club dinner to celebrate 50 years since the historic 1958 Cup Final victory. Grattan, Child Protection Officer at the Irish Football Association, embarrassingly had to resign after only three days due to his full-time commitments with the IFA which had vetoed the appointment.

Despite, the faux-pas in the managerial appointment, off the field the club was in rude health. All Irish League clubs had been extensively assessed over two years by an independent panel ahead of the formation of the (again) newly restructured 12-team IFA Premiership for the 2008/09 season. Across a number of criteria. Ballymena were ranked second in from all applicant clubs, behind only Linfield.

⚽ *2008/2009* ⚽

Roy Walker was coaxed back into management with United in May 2008. Having won Irish League Championships with Crusaders in 1995 and 1997,

Roy Walker. Courtesy of Presseye

Walker had been out of football for almost eight years before coming back into management. The lay preacher told the gathered media upon his unveiling that he believed it was 'God's path' that brought him to Ballymena.

It was a summer of unrest at the Showgrounds as captain Albert Watson and team-mate Craig McClean almost instantly submitted transfer requests upon the new manager's appointment. Whilst talisman Kevin Kelbie was the subject of relentless interest from Linfield throughout pre-season. Kevin openly admitted he wished to leave but was resigned to staying at the Braid after the club's board rejected a final £40,000 offer from the Windsor Blues. The Scottish forward signed an improved two year contact.

Tommy Wright had already started the building blocks for the new season before he left with a trio of pre-contract signings. Former Southampton goalkeeper Alan Blayney joined from Bohemians, midfielder Joe McDonnell (Newry City) and Dublin centre-half Gavin McDonnell (Glenavon) all penning advanced deals for the 2008/09 campaign and they would be joined by former Sunderland striker Neil Teggart.

Walker dismantled the team that had comfortably finished sixth the previous season as out went Paul Murphy (Newry), Simon Kelly (Dundalk), Garth Scates (Glenavon), Lee Patrick & Stephen Lowry (both Limavady) and Darren Fitzgerald (Ards).Long serving defender Nigel Boyd left to join newly promoted Bangor after 376 appearances during 13 seasons at his hometown club.

Much promotion and fanfare had accompanied the launch of the new IFA Premiership in August 2008 but it was delayed in two successive weekends due to a referee's strike and then freak weather conditions. Ballymena United eventually lined out under their new manager in the first round of the County Antrim Shield at home to Ballyclare Comrades. Neil Teggart scored twice and Davitt Walsh got one in a comfortable 3-0 victory.

The league campaign eventually started but in disastrous fashion as Ballymena lost 5-1 at home to Cliftonville in front of an expectant crowd. Alarm bells started to ring after a worrying start to the new league with no wins and only three points from the opening ten

The new IFA Premiership was launched with increased publicity including billboards featuring United goalkeeper Alan Blayney

games. Roy Walker's beleaguered Sky Blues were already cut adrift at the bottom of the table and had been unceremoniously dumped out of the County Antrim Shield by Glentoran, losing 6-1 at the Oval.

On 11th October, tragedy struck the club with the sudden death of the mother of teenage defender Aaron Stewart (and wife of former player and now reserve team manager, Alfie Stewart) as she drove her son to the home game against Linfield at the Showgrounds. Amidst the sombre atmosphere, Ballymena United fittingly produced their best performance of the season, defeating the reigning champions 2-0, with both goals coming from Kevin Kelbie. The Scottish forward dedicated his two goals to the late Lorraine Stewart after the game.

Despite still propping up the rest of the league, draws with Glentoran and Cliftonville boosted confidence ahead of the club's landmark first live televised game in the club's history. Sky Sports had selected the game against Newry City as part of their live Monday football schedule. The large crowd gathered at the Ballymena Showgrounds could only watch on with the rest of the UK audience as the Sky Blues lost an entertaining encounter 3-2.

By late November, Walker's side had only managed the one league victory in 17 games and travelled to Glenavon knowing defeat would cut the club 10 points adrift at the bottom of the league. However a spirited 3-1 win with goals from Stuart King, David Cushley and Paul McNeill sparked the club on a mini-revival over the Christmas period. It was the first of five successive league victories for the

Sky Blues, winning Roy Walker the Manager of the Month award for December 2008.

By January, United had now won seven of the their last nine games and gradually moved away from the bottom of the league. It had come at a cost as captain Gary Haveron broke his leg against Bangor before Christmas, and in-form vice-captain Stuart King broke his ankle in the 2-0 Boxing Day win against Coleraine. Striker Kevin Kelbie would captain the team for the remainder of the season. As cover for the injuries Walker welcomed defender Paul Muir back to the club after almost ten years away, along with striker Nathan McConnell and teenage full-back Michael Smith from Ballyclare Comrades for a £5,000 fee.

Paul Muir and George Young. Courtesy of Presseye

Ballymena United headed into the Irish Cup in-form but despite a comfortable fifth round victory over Ballyclare, the 1-0 defeat at home to eventual winners Crusaders on Valentines' Day effectively ended the Braidmen's season. Despite a 1-0 derby win against Coleraine, thanks to a Paul Muir free-kick, Ballymena United were unsurprisingly condemned to the bottom of half of the table as IFA Premiership split into two sections for the final five games of the season.

Tenth place from the twelve teams was the final verdict on a dismal first season for Roy Walker, who responded by the promise of weeding out his under-performing players. True to his word, ten of his squad were released or transfer-listed come the end of the season including leading goalscorer Neil Teggart, former captain Albert Watson and the previous season's player of the year Gavin Melaugh.

More positively, whilst established players underperformed during forgettable 2008/09 campaign, the emergence of young players such as player of the year Lee Colligan (who Walker wildly claimed should be worth £1million to the club). Aaron Stewart, Sean O'Neill, Ryan Deans, Michael Smith and George Young all featured prominently in the first team. Colligan and O'Neill also both merited appearances for the Northern Ireland Under-21 team, making history as the first two players to represent the club at this level during the same season.

⚽ *2009/2010* ⚽

Manager Roy Walker was left with a major rebuilding job ahead of the 2009/10 season after the mass exodus of players from the Showgrounds. Goalkeeper Alan Blayney had signed a pre-contract with Linfield and just under a dozen other departures including Neil Teggart (Portadown), Gavin Melaugh (Lisburn Distillery), Michael Ward & Craig McClean (both Dungannon Swifts), Thomas Wray (Institute) and Gavin McDonnell (Newry City).Stuart King, who had previously agreed a new three-year contract with Walker, joined Glenavon.

Andy Smith. Courtesy of Presseye

This allowed the management team to work with a blank slate for their team, albeit with a reduced budget. The marquee summer signing was former Glentoran and Preston North End striker Andy Smith. The 18 cap Northern Ireland international had recently left Portadown following a self-imposed year long exile from football.

Veteran midfielder Darren Lockhart and Noel Anderson both joined from relegated Bangor, Philip Carson joined from Glentoran. Walker utilised the lower leagues for signings with Nigerian born winger Orman Okunaiya from Carrick Rangers, ex-Peterborough trainee Gavin Taggart from Newington YC and local utility player Mark Surgenor from Ballymoney United all joining the club.

Cliftonville again opened domestic proceedings at the Showgrounds but despite a 1-0 defeat the signs of improvement were plain to see in comparison with the 5-1 reversal, twelve months before. The following Tuesday night a four goal County Antrim Shield win over Harland & Wolff Welders got the Sky Blues up and running with the mercurial Andy Smith opening his account for his new club.

Ballymena United's players, officials and supporters were blissfully unaware of the repercussions of United's trip to Dungannon Swifts in August. Referee Trevor Mountray, (backed by an Irish FA appointed observer in the stands) alleged that visiting Ballymena United supporters had made racist chants towards the Swifts' Caribbean goalkeeper Alvin Rouse. Much to the bewilderment of all supporters when the story appeared in the local press the next day. The club were given an unprecedented fine of £1,250 which was unsuccessfully appealed later in the season.

Gary Haveron. Courtesy of Presseye

On the pitch, the team struggled for form and surrendered a two goal lead away at Coleraine, losing the game 3-2. Captain Gary Haveron cruelly suffered a second leg break in nine months against his former club. The first league win of the season came at the Oval stunning reigning champions Glentoran. United had developed a fantastic record at the East Belfast venue and two goals from Kevin Kelbie secured a 2-1 against Alan McDonald's side.

The Sky Blues had begun to hit form throughout the autumn with wins again Institute, Lisburn Distillery and a dramatic late 2-1 victory over Portadown thanks to Kevin Kelbie's stoppage time goal. The Scotsman had recaptured his form of old, but his strike partner Smith had yet to break any delph in a Ballymena shirt until a midweek trip to Solitude in October. Named as captain for the evening, Smith turned out an exemplary performance scoring the second goal in an impressive 2-0 win against title-chasing Cliftonville. The game also marked the debut of teenage defender Chris Ramsey who signed from Manchester City.

Home wins against Coleraine and Crusaders pushed the Braidmen into the top half of the table for the first time since the league restructuring. It was a home defeat against Glentoran that shattered the fragile confidence of Walker's inexperienced side. They had led by two Nathan McConnell goals with only seven minutes to go before capitulating to lose the game 3-2, Colin Nixon's injury time winner capped a stunning comeback by the champions.

The Glentoran defeat was the catalyst for a nine game run without a victory. Having already exited the County Antrim Shield to Crusaders at the semi-final stage, Institute knocked United out of the League Cup at the first hurdle. Bottom placed Lisburn Distillery appointed former United manager Tommy Wright and claimed a 1-0 victory at the Showgrounds in his first game in charge. This was followed a few days later with a frustrating defeat to Newry Town in which Andy

Smith picked up a needless six game suspension for attempting to head-butt an opponent.

Off the field, United were back in financial trouble as the economic downturn had affected both attendances and sponsorship. The club campaigned for supporters to back a new share issue with the aim of raising £90,000 to secure the immediate future of the club. This was a season besieged with financial fears for many Irish League clubs which eventually led to budget controls and wage caps being put in place to help clubs live within their means.

Speculation was rife that Kevin Kelbie was to be sold to Glentoran in the January transfer window as he was entering the last six months of his contract at Warden Street. He had proved his worth in mid-December when Ballymena got back to winning ways with a superb 2-0 victory over Linfield; Kelbie following up Darren Lockhart's opener with a superbly taken finish to provide supporters with an early Christmas present of three points.

Ballymena United players celebrate scoring against Linfield in December 2009 at the Showgrounds. Courtesy of Presseye

This was the last game for almost a month, as the harsh winter weather curtailed any of the scheduled holiday fixtures. It would not be until 16th January and the Irish Cup fifth round that the club would be back in action, drawing 0-0 with Championship (the rebranded First Division) side Ards, before winning 1-0 in the replay a few days later with Kelbie scoring the winner. Kelbie scored a hat-trick in a 5-2 victory in the following round against Ballinamallard United, having decided to stay at the club until the end of the year.

The racism dispute from August, returned to the fore as Ballymena United were to travel to Stangmore Park in February 2010. The club's committee had appealed the initial fine of £1,750 having conducted a thorough investigation and despite providing video evidence the club's appeal was not heard. Angry Ballymena United supporters, disgusted with having the club's reputation tarnished held a boycott of Dungannon Swifts for the fixture - instead attending the corresponding Reserve team fixture at the Showgrounds on the same evening.

The low-key 2-1 defeat to Dungannon Swifts effectively spelt the end of lingering hopes of a top six finish before the league split.

Attentions turned to the quarter-finals of the Irish Cup and after a thrilling 3-3 draw with Glenavon at Mourneview Park, the Sky Blues secured a first Irish Cup semi-final in five years defeating the Lurgan Blues 2-0 in the replay with goals from Andy Smith and Noel Anderson.

Devoid of any league form Ballymena travelled to Windsor Park for an evening

Celebrations as Ballymena United equalise in the Irish Cup semi-final. Courtesy of Presseye

Heartbreak for Mark Surgenor after the penalty shoot-out. Courtesy of Presseye

kick-off against Portadown. The teams were evenly matched throughout the 1-1 draw with former Ports' striker Andy Smith scoring the equaliser against his former club. Mark Surgenor would rue missing a gilt-edged change to win the game in injury time. Penalties were the cruel decider and it was Aaron Stewart who saw his decisive penalty saved by David Miskelly to send Portadown into the final against Linfield.

Having been condemned to the bottom half of the table, the low-key end of the league season split meant that United disappointingly finished tenth for a second consecutive season. Off the field work began on the redevelopment of the Warden Street stand at the Showgrounds as the face of the club continued to development thanks to almost £1 million funding from Sport NI. This brought the total capacity of the now all seated arena to 3,900.

Back row: Colin Sewell (Coach), Denver Gage, Richard Gibson, Albert Watson, Ryan Brown, Bertnel Thompson (Team Attendant), Dwayne Nelson,
Aaron Stewart, Gavin Taggart, Andy Smith, Gordon McCartney (Sports Therapist).
Front row: Gary McCutcheon, Ryan Berry, Lee Colligan, Wesley Gregg (Assistant Manager), Gary Haveron, Roy Walker (Manager), Eamonn Murray,
Maurice McDowell, Michael Smith.

🅐 2010/2011 🅐

After another disappointing campaign, Roy Walker started rebuilding his side again in search of success. The highest profile summer departure was top scorer Kevin Kelbie who was not offered a new contract. The Scot's performances were not meeting the value of his high wages in the manager's eyes and he left the club after 75 goals in 181 games in five seasons. His direct replacement was another Scot in the form of 31-year-old Gary McCutcheon, a proven Irish League goalscorer with Portadown and Larne who had previously had spells with Kilmarnock and Stranraer.

Adian Watson (Crusaders), Chris Ramsey (Portadown), Darren Lockhart (Ards) would move on during the summer, alongside the talented youngsters David Cushley (Lisburn Distillery) and Sean O'Neill (Dungannon Swifts) who did not fit into Walker's plans for the club. In came goalkeeper Ryan Brown (Larne), wingers Eamonn Murray (Glenavon) and Mo McDowell (Carniny Rangers) and Ryan Berry (Glentoran).

In a true 'Roy of the Rovers' scenario, Walker signed Clough central defender Denver Gage who had been impressing for Ballymoney United in the Championship. Gage, a life-long United supporter from an avid family of Sky Blue followers, was also a shareholder in the club before signing. During contract negotiations between Walker and Gage, the latter was asked about money – prompting the innocent question 'How much do you want me to pay?!'.

The Irish League season started with an encouraging scoreless draw against champions Linfield at Windsor Park but the following week, the opening home fixture against newly promoted Donegal Celtic, the West Belfast hoops shocked

Gary McCutcheon and Denver Gage. Courtesy of Presseye

the home crowd with a 4-0 win. Early season pressure had already mounted on the manager to strengthen his team and the arrivals of young midfielders Nathan Hanley (from Hull City) and Rory Carson (from Bradford City) followed immediately.

The Sky Blues bounced back quickly with a superb 3-1 win over Portadown at Shamrock Park, with Hanley scoring on his debut. This sparked a change in fortunes for the Sky Blues who chalked up wins over Glenavon, Newry City and Glentoran to move into third place in the table at the end of September Ballymena were now playing a welcome brand of attractive football buoyed by the strike partnership of McCutcheon and Gibson, the electrifying pace of Eamonn Murray, the industry of Hanley and the reliability of Watson and Gage in the centre of defence.

There were virtually no fixtures played over the Christmas period due to the sub-zero temperatures which brought the province to a stand-still. United started their Irish Cup journey against Glentoran in the opening round and came from behind to draw 1-1 in the first game thanks to Denver Gage's first goal for the club. The replay was a cup thriller at the Oval and extra time was needed to separate the two evenly matched sides. Andy Waterworth's goal eventually won the tie for the Glens despite an onslaught of late pressure from Walker's men. Either side of the two cup games the Sky Blues crashed out of the League Cup at the quarter-final stage to Crusaders.

Impressed by his team's first half of the season, in January the manager offered new contracts to many of his key players. Some simply 'shook hands' but never formally signed agreements. Towards the end of the transfer window, Nathan Hanley and Richard Gibson both negated on their agreements and signed formal pre-contract agreements with Linfield and Glentoran. News of Gibson's pre-contract filtered through the day of the Irish Cup replay at the Oval, a game in which he surprisingly played. Furious with both players for breaking their promise to the club, Walker released both to be transferred to their future clubs immediately.

The club made a few late transfers towards the end of the transfer window; bringing in Portadown midfielder Neil McCafferty on loan, teenage striker Aaron Boyd from Linfield and ex-Donegal Celtic and Linfield midfielder Paul McAreavey. However the contractual chaos and the loss the two key players rocked United's form. Despite creditable draws away to both Linfield and Cliftonville, Walker's side would only manage one league win from January until the league split in March, sacrificing their previously secure top six place to eventually finish a hugely disappointing ninth place in the table.

At the start of April, striker Andy Smith (who had missed large periods of the season through injury) packed his bags and moved on. The ex-Northern Ireland international's form had dropped dramatically from his encouraging first season at the club, but only managed one goal in his second season. He was released by mutual consent and after a sensational move to Vietnam fell through at the last minute he eventually resurfaced at Belgian Third Division side UR Namur the following term.

Another disappointing departure on the final day of the season was long-serving Albert Watson. The 25-year-old signed a pre-contract agreement with Linfield after an impressive tally of 316 appearances during 10 seasons at the Showgrounds. Watson thrived at Windsor Park over the next two seasons before emigrating to Canada to captain the new North American Soccer League franchise FC Edmonton.

Albert Watson. Courtesy of Presseye

⚽ *2011/2012* ⚽

Ballymena United supporters were by now unfazed by the roller-coaster nature of the Showgrounds.

It was yet another summer of change as the Sky Blues tried to improve on a disappointing ninth place finish during the previous season. This wasn't aided by the departure of key players; Albert Watson ended his nine year association with the club to join champions Linfield, Michael Smith secured a move to professional football with Bristol Rovers and Lee Colligan immigrated to Australia. Club captain Gary Haveron also said farewell as his work commitments took priority and joined Larne Tech OB.

Manager Roy Walker took little time in replacing those departed and his marquee signing of Greenock Morton's Allan Jenkins as new club captain signaled

Allan Jenkins. Courtesy of Presseye

the intent of his rebuilding job at the club. Stranraer based Jenkins (a close friend of McCutcheon) had recently played with Gretna in the Scottish Premier League during their meteoric rise and fall to the top flight of Scottish football. In the revolving door also came Davy Munster, Conor Downey and Ross Black from relegated Newry City, Portadown duo Alan Teggart and Jordan Baker, Glenavon's James Costello, goalkeeper Aaron Kerr from Ards and finally full-backs Curtis Woods (Burnley) and Tony Kane (Cliftonville).

Following a pre-season campaign in which United plundered goals against tame Championship opposition and also held Kenny Shiels' Kilmarnock to a creditable draw, the Braidmen started their season with a bang sitting proudly on top of the league after one game! A four goal blitz of Lisburn Distillery at New Grovenor had supporters positively salivating at this free-scoring Ballymena United side.

Those fans came crashing down to reality the following week after the first home game against Glenavon as a host of individual errors caused Ballymena

Back row: Colin Sewell (Coach), Denver Gage, Mark Surgenor, Jordan Baker, James Costello, Aaron Black, Gavin Taggart, Tony Kane, Chris Rodgers.
Third row: Terry Moore (Assistant Manager), Gordon McCartney (Sports Therapist), Michael Smith, Curtis Woods, Ross Black, Dwayne Nelson,
Aaron Kerr, Conor Downey, Rory Carson, Bertnel Thompson (Team Attendant), Iain Black (Committee), David Wells (Goalkeeping coach).
Second row: (All committee) Jim Somerville, Neil Coleman (Company Secretary), Billy Bell, Maurice Smyth, Bill Wray, Nigel McIlrath, Don Stirling
(Football Secretary), Noel Millar (Treasurer), Brian Thompson.
Front row: John Taggart (Committee), Norman McBurney (President), Eamonn Murray, Aaron Stewart, Gary McCutcheon, Roy Walker (Manager),
Allan Jenkins, Alan Teggart, Robert Cupples (Chairman), John Blair (Vice-Chairman).

to surrender a 3-0 lead and eventually draw 3-3. The combination of individual mistakes and poor home form would be a regular occurrence during the season. This was in stark contrast to Ballymena's stunning away form were they picked up five wins in their first five games on their travels, including coming from behind against Donegal Celtic and Cliftonville.

The now routine annual win at the Oval against Glentoran was sealed by Gary McCutcheon scoring a hat-trick to send him into double figures before September was over. The away victories merely seemed to paper over the cracks, as worrying home defeats to Crusaders and newly promoted Carrick Rangers coupled with a five goal mauling from derby rivals Coleraine meant that any early season optimism had now quickly evaporated.

Walker quickly sought reinforcements to address the alarming downturn in form with defenders Richard Vauls joining from Coleraine and Liam Watson from Donegal Celtic. Northern Ireland Under-21 goalkeeper Wayne Drummond was brought in to replace the injured Aaron Kerr. Results in the league continued to be inconsistent but an overdue stroke of luck was dealt in the League Cup as (having already been dumped out of the County Antrim Shield by Linfield) Ballymena beat Chimney Corner, Bangor and Dergview to set up the semi-final clash against Crusaders in December.

With growing concern from the terraces the seven goal annihilation at the hands of a rampant Cliftonville at the Showgrounds signaled the beginning of the end for manager Roy Walker. Rory Donnelly had inspired the in-form Reds with four goals in the 7-3 win. The following week Walker issued an ambiguous statement to supporters that if results did not improve by the end of the year, changes would be made.

Ultimately he didn't make it that far as despite a resurgent win against Donegal Celtic the next week, a dismal defeat to relegation threatened Glenavon at Mourneview Park followed by a 1-0 defeat to Crusaders in the League Cup semi-final at home was more than enough for Roy Walker. He resigned on the 13th December after three and a half years at the helm, with assistant Terry Moore in tow.

Joe McCall had recently returned to the club as Head of Youth Development and quickly stepped in as caretaker manager with Colin Sewell as his assistant. The remit was to steer the team through the Christmas period as the search began for a successor. McCall was in charge for three games losing to Coleraine on Boxing Day and earning draws against Dungannon Swifts and Donegal Celtic.

On 31st December, 2011 former Linfield and Northern Ireland striker Glenn

Glenn Ferguson. Courtesy of Presseye

Ferguson was appointed as the new manager of Ballymena United FC after with Norman Kelly as assistant manager and Lee Doherty as first-team coach. As fate would have it, Ferguson's first game in charge was against the Windsor Blues. Despite a spirited performance a 2-1 defeat to the reigning Irish League champions in front of the biggest home crowd of the season was enough to at least give United's long suffering supporters some encouragement for the remainder of the season.

It couldn't have been a more difficult start for 'Spike' as his first five league games in charge of struggling Ballymena Untied were all against teams residing in the top six of the table. Two heartbreaking last minute defeats to both Portadown and Cliftonville at home meant that chances of a top six league finish before the 'split' had quickly evaporated. Ferguson wasted little time stamping his authority on the side as Wayne Drummond, Aaron Kerr and Curtis Woods were all released and joined the winter exodus of Walker's squad which included Eamonn Murray (to Glentoran), Aaron Boyd (Coleraine) and Liam Watson. Young players such as Neil Lowry and Jamie Davidson were promoted to the first-team panel while defender Johnny Taylor joined from Glentoran on loan along with by midfielder Alan Davidson from Glenavon.

Davidson was to make a bigger impact on United's season that he could have imagined as United reached the quarter-final of the Irish Cup. Fifth and sixth round victories over Lisburn Distillery and Derriaghy CC set United up with a quarter-final trip to Championship side Newry City. Davidson proved the hero after scoring the winning goal in a 2-1 win at his former club but within hours it was apparent there was trouble afoot immediately after the game, as Newry had appealed the player's eligibility.

Davidson was deemed by the IFA to have been registered after the Irish Cup deadline for new signings. The battle even reached the courtroom were the IFA Appeals Committee upheld their decision to eliminate the Sky Blues from the Irish Cup and miss out on a semi-final against Linfield.

Undeterred by the legal circus, Ferguson galvanized his inherited squad as despite no chance of top six qualification the team went on an unbeaten run stretching 12 games to finish eventually finish seventh in the table, James Costello who had struggled for goals all season flourished under the new manager and scored seven goals in the final five games to claim the Football Writer's April Player of the Month award.

⚽ 2012/2013 ⚽

McBurney Transport celebrated a record breaking 25th year of being the main shirt sponsor of the club. Honorary club President Norman McBurney (who would also celebrate being awarded an OBE for service to the community) had begun sponsoring the football club in January 1988 and this was now the longest

Back row: Tony Kane, Gary Thompson, Jordan Baker, Mark Surgenor, Chris Rodgers, Jamie Davidson, Gavin Taggart, David Reid, David Cushley.
Middle row: Gordon McCartney (Sports Therapist), Ross Black, Denver Gage, David Munster, Stuart Addis, Dwayne Nelson, Neil Lowry, James Costello, Johnny Taylor, Bertnel Thompson (Team Attendant).
Front row: Norman Kelly (Assistant Manager), Wes Lamont (Goalkeeping Coach), Alan Teggart, Aaron Stewart, Glenn Ferguson (Manager), Allan Jenkins, Richard Vauls, Lee Doherty (Coach), Clifford Adams (Performance Analyst).

Norman McBurney

sponsorship in senior British football history and the third longest in Europe behind only Celta Vigo and PSV Eindhoven.

On the flip side the club saw the withdrawal of a key sponsor following the decision to compete in a low-key pre-season tournament in Dublin to mark the 130th anniversary of former League of Ireland side St. James' Gate as the final of the two day competition was played on a Sunday. Ferguson continued with the pre-season preparations as Ballymena United won the competition beating Welsh side Port Talbot Town and the hosts to win the mini-tournament.

Ulster Footballer of the Year, Gary McCutcheon left the club to join Crusaders. The veteran striker felt he had more opportunity to win medals at Seaview in his final few seasons of his career. Without McCutcheon, the management team tried in vain all summer to replace his 34 goals with no success as the talented David Cushley returned to the club from Distillery alongside midfielder Gary Thompson as the only major signings. Teenage defender Michael Ruddy signed from Crusaders but there was no place in the squad for Rory Carson and Conor Downey who were both released.

The Sky Blues started the season with a bang as local teenager Jamie Davidson stunned champions Linfield on the first day of the new league season with both goals in the 2-0 win. Ferguson's men continued their unbeaten form into the new season as the team moved top of the table at the end of August following the 2-0 home win against Distillery.

September was a different story for the Sky Blues as they failed to win any of the next four games and lost heavily to Coleraine at the Ballycastle Road. This went from one extreme to another as Ballymena continued the busy schedule by going nine games unbeaten and moved back into the top six league places. United secured a place in the County Antrim Shield final after successfully defeating Cliftonville in the quarter-final and Donegal Celtic in the semi-final.

With influential defender Johnny Taylor ruled out for the rest of the season through injury, preparations for a first final in six years were not helped by a humiliating 8-0 defeat to title chasing Cliftonville at the Showgrounds in November. This was the first home league defeat the team had suffered since February but was also off the back of a disappointing six goal exit to Linfield in the League Cup quarter-final two weeks previously.

Ten days after the Cliftonville debacle an under-strength Ballymena United squared up to Linfield at the Oval in the Shield final. It proved to be one of the most memorable nights in the club's history as the 23 year trophy famine ended following a dramatic penalty shoot-out. Defender Davy Munster had headed his team in front after 23 minutes but the same player gave away the second half penalty which allowed Linfield's Brian McCaul to equalize. Goalkeeper Stuart Addis made himself the hero saving penalties from David Armstrong and Daryl Fordyce and allowed Alan Davidson the opportunity to drive home the winning spot-kick.

The large 2,000 strong Ballymena support were sent into raptures and there was tangible relief once stand-in captain and man of the match, Aaron Stewart

Davy Munster wheels away in celebration after opening the scoring. Courtesy of Presseye

Stuart Addis saves Daryl Fordyce's penalty. Courtesy of Presseye

Winning penalty scorer Alan Davidson is mobbed by his team-mates. Courtesy of Presseye

Allan Jenkins and Aaron Stewart lift the County Antrim Shield. Courtesy of Presseye

lifted the famous old Shield alongside Allan Jenkins. The first silverware the club had won since the 1989 Irish Cup final and the first of Glenn Ferguson's blossoming managerial career, he graciously gave his winning medal to long serving ball-boy Paul Kelly.

The hangover from the Shield win lasted until January as the team failed to win another game during the calendar year. The lack of any goalscoring threat had started to catch up with the team. Ferguson invested in Dublin striker Shane Dolan from Donegal Celtic and Gary Liggett from Lisburn Distillery to fire his team into the top six for the first time. Out-of-form James Costello was freed to join Dungannon Swifts.

January also brought a hastily arranged away friendly in Rotterdam to Dutch third-tier side RSKV Leonidas which United (accompanied by some international trialists) lost 1-0. It was the club's first away friendly outside of the UK and Ireland and was facilitated by the Dutch club's Irish owner. The team building exercise had a temporary positive affect on the team with wins over Warrenpoint Town (in the Irish Cup) and Glentoran.

The manager admitted at the end of the campaign that his players and staff had become complacent after winning the Shield in November as the club went ten games without a win and crashed out of the Irish Cup to rivals Coleraine at home and they also suffered another drubbing – losing 7-0 to Glenavon at Mourneview Park in February. This ruled the Braidmen out of any contention for a place in the top half of the league split. The expected goals of Liggett and Dolan never truly materialised and it would be April before the fans would taste victory again.

United returned to winning ways in the low key post-split games with a stunning 6-1 Easter Tuesday victory against Portadown with David Cushley scoring a superb hat-trick. The 2-0 win over Distillery at New Grosvenor Park was the final nail in the coffin of the Whites who were relegated to the Championship as Ballymena United had to settle for eighth place – a position held almost exclusively throughout 2013.

2013/2014

Manager Glenn Ferguson had outlined to shareholders at the AGM that the team would be harder to beat this season and would not suffer any of the heavy defeats that were commonplace the previous season – those words seemed hollow to astonished United supporters on the opening day of the 2013/2014 season – as they were 4-0 down at half-time to Glenavon at the Showgrounds, eventually losing 6-3.

Ferguson's men bounced back though with three wins in their next four games against Crusaders, Dungannon Swifts and Portadown – the last of which included new signing Michael McLellan scoring against the Ports just days after switching to United on transfer deadline day. Long term target McLellan had spent the past season at Shamrock Park, after returning from England and had appeared for the Sky Blues the previous summer, despite his promising debut – he failed to hold down a regular place in the team and was eventually released.

After the Portadown win, the team struggled for form and struggled for goals. Defeats to Cliftonville and Linfield weren't unexpected but concerns started to rise with back-to-back defeats to strugglers Ballinamallard United and Warrenpoint Town (promoted to the top division for the first time in their history). Having lost faith in his misfiring strikers and languishing in the bottom half of the table,

Ferguson resorted to using captain Allan Jenkins as a makeshift lone striker through until the transfer window reopened.

The upturn in fortunes was instantaneous as arguably the performance of the season in the quarter-final of the League Cup against Portadown. Ballymena dominated throughout the whole game, winning 4-0 at a canter to progress to the semi-final of the competition. Three consecutive league wins followed in the run-up to a League Cup semi-final showdown at Seaview against Crusaders. David Cushley stunned the Crues with a superb first half hat-trick but the resilience North Belfast men fought back to win 4-3 and clinch a place in the final.

A large Boxing Day crowd at the Ballycastle Road Showgrounds witnessed Ballymena United get the better of their fierce rivals with the Sky Blues' first

Captain Allan Jenkins celebrates scoring at the Coleraine Showgrounds in the 2013 Boxing Day derby. Courtesy of Presseye

derby win since 2009. Allan Jenkins' two goals secured a 3-2 win that not only gave United fans the Christmas bragging rights but also moved the Sky Blues into the top six for the first time this season.

December marked a goalkeeping crisis at the club as both Dwayne Nelson and Stuart Addis were both ruled out for the remainder of the season with serious injuries. Crusaders' French stopper Yohann Lacroix came in on a short-term loan and Dundalk goalkeeper Aaron Shanahan came in for the rest of the season. In-form forward Darren Boyce also joined the club from Coleraine (having been on loan at Dungannon for the first half of the season) to replace Gary Liggett and Shane Dolan who were released to join Dungannon and Shelbourne, respectively. Linfield stalwart Jim Ervin came in during the transfer window and quickly established himself at full-back.

Darren Boyce wasted no time making himself a hero at the Braid, as he scored a late equaliser against Harland & Wolff Welders in the Irish Cup fifth round to spare United blushes. United won the replay by a single goal to set up a daunting sixth round tie against Linfield at Windsor Park. Goals from Allan Jenkins and David Cushley secured a memorable cup win against the Blues as Ballymena

United stunned the hosts with a 2-1 win, as United supporters began to believe that their name was on the cup.

By March, United had once again fallen out of contention for the top half split having dropped to the bottom six in the table following defeats to Glentoran and Crusaders, United would eventually finish in seventh place. All attention was focused on the Irish Cup.

David Cushley beats Linfield goalkeeper Johnny Tuffey for the winner in the Irish Cup quarter-final. Courtesy of Presseye

Dungannon Swifts provided little opposition in the quarter-final, as Ballymena won 4-1 at the Showgrounds. Championship 2 side Queen's University awaited in the semi-final but despite their impressive run to the last four, Ballymena professionally progressed thanks to two Alan Davidson goals to reach the cup final for the first time since 1989.

Ballymena United players line-up before the 2014 Irish Cup final against Glenavon at Windsor Park.
Back row: Darren Boyce, Gary Thompson, Allan Jenkins, Aaron Shanahan, David Munster, Johnny Taylor.
Front row: Alan Teggart, Tony Kane, David Cushley, Stephen McBride, Jim Ervin. Courtesy of Presseye

Davy Munster and David Cushley celebrate with captain Allan Jenkins after the Scot's equalising cup final goal. Courtesy of Presseye

Cup final fever hit the town, as shirts and memorabilia flew off the shelves and upwards of 3,500 Ballymena United fans descended on Windsor Park for the Cup final against Glenavon in May. The day proved an anti-climax in a game marred by bizarre refereeing decisions as Ballymena United lost 2-1 to the Lurgan Blues. Allan Jenkins' equaliser had failed to spark a revival for the Sky Blues, who finished the game with nine men following the dismissals of Gary Thompson and Tony Kane.

⚽ 2014/2015 ⚽

There was very little summer activity in the aftermath of the Irish Cup final defeat, as Ferguson rewarded the vast majority of his squad with new contracts in the hope that another year's experience could take United one step further and deliver a major trophy.

Cup final goalkeeper Aaron Shanahan returned to the League of Ireland with Bohemians as regular stoppers Nelson and Addis returned to fitness for

Matthew Tipton. Courtesy of Presseye

the new season, whilst enigmatic winger Neil Lowry drifted out of senior football to Ahoghill Thistle and Michael McLellan joined the Welders. In came Veteran Welsh striker Matthew Tipton and Kyle McVey both from Linfield alongside midfielder Brian McCaul from Glenavon.

The progressive NI Football League decided brought a return of the Charity Shield as a curtain-raiser for the 2014/15 season for the first time since 2000. League champions Cliftonville had been due to face the Irish Cup winners Glenavon, but due to other pre-season commitments the Lurgan blues passed up on the opportunity which allowed Ballymena United to participate for the first time, as Irish Cup runners-up. The scoreless draw at Solitude was followed by penalties which the home side won 4-2 to claim the first silverware of the season.

Despite the disappointment of the Charity Shield defeat, Ballymena started the season in fine form with wins against Warrenpoint, Portadown, Dungannon and Institute (and a draw against Crusaders at Seaview) to leave the club as the early pacesetters in the Gibson Cup race. Sitting top of the Premiership at the end of August, Glenn Ferguson was deservedly awarded the writers' manager of the month award.

Although setback by away defeats to both Glenavon and Ballinamallard – the Braidmen continued to impress during September plenty of excitement and drama as they showed their character coming from behind to salve last-gasp draws with top six rivals Glentoran and Cliftonville and also claim the first derby win over the season at the Coleraine Showgrounds, with defender Michael Ruddy becoming the unlikely hero with a late winner in a 2-1 win to move United back into second place.

It was into the autumn though that injuries began to mount up on Ferguson's squad with Aaron Stewart, Kyle McVey and Gavin Taggart being ruled out for the season with serious injuries and talisman David Cushley also requiring knee surgery. Taggart in particular had won many plaudits for his superb start to the season in the engine room and was badly missed as the team could only manage one win from the next 12 league games and also were cruelly knocked out of the County Antrim Shield in the quarter-final by Cliftonville in a thrilling encounter which ended 4-3 to the North Belfast Reds.

There still had been some success in Ferguson's favoured cup competitions as Ballymena comfortably progressed to the semi-final of the League Cup following wins against Newington YC, Ballyclare Comrades and Dungannon Swifts. The long mid-week trip to County Fermanagh in December presented the Sky Blues with the task of winning against Ballinamallard United at Ferney Park for the first time for a place in the final. Davy Munster's late, late winner sparked scenes of delirium in yet another entertaining game as Ballymena sneaked a 3-2 win to seal a first League Cup final for the club.

Having since dropped out of the top six, the cup win sparked a mini-revival and provided a Christmas cracker on Boxing Day as Ballymena beat Coleraine 4-3 in a pulsating derby in front of a packed Warden Street Showgrounds, Matthew Tipton grabbing the winner for the home side to end 2014 on a high note.

The New Year started with even more reason for optimism as striker Gary McCutcheon returned to the club after two and a half years with Crusaders. A stunning long range strike against Glenavon at the Showgrounds on his second debut was unfortunately the highlight for a more subdued second spell at the club as the defeat to the Lurgan side in early January meant that it was unlikely the Ferguson would achieve the goal of a top six finish for the club this season. Ferguson also added Paddy McNally (Glenavon), Eamon McAllister (Ards) and Australian goalkeeper Tim Allen to the ranks during the transfer window.

The Sky Blues warmed up for the League Cup final with a bizarre 5-5 draw with Portadown at Shamrock Park but didn't heed the warning of the defensive frailties at Windsor Park against Cliftonville in the showpiece final as it took the league's top goalscorer Joe Gormley only 55 seconds to open the scoring. Gormley added a second before half-time but a superb double from the returning David Cushley sparked a superb comeback to level the score, only for Cliftonville's Martin Donnelly to steal the winner with ten minutes remaining and deprive Ballymena United of a first League Cup on the sideboard.

David Cushley celebrates scoring in the League Cup final against Cliftonville. Courtesy of Presseye

In a bizarre twist of fate, the Irish Cup sixth round draw paired United with the Solitude men, in the sixth of seven meetings between the sides over the course of the season – including in every cup competition. The tense cup tie seemed to be going the way of many of the previous encounters – with Cliftonville holding a slender 1-0 win going into the final minutes. Out of no-where David Cushley's deflected free-kick sent the travelling support into raptures with the equaliser, but having barely had the chance to sit back down the Belfast winger stunned the Champions with the goal of season. Tony Kane tipped the ball off to Cushley who drilled an inch perfect thunderbolt past Cherrie in the Reds' goal to send United to the quarter-final.

With top six now an impossibility, United pinned all hopes on a return to the Irish Cup final and faced the tricky task of Harland & Wolff Welders in the last eight. The Championship side stunned the visitors at the rain-soaked Tillysburn Park when Michael McLellan struck twice against his former employers to leave United on the verge of elimination from the competition. The late drama which followed epitomised the roller-coaster nature of Ballymena's season as three goals in the final ten minutes saw a relieved Glenn Ferguson and his team through to the semi-finals. Gary

Wild celebrations at Tillysburn Park as Gary Thompson's late winner sends United into the Irish Cup semi-final. Courtesy of Presseye

Thompson's winner came deep into the 95th minute and sparked wild pitch invasions from the large travelling support.

If the previous rounds had produced sparked some of the wildest celebrations and greatest comebacks seen from a Ballymena United side in years, the semi-final proved a major anti-climax. The disastrous three goal first half capitulation against Portadown at the Oval gave the Braidmen too big a mountain to climb in the second half, and despite Darren Boyce's consolation – the season's great entertainers went out of the Irish Cup with a mere whimper.

The Premiership campaign surprisingly ended positively after the cup exit, as United won their final six games in succession to finish the season in seventh place – this was the first time since 1968 that the club had won six top-flight league games in a row.

Club Honours

Number of times competition won or runners-up in brackets and honours won by Ballymena FC highlighted with an asterisk.

Irish Cup
Winners: (6)   1928/29*, 1939/40, 1957/58, 1980/81, 1983/84, 1988/89
Finalists: (9)   1929/30*, 1930/31*, 1938/39, 1950/51, 1958/59, 1969/70, 1973/74, 1977/78, 2013/14

Irish League
Winners: None
Runners-Up: (2) 1938/39, 1979/80

Irish League First Division
Winners: (1)   1996/97
Runners-Up: (2) 1995/96, 2002/03

Gold Cup
Winners: (1)   1974/75
Finalists: (4)   1931/32*, 1975/76, 1979/80, 1981/82

City Cup
Winners: (1)   1971/72
Runners-Up: (2) 1928/29*, 1960/61

Ulster Cup
Winners: (2)   1960/61, 1980/81
Runners-Up: (3) 1949/50, 1971/72, 2002/03

County Antrim Shield
Winners: (5)   1947/48, 1950/51, 1975/76, 1979/80, 2012/13
Finalists: (9)   1937/38, 1953/54, 1965/66, 1985/86, 1987/88, 1996/97, 2002/03, 2005/06

Festival of Britain Cup
Winners: (1)   1951/52

League Cup
Finalists: (1)   2014/15

Floodlit Cup
Finalists: (1)   1992/93

Blaxnit All-Ireland Cup
Finalists: (1)   1973/74

Irish News Cup
Finalists: (2)   1997/98, 1998/99

County Antrim Centenary Chalice
Finalists: (1)   1987/88

Other honours won by Ballymena United Reserves or Ballymena United Thirds

Steel and Sons Cup
Winners: (1)   1995/96

Irish Reserve League
Winners: (1)   2006/07

George Wilson Cup
Winners: (2)   1989/90, 1990/91

Harry Cavan IFA Youth Cup
Winners: (1)   2008/09

IFA Youth League Cup
Winners: (1)   2009/10

Louis Moore Youth Cup
Winners: (1)   1952/53

Club Records

Wins

Biggest win (all competitions)

> 1965/66 v. Cliftonville (home) – won 8-0 – Irish League
> 1974/75 v. Glenavon (home) – won 8-0 – Irish League
> 1979/80 v. Distillery (home) – won 8-0 – Irish League
> 1994/95 v. Newry Town (away) – won 8-0 – Irish League
> 2002/03 v. Ballymoney United (home) – won 8-0 – County Antrim Shield
> 2007/08 v. Orangefield OB (home) – won 8-0 – County Antrim Shield

Consecutive wins

(all competitions)	8 (Mar 1929 – Apr 1929 & Oct 2002 – Nov 2002)
(league only)	8 (Mar 1996 – Aug 1996 in First Division)
(top division)	7 (Dec 1965 - Jan 1966)

Consecutive games unbeaten

(all competitions)	16 (Sept 1971 – Nov 1971)

Most wins in a season

(all competitions)	29 (1979/80 in 47 games)
(league only)	21 (1996/97 in 28 games in First Division)
(top division)	15 (1938/39 & 1939/40 both in 26 games)

Fewest wins in a season

(all competitions)	5 (1976/77 in 40 games)
(league only)	3 (1956/57 in 22 games)

First win

(Ballymena FC)	08/09/1928 v. Ards (away) – won 2-1 – Gold Cup
(Ballymena Utd)	22/08/1934 v. Coleraine (home) – won 3-1 – Irish League

Draws

Consecutive draws

(all competitions)	4 (April 1967; Aug 1999 – Sept 1999; Dec 1999; Nov 2004 – Dec 2004)

Most draws in a season

(all competitions)	17 (1962/63 in 45 games)
(league only)	16 (1999/00 in 36 games)

Fewest draws in a season

(all competitions)	2 (1955/56 in 41 games)
(league only)	0 (1955/56 in 22 games)

First draw

(Ballymena FC)	25/08/1928 v. Larne (away) – drew 2-2 – Irish League
(Ballymena Utd)	18/08/1934 v. Glentoran (away) – drew 1-1 – Irish League

Defeats

Biggest defeat

(all competitions)	1946/47 v. Belfast Celtic (away) lost 1-10 – Regional League
	1963/64 v. Crusaders (home) – lost 1-10 – Ulster Cup

First defeat

(Ballymena FC)	20/08/1928 v. Belfast Celtic (home) – lost 0-3 – Irish League
(Ballymena Utd)	29/08/1934 v. Linfield (home) – lost 2-4 – Gold Cup

Goals

Most individual goals (all competitions)

Mal McDonnell (137)

Most individual goals scored in a season

Bob Sclater (50 goals in 1937/38)

Most individual goals scored in a single match

Bob Sclater (6 goals on 10/12/1938 v. Ards)

Most team goals scored in a season

129 (1930/31)

Appearances

#	Years	Player	Apps	Goals
1	1948 -1962	Eric Trevorrow	559	16
=	1957-1966 & 1968-1975	Eddie Russell	559	89
3	1951-1953 & 1955-1965	Billy Cubitt	485	13
4	1973-1976 & 1977-1986	John Sloan	478	85
5	1992-2003	Mark Carlisle	436	2
6	1988-1999	Des Loughery	376	111
=	1995-2008	Nigel Boyd	376	22
8	1957-1961 & 1970-1976	Arthur Stewart	372	33
9	1968-1972 & 1973-1978	Bobby Averell	328	19
10	1928-1936	John McNinch*	316	15
=	1948-1949 & 1949-1957	Harry Murphy	316	6
=	2001-2011	Albert Watson	316	10
13	1985-1996	John Heron	300	13
14	1970-1977	Tom Gowdy	299	3
15	1960-1969	Roy Dobbin	297	5
16	1983-1992	Michael Smyth	275	17
17	1969-1977	Quinton McFall	273	26
18	1972-1979 & 1981-1982	Sammy McAuley	272	4
19	1987-1994	Stephen Young	263	20
20	1987-1995	Damien Grant	259	0
21	1971-1981	Alec Donald	251	16
22	1952-1960	Des Brown	243	3
23	1968-1972 & 1975-1977	Jimmy Martin	242	126
24	1995-2001	Jason Allen	241	8
25	1985-1992	Ian Hamilton	232	9
=	1928-1930	James McCambridge $	49	71
=	1986-1991	Billy Pyper	49	209
21	1971-81	Alec Donald	251	16
22	1952-60	Des Brown	243	3
23	1968-72 & 1975-77	Jimmy Martin	242	126
24	1995-2001	Jason Allen	241	8
25	1985-92	Ian Hamilton	232	9

Includes 238 appearances (and 12 goals) for Ballymena FC

Goals

#	Years	Player	Goals	Apps
1	1963-1968	Mal McDonnell	137	182
2	1937-1940	Bob Sclater	136	114
3	1968-1972 & 1975-1977	Jimmy Martin	126	242
4	1928-1931 & 1932-1934	Jamie Shiels *	125	183
5	1979-1984	Paul Malone	115	194
6	1988-1999	Des Loughery	111	376
7	1957-1966 & 1968-1975	Eddie Russell	89	559
8	1983-1984, 1985-1987 & 1992-1995	Johnny Speak	88	221
9	1957-1966 & 1968-1975	John Sloan	85	478
10	1956-1959	Jimmy McGhee	77	114
11	2005-2010	Kevin Kelbie	75	181
12	1954-1955 & 1959-1961	Hubert Barr	71	84
13	1978-1983	Sammy McQuiston	70	181
14	2001-2004	Shea Campbell	69	141
15	1994-2000	Barry Patton	62	211
16	1936-1940	William Moore	58	163
17	1964-1965	Arthur Thomas	57	56
18	1929-1932	Jamie Murphy*	56	97
19	1968-1970 & 1972-1975	Gary Erwin	55	159
20	1998-2001	Glenn Hunter	54	129
21	1968-1969 & 1975-1978	Barry Brown	52	99
=	2010-2012 & 2015	Gary McCutcheon	52	99
23	1990-1993 & 1997-1998	Neil Candlish	51	160
24	1946-1949	Norman Kernaghan	50	92
25	2006-2010 & 2012-2015	David Cushley	49	200
=	1928-1930	James McCambridge *	49	71
=	1986-1991	Billy Pyper	49	209

* All appearances and goals for Ballymena FC

Individual Honours

Ulster Footballer of the Year

(Presented by the Castlereagh Glentoran Supporters' Club)

1952	Eric Trevorrow
1974	Arthur Stewart
2012	Gary McCutcheon

Ulster Young Footballer of the Year

(Presented by the Castlereagh Glentoran Supporters' Club)

1978	Tom Sloan
1980	Tony McCall
1981	Nigel Worthington
1984	Jonathan Speak
1989	Lindsay Curry

Northern Ireland PFA Most Promising Newcomer

1980	Tony McCall
1981	Nigel Worthington
1989	Lindsay Curry

Northern Ireland Football Personality of the Year

1979	Freddie McFaul

NI Football Writers Association Merit Trophy

1991	Billy McCready
2014	Don Stirling

Irish League First Division Player of the Year

2003	Shea Campbell

County Antrim FA Personality of the Senior Shield

1997	Des Loughery

Member of the Irish League Team of the Year

2011	Michael Smith
2012	Gary McCutcheon

NI Football Writers Association Player of the Month

1974/75	Paul Kirk (August) & Bobby Brown (November)
1980/81	Gerry Mullan (September) & David Neill (January)
1981/82	Denis Matthews (October)
1983/84	John Sloan (March)
1984/85	Alan Harrson (November)
1987/88	Steve Conville (December)
1989/90	Lindsay Curry (December)
1990/91	Damien Grant (April)
1996/97	Des Loughery (September & November)
2011/12	James Costello (April)
2014/15	Johnny Taylor (September)

NI Football Writers Association Manager of the Month

1996/97	Alan Fraser (March)
1997/98	Alan Fraser (October)
2007/08	Tommy Wright (December)
2008/09	Roy Walker (December)
2011/12	Glenn Ferguson (April)
2014/15	Glenn Ferguson (August)

Ballymena United Player of the Year awards

Members' Player of the Year		Players' Player of the Year	
1992/1993	Mark Carlisle	2014/2015	Stephen McBride
1991/1992	Michael Smyth	2013/2014	Gary Thompson
1990/1991	Des Loughery	2012/2013	Dwayne Nelson
1989/1990	John Garrett	2011/2012	Gary McCutcheon
1988/1989	John McKee	2010/2011	Albert Watson
1987/1988	Michael Smyth	2009/2010	Michael Smith
1986/1987	Stevie Conville	2008/2009	Lee Colligan
1985/1986	Ronnie Burns	2007/2008	Gavin Melaugh
1984/1985	John Sloan	2006/2007	Albert Watson
1983/1984	John Sloan	2005/2006	Gary Smyth
1982/1983	Stephen Penney	2004/2005	Ciaran Donaghy
1981/1982	Denis Matthews	2003/2004	Nigel Boyd
1980/1981	Paul Malone	2002/2003	Shea Campbell
1979/1980	Ronnie McCullough	2001/2002	Peter Withnell
1978/1979	Ronnie McCullough	2000/2001	Nigel Boyd
1977/1978	Alec Donald	1999/2000	Glenn Hunter
1976/1977	David Malcolmson	1998/1999	Mark Carlisle
1975/1976	John Sloan	1997/1998	Barry Patton
1974/1975	Tommy Gowdy	1996/1997	Mark Carlisle
1973/1974	Bobby Averell	1995/1996	Jason Allen
1972/1973	Sammy McAuley	1994/1995	Award withheld
1971/1972	Jim Martin	1993/1994	John Heron
1970/1971	Roy Torrens	1992/1993	Mark Carlisle
1969/1970	Jim Platt	1991/1992	John Heron
1968/1969	Bobby Averell	1990/1991	Des Loughery
1967/1968	Roy Dobbin	1989/1990	John Garrett
1966/1967	Tommy Stewart	1988/1989	John McKee
1965/1966	Tommy Brannigan	1987/1988	Stevie Conville & Michael Smyth (shared)
		1986/1987	Stevie Conville
1964/1965	Arthur Thomas	1985/1986	Ronnie Burns
1963/1964	David Cloughley	1984/1985	Brian Crockard
1962/1963	John Eric Smith	1983/1984	Brian Crockard
1961/1962	Eric Trevorrow	1982/1983	Tommy Huston
1960/1961	Billy Cubitt	1981/1982	Denis Matthews
1959/1960	Unknown	1980/1981	Nigel Worthington
1958/1959	Harry Bond	1979/1980	George Beattie
1957/1958	Tommy Lowry		

Internationals

Full internationals (4)

3 caps

McNinch, John^ ('31 v. Scotland, Scotland & Wales)

2 caps

McCambridge, James^ ('30 v. Scotland & Wales)

1 cap

Jack Mahood^ ('33 v. Scotland); Platt, Jim ('84 v. England)

'B' internationals (1)

1 cap

Barr, Hubert ('59 v. France)

Under-23 internationals (5)

2 caps

Stewart, Aaron ('10 v. Poland & Portugal); Watson, Albert ('07 v. Belgium & Republic of Ireland)

1 cap

Clarke, Norman ('62 v. Wales); McClean, Craig ('08 v. Republic of Ireland); Smith, Michael ('09 v. Wales)

Under-21 internationals (5)

9 caps

Callaghan, Aaron ('06 v. Germany, '07 v. Wales, Romania, Scotland, Moldova, Finland, Luxembourg, Luxembourg & Moldova)

4 caps

O'Neill, Sean ('09 v. Ukraine, Portugal & Iceland, '10 v. San Marino)

1 cap

Campbell, Shea ('03 v. Spain); Colligan, Lee ('08 v. Scotland); Sloan, Tom ('78 v. Republic of Ireland)

Amateur internationals (33)

6 caps

Clarke, Norman ('59 v. Wales, Scotland & England, '60 v. Wales & Scotland, '61 v. England); Cloughley, David ('65 v. Scotland & England, '66 v. Wales & Scotland, '67 v. Wales & Scotland)

5 caps

Barr, Hubert ('59 v. England, '60 v. Wales, Scotland & England, '61 v. Scotland);
Stewart, Arthur ('59 v. England, '60 v. Wales, Scotland & England, '61 v. Scotland)

4 caps

Averell, Bobby ('69 v. Scotland & England, '70 v. Wales & Scotland), Johnston, Eddie
('58 v. England, '59 v. Wales & Scotland, '60 v. Scotland), Moore, William ('38 v.
England & Scotland, '39 v. England & Scotland), Wallace, John ('38 v. England &
Scotland, '39 v. England & Scotland)

3 caps

Connell, Alex ('36 v. England & Scotland, '38 v. Scotland); Coyle, Roy ('68 v.
England, '69 v. Wales & Scotland); Cubitt, Billy ('52 v. Scotland, '53 v. England &
Scotland); Torrens, Roy ('68 v. Scotland & Wales, '71 v. Scotland)

2 caps

Erwin, Gary ('69 v. Wales & Scotland); Kavanagh, David ('49 v. Scotland, '50 v.
England); McCann, Sean ('49 v. England & Scotland); Olphert, Richard ('39 v.
England & Scotland); Platt, Jim ('70 v. Wales & Scotland); Russell, Eddie ('58 v. Wales
& Scotland); Smith, John Eric ('60 v. Scotland & England)

1 cap

Aiken, Thomas ('66 v. England); Anderson, Billy ('47 v. England); Horner, Richard
('39 v. England); McAuley, Sammy ('73 v. Wales); McCartney, David ('57 v. Wales);
McDowell. William ('35 v. England); McIlroy, Charles^ ('34 v. England); Orr, Des ('74
v. Wales); Shaw, Richard^ ('29 v. England); Simpson, James ('53 v. Scotland); Stewart,
Thomas ('57 v. Scotland); Todd, Brian ('74 v. Wales); Vincent, Blair ('39 v. Scotland);
White, Jim ('53 v. Scotland)

Irish League Representatives (39)

12 caps

Trevorrow, Eric ('50 v. League of Ireland & League of Ireland, '51 v. Western
Command, Welsh League, Welsh League & Scottish League, '52 v. Football League,
Western Command, Scottish League & Football League, '53 v. League of Ireland &
Scottish League)

9 caps

Twentyman, Geoff ('60 v. Scottish League & Football League, '61 v. League of Ireland,
League of Ireland, Scottish League & Football League, '62 v. Italian Semi-Pro League,
League of Ireland & Football League)

5 caps

Sloan, John ('78 v. Scottish League, '80 v. Scottish League & Canada, '81 v. League
of Ireland, '82 v. OFK Belgrade); Smith, John Eric ('61 v. Scottish League & Football

League, '63 v. Italian Semi-Pro League & Scottish League, '64 v. League of Ireland)

3 caps

Barr, Hubert ('60 v. Scottish League, '61 v. League of Ireland & League of Ireland); Cassidy, Joseph^ ('30 v. League of Ireland, Football League & Scottish League); McNinch, John^ ('31 v. Football League & Scottish League, '34 v. Football League); Mullan, Gerry ('80 v. Scottish League, Canada & Canada); Russell, Eddie ('58 v. Football League, '59 v. Football League & Scottish League); Sclater, Bob ('38 v. League of Ireland, '39 v. League of Ireland & Scottish League); Smyth, Michael ('90 v. Manchester United, '91 v. League of Ireland, '92 v. Everton)

2 caps

Candlish, Neil ('91 v. League of Ireland, '92 v. Everton); Clarke, Norman ('60 v. Scottish League, '61 v. Scottish League); Malone, Paul ('80 v. Scottish League, '81 v. League of Ireland); McCambridge, James^ ('29 v. League of Ireland, '30 v. League of Ireland); McCrae, Alex ('57 v. Western Command, '58 v. League of Ireland); McQuiston, Sammy ('80 v. Scottish League, '81 v. League of Ireland); Neill, David ('80 v. Canada & Canada); Reid, David^ ('29 v. Football League & Scottish League); Stewart. Arthur ('70 v. Football League, '74 v. League of Ireland)

1 cap

Barr, Albert ('40 v. League of Ireland); Bonnar, Paddy ('53 v. League of Ireland); Brannigan, Thomas ('66 v. Football League); Burke, Robert ('63 v. League of Ireland); Canning, David ('47 v. League of Ireland); Currie. Jack ('51 v. Welsh League); Fox, Graham ('80 v. Scottish League); Harrison, Alan ('84 v. League of Ireland); McCutcheon, Gary ('12 v. Manchester United); McDonnell, Mal ('67 v. League of Ireland); McFall, Quinton ('74 v. League of Ireland); McMullan, Charles ('53 v. League of Ireland); McMullan, Trevor ('95 v. League of Ireland); McPherson, James^ ('32 v. Football League); Mitchell, Steve ('38 v. League of Ireland); Mitten, John ('52 v. Scottish League); Murphy, Jamie^ ('30 v. League of Ireland); Shiels, Jim ('62 v. Football League); Worthington, Nigel ('81 v. League of Ireland)

Office Bearers

All office bearers of Ballymena FC noted with ^.

Chairman

1928 - 1934	Albert McClelland^
1934 - 1935	Simon McCrory
1935 - 1937	D.B. Elliott
1937 - 1940	R. Craig
1946 - 1948	Samuel Callender
1948 - 1949	Simon McCrory
1949 - 1950	John Watt
1950 - 1953	Samuel Callender
1953 - 1964	Samuel Graham
1964 - 1982	David McKeown
1982 - 1983	Brian Millar
1983 - 1987	Leonard Wiseman
1987 - 1991	Gordon McIlrath
1991 - 1993	Ken Hood
1993 - 1996	Norman McBurney OBE
1996 - 2000	Edwin McLaughlin
2000 - 2014	Robert Cupples
2014 -	John Taggart

Treasurer

1928 - 1934	John Watt
1934 - 1935	J.P. Delaney
1935 - 1936	John Watt
1936 - 1940	Samuel Callender
1946 - 1948	James Andrews & Alfred Kennedy
1948 - 1949	Alfred Kennedy
1949 - 1950	James Eaton
1950 - 1953	William Ward
1953 -1954	James O'Neill
1954 - 1955	James Owens
1955 - 1957	William McNeice
1957 - 1959	James Andrews
1959 - 1961	Robert Gribben
1961 - 1966	Robert Read
1966 - 1968	Herbert Magill
1968 - 1969	Hugo Colgan
1969 - 1970	Guy McCullough
1970 - 1991	Ken Hood
1991 - 1997	Jimmy Gray
1997 - 2000	Robert Cupples
2000 - 2012	Noel Millar
2012 -	Bill Parkinson

Vice Chairman

1946 - 1948	Simon McCrory
1948 - 1949	John Watt
1949 - 1950	Alfred Kennedy
1950 - 1951	Simon McCrory
1951 - 1952	Leslie Woodside
1952 - 1953	Samuel Graham
1953 - 1956	John Wallace
1956 - 1957	R.J. Hamilton
1957 - 1965	James Rock
1966 - 1968	Billy Swann
1969 - 1973	James Rock
1973 - 1975	Tom Cubitt
1975 - 1978	Samuel Magill
1978 - 1982	Brian Millar
1982 - 1985	David McKeown
1985 - 1987	Gordon McIlrath
1987 - 1989	Jimmy Gray
1989 - 1993	Norman McBurney OBE
1993 – 1999	Gordon McIlrath
1999 - 2010	Maurice Smyth
2010 - 2011	John Blair
2012 - 2014	John Taggart
2014 -	Don Stirling

Secretary

1928 - 1934	Samuel Eagleson
1934 - 1971	William McNeice
1971 - 1986	Jimmy Coulter
1986 - 1987	Ken Barr
1987 - 2000	Don Stirling
2000 - 2002	Billy Bell
2002 -	Don Stirling

Company Secretary

2002 - 2003	Jim Bolon
2003 - 2010	Kenny Whitbread
2010 - 2013	Neil Coleman
2013 - 2015	George Dillon
2015 -	John Torrington

Managers

All periods where no individual manager was appointed, team affairs were managed by a selection committee consisting of members of the club management committee.

Jul 1934 - May 1935	Joe Miller
Sep 1937 - Nov 1938	Steve Mitchell
Jun 1946 - Sep 1946	William Reid
Jun 1947 - May 1949	Bob McKay
Aug 1949 - May 1950	Billy McMillan
May 1950 - Mar 1951	Norman Kernaghan
Aug 1953 - Jun 1954	Samuel Picken
Aug 1954 - May 1955	Walter Rickett
Oct 1957 - Jan 1960	Alex McCrae
Mar 1960 - May 1963	Geoff Twentyman
Nov 1963 - Dec 1964	David Hickson
Jan 1965 - Oct 1966	George Smith
Dec 1966 - Jan 1967	Norman Clarke (caretaker)
Sep 1967 - Dec 1967	David Hickson
Jan 1968 - Dec 1969	Alex Parker
Dec 1969 - Aug 1971	Alex McCrae
Aug 1971 - Mar 1976	Arthur Stewart
Mar 1976 - Apr 1977	Eddie Russell
Apr 1977 - May 1977	Alex McKee (caretaker)
May 1977 - Jan 1979	Billy Johnston
Feb 1979 - Feb 1982	Alan Campbell
Feb 1982 - Feb 1983	Ivan Murray
Feb 1983 - Apr 1983	Alec Donald (caretaker)
Apr 1983 - Nov 1983	Ian Russell
Nov 1983 - Dec 1983	Alec Donald (caretaker)
Dec 1983 - Jun 1984	Jim Platt
Jun 1984 - Apr 1985	Alan Campbell
May 1985 - Sep 1987	Jimmy Brown
Sep 1987 - Apr 1991	Alex McKee
May 1991 - Sep 1993	Jim Hagan
Oct 1993 - Oct 1994	Tommy Jackson
Oct 1994 - Mar 1995	Gary Erwin
Mar 1995 - Apr 1999	Alan Fraser
Apr 1999 - May 1999	Shay Hamill (caretaker)
May 1999 - Dec 2000	Nigel Best
Dec 2000 - Jan 2001	George Magill (caretaker)
Jan 2001 - May 2005	Kenny Shiels
May 2005 - Apr 2008	Tommy Wright
Apr 2008 - May 2008	Jim Grattan
May 2008 - Dec 2011	Roy Walker
Dec 2011	Joe McCall (caretaker)
Dec 2011 - Present	Glenn Ferguson

Results

Competition key:

League competitions
IL – Irish League (including Premier Division post 1995); NRL – Northern Regional League; FD – First Division

Domestic Cup competitions
IC – Irish Cup; GC – Gold Cup; CC – City Cup; CAS – County Antrim Shield; UC-Ulster Cup; FBC – Festival of Britain Cup; TFT – Top Four Trophy; CBC – Carlsberg Cup; LC – League Cup; FC – Floodlit Cup; CAC – County Antrim Centenary Chalice; CS – Charity Shield

All-Ireland and UK competitions
ICC – Inter-City Cup; AIC – Blaxnit All-Ireland Cup; TXC – Texaco Cup; TC – Tyler All-Ireland Cup; INC – Irish News Cup

European competitions
ECWC – European Cup Winners' Cup; UEFA – UEFA Cup; INT – UEFA Intertoto Cup

Misc.
TEST – Testimonial; FR – Friendly

Ballymena Football & Athletic Club Results (1928 – 1934)

Played: 46, won: 24, drawn: 10, lost: 12, goals scored: 127, goals conceded: 82

Irish League: 6th; Irish Cup: Winners; Gold Cup: Round 1; City Cup: Runners-up; County Antrim Shield: Quarter-final

Date	Comp	Venue	Opponents	Result	Scorers
20/08/1928	IL 1	H	Belfast Celtic	L 0-3	-
25/08/1928	IL 2	A	Larne	D 2-2	McCambridge; D. Reid
01/09/1928	IL 3	A	Coleraine	D 3-3	McCambridge; Shiels 2
05/09/1928	GC rd1	A	Ards	L 0-2	-
08/09/1928	IL 4	A	Ards	W 2-1	Shiels; McCambridge
15/09/1928	IL 5	H	Cliftonville	W 4-0	Shiels 2; McCambridge; Mitchell
29/09/1928	IL 6	A	Glentoran	D 2-2	J. Reid; Shaw
06/10/1928	IL 7	H	Distillery	W 5-3	Shiels 3, McCambridge; Cunning
13/10/1928	IL 8	A	Bangor	D 2-2	J. Reid; Shiels
20/10/1928	IL 9	H	Linfield	W 4-2	Shaw; McCambridge 2; Shiels
27/10/1928	IL 10	A	Glenavon	D 1-1	McCambridge
03/11/1928	IL 11	A	Newry Town	D 2-2	Shaw; Shiels
10/11/1928	IL 12	H	Queen's Island	W 7-3	Shiels 5; Mitchell; D. Reid
17/11/1928	IL 13	A	Portadown	W 5-3	McCambridge 2; Mitchell; Clarke; Shiels
24/11/1928	IC rd1	A	Glentoran	D 3-3	Shaw; McCambridge 2
28/11/1928	IC rd1 rep	H	Glentoran	W 2-1	McCambridge 2
01/12/1928	IL 14	A	Belfast Celtic	L 2-3	Gilmore; McCambridge
08/12/1928	IL 15	H	Larne	W 2-1	D. Reid; McCambridge
15/12/1928	IL 16	A	Coleraine	D 0-0	-
22/12/1928	IL 17	H	Ards	W 4-2	Shiels 2; Clarke 2
25/12/1928	IL 18	A	Cliftonville	L 2-3	Shiels; Morrow
26/12/1928	IL 19	H	Glentoran	W 3-0	Morrow; McCambridge; Shiels
29/12/1928	IL 20	A	Distillery	L 1-5	McCambridge
05/01/1929	IL 21	H	Bangor	L 1-2	McNinch
12/01/1929	IC qf	H	Broadway United	W 4-1	Mitchell 2; McCambridge; Gilmore
19/01/1929	IL 22	H	Glenavon	D 2-2	Quigley; Morrow
26/01/1929	IL 23	A	Newry Town	L 0-1	-
02/02/1929	IL 24	H	Queen's Island	W 7-0	Shiels 5; Cassidy; Mitchell
09/02/1929	IC sf	N	Coleraine	W 3-0	McCambridge 2; Mitchell
16/02/1929	CC 1	H	Belfast Celtic	W 2-1	Mitchell; Cassidy
20/02/1929	CAS qf	H	Linfield	L 1-2	D. Reid
23/02/1929	IL 25	H	Portadown	L 1-3	McCambridge
25/02/1929	IL 26	A	Linfield	L 0-6	-
02/03/1929	CC 2	A	Portadown	L 3-4	McCambridge; Shiels; D. Reid
16/03/1929	CC 3	H	Ards	W 3-0	Shiels 3
23/03/1929	CC 4	A	Coleraine	W 2-0	Morrow; Howard
30/03/1929	IC f	N	Belfast Celtic	W 2-1	Shiels; McCambridge
01/04/1929	CC 5	H	Larne	W 5-1	Shiels 3; Mitchell 2
02/04/1929	CC 6	A	Cliftonville	W 4-1	Cassidy; Shiels; McCambridge; Mitchell
06/04/1929	CC 7	H	Glentoran	W 4-2	Shiels 2; McCambridge; Mitchell
13/04/1929	CC 8	A	Distillery	W 3-0	McCambridge 2; Cassidy
20/04/1929	CC 9	H	Newry Town	W 7-1	Mitchell 4; Shiels 2; D. Reid
27/04/1929	CC 10	A	Queen's Island	D 3-3	Mitchell 2; Shiels
29/04/1929	FR	H	Kilmarnock	L 0-1	-
04/05/1929	CC 11	H	Bangor	W 8-2	McCambridge 2; Cassidy 2; Mitchell 2; Shiels; J. Reid
11/05/1929	CC 12	A	Linfield	L 0-3	-
15/05/1929	CC 13	H	Glenavon	W 4-1	Mitchell; Girvan; Shiels; McCambridge
18/05/1929	FR	A	Shamrock Rovers	W 2-1	Cassidy; Shiels

Notes

09/02/1929 v. Coleraine: Match played Windsor Park

30/03/1929 v. Belfast Celtic: Match played at Solitude

Player Appearances and Goals

BENTLEY	7	0	McDAIRMID Gordon	45	0
BONNAR	1	0	McNINCH John	41	1
CASSIDY Joseph	17	6	MITCHELL James	37	21
CLARKE William	28	2	MORROW John	13	4
CUNNING David	7	1	NELSON David	7	0
EVANS	2	0	PARKINSON William	1	0
GILMORE H	13	2	QUIGLEY Edward	1	1
GIRVAN William	3	1	REID David	42	6
GOUGH John	44	0	REID John	39	3
HANNA Thomas	2	0	SHAW Richard	28	4
HOWARD Sydney	36	1	SHIELS Jamie	37	42
KIMLIN William	2	0	WEBSTER Sydney	5	0
McCAMBRIDGE James	44	32	WOODROW James	4	0

Date	Comp	Venue	Opponents	Result	Scorers
21/08/1929	IL 1	H	Portadown	D 2-2	Cassidy; McCambridge
24/08/1929	IL 2	A	Newry Town	L 0-2	-
31/08/1929	IL 3	A	Derry City	D 1-1	Arlow
04/09/1929	GC rd1	H	Belfast Celtic	L 0-3	-
07/09/1929	IL 4	H	Belfast Celtic	D 1-1	Shiels
14/09/1929	IL 5	A	Ards	W 2-0	Hanna 2
21/09/1929	IL 6	H	Linfield	L 1-4	Bassnett
28/09/1929	IL 7	A	Cliftonville	W 2-0	Gilmore; McCambridge
05/10/1929	IL 8	H	Glenavon	W 5-0	Gilmore 2; Shiels 2; McCambridge
12/10/1929	IL 9	A	Larne	W 2-1	Shiels 2
26/10/1929	IL 10	H	Coleraine	L 0-1	-
02/11/1929	IL 11	A	Distillery	L 1-3	Kilpatrick
09/11/1929	IL 12	H	Bangor	W 4-0	McCambridge; Shiels; Cassidy 2
16/11/1929	IL 13	A	Glentoran	W 2-1	Girvan; Murphy
23/11/1929	IL 14	A	Portadown	L 3-5	Shiels 2; Cassidy
30/11/1929	IC rd1	A	Derry City	W 4-1	Cassidy; Shiels 2; Howard
07/12/1929	IL 15	H	Newry Town	W 3-0	Arlow; Shiels; Howard
14/12/1929	IL 16	A	Derry City	W 4-0	McCambridge; Murphy; Shiels; D. Reid
21/12/1929	IL 17	A	Belfast Celtic	L 3-4	Cassidy 2; Shiels
25/12/1929	IL 18	H	Ards	L 1-3	McCambridge
26/12/1929	IL 19	A	Linfield	W 7-4	McCambridge 3; Cassidy 3; Shiels
28/12/1929	IL 20	H	Cliftonville	W 7-1	Murphy 3; Shiels; McCambridge 3
11/01/1930	IC qf	A	Belfast Celtic	W 3-2	Cassidy; McCambridge 2
18/01/1930	IL 21	A	Coleraine	L 1-2	McCambridge
22/01/1930	IL 22	H	Larne	W 3-1	D. Reid; Kilpatrick; Shiels
25/01/1930	IL 23	H	Distillery	W 6-3	D. Reid; Shiels 3; Arlow; McCambridge
29/01/1930	CAS rd1	H	Bangor	L 1-5	Murphy
01/02/1930	IL 24	A	Glenavon	L 1-3	Cassidy
08/02/1930	IC sf	N	Newry Town	W 3-1	Cassidy; McCambridge; Murphy
15/02/1930	IL 25	H	Glentoran	W 2-1	Murphy; Cassidy
19/02/1930	IL 26	A	Bangor	L 1-3	Dalrymple
22/02/1930	CC 1	H	Cliftonville	W 4-0	Murphy; Shiels 2; Howard
08/03/1930	CC 2	A	Coleraine	D 2-2	Shiels; Cassidy
15/03/1930	CC 3	H	Linfield	D 2-2	Dalrymple; Shiels
22/03/1930	CC 4	A	Portadown	L 2-3	Shiels; Gilmore
29/03/1930	IC f	N	Linfield	L 3-4	D. Reid; Shiels 2
05/04/1930	CC 5	A	Ards	L 0-2	-
12/04/1930	CC 6	H	Belfast Celtic	W 3-0	Murphy 2; Shiels
15/04/1930	FR	H	Everton	W 2-1	Shiels; Cassidy
19/04/1930	CC 7	A	Newry Town	W 2-1	O'Reilly; Shiels
21/04/1930	CC 8	H	Glenavon	L 1-3	Murphy
22/04/1930	CC 9	A	Derry City	L 0-2	-
26/04/1930	CC 10	A	Glentoran	D 4-4	Gilmore; D. Reid; Murphy; Dalrymple
30/04/1930	FR	H	Kilmarnock	W 3-1	Murphy 2; Gilmour
02/05/1930	CC 11	A	Larne	L 1-2	Moore
09/05/1930	CC 12	H	Bangor	L 0-2	-
14/05/1930	CC 13	A	Distillery	W 3-2	Shiels 2; Armstrong
17/05/1930	FR	A	Bohemians	L 2-5	D. Reid; Shiels

Notes

08/02/1930 v. Newry Town: Match played at Solitude

29/03/1930 v. Linfield: Match played Celtic Park

Player Appearances and Goals

ARLOW George	9	3	McDAIRMID Gordon	40	0
ARMSTRONG	2	1	McKEAN James	3	0
BASSNETT Alfred	33	1	McNINCH John	35	0
CASSIDY Joseph	29	15	MITCHELL James	8	0
DALRYMPLE Jonathan	25	3	MOORE	1	1
GILMORE H	13	5	MURPHY Jamie	32	13
GIRVAN William	8	1	NELSON David	15	0
GOUGH John	39	0	O'BRIEN John	1	0
HANNA Thomas	2	2	O'REILLY	9	1
HOWARD Sydney	44	3	REID David	39	5
KILPATRICK Thomas	30	2	SHANNON	3	0
KIRKWOOD James	3	0	SHIELS Jamie	44	30
McCAMBRIDGE James	27	17	WILSON R	1	0

Date	Comp	Venue	Opponents	Result	Scorers
20/08/1930	IL 1	A	Cliftonville	L 3-4	Murphy; Howard; Kimlin
23/08/1930	IL 2	H	Distillery	W 4-0	Kimlin; Murphy 2; Dalrymple
30/08/1930	IL 3	A	Coleraine	D 1-1	Rainey og.
03/09/1930	GC rd1	H	Newry Town	W 7-0	Shiels 3; Murphy 3; Kilpatrick
06/09/1930	IC 4	H	Portadown	W 7-1	Cassidy; Stewart; Shaw; Murphy 2; Kimlin; Dalrymple
13/09/1930	IL 5	H	Glentoran	L 2-4	Cassidy; Murphy
17/09/1930	GC qf	A	Linfield	L 0-5	-
20/09/1930	IL 6	A	Ards	W 6-3	Murphy 3; Turkington 3
27/09/1930	IL 7	H	Linfield	D 2-2	Murphy; McNinch
04/10/1930	IL 8	A	Newry Town	W 1-0	Nelson
11/10/1930	IL 9	H	Derry City	W 4-1	Murphy 3; Cassidy
18/10/1930	IL 10	A	Glenavon	D 1-1	Dalrymple
25/10/1930	IL 11	H	Larne	W 3-1	Howard 2; Murphy
01/11/1930	IL 12	A	Bangor	W 6-2	Howard 2; Cassidy 2; Shiels; Dalrymple
08/11/1930	IL 13	H	Belfast Celtic	W 4-1	Murphy 3; McCandless
19/11/1930	IL 14	H	Cliftonville	D 2-2	Shiels 2
22/11/1930	IL 15	A	Distillery	W 2-1	Howard; Gilmour
29/11/1930	IC rd1	H	Cliftonville	W 2-1	Dalrymple; Murphy
06/12/1930	IL 16	H	Coleraine	L 2-3	Murphy; Gilmour
13/12/1930	IL 17	A	Portadown	L 1-3	Gilmour
20/12/1930	IL 18	A	Glentoran	D 2-2	Gilmour 2
25/12/1930	IL 19	H	Ards	W 5-1	Cassidy; Gilmour 4
26/12/1930	IL 20	A	Linfield	L 1-2	Gilmour
27/12/1930	IL 21	H	Newry Town	W 6-1	Howard 3; Gilmour 2; Nelson
03/01/1931	IL 22	A	Derry City	W 2-1	Shiels; Shaw
10/01/1931	IC qf	A	Bangor	D 2-2	Gilmour 2
14/01/1931	IC qf rep	H	Bangor	W 2-0	Shaw; Shiels
17/01/1931	IL 23	A	Larne	L 0-4	-
21/01/1931	IL 24	H	Glenavon	W 6-1	Murphy; Gilmour 3; Cassidy; Shiels
24/01/1931	IL 25	H	Bangor	L 1-4	Kimlin
28/01/1931	CAS rd1	H	Ards	D 1-1	Dalrymple
31/01/1931	IL 26	A	Belfast Celtic	L 1-4	Shaw
02/02/1931	CAS rd1 rep	A	Ards	L 1-4	Turkington
07/02/1931	IC sf	N	Derry City	W 2-1	Gilmour; Kilpatrick
11/02/1931	CC 1	H	Cliftonville	W 4-2	Murphy; Gilmour 3
14/02/1931	CC 2	A	Derry City	L 1-5	Shiels
28/02/1931	CC 3	H	Portadown	D 4-4	Cassidy; Gilmour; Murphy; Kilpatrick
07/03/1931	CC 4	A	Belfast Celtic	D 2-2	Gilmour 2
14/03/1931	CC 5	A	Distillery	L 2-4	Kimlin; Murphy
21/03/1931	CC 6	A	Ards	D 3-3	Howard 2; Murphy
28/03/1931	IC f	N	Linfield	L 0-3	-
04/04/1931	CC 7	H	Linfield	L 2-4	Shiels; McCready
06/04/1931	CC 8	A	Newry Town	L 0-1	-
07/04/1931	CC 9	H	Glentoran	L 1-5	McCready
11/04/1931	CC 10	A	Coleraine	W 3-2	Reid; Murphy 2
18/04/1931	CC 11	H	Glenavon	W 5-1	Murphy 2; Cameron; McCready 2
25/04/1931	CC 12	A	Larne	W 4-3	Gilmour; Murphy; Shiels; Cameron
02/05/1931	CC 13	H	Bangor	W 6-1	Murphy 4; Shiels 2

Notes

07/02/1931 v. Derry City: Match played at Solitude

28/03/1931 v. Linfield: Match played The Oval

Player Appearances and Goals

BLACK	17	0	McCREADY William	11	4
BLAIR Robert	9	0	McKEAN James	17	0
BLAKE John	2	0	McNINCH John	41	1
CAMERON Ronald	3	2	MURPHY Jamie	37	36
CASSIDY Joseph	38	8	NELSON David	39	2
DALRYMPLE Jonathan	28	6	O'REILLY	7	0
GILMOUR James	21	25	REID David	47	1
HOWARD Sydney	20	11	SHAW Richard	15	4
JAMIESON	1	0	SHIELS Jamie	32	14
KILPATRICK Thomas	30	3	SIMPSON	1	0
KIMLIN William	14	5	STEWART Robert	43	1
McCANDLESS William	47	1	TURKINGTON George	5	4
McCANN Patrick	1	0	WOODS	1	0
McCARTNEY	1	0			

Played: 48, won: 25, drawn: 7, lost: 16, goals scored: 114, goals conceded: 77

Irish League: 6th; Irish Cup: Quarter-final; Gold Cup: Finalists; City Cup: 5th; County Antrim Shield: Quarter-final

Date	Comp	Venue	Opponents	Result	Scorers
20/08/1931	IL1	H	Derry City	D 0-0	-
22/08/1931	IL 2	A	Portadown	L 0-1	-
29/08/1931	IL 3	H	Cliftonville	L 3-5	Lamont; McNinch; Mitchell
02/09/1931	GC rd1	H	Distillery	W 1-0	Cameron
05/09/1931	IL 4	A	Larne	L 0-3	-
12/09/1931	IL 5	A	Linfield	L 0-2	-
16/09/1931	GC qf	H	Ards	W 3-1	Cox; Cameron; McCandless
19/09/1931	IL 6	H	Ards	W 6-2	Barr 2; Cox; Cameron; Stoddart 2
26/09/1931	IL 7	A	Newry Town	D 1-1	Murphy
03/10/1931	IL 8	H	Coleraine	W 7-0	McCready; Cox; Barr 2; Flannagan; Stewart; Murphy
10/10/1931	IL 9	A	Glenavon	W 4-0	Murphy; McNinch; Haddow; Cox
21/10/1931	GC sf	N	Linfield	W 3-0	Barr 3
24/10/1931	IL 10	H	Bangor	W 6-4	Barr 4; Murphy; McNinch
31/10/1931	IL 11	A	Belfast Celtic	L 1-2	McNinch
07/11/1931	IL 12	H	Distillery	W 4-0	Barr 3; Haddow
14/11/1931	IL 13	A	Glentoran	L 0-3	-
21/11/1931	IL 14	A	Derry City	D 2-2	Barr; Stoddart
28/11/1931	IC rd1	H	Distillery	W 3-1	Cox; Haddow; Murphy
09/12/1931	GC f	N	Coleraine	L 0-3	-
12/12/1931	IL 15	H	Portadown	L 2-3	Stoddart; McCready
19/12/1931	IL 16	A	Cliftonville	D 1-1	J.P. Surgenor
25/12/1931	IL 17	H	Larne	W 2-0	Barr; Cox
29/12/1931	IL 18	A	Ards	D 1-1	Stoddart
02/01/1932	IL 19	H	Newry Town	W 6-2	Haddow; J.P. Surgenor 3; Stoddart 2
09/01/1932	IC qf	H	Glentoran	D 2-2	McMeekin og; Barr
13/01/1932	IC qf rep	A	Glentoran	L 1-3	McNinch
16/01/1932	IL 20	H	Glenavon	W 4-1	McNinch; Stoddart 2; Stewart
21/01/1932	IL 21	A	Coleraine	L 1-4	Barr
23/01/1932	IL 22	A	Bangor	W 3-2	Barr 3
27/01/1932	CAS rd1	A	Brantwood	W 4-1	Stewart; Stoddart; Cox; Barr
30/01/1932	IL 23	H	Belfast Celtic	W 6-0	Cox 2; Barr 3; Haddow
06/02/1932	IL 24	A	Distillery	L 0-2	-
13/02/1932	IL 25	H	Glentoran	W 5-0	Stoddart; Barr 3; Murphy
20/02/1932	CC 1	H	Belfast Celtic	L 1-2	Hood
24/02/1932	CAS qf	A	Belfast Celtic	L 0-2	-
27/02/1932	CC 2	A	Bangor	L 0-2	-
02/03/1932	IL 26	H	Linfield	W 2-0	Cameron; Haddow
05/03/1932	CC 3	A	Coleraine	W 4-0	Stoddart 2; Barr; McNinch
12/03/1932	CC 4	A	Glentoran	W 3-2	Cameron 2; Haddow
19/03/1932	CC 5	H	Larne	W 3-1	Cameron; Haddow; Murphy
26/03/1932	FR	H	Bedouins	W 6-0	Stewart; Cameron 3; Haddow 2
28/03/1932	CC 6	A	Glenavon	W 3-1	Cameron; Barr; Stoddart
29/03/1932	CC 7	H	Derry City	D 2-2	Stewart; Stoddart
02/04/1932	CC 8	A	Cliftonville	W 3-2	Barr; Haddow; Stoddart
09/04/1932	CC 9	H	Ards	W 4-1	Haddow 3; Cameron
16/04/1932	CC 10	A	Linfield	L 0-4	-
23/04/1932	CC 11	H	Newry Town	W 3-0	Haddow 2; Stoddart
30/04/1932	CC 12	A	Distillery	L 1-4	Barr
07/05/1932	CC 13	A	Portadown	W 3-2	Flannagan; Mitchell; Haddow

Notes

21/10/1931 v. Linfield: Match played at Celtic Park
09/12/1931 v. Coleraine: Match played Solitude

Player Appearances and Goals

BARR John	38	32	McCANDLESS William	44	1
BEGGS Joseph	1	0	McCREADY William	12	2
BLAIR Robert	1	0	McDOWELL William	3	0
CAMERON Ronald	19	9	McNINCH John	46	7
COX Walter	34	9	McQUILLAN H	3	0
DAVISON Robert	6	0	MITCHELL James	16	2
DUNLOP W	1	0	MURPHY Jamie	28	7
FISHER	1	0	NELSON David	12	0
FLANNIGAN David	28	2	RUSSELL	1	0
GRAHAM	1	0	STEWART Robert	48	4
HADDOW Andrew	37	15	STODDART Robert	33	17
HODGE David	6	0	SURGENOR J.P.	28	0
HOOD William	26	1	SURGENOR James	5	4
KING James	44	0	TILLY Harold	2	0
LAMONT Thomas	3	1	WYLIE	1	0

Date	Comp	Venue	Opponents	Result	Scorers
20/08/1932	IL 1	A	Newry Town	W 5-3	Shiels 2; Stewart 2; Patterson
24/08/1932	IL 2	H	Glentoran	L 2-3	Patterson 2
27/08/1932	IL 3	A	Coleraine	L 0-3	-
03/09/1932	IL 4	H	Glenavon	W 3-1	McPherson; Barr; McClelland
07/09/1932	GC qf	H	Larne	W 5-1	Patterson; Lee; Barr; McNinch; McPherson
10/09/1932	IL 5	A	Ards	W 4-0	McClelland; Lee; McPherson; McNinch
24/09/1932	IL 6	H	Larne	W 2-1	Shiels; Lee
08/10/1932	IL 7	A	Linfield	L 0-2	-
15/10/1932	IL 8	H	Distillery	L 1-3	Lee
22/10/1932	IL 9	A	Derry City	L 0-1	-
26/10/1932	IL 10	H	Portadown	W 5-1	Shiels 3; McClelland; McPherson
29/10/1932	IL 11	A	Bangor	L 3-5	Patterson; Shiels 2
05/11/1932	IL 12	H	Belfast Celtic	D 1-1	McNinch
09/11/1932	GC sf	N	Linfield	D 2-2	Lee; Patterson
12/11/1932	IL 13	A	Cliftonville	L 1-6	McElfatrick
16/11/1932	GC sf rep	A	Linfield	L 1-2	Paterson
19/11/1932	IL 14	H	Newry Town	W 2-1	Murphy; McPherson
26/11/1932	IL 15	A	Glentoran	L 1-6	Murphy
03/12/1932	IL 16	H	Coleraine	W 2-1	Lee; Stewart
10/12/1932	IL 17	A	Glenavon	W 1-0	McElfatrick
17/12/1932	IL 18	H	Ards	W 8-2	McElfatrick 5; Patterson; Lee 2
24/12/1932	IL 19	A	Larne	D 2-2	McElfatrick; Shiels
26/12/1932	IL 20	H	Linfield	L 0-1	-
27/12/1932	IL 21	A	Distillery	D 2-2	Lee; McElfatrick
31/12/1932	IL 22	H	Derry City	W 3-1	Shiels; McElfatrick; McPherson
07/01/1933	IL 23	A	Portadown	W 4-1	Lee; Shiels; McElfatrick 2
14/01/1933	IC rd1	H	Cliftonville	L 2-4	Paterson; Shiels
21/01/1933	IL 24	H	Bangor	L 1-3	Shiels
28/01/1933	IL 25	A	Belfast Celtic	L 2-7	McElfatrick; Barr
31/01/1933	CAS rd1	A	Larne	W 5-1	McPherson 2; Paterson; McClelland; Barr
04/02/1933	IL 26	H	Cliftonville	D 1-1	Lee
18/02/1933	CC 1	A	Distillery	L 1-2	McPherson
22/02/1933	CC 2	H	Cliftonville	W 7-0	McClelland 2; Lee 2; Stewart; Shiels; Barr
25/02/1933	CC 3	H	Coleraine	W 3-1	Barr 2; J.P. Surgenor
02/03/1933	CAS qf	A	Ards	L 0-1	-
04/03/1933	CC 4	A	Portadown	D 1-1	J.P. Surgenor
18/03/1933	CC 5	H	Ards	D 1-1	J.P. Surgenor
20/03/1933	CC 6	A	Glentoran	L 0-4	-
25/03/1933	CC 7	A	Linfield	L 0-1	-
01/04/1933	CC 8	H	Newry Town	W 1-0	Shiels
15/04/1933	CC 9	A	Derry City	L 0-4	-
17/04/1933	CC 10	A	Glenavon	W 2-1	Paterson; McPherson
18/04/1933	CC 11	A	Larne	L 1-3	Lee
22/04/1933	CC 12	H	Bangor	L 2-3	J.P. Surgenor; Lee
29/04/1933	CC 13	A	Belfast Celtic	L 2-4	McClelland; Shiels

Notes

09/11/1932 v. Linfield: Match played at Grosvenor Park

Player Appearances and Goals

BAILIE	13	0	McPHERSON James	43	10
BARR John	26	7	McQUILLAN H	2	0
DAVIDSON Robert	7	0	MITCHELL	3	0
KING James	31	0	MURPHY	2	2
LEE Patrick	40	15	PATERSON William	45	3
McALLISTER Daniel Martin	3	0	PATTERSON Daniel	27	8
McCANDLESS William	42	0	RUSSELL	3	0
McCLELLAND James	34	7	SHIELS Jamie	34	16
McDOWELL William	11	0	STEWART Robert	44	4
McELFATRICK Alistair	19	13	SURGENOR J.P.	10	4
McILROY Charles	2	0	SURGENOR James	13	0
McNINCH John	41	3			

Played: 42, won: 16, drawn: 9, lost: 17, goals scored: 88, goals conceded: 92

Irish League: 5th; Irish Cup: Quarter-final; Gold Cup: Quarter-final; City Cup: 13th; County Antrim Shield: Round 1

Date	Comp	Venue	Opponents	Result	Scorers
21/08/1933	IL 1	A	Newry Town	D 2-2	S. Mahood; Shiels
23/08/1933	IL 2	H	Larne	W 4-2	Shiels 2; J. Mahood; S. Mahood
26/08/1933	IL 3	A	Linfield	L 0-3	-
02/09/1933	IL 4	H	Coleraine	W 4-2	McIlroy 2; Lucas 2
05/09/1933	GC rd1	A	Larne	D 1-1	J. Mahood
09/09/1933	IL 5	A	Distillery	L 0-1	-
13/09/1933	GC rd1 rep	H	Larne	W 3-0	S. Mahood; McIlroy; Lucas
16/09/1933	IL 6	H	Portadown	W 1-0	O'Hara
23/09/1933	IL 7	A	Cliftonville	W 3-0	Shiels; S. Mahood; McIlroy
07/10/1933	IL 8	H	Derry City	W 2-1	Lucas 2
11/10/1933	GC qf	H	Glentoran	L 1-2	Lucas
19/10/1933	IL 9	A	Bangor	W 3-2	Shiels 2; Lucas
21/10/1933	IL 10	H	Belfast Celtic	W 2-1	Lucas 2
28/10/1933	IL 11	H	Ards	D 2-2	Williamson; McCormick
11/11/1933	IL 12	A	Glentoran	D 1-1	McIlroy
18/11/1933	IL 13	A	Glenavon	D 3-3	Shiels 2; McIlroy
25/11/1933	IL 14	H	Newry Town	W 7-0	Lucas 5; Shiels; S. Mahood
02/12/1933	IL 15	H	Larne	W 3-0	McIlroy 2; Lucas
09/12/1933	IL 16	H	Linfield	L 2-4	McIlroy 2
16/12/1933	IL 17	A	Coleraine	D 0-0	-
23/12/1933	IL 18	H	Distillery	W 4-2	Lucas 2; Shiels; McCormick
25/12/1933	IL 19	A	Portadown	L 0-1	-
26/12/1933	IL 20	H	Cliftonville	L 1-4	Shiels
30/12/1933	IL 21	A	Derry City	D 2-2	Shiels; S. Mahood
06/01/1934	IL 22	H	Bangor	W 5-0	Wallace 2; Shiels 2; Williamson
13/01/1934	IC rd1	A	Glenavon	W 3-1	Shiels 2; Hoy og
20/01/1934	IL 23	A	Belfast Celtic	L 2-3	Shiels; Williamson
27/01/1934	IL 24	A	Ards	L 1-2	McIlroy
31/01/1934	CAS rd1	A	Linfield	L 1-6	Williamson
03/02/1934	IL 25	H	Glentoran	W 3-1	Williamson 2; Shiels
10/02/1934	IC qf	A	Belfast Celtic	L 1-4	Shiels
14/02/1934	IL 26	A	Glenavon	L 2-7	McCormick; Shiels
17/02/1934	CC 1	H	Coleraine	D 3-3	S. Mahood; Williamson; Shiels
24/02/1934	CC 2	A	Glenavon	L 1-5	Wallace
03/03/1934	CC 3	H	Ards	W 7-2	McIlroy; McCormick 3; Shiels; S. Mahood; Williamson
12/03/1934	CC 4	A	Linfield	L 0-6	-
17/03/1934	CC 5	H	Newry Town	W 5-1	Shiels 3; McCormick; Lunn og
24/03/1934	CC 6	A	Larne	L 1-2	Williamson
31/03/1934	CC 7	H	Distillery	L 1-4	Shiels
02/04/1934	CC 8	A	Derry City	L 0-5	-
03/04/1934	CC 9	H	Portadown	D 0-0	-
07/04/1934	CC 10	A	Bangor	L 1-4	McLoughlin og

Player Appearances and Goals

Player	Apps	Goals	Player	Apps	Goals
CASSON	6	0	McILROY Charles	39	12
DAVISON Robert	5	0	McNEILL	1	0
FEE	4	0	McNINCH John	34	0
FLANNIGAN David	26	0	MILLS	1	0
GILL	3	0	MORGAN Gerard	8	0
HANSON	1	0	O'HARA	1	1
HERBISON	5	0	POLLOCK	1	0
KING James	36	0	RUSSELL	2	0
LECKEY Ernest	4	0	SHIELS Jamie	36	26
LUCAS Frank	18	17	SMITH	1	0
MAGEE	5	0	STEWART Robert	42	0
MAHOOD Jack	11	1	SURGENOR J.P.	4	0
MAHOOD Stanley	37	9	SURGENOR Jamie	1	0
McALLISTER Daniel Martin	1	0	WALLACE Jack	21	3
McCORMICK Edward	28	7	WILLIAMSON John	38	9
McDIARMID Gordon	42	0			

Ballymena United Football Club Results (1934 – 2015)

Date	Comp	Venue	Opponents	Result	Scorers
18/08/1934	IL 1	A	Glentoran	D 1-1	Campbell
22/08/1934	IL 2	H	Coleraine	W 3-1	E. Mitchell 2; Williamson
25/08/1934	IL 3	A	Glenavon	D 1-1	Moir
29/08/1934	GC rd1	H	Linfield	L 2-4	Williamson; E. Mitchell
01/09/1934	IL 4	A	Bangor	W 4-1	McGowan 2; E. Mitchell; Conlin
08/09/1934	IL 5	H	Linfield	L 1-3	McGowan
15/09/1934	IL 6	A	Newry Town	L 0-2	-
22/09/1934	IL 7	H	Distillery	L 1-4	McGowan
29/09/1934	IL 8	A	Ards	D 2-2	Campbell; McGowan
06/10/1934	IL 9	H	Derry City	L 0-2	-
13/10/1934	IL 10	A	Portadown	W 2-0	McGowan 2
27/10/1934	IL 11	H	Larne	D 1-1	Campbell
03/11/1934	IL 12	A	Belfast Celtic	L 0-3	-
10/11/1934	IL 13	H	Cliftonville	W 5-1	Wallace; Conlin; Berry 2; McGowan
17/11/1934	IL 14	H	Glentoran	L 0-3	-
24/11/1934	IL 15	A	Coleraine	L 1-2	McGowan
01/12/1934	IL 16	H	Glenavon	W 5-1	McNinch; Wallace; Campbell; R. Hargreaves; J. Mitchell
08/12/1934	IL 17	H	Bangor	D 4-4	Wallace; R. Hargreaves 3
15/12/1934	IL 18	A	Linfield	L 0-6	-
22/12/1934	IL 19	H	Newry Town	W 5-2	R. Hargreaves 4; Russell og
25/12/1934	IL 20	A	Distillery	L 2-3	Wallace; R. Hargreaves
26/12/1934	IL 21	H	Ards	W 5-1	R. Hargreaves 2; Campbell 2; E. Hargreaves
29/12/1934	IL 22	A	Derry City	L 3-7	R. Hargreaves; J. Mitchell; E. Hargreaves
05/01/1935	IL 23	H	Portadown	L 1-3	R. Hargreaves
12/01/1935	IL 24	A	Larne	L 0-4	-
19/01/1935	IC rd1	A	Cliftonville	W 1-0	McNinch
26/01/1935	IL 25	H	Belfast Celtic	L 0-3	-
02/02/1935	IL 26	A	Cliftonville	L 1-4	Wallace
09/02/1935	CC 1	H	Belfast Celtic	L 0-5	-
12/02/1935	CAS qf	H	Larne	W 4-2	R. Hargreaves 2; Wallace; E. Hargreaves
16/02/1935	CC 2	H	Bangor	D 2-2	Wallace; McNinch
23/02/1935	IC qf	A	Distillery	W 3-2	McNinch; R. Hargreaves; Campbell
27/02/1935	CC 3	A	Derry City	L 1-7	R. Hargreaves
02/03/1935	CC 4	A	Larne	L 0-2	-
06/03/1935	CAS sf	N	Linfield	L 0-4	-
09/03/1935	CC 5	H	Glentoran	L 2-3	Campbell; R. Hargreaves
16/03/1935	IC sf	N	Glentoran	L 0-3	-
21/03/1935	CC 6	A	Portadown	D 1-1	E. Mitchell
23/03/1935	CC 7	H	Newry Town	W 4-2	R. Hargreaves 3; J. Mitchell
30/03/1935	CC 8	A	Linfield	L 0-2	-
13/04/1935	CC 9	H	Ards	W 3-0	J. Mitchell 2; R. Hargreaves
20/04/1935	CC 10	A	Coleraine	W 1-0	R. Hargreaves
22/04/1935	CC 11	A	Distillery	L 2-3	E. Hargreaves; Campbell
23/04/1935	CC 12	H	Glenavon	W 2-1	R. Hargreaves; E. Mitchell
27/04/1935	CC 13	A	Cliftonville	W 2-0	E. Mitchell; R. Hargreaves

Notes

06/03/1935 v. Linfield: Match played at Grosvenor Park

16/03/1935 v. Glentoran: Match played at Solitude

Player Appearances and Goals

AGNEW John	7	0	MATTHEWS Vincent	6	0
BARBOUR	5	0	McDOWELL William	17	0
BERRY	5	2	McGOWAN John	16	9
BLAIR Robert	10	0	McNINCH John	43	2
BUCKLEY Adam	15	0	MILLER Joseph	27	0
CAMPBELL Robert	36	8	MITCHELL Edward	20	7
CONLIN George	41	2	MITCHELL Jonathan	26	5
CORRY	2	0	MITCHELL Steve	45	0
DIFFIN Jack	5	0	MOIR James	6	1
DRAIN	1	0	ORR Hugh	1	0
GIFFEN	1	0	PRATT William	16	0
HARGREAVES Edgar	22	4	SMYTHE	1	0
HARGREAVES Richard	28	24	STEWART	1	0
HILL	1	0	STIRLING George	1	0
HUME	2	0	TIMPERLEY	5	0
KING James	13	0	WALLACE John	35	7
LECKEY Ernest	9	0	WILKINSON Robert	9	0
LEWIS	4	0	WILLIAMSON John	13	2

Played: 44, won: 11, drawn: 9, lost: 24, goals scored: 69, goals conceded: 106

Irish League: 11th; Irish Cup: Round 1; Gold Cup: Semi-final; City Cup: 12th; County Antrim Shield: Round 1

Date	Comp	Venue	Opponents	Result	Scorers
17/08/1935	IL 1	H	Belfast Celtic	L 1-3	Gray
20/08/1935	IL 2	A	Newry Town	L 1-5	J.P. Surgenor
24/08/1935	IL 3	H	Distillery	W 1-0	Barr
31/08/1935	IL 4	A	Derry City	L 0-1	-
04/09/1935	GC rd1	A	Cliftonville	W 4-2	Barr 2; Quinn og; Wa. Jones
07/09/1935	IL 5	H	Bangor	W 4-3	Barr 2; Wi. Jones; Wa. Jones
14/09/1935	IL 6	A	Portadown	L 1-8	Connell
18/09/1935	GC qf	H	Glentoran	W 3-2	Wa. Jones 2; Buckley
21/09/1935	IL 7	A	Linfield	L 2-3	Barr 2
28/09/1935	IL 8	H	Cliftonville	W 2-1	Barr; J. Surgenor
05/10/1935	IL 9	A	Ards	W 5-1	J. Mitchell 4; Wi. Jones
12/10/1935	IL 10	H	Coleraine	W 1-0	Doherty
26/10/1935	IL 11	A	Glentoran	D 2-2	Millar og; J.P. Surgenor
02/11/1935	IL 12	H	Glenavon	W 2-1	Olphert; J. Mitchell
06/11/1935	GC sf	N	Distillery	L 1-2	Wi. Jones
09/11/1935	IL 13	A	Larne	L 1-3	Barr
16/11/1935	IL 14	A	Belfast Celtic	L 0-2	-
23/11/1935	IL 15	H	Newry Town	L 2-3	Wi. Jones; Kerr
30/11/1935	IL 16	A	Distillery	L 0-1	-
07/12/1935	IL 17	H	Derry City	D 2-2	J. Mitchell; J.P. Surgenor
14/12/1935	IL 18	A	Bangor	L 1-2	J.P. Surgenor
21/12/1935	IL 19	H	Portadown	D 2-2	Kerr; Allen og
25/12/1935	IL 20	H	Linfield	D 1-1	Wallace
26/12/1935	IL 21	A	Cliftonville	L 4-5	Wallace; McNinch; Wi. Jones; Davison
28/12/1935	IL 22	H	Ards	D 1-1	Wallace
04/01/1936	IL 23	A	Coleraine	L 0-1	-
11/01/1936	IC rd1	A	Portadown	L 1-3	J.P. Surgenor
18/01/1936	IL 24	H	Glentoran	L 2-4	Millar; Wallace
25/01/1936	IL 25	A	Glenavon	L 0-2	-
01/02/1936	IL 26	H	Larne	W 3-2	J. Mitchell; Wallace 2
08/02/1936	CC 1	H	Glenavon	L 0-1	-
12/02/1936	CAS rd1	A	Distillery	L 1-4	Buckley
15/02/1936	CC 2	A	Derry City	L 0-6	-
22/02/1936	CC 3	H	Coleraine	D 1-1	Tyson
29/02/1936	CC 4	A	Cliftonville	D 2-2	J. Mitchell; Goodall
07/03/1936	CC 5	H	Distillery	L 2-4	McClelland; Tyson
14/03/1936	CC 6	A	Belfast Celtic	D 2-2	Wallace; Fisher
25/03/1936	CC 7	H	Linfield	W 3-0	Billingsley 2; J. Mitchell
28/03/1936	CC 8	A	Glentoran	L 0-4	-
11/04/1936	CC 9	H	Newry Town	D 2-2	Fisher 2
13/04/1936	CC 10	A	Bangor	L 1-2	Fisher
14/04/1936	CC 11	H	Ards	W 4-1	Fisher 3; J. Mitchell
18/04/1936	CC 12	A	Larne	L 2-3	Dalrymple; Fisher
25/04/1936	CC 13	A	Portadown	L 0-2	-
29/04/1936	TEST	H	Linfield	D 4-4	Fisher; Gourley 2; McCartney

Notes

06/11/1935 v. Distillery: Match played at Solitude

29/04/1936 v. Linfield: Testimonial for John McNinch

Player Appearances and Goals

BARR Albert	18	9	McCLELLAND	2	1
BILLINGSLEY James	13	2	McGONNIGLE	1	0
BLAIR Robert	38	0	McKINSTRY	1	0
BUCKLEY Adam	39	2	McNINCH John	35	1
CONNELL Alexander	37	1	MILLAR William	4	1
CRONE	1	0	MITCHELL Jonathan	37	10
CURRAN	3	0	MITCHELL Steve	44	0
DALRYMPLE Jonathan	5	1	MORRIS	1	0
DAVISON Robert	10	1	O'HARA	1	0
DOHERTY	1	1	OLPHERT Robert	14	1
FISHER Daniel	7	8	OWENS W	2	0
GOODALL Bernard	10	1	PENNIE	2	0
GOURLEY Robert	1	0	PHEONIX Frederick	12	0
GRAY Alexander	1	1	SPROULE	1	0
JONES Walter	26	5	SURGENOR J.P.	15	5
JONES William	8	4	SURGENOR James	34	1
KERR	9	2	TYSON William	15	2
LILBURN	1	0	WALLACE Jack	25	7
LYNAS	1	0	WILKINSON Robert	2	0
McALLISTER Daniel Martin	5	0	WILLIAMSON John	2	0

Date	Comp	Venue	Opponents	Result	Scorers
15/08/1936	IL 1	H	Newry Town	L 1-3	McAllister
19/08/1936	IL 2	A	Linfield	L 0-4	-
22/08/1936	IL 3	H	Coleraine	W 1-0	McAllister
29/08/1936	IL 4	A	Ards	L 1-6	W.R. Moore
05/09/1936	IL 5	A	Distillery	D 2-2	Lingwood; McAllister
09/09/1936	GC rd1	A	Distillery	L 3-4	Lingwood; W.R. Moore; Fisher
12/09/1936	IL 6	H	Glenavon	L 1-3	McAllister
19/09/1936	IL 7	A	Cliftonville	L 1-4	McAllister
26/09/1936	IL 8	H	Bangor	L 2-5	Lingwood; Hutchinson
03/10/1936	IL 9	A	Derry City	L 0-2	-
10/10/1936	IL 10	H	Belfast Celtic	L 0-2	-
17/10/1936	IL 11	A	Larne	W 2-1	Lingwood; W.R. Moore
24/10/1936	IL 12	H	Portadown	L 1-3	W.R. Moore
07/11/1936	IL 13	A	Glentoran	L 2-8	McAllister 2
14/11/1936	IL 14	A	Newry Town	L 3-5	W.R. Moore; McAllister 2
21/11/1936	IL 15	H	Linfield	L 0-7	-
28/11/1936	IL 16	A	Coleraine	L 0-1	-
05/12/1936	IL 17	H	Ards	W 4-1	Brown 3; Lingwood
12/12/1936	IL 18	H	Distillery	W 3-1	W.R. Moore 2; Brown
19/12/1936	IL 19	A	Glenavon	L 2-5	Brown; Roberts
25/12/1936	IL 20	H	Cliftonville	L 1-3	Wallace
26/12/1936	IL 21	A	Bangor	L 0-2	-
02/01/1937	IL 22	H	Derry City	L 1-4	Carlyle og
09/01/1937	IC rd1	H	Ards	W 5-1	Fisher 3; Buckley; W.R. Moore
16/01/1937	IL 23	A	Belfast Celtic	L 0-4	-
23/01/1937	IL 24	H	Larne	L 1-3	Wallace
27/01/1937	CAS rd1	H	Glentoran	L 1-5	McAllister
30/01/1937	IL 25	A	Portadown	L 1-4	McAllister
06/02/1937	IL 26	H	Glentoran	D 4-4	Fisher; McDowell 3
13/02/1937	CC 1	A	Glenavon	W 2-1	McDowell 2
20/02/1937	IC qf	H	Derry City	W 1-0	Brown
24/02/1937	CC 2	H	Belfast Celtic	W 2-0	Brown; McDowell
27/02/1937	CC 3	H	Coleraine	D 1-1	McDowell
06/03/1937	CC 4	A	Glentoran	W 2-1	Wallace; W.R. Moore
20/03/1937	IC sf	N	Belfast Celtic	D 1-1	W. Moore
22/03/1937	IC sf rep	N	Belfast Celtic	L 0-3	-
27/03/1937	CC 5	A	Larne	D 1-1	McDowell
29/03/1937	CC 6	H	Linfield	D 1-1	McDowell
30/03/1937	CC 7	A	Derry City	L 1-5	Brown
01/04/1937	CC 8	A	Bangor	L 0-3	-
03/04/1937	CC 9	H	Distillery	W 4-0	Wallace 2; Brown; D. McAllister
07/04/1937	CC 10	H	Newry Town	L 1-3	Fisher
17/04/1937	CC 11	A	Cliftonville	L 1-5	W.R. Moore
24/04/1937	CC 12	H	Portadown	L 0-2	-
01/05/1937	CC 13	A	Ards	L 0-3	-

Notes

20/03/1937 v. Linfield: Match played at Grosvenor Park

22/03/1937 v. Linfield: Match played at Grosvenor Park

Player Appearances and Goals

Player	Apps	Goals	Player	Apps	Goals
AUSTIN	1	0	MATHEISON	24	0
BLAIR	5	0	McALLISTER Daniel	39	12
BROWN	25	9	McALLISTER Daniel Martin	4	0
BUCKLEY Adam	22	1	McATEER	1	0
CLARK	2	0	McCABE	4	0
CUMMING	12	0	McDAID John	16	0
DAVISON Robert	8	0	McDOWELL James	19	9
DUNSEITH	2	0	McMULLAN John	33	0
FISHER Daniel	33	6	MITCHELL Steve	42	0
FORSYTHE	2	0	MOORE William R.	41	10
GIBB	1	0	MOORE William	4	1
GOODALL Bernard	14	0	NELSON	1	0
HANSON	7	0	ROBERTS Fred	2	1
HOWARD	1	0	SMALLMAN Joseph	38	0
HUTCHINSON	6	1	SURGENOR J.P.	12	0
JONES	4	0	TAGGART John	6	0
KERNOHAN	2	0	THOMPSON	1	0
LINGWOOD	17	5	TURTLE John	3	0
LYNN	2	0	WALLACE John	38	5
MAILEY	1	0			

Date	Comp	Venue	Opponents	Result	Scorers
21/08/1937	IL 1	H	Glentoran	L 0-1	-
23/08/1937	IL 2	A	Derry City	L 1-9	Jones
25/08/1937	IL 3	A	Distillery	D 4-4	Wallace; Moore 2; Surgenor
28/08/1937	IL 4	H	Newry Town	D 2-2	Surgenor 2
04/09/1937	IL 5	A	Belfast Celtic	L 1-3	Surgenor
11/09/1937	IL 6	H	Ards	L 1-4	Wilson og
14/09/1937	GC rd1	A	Belfast Celtic	L 0-3	-
18/09/1937	IL 7	A	Glenavon	L 0-2	-
25/09/1937	IL 8	H	Coleraine	W 6-2	Olphert 2; Wallace 3; Surgenor
02/10/1937	IL 9	A	Linfield	D 1-1	Wallace
09/10/1937	IL 10	H	Larne	W 3-2	Sclater; Wallace; Gourley
16/10/1937	IL 11	A	Cliftonville	W 3-1	Olphert; Moore; Sclater
30/10/1937	IL 12	H	Portadown	D 1-1	Sclater
06/11/1937	IL 13	A	Bangor	W 3-0	Sclater 3
13/11/1937	IL 14	H	Glentoran	W 2-1	Sclater; Wallace
20/11/1937	IL 15	H	Derry City	W 5-0	Wallace; Sclater 2; Gourley; Moore
27/11/1937	IL 16	H	Distillery	W 5-1	Sclater 4; Gourley
04/12/1937	IL 17	A	Newry Town	L 2-5	Sclater 2
18/12/1937	IL 18	A	Ards	W 3-1	Wallace 2; Moore
25/12/1937	IL 19	H	Glenavon	W 7-2	Sclater 4; McDaid; Moore 2
27/12/1937	IL 20	A	Coleraine	W 6-3	Sclater 4; Wallace; Moore;
29/12/1937	IL 21	H	Belfast Celtic	W 1-0	Sclater
01/01/1938	IL 22	A	Linfield	D 2-2	Surgenor; Sclater
08/01/1938	IC rd1	H	Linfield	W 3-2	Sclater; Moore; Gourley
15/01/1938	IL 23	A	Larne	W 6-2	Gourley; Moore; Wallace; Sclater 3
22/01/1938	IL 24	H	Cliftonville	W 3-1	Wallace; Gourley; Sclater
26/01/1938	CAS qf	H	Bangor	W 3-0	Sclater; Moore; Gourley
29/01/1938	IL 25	A	Portadown	L 2-4	Sclater; Gourley
05/02/1938	IL 26	H	Bangor	W 2-1	Sclater 2
12/02/1938	CC 1	A	Coleraine	W 4-0	Sclater 3; Moore
19/02/1938	CC 2	H	Glentoran	W 4-2	Brand 2; Sclater; Gourley
26/02/1938	IC qf	A	Belfast Celtic	D 0-0	-
02/03/1938	IC qf rep	H	Belfast Celtic	D 0-0	-
05/03/1938	CC 3	H	Bangor	L 1-4	Brand
07/03/1938	IC qf rep 2	A	Belfast Celtic	L 0-1	-
12/03/1938	CC 4	A	Glenavon	L 1-4	Sclater
17/03/1938	CC 5	A	Distillery	L 2-3	Wallace; Connell
19/03/1938	CC 6	H	Portadown	W 2-0	Sclater 2
23/03/1938	CAS sf	N	Cliftonville	W 3-2	Olphert; Wallace; Sclater
26/03/1938	CC 7	A	Ards	W 2-1	Sclater; Brand
02/04/1938	CC 8	H	Cliftonville	L 2-3	Sclater 2
16/04/1938	CC 9	A	Belfast Celtic	D 1-1	Sclater
18/04/1938	CC 10	H	Larne	W 6-1	Brand 2; Sclater 3; Gourley
19/04/1938	CC 11	A	Newry Town	D 2-2	Sclater; Brand
23/04/1938	CC 12	H	Linfield	L 0-1	-
27/04/1938	CAS f	N	Linfield	L 2-3	Wilkins; Mitchell
30/04/1938	CC 13	H	Derry City	D 0-0	-

Notes

Notes:

23/03/1938 v Cliftonville: Match played at Grosvenor Park

27/04/1938 v Linfield: Match played at Grosvenor Park

Player Appearances and Goals

BAILIE	2	0	MOORE William R.	39	12
BRAND	15	7	NELSON	1	0
CONNELL Alexander	5	1	O'KANE Patrick	35	0
DONALDSON	1	0	OLPHERT Robert	13	4
GOURLEY Robert	32	10	O'NEILL	3	0
JONES	4	1	REDMOND Matthew	34	0
LYNESS Robert	4	0	RUSSELL	2	0
McCARTNEY John	37	0	SCLATER Robert	37	50
McDAID John	40	1	SMALLMAN Joseph	42	0
McMANUS	2	0	SURGENOR J.P.	42	6
McMULLAN John	11	0	WALLACE John	42	15
MITCHELL Steven	43	1	WILKINS	31	1
McCAMBRIDGE James	44	32	WOODROW James	4	0

Date	Comp	Venue	Opponents	Result	Scorers
20/08/1938	IL 1	A	Derry City	W 5-3	Hood og; W.R. Moore; Sclater 2; Grant
22/08/1938	IL 2	H	Newry Town	W 1-0	Wilkins
24/08/1938	IL 3	H	Cliftonville	W 7-2	W.R. Moore 2; Mitchell; Horner; Grant; Wilkins 2
27/08/1938	IL 4	A	Glenavon	L 0-7	-
03/09/1938	IL 5	H	Ards	D 1-1	W.R. Moore
10/09/1938	IL 6	A	Distillery	D 0-0	-
14/09/1938	GC rd1	H	Ards	W 5-3	Grant; W. Moore 2; Sclater 2
17/09/1938	IL 7	H	Larne	W 7-3	Sclater 3; Olphert; Mitchell; W.R. Moore; Pierson
24/09/1938	IL 8	A	Coleraine	W 2-1	Sclater 2
01/10/1938	IL 9	H	Glentoran	W 1-0	Sclater
12/10/1938	GC qf	A	Belfast Celtic	L 3-9	Grant; Sclater 2
15/10/1938	IL 10	A	Linfield	W 2-1	Sclater; Wallace
22/10/1938	IL 11	H	Portadown	L 2-4	Dowall; Wallace
29/10/1938	IL 12	A	Bangor	D 3-3	Pierson; W.R. Moore; Olphert
05/11/1938	IL 13	H	Belfast Celtic	L 0-8	-
12/11/1938	IL 14	H	Derry City	W 1-0	Pierson
19/11/1938	IL 15	A	Newry Town	L 1-3	Mitchell
26/11/1938	IL 16	A	Cliftonville	W 3-0	Horner; Sclater; W.R. Moore
03/12/1938	IL 17	H	Glenavon	D 1-1	Sclater
10/12/1938	IL 18	A	Ards	W 6-2	Sclater 6
17/12/1938	IL 19	H	Distillery	W 3-0	Sclater; Pierson; W.R. Moore
24/12/1938	IL 20	A	Larne	D 2-2	Sclater; Pierson
26/12/1938	IL 21	H	Coleraine	W 4-0	Pierson; Olphert 2; Horner
27/12/1938	IL 22	A	Glentoran	W 3-1	Sclater 3
31/12/1938	IL 23	H	Linfield	W 2-1	Sclater 2
07/01/1939	IL 24	A	Portadown	L 2-7	Sclater 2
14/01/1939	IL 25	H	Bangor	L 2-3	W. Moore; Horner
21/01/1939	IC rd1	H	Glentoran	W 1-0	Sclater
28/01/1939	IL 26	A	Belfast Celtic	W 2-1	Olphert; Sclater
01/02/1939	CAS qf	A	Linfield	L 3-4	Horner; Sclater; Grant
04/02/1939	CC 1	A	Bangor	W 1-0	W. Moore
11/02/1939	CC 2	H	Glenavon	W 2-1	Olphert; Sclater
15/02/1939	CC 3	A	Distillery	W 2-1	Sclater; W.R. Moore
25/02/1939	IC qf	H	Belfast Celtic	W 3-1	Sclater 2; Kirby
04/03/1939	CC 4	A	Coleraine	W 4-1	Bowden og; Kirby Olphert; W.R. Moore
18/03/1939	CC 5	H	Linfield	L 2-3	Sclater; Horner
22/03/1939	CC 6	H	Cliftonville	W 5-3	Sclater; W.R. Moore 2; Kirby 2
25/03/1939	CC 7	A	Ards	L 2-3	W.R. Moore; Sclater
01/04/1939	IC sf	N	Portadown	W 3-2	Sclater; W.R. Moore 2
08/04/1939	CC 8	A	Glentoran	L 1-5	W.R. Moore
10/04/1939	CC 9	H	Newry Town	W 5-1	Kirby; Grant 2; W.R. Moore 2
11/04/1939	CC 10	A	Derry City	L 0-3	-
15/04/1939	CC 11	H	Larne	W 4-3	Wallace; W.R. Moore; Kirby; Sclater
20/04/1939	CC 12	H	Portadown	D 0-0	-
22/04/1939	CC 13	H	Belfast Celtic	L 0-5	-
29/04/1939	IC f	N	Linfield	L 0-2	-

Notes

01/04/1939 v. Portadown: Match played at The Oval

29/04/1939 v. Linfield: Match played at Solitude

Player Appearances and Goals

DOWALL William	7	1	MOORE William	9	4
ESLER John	1	0	NELSON Michael	1	0
FRASER	1	0	O'HARA	2	0
FULLERTON John	14	0	OLPHERT Robert	23	7
GRANT John	27	7	OWENS	1	0
HAGAN	1	0	PIERSON John	22	6
HERNON John	2	0	REDMOND Matthew	45	0
HOGG Robert	6	0	SCLATER Robert	35	42
HORNER Richard	40	6	SMALLMAN Joseph	1	0
KIRBY John	14	6	STOKES Edward	2	0
McCARTNEY John	46	0	SURGENOR J.P.	38	0
McDAID John	43	0	VINCENT Blair	18	0
McGILLEON	1	0	WALLACE John	41	3
MITCHELL Steven	18	3	WILKINS	5	3
MOORE William R.	42	19			

Played: 47, won: 25, drawn: 6, lost: 16, goals scored: 126, goals conceded: 95

Irish League: 4th; Irish Cup: Winners; Gold Cup: Round 1; City Cup: 11th; County Antrim Shield: Semi-final

Date	Comp	Venue	Opponents	Result	Scorers
19/08/1939	CC 1	A	Ards	W 2-1	Sclater; Moore
23/08/1939	CC 2	H	Newry Town	L 1-2	Grant
26/08/1939	CC 3	A	Coleraine	L 1-3	Grant
02/09/1939	CC 4	H	Linfield	L 1-2	Vincent
06/09/1939	CC 5	A	Portadown	L 0-2	-
09/09/1939	CC 6	H	Distillery	L 3-4	Sclater 2; McPeake
13/09/1939	GC rd1	A	Newry Town	L 2-5	Gamble 2
16/09/1939	CC 7	A	Larne	D 1-1	Sclater
23/09/1939	CC 8	H	Cliftonville	W 3-1	Shannon; Sclater 2
30/09/1939	CC 9	A	Derry City	L 0-3	-
07/10/1939	CC 10	H	Belfast Celtic	L 1-5	Sclater
14/10/1939	CC 11	A	Glenavon	D 4-4	Grant 2; Gamble; Sclater
21/10/1939	CC 12	H	Glentoran	W 4-1	Grant; Olphert; Sclater; Shannon
04/11/1939	CC 13	A	Bangor	W 2-0	Sclater 2
11/11/1939	IL 1	A	Portadown	L 2-4	Sclater; Shannon
18/11/1939	IL 2	H	Larne	W 5-1	Moore; Olphert; Grant; Sclater 2
25/11/1939	IL 3	A	Distillery	D 3-3	Moore; Olphert 2
02/12/1939	IL 4	H	Coleraine	W 6-1	Grant 2; Sclater; Olphert; Moore 2
09/12/1939	IL 5	A	Bangor	D 2-2	Moore 2
16/12/1939	IL 6	H	Linfield	W 2-1	Grant 2
23/12/1939	IL 7	A	Glenavon	L 2-4	Olphert; Sclater
25/12/1939	IL 8	H	Newry Town	W 8-2	Sclater 4; Weir; Grant; Moore 2
26/12/1939	IL 9	H	Glentoran	L 2-3	Moore; Fullerton
30/12/1939	IL 10	A	Cliftonville	W 1-0	Grant
06/01/1940	IL 11	H	Derry City	W 4-1	Sclater 3; Grant
11/01/1940	CAS rd1	A	Bangor	W 3-2	Moore; Grant; Sclater
13/01/1940	IL 12	A	Ards	W 2-0	Sclater 2
27/01/1940	IL 13	H	Belfast Celtic	L 1-5	Weir
03/02/1940	IL 14	H	Portadown	W 2-1	Grant; Weir
07/02/1940	CAS qf	H	Cliftonville	W 6-2	Moore 2; Grant 3; Olphert
10/02/1940	IL 15	A	Larne	W 4-2	Moore; Olphert 2; Weir
14/02/1940	IC rd1	H	Bangor	W 3-1	Sclater 2; Grant
17/02/1940	IL 16	H	Distillery	W 4-0	Weir 2; Olphert; Shannon
24/02/1940	IC qf	H	Dundela	W 3-2	Weir; Olphert; Shannon
02/03/1940	IL 17	H	Bangor	W 6-0	Moore; Sclater 3; Grant 2
09/03/1940	IL 18	A	Linfield	L 1-2	Shannon
13/03/1940	CAS sf	N	Glentoran	L 0-2	-
16/03/1940	IL 19	H	Glenavon	D 2-2	Olphert; Sclater
20/03/1940	IL 20	A	Coleraine	W 4-2	Weir; Olphert; Sclater 2
23/03/1940	IL 21	A	Newry Town	W 3-1	Sclater; Moore; Grant
25/03/1940	IL22	A	Glentoran	L 2-4	Sclater 2
26/03/1940	IL 23	H	Cliftonville	W 4-3	Weir 2; McPeake; Sclater
30/03/1940	IL 24	A	Derry City	L 2-5	Sclater; Grant
06/04/1940	IC sf	N	Belfast Celtic	W 2-0	Sclater; Grant
13/04/1940	IL 25	A	Belfast Celtic	D 3-3	Weir 2; Grant
20/04/1940	IC f	N	Glenavon	W 2-0	Moore; Sclater
24/04/1940	IL 26	H	Ards	W 5-0	Grant 2; Sclater 3
30/04/1940	FR	H	Dundalk	W 6-4	Grant 2; Sclater 2; McPeake; Weir

Notes

13/03/1940 v. Glentoran: Match played at Grosvenor Park

06/04/1940 v. Belfast Celtic: Match played at Solitude

20/04/1940 v. Glenavon: Match played at Windsor Park

Player Appearances and Goals

ARMOUR S	1	0	MOORE William R.	41	17
BARR Albert	22	0	OLPHERT Robert	33	13
CARSON	1	0	REDMOND Matthew	44	0
CASSON	2	0	ROSBOTHAM James	14	0
FINLAY Hugh	7	0	SCLATER Robert	42	44
FULLERTON John	31	1	SCOTT William	1	0
GAMBLE	9	3	SHANNON Alexander	36	6
GRANT George	47	27	SUMMERS David	9	0
HORNER Richard	11	0	SWANN John	46	0
McCARTNEY John	42	0	TWEED John	3	0
McCREADY William	23	0	VINCENT Blair	14	1
McPEAKE Matthew	7	2	WEIR Alexander	30	12
MILLS	1	0			

Ballymena United Football Club withdrew from the Irish League and all associated competitions in July 1940 due to the Ballymena Showgrounds being used by the military during the Second World War. Ballymena United returned to competitive football in August 1946.

Date	Comp	Venue	Opponents	Result	Scorers
17/08/1946	GC 1	H	Distillery	W 2-1	Neilson 2
20/08/1946	GC 2	A	Belfast Celtic	L 1-5	Collins
24/08/1946	GC 3	H	Coleraine	W 6-2	Currie 3; Neilson 2; Collins
29/08/1946	GC 4	A	Linfield	L 0-6	-
31/08/1946	GC 5	H	Cliftonville	W 5-1	McIlroy; Neilson 4
05/09/1946	GC 6	A	Derry City	W 2-1	McIlroy; Neilson
07/09/1946	GC 7	H	Glentoran	L 1-2	Collins
12/09/1946	GC 8	A	Distillery	L 1-2	Kernaghan
14/09/1946	GC 9	H	Belfast Celtic	L 0-5	-
21/09/1946	GC 10	A	Coleraine	W 4-2	Burch; Neilson 2; Kernaghan
05/10/1946	GC 11	H	Linfield	D 2-2	McWilliams og; Neilson
12/10/1946	GC 12	A	Cliftonville	W 5-1	Neilson 3; Bavin; Montgomery
19/10/1946	GC 13	H	Derry City	W 4-1	Bavin; Currie; Neilson 2
26/10/1946	GC 14	A	Glentoran	L 1-3	Neilson
02/11/1946	NRL 1	H	Glentoran	D 1-1	Montgomery
09/11/1946	NRL 2	A	Cliftonville	D 5-5	Neilson 3; Clarke; J. Robinson
16/11/1946	NRL 3	H	Coleraine	D 1-1	J. Davidson
23/11/1946	NRL 4	A	Belfast Celtic	L 1-10	J. Davidson
30/11/1946	NRL 5	H	Derry City	W 3-2	Neilson 2; J. Davidson
07/12/1946	NRL 6	A	Distillery	W 2-0	Neilson; Kernaghan
14/12/1946	NRL 7	H	Linfield	L 0-1	-
21/12/1946	NRL 8	A	Glentoran	L 1-5	Clarke
25/12/1946	NRL 9	H	Cliftonville	W 5-1	Kernaghan 5
26/12/1946	NRL 10	A	Coleraine	L 0-1	-
28/12/1946	NRL 11	H	Belfast Celtic	D 1-1	Currie og
04/01/1947	NRL 12	A	Derry City	W 4-3	Kernaghan 3; J. Davidson
11/01/1947	NRL 13	H	Distillery	W 1-0	Kernaghan
22/01/1947	NRL 14	A	Linfield	L 1-2	Neilson
29/01/1947	NRL 15	H	Glentoran	L 3-5	Montgomery; J. Davidson; Clarke
01/02/1947	NRL 16	A	Cliftonville	D 2-2	Hegarty og; J. Robinson
08/02/1947	NRL 17	H	Coleraine	W 3-0	Kernaghan 2; J. Robinson
15/02/1947	IC qf leg 1	A	Cliftonville	W 2-0	Kernaghan; Currie
04/03/1947	IC qf leg 2	H	Cliftonville	W 3-0	Kernaghan 3
08/03/1947	NRL 18	H	Linfield	L 3-5	Martin 2; Kernaghan
19/03/1947	CAS rd1	H	Belfast Celtic	L 2-3	Sneddon 2
22/03/1947	NRL 19	H	Cliftonville	W 4-3	Kernaghan; Sneddon 2; Martin
29/03/1947	IC sf	N	Glentoran	D 1-1	Kernaghan
02/04/1947	IC sf rep	N	Glentoran	D 1-1	Clarke
05/04/1947	NRL 20	H	Belfast Celtic	L 2-4	Martin 2
08/04/1947	NRL 21	A	Derry City	L 1-2	Anderson
09/04/1947	NRL 22	A	Distillery	L 1-6	McInally
12/04/1947	NRL 23	H	Distillery	W 2-0	Martin; Kernaghan
14/04/1947	IC sf rep 2	N	Glentoran	L 1-2	Sneddon
17/04/1947	NRL 24	A	Coleraine	L 0-3	-
19/04/1947	NRL 25	A	Linfield	L 0-6	-
23/04/1947	NRL 26	H	Derry City	D 3-3	Kernaghan; McInally 2
01/05/1947	NRL 27	A	Belfast Celtic	D 1-1	McInally
03/05/1947	FR	H	Coleraine	D 3-3	Craig og; Sneddon; Anderson
07/05/1947	FR	H	Fulham	W 3-1	McDowell; Doherty 2
12/05/1947	NRL 28	A	Glentoran	L 1-3	Sneddon
16/05/1947	FR	A	Coleraine	L 1-4	Sneddon

Notes

04/03/1947 v. Cliftonville: Ballymena United won 5-0 on aggregate

29/03/1947 v. Glentoran: Match played at Windsor Park

02/04/1947 v. Glentoran: Match played at Windsor Park

14/04/1947 v. Glentoran: Match played at Windsor Park

Player Appearances and Goals

Player	Apps	Goals	Player	Apps	Goals
ANDERSON William	19	1	LOWE	1	0
BARR Albert	1	0	MARTIN David	6	6
BARR William	2	0	McCAMBRIDGE David	1	0
BAVIN Charles	20	2	McILROY Sydney	35	2
BURCH David	8	1	McINALLY John	9	4
CANNING Michael	41	0	McMINN	2	0
CASSIDY	2	0	MONTGOMERY	23	3
CATHCART	2	0	MOORE William	2	0
CLARKE William	29	4	MULGREW	1	0
COLLINS John	8	3	NEILL Thomas	2	0
CURRIE Albert	39	5	NEILSON John	26	25
DAVIDSON J	11	5	PLATT	10	0
DAVIDSON S	3	0	PRITCHARD	1	0
DOBBIN Jack	2	0	REDMOND Matthew	41	0
FULLERTON John	1	0	REGAN	1	0
FULLERTON R	4	0	ROBINSON John	35	3
GREER	6	0	ROBINSON W	1	0
HEFFRON Charles	3	0	RYAN Thomas	3	0
HENDERSON	2	0	SMITH	2	0
HILL Frank	25	0	SNEDDON Walter	7	6
HOUGHTON Frank	39	0	TOWELL	1	0
IRVINE	3	0	TURTLE	4	0
KERNAGHAN Norman	40	23	VENNARD	1	0
LAWS	1	0	WALSH	1	0
LOGAN	1	0			

Played: 43, won: 18, drawn: 12, lost: 13, goals scored: 98, goals conceded: 84

Irish League: 3rd; Irish Cup: Round 1; Gold Cup: Quarter-final; City Cup: 6th; County Antrim Shield: Winners; Inter City Cup: Quarter-final

Date	Comp	Venue	Opponents	Result	Scorers
16/08/1947	CC 1	H	Bangor	W 6-4	Kernaghan 2; D'Arcy; McStay 3
23/08/1947	CC 2	A	Cliftonville	W 2-0	Spalding; McStay
27/08/1947	GC rd1	H	Glenavon	W 4-2	McStay; D'Arcy 2; McInally
30/08/1947	CC 3	A	Ards	D 1-1	McStay
03/09/1947	GC qf	A	Portadown	L 1-2	McInally
06/09/1947	CC 4	H	Coleraine	D 1-1	D'Arcy
13/09/1947	CC 5	A	Glentoran	D 0-0	-
20/09/1947	CC 6	H	Linfield	L 1-5	Kernaghan
27/09/1947	CC 7	H	Derry City	L 2-4	D'Arcy; Kernaghan
11/10/1947	CC 8	A	Belfast Celtic	L 0-4	-
18/10/1947	CC 9	H	Glenavon	W 6-2	Spalding 2; Kernaghan; Fullerton; McInally 2
25/10/1947	CC 10	H	Distillery	D 1-1	D'Arcy
01/11/1947	CC 11	A	Portadown	D 2-2	D' Arcy; McInally
08/11/1947	IL 1	A	Glenavon	W 2-1	McInally; Spalding
15/11/1947	IL 2	H	Bangor	W 2-0	Spalding; D'Arcy
22/11/1947	IL 3	H	Linfield	L 1-2	Houghton
29/11/1947	IL 4	A	Glentoran	D 2-2	Spalding 2
06/12/1947	IL 5	H	Derry City	W 6-0	Spalding; Kernaghan 2; Anderson; Houghton; D'Arcy
13/12/1947	IL 6	H	Distillery	W 2-1	Kernaghan 2
20/12/1947	IL 7	A	Ards	D 2-2	Welsh 2
25/12/1947	IL 8	H	Cliftonville	W 5-2	D'Arcy; Spalding; Kernaghan; McInally 2
26/12/1947	IL 9	A	Coleraine	L 0-4	-
27/12/1947	IL 10	H	Portadown	W 5-2	D'Arcy 2; Kernaghan 2; Spalding
03/01/1948	IL 11	A	Belfast Celtic	L 0-2	-
10/01/1948	IL 12	H	Glenavon	W 4-2	Spalding; Kernaghan 2; Anderson
17/01/1948	IL 13	A	Bangor	W 7-3	McInally 2; D' Arcy 4; Spalding
24/01/1948	IC rd1	H	Linfield	L 3-4	D'Arcy; Spalding; Kernaghan
31/01/1948	IL 14	A	Linfield	L 1-3	D'Arcy
07/02/1948	IL 15	H	Glentoran	D 1-1	Kernaghan
21/02/1948	IL 16	A	Derry City	D 1-1	Kernaghan
28/02/1948	IL 17	A	Distillery	D 2-2	Kernaghan; D'Arcy
06/03/1948	IL 18	H	Ards	L 0-1	-
13/03/1948	IL 19	A	Cliftonville	D 1-1	McInally
27/03/1948	IL 20	H	Coleraine	W 3-2	Sneddon; McCormack 2
30/03/1948	IL 21	A	Portadown	D 1-1	McInally
03/04/1948	IL 22	H	Belfast Celtic	W 4-3	McCormack; Kernaghan 3
07/04/1948	ICC rd1 leg 1	H	Shelbourne	W 4-1	McDonald; Kernaghan; Anderson; Spalding
14/04/1948	FR	H	Airdrieonians	L 1-4	McCormack
15/04/1948	CAS qf	A	Bangor	W 3-2	McInally ; McCormack 2
17/04/1948	ICC rd1 leg 2	A	Shelbourne	L 0-1	-
24/04/1948	CAS sf	N	Ards	W 4-1	McDonald; Spalding; McCormack; McInally
27/04/1948	ICC qf leg 1	A	Shamrock Rovers	L 1-4	McDonald
01/05/1948	ICC qf leg 2	H	Shamrock Rovers	L 2-4	McDonald 2
04/05/1948	FR	H	Charlton Athletic	L 2-4	McDowell; Kernaghan
08/05/1948	FR	H	Newcastle United	L 2-3	McDowell; McCormack
10/05/1948	FR	H	Luton Town	L 0-1	-
18/05/1948	CAS f	N	Linfield	W 2-1	McDonald 2

Notes

07/04/1948 v. Shelbourne: Match played at Solitude

17/04/1948 v. Shelbourne: Ballymena United won 4-2 on aggregate

24/04/1948 v. Ards: Match played at Grosvenor Park

01/05/1948 v. Shamrock Rovers: Match played at Solitude & Ballymena United lost 8-3 on aggregate

18/05/1948 v. Linfield: Match played at Celtic Park

Player Appearances and Goals

Player	Apps	Goals	Player	Apps	Goals
ANDERSON William	25	3	McCONNELL	1	0
ARCHER Charles	11	0	McDONALD John	8	7
BARR William	24	0	McILREAVY John	16	0
CURRIE Jack	3	0	McILROY Sydney	41	0
D'ARCY Seamus	30	19	McINALLY John	36	14
DOBBIN Jack	3	0	McSTAY James	13	6
FRASER	3	0	McWILLIAMS Michael	3	0
FULLERTON R	2	1	NEILL Thomas	3	0
GAVIN Charles	37	0	REDMOND Matthew	40	0
GILLEN	4	0	RUSSELL Thomas	1	0
HOUGHTON Frank	25	2	SNEDDON Walter	6	1
JACKSON James	40	0	SPALDING William	42	15
KERNAGHAN Norman	35	22	TREVORROW Eric	1	0
McAULEY John	8	0	WELSH	6	2
McCORMACK Thomas	6	6			

Played: 39, won: 11, drawn: 9, lost: 29, goals scored: 66, goals conceded: 97

Irish League: 10th; Irish Cup: Round 1; Gold Cup: Quarter-final; City Cup: 7th; County Antrim Shield: Quarter-final; Inter City Cup: Quarter-final

Date	Comp	Venue	Opponents	Result	Scorers
21/08/1948	CC 1	A	Cliftonville	D 1-1	Williamson
25/08/1948	GC rd1	A	Ards	W 2-0	Williamson; McCormack
28/08/1948	CC 2	H	Linfield	L 0-1	-
02/09/1948	GC qf	A	Glenavon	D 1-1	McCormack
04/09/1948	CC 3	A	Glenavon	L 1-6	McDonald
08/09/1948	GC qf rep	H	Glenavon	L 2-4	Williamson 2
11/09/1948	CC 4	H	Derry City	W 2-1	McDonald; McCormack
18/09/1948	CC 5	A	Portadown	L 2-5	McCormack 2
25/09/1948	CC 6	H	Glentoran	W 2-1	McDonald; Williamson
02/10/1948	CC 7	H	Distillery	W 6-1	McDonald 3; Kernaghan 2; Williamson
16/10/1948	CC 8	A	Coleraine	W 2-1	Kernaghan; Giffen
23/10/1948	CC 9	H	Ards	L 2-3	Dobbin; McDonald
30/10/1948	CC 10	A	Bangor	L 3-4	Dobbin; McDonald; Jackson
13/11/1948	CC 11	H	Belfast Celtic	L 0-3	-
20/11/1948	IL 1	H	Coleraine	W 5-2	Spalding 2; McIntyre; McDonald 2
27/11/1948	IL 2	A	Distillery	L 2-6	Spalding; Giffen
04/12/1948	IL 3	H	Derry City	W 3-2	McDonald; Williamson; Sneddon
11/12/1948	IL 4	A	Bangor	D 2-2	Giffen; McDonald
18/12/1948	IL 5	A	Glentoran	L 2-4	Sneddon; McDonald
25/12/1948	IL 6	H	Belfast Celtic	L 0-5	-
26/12/1948	IL 7	A	Cliftonville	D 1-1	Williamson
08/01/1949	IL 8	H	Portadown	D 1-1	Williamson
15/01/1949	IL 9	H	Linfield	L 0-3	-
22/01/1949	IC rd1	H	Coleraine	L 1-2	McDonald
29/01/1949	IL 10	H	Glenavon	D 0-0	-
05/02/1949	IL 11	A	Coleraine	W 2-1	McDonald; Jackson
12/02/1949	IL 12	A	Ards	L 0-8	-
19/02/1949	IL 13	H	Distillery	W 7-5	Corr; Cronin 2; Williamson 3; Kernaghan
26/02/1949	IL 14	A	Derry City	W 2-1	Corr 2
05/03/1949	IL 15	H	Bangor	D 1-1	Dobbin
12/03/1949	IL 16	H	Glentoran	D 1-1	Kernaghan
19/03/1949	IL 17	A	Belfast Celtic	L 2-3	McDonald; Williamson
02/04/1949	IL 18	H	Cliftonville	L 3-4	Corr 2; Murphy
06/04/1949	CAS qf	A	Glentoran	L 0-1	-
09/04/1949	IL 19	H	Ards	W 1-0	McDonald
19/04/1949	IL 20	A	Portadown	L 0-2	-
26/04/1949	IL 21	A	Linfield	L 2-4	McDonald; Corr
30/04/1949	IL 22	A	Glenavon	D 2-2	Williamson; Cronin
06/05/1949	ICC qf	H	Drumcondra	L 0-4	-
01/05/1949	TEST	H	Irish League Select	L 1-2	McDonald

Notes

01/05/1949 v. Irish League Select: Testimonial for Matt Redmond

Player Appearances and Goals

BARR William	16	0	MANDELSON	1	0
CORR Patrick	12	6	McCANN Sean	32	0
COULTER W.J.	1	0	McCORMACK Thomas	8	5
CRONIN Patrick	11	3	McDONALD John	36	18
CURRIE	1	0	McILREAVEY John	34	0
DOBBIN Jack	18	3	McILROY Sydney	8	0
FULLERTON	1	0	McINTYRE	4	1
GIFFEN James	19	3	McMURRAY R	3	0
GODFREY	4	0	McWILLIAMS Michael	7	0
IRVINE	1	0	MONTGOMERY	1	0
JACKSON James	36	2	MURPHY Harold	34	1
JOHNSTON Patrick	1	0	REDMOND Matthew	7	0
JONES Sydney	1	0	SNEDDON Walter	12	2
KENNEDY Joseph	4	0	SPALDING William	14	3
KERNAGHAN Norman	21	5	TREVORROW Eric	39	0
KIDD Arthur	2	0	WILLIAMSON Thomas	38	14
LUNEY William	2	0			

Played: 43, won: 13, drawn: 10, lost: 20, goals scored: 59, goals conceded: 79

Irish League: 8th; Irish Cup: Round 1; Gold Cup: Quarter-final; Ulster Cup: Finalists; City Cup: 7th; County Antrim Shield: Quarter-final

Date	Comp	Venue	Opponents	Result	Scorers
20/08/1949	CC 1	A	Distillery	D 2-2	Morrison; McKnight
25/08/1949	GC rd1	H	Derry City	D 1-1	Trevorrow
27/08/1949	CC 2	H	Cliftonville	D 1-1	Corr
01/09/1949	GC rd1 rep	A	Derry City	W 4-1	Mulgrew; Lavery 2; Dobbin
03/09/1949	UC 1	H	Coleraine	W 3-2	Dobbin 2; Giffen
10/09/1949	CC 3	A	Portadown	L 0-2	-
17/09/1949	UC 2	A	Derry City	W 1-0	Dobbin
21/09/1949	UC 3	H	Ulsterville	W 4-0	Morrison 2; Vennard; Giffen
24/09/1949	CC 4	H	Glentoran	W 2-1	Dobbin; Vennard
28/09/1949	GC qf	A	Distillery	L 0-1	-
08/10/1949	CC 5	A	Derry City	L 0-2	-
15/10/1949	CC 6	H	Linfield	L 1-2	Trevorrow
22/10/1949	CC 7	A	Crusaders	D 2-2	Lavery; Dobbin
29/10/1949	CC 8	H	Glenavon	W 2-1	Lavery; Douglas
05/11/1949	CC 9	A	Bangor	L 0-4	-
12/11/1949	CC 10	A	Ards	D 0-0	-
19/11/1949	CC 11	H	Coleraine	W 2-1	Kavanagh 2
26/11/1949	IL 1	A	Cliftonville	D 2-2	Corr; Doris
03/12/1949	IL 2	A	Ards	D 1-1	Doris
10/12/1949	IL 3	H	Crusaders	L 1-3	McCullough
17/12/1949	IL 4	A	Glentoran	L 0-5	-
24/12/1949	IL 5	H	Portadown	L 1-2	Milligan
26/12/1949	IL 6	A	Linfield	L 1-6	Doris
27/12/1949	IL 7	H	Coleraine	W 4-1	Corr; Lavery 2; Kavanagh
31/12/1949	IL 8	H	Distillery	L 0-3	-
07/01/1950	IL 9	A	Bangor	L 0-3	-
14/01/1950	IL10	H	Glenavon	D 1-1	Kavanagh
21/01/1950	IC rd1	A	Bangor	L 1-2	Douglas
28/01/1950	IL 11	H	Derry City	D 1-1	Dobbin
11/02/1950	IL 12	H	Cliftonville	W 6-0	Vennard; Mackey 4; Luney
18/02/1950	IL 13	H	Ards	D 0-0	-
25/02/1950	IL 14	A	Crusaders	W 1-0	Vennard
04/03/1950	IL 15	H	Glentoran	L 1-5	Corr
11/03/1950	IL 16	A	Portadown	W 3-1	Kavanagh; Vennard 2
18/03/1950	IL 17	H	Linfield	L 1-3	Kavanagh
01/04/1950	IL 18	A	Coleraine	W 1-0	Kavanagh
05/04/1950	CAS qf	H	Bangor	L 1-2	Douglas
08/04/1950	IL 19	A	Distillery	L 1-2	Mackey
15/04/1950	IL 20	A	Glenavon	L 1-3	Chambers
11/04/1950	IL 21	H	Bangor	L 1-2	Trevorrow
19/04/1950	UC sf	N	Glentoran	W 2-1	Chambers; Douglas
27/04/1950	UC f	N	Larne	L 1-2	Douglas
29/04/1950	IL 22	A	Derry City	L 1-5	McIlreavey

Notes

19/04/1950 v. Glentoran: Match played at Windsor Park

27/04/1950 v. Larne: Match played at Grosvenor Park

Player Appearances and Goals

Player	Apps	Goals	Player	Apps	Goals
CAMERON	2	0	McCULLOUGH James	3	1
CHAMBERS	10	2	McFARLAND	6	0
CORR Patrick	39	4	McILREAVEY John	9	1
CUNNING John	2	0	McILROY Hugh	19	0
DOBBIN Jack	25	7	McKNIGHT	2	1
DORIS John	9	3	McMILLAN William	25	0
DOUGLAS Joseph	39	5	MILLIGAN Dudley	3	1
DUNWOODY R	17	0	MOORE William	1	0
FLANNIGAN Liam	35	0	MORRISON	6	3
FORSYTHE Robert	2	0	MULGREW Andrew	5	1
GIFFEN James	21	2	MURPHY Harold	19	0
GILLESPIE Samuel	4	0	O'KANE	1	0
IRVINE	4	0	SIMPSON Reginald	39	0
KAVANAGH David	25	7	SMITH	1	0
KELLY	2	0	SMYTH W	4	0
LAVERY Daniel	14	6	TREVORROW Eric	40	3
LUNEY William	15	1	VENNARD	12	6
MACKEY	13	5			

Played: 46, won: 18, drawn: 8, lost: 20, goals scored: 76, goals conceded: 95

Irish League: 10th; Irish Cup: Finalists; Gold Cup: Semi-final; Ulster Cup: Group stage; City Cup: 6th; County Antrim Shield: Winners

Date	Comp	Venue	Opponents	Result	Scorers
19/08/1950	UC 1	H	Ulsterville	W 4-0	Moore; Williamson; G. Bell 2
22/08/1950	GC qf	A	Cliftonville	W 3-2	Morrison 2; Moore
26/08/1950	CC 1	H	Distillery	L 0-2	-
28/08/1950	UC 2	H	Derry City	W 3-0	Douglas; Moore; Donaghy
02/09/1950	UC 3	A	Coleraine	L 0-2	-
09/09/1950	CC 2	A	Cliftonville	W 4-3	Moore; Lunn; G. Bell 2
12/09/1950	GC sf	N	Linfield	L 1-4	Douglas
16/09/1950	CC 3	H	Portadown	W 1-0	G. Bell
23/09/1950	CC 4	A	Glentoran	L 0-5	-
30/09/1950	CC 5	H	Derry City	D 2-2	Moore 2
14/10/1950	CC 6	A	Linfield	L 1-5	Morrison
21/10/1950	CC 7	H	Crusaders	W 2-0	G. Bell; Douglas
28/10/1950	CC 8	A	Glenavon	W 2-1	Anderson; Murphy
04/11/1950	CC 9	H	Bangor	D 0-0	-
11/11/1950	CC 10	H	Ards	W 6-2	Murphy; Small; Morrison; Trevorrow; Williamson; Anderson
18/11/1950	CC 11	A	Coleraine	L 0-2	-
25/11/1950	IL 1	A	Glenavon	L 0-4	-
02/12/1950	IL 2	H	Ards	W 4-2	Trevorrow; Small; Williamson; Imrie og
09/12/1950	IL 3	H	Portadown	L 0-2	-
23/12/1950	IL 4	A	Crusaders	D 3-3	Williamson; Murphy; Dunkley
25/12/1950	IL 5	H	Cliftonville	W 4-0	Lunn 3; Morrison
26/12/1950	IL 6	A	Coleraine	L 0-3	-
27/12/1950	IL 7	A	Bangor	L 1-4	Douglas
30/12/1950	IL 8	H	Derry City	W 2-1	Currie; Johnston
13/01/1951	IL 9	H	Linfield	W 3-2	Johnston; Currie 2
20/01/1951	IC rd1	H	Coleraine	W 2-1	Barr; Douglas
27/01/1951	IL 10	A	Glentoran	L 0-2	-
31/01/1951	IL 11	A	Distillery	W 2-1	Currie; Barr
03/02/1951	IL 12	H	Glenavon	L 1-5	O'Hara
10/02/1951	IL 13	A	Ards	D 1-1	Currie
17/02/1951	IC qf	A	Cliftonville	D 2-2	Jackson; Currie
22/02/1951	IC qf rep	H	Cliftonville	W 2-0	Currie; Jackson
24/02/1951	IL 14	A	Portadown	L 2-7	Shaw og; Morrison
03/03/1951	IL 15	H	Bangor	L 0-2	-
10/03/1951	IL 16	H	Crusaders	L 1-2	Morrison
17/03/1951	IL 17	A	Cliftonville	L 0-2	-
24/03/1951	IL 18	H	Coleraine	L 2-3	Ewart; Currie
27/03/1951	IL 19	A	Derry City	L 1-3	Barr
31/03/1951	IL 20	H	Distillery	D 2-2	Currie; O'Hara
07/04/1951	IC sf	N	Portadown	W 2-1	Ewart; Anderson
14/04/1951	IL 21	A	Linfield	D 1-1	Ewart
18/04/1951	CAS qf	A	Linfield	W 4-1	Gray; Ewart; Currie; O'Hara
21/04/1951	IL 22	H	Glentoran	L 0-2	-
28/04/1951	IC f	N	Glentoran	L 1-3	Currie
05/05/1951	CAS sf	N	Brantwood	W 2-1	Morrison 2
16/05/1951	CAS f	N	Cliftonville	D 2-2	Douglas; Currie

Notes

12/09/1950 v. Linfield: Match played at the Oval

07/04/1951 v. Portadown: Match plated at Windsor Park

28/04/1951 v. Glentoran: Match played at Windsor Park

05/05/1951 v. Brantwood: Match played at Solitude

16/05/1951 v. Cliftonville: Match played at Windsor Park and replay held over to start of 1951/52 season

Player Appearances and Goals

Player	Apps	Goals	Player	Apps	Goals
ADAMS	1	0	KERNAGHAN Harold	6	0
ANDERSON William	26	3	LONG Walter	33	0
BARR Joseph	31	3	LUNEY William	6	0
BELL George	10	6	LUNN Ferris	22	4
BELL William	12	0	McCALLUM Norman	6	0
CUNNINGHAM	2	0	McDONALD Angus	2	0
CURRIE Jack	29	12	McILREAVEY John	26	0
DONAGHY	5	1	McKEEGAN	2	0
DOUGLAS Joseph	34	6	MOORE Alexander	13	6
DUNKLEY Robert	15	1	MORRISON Vincent	37	9
EWART R	9	4	MURPHY Harold	44	3
FEGAN Gerald	2	0	O'HARA Gerald	21	3
GRAHAM Albert	3	0	RODGERS James	13	0
GRAY George	20	1	SMALL James	3	2
JACKSON	10	2	TREVORROW Eric	40	2
JOHNSTON	3	2	WILLIAMSON Thomas	20	4

Played: 52, won: 20, drawn: 16, lost: 16, goals scored: 99, goals conceded: 91

Irish League: 5th; Irish Cup: Semi-final; Gold Cup: Round 1; City Cup: 9th; County Antrim Shield: Quarter-final; Festival of Britain Cup: Winners

Date	Comp	Venue	Opponents	Result	Scorers
18/08/1951	CC 1	A	Distillery	W 4-1	Mullen 4
20/08/1951	CAS (50/51) f	N	Cliftonville	W 3-0	Cubitt; Currie 2
23/08/1951	FBC 1	H	Coleraine	W 5-4	J. Mitten 3; Currie; Douglas
25/08/1951	CC 2	H	Cliftonville	L 0-3	-
28/08/1951	GC rd1	H	Ards	L 3-4	Lyness; J. Mitten; H. Murphy
30/08/1951	FBC 2	A	Coleraine	L 1-4	Cubitt
01/09/1951	CC 3	A	Portadown	L 1-2	Currie
08/09/1951	CC 4	H	Glentoran	D 1-1	Currie
15/09/1951	CC 5	A	Derry City	L 1-2	Mullen
20/09/1951	FBC 3	A	Derry City	W 3-2	Lyness; Mullen; Barr
22/09/1951	CC 6	H	Linfield	D 0-0	-
29/09/1951	CC 7	A	Crusaders	W 2-0	Lyness; S. Mitten
03/10/1951	FBC 4	H	Derry City	W 5-0	Currie 2; S. Mitten 3
13/10/1951	CC 8	H	Glenavon	L 1-3	Lyness
20/10/1951	CC 9	A	Bangor	D 1-1	J. Mitten
27/10/1951	CC 10	A	Ards	L 0-3	-
03/11/1951	CC 11	H	Coleraine	W 3-2	Mullen; Johnston 2
10/11/1951	IL 1	A	Portadown	L 0-5	-
17/11/1951	IL 2	H	Cliftonville	W 2-1	S. Mitten 2
24/11/1951	IL 3	A	Bangor	L 4-5	Lyness; Currie; Fegan; S.Mitten
01/12/1951	IL 4	H	Crusaders	W 3-1	S. Mitten 2; Currie
08/12/1951	IL 5	A	Linfield	D 2-2	Lyness; Currie
15/12/1951	IL 6	H	Glentoran	D 2-2	Douglas; S. Mitten
22/12/1951	IL 7	A	Glenavon	L 1-2	Currie
25/12/1951	IL 8	H	Distillery	D 3-3	Cubitt 2; J. Mitten
26/12/1951	IL 9	A	Derry City	D 2-2	S. Mitten; Cubitt
29/12/1951	IL 10	A	Ards	L 1-4	S. Mitten
05/01/1952	IL 11	H	Coleraine	D 1-1	Currie
12/01/1952	IL 12	H	Portadown	L 0-2	-
19/01/1952	IC rd1	H	Distillery	D 2-2	Lyness; S. Mitten
26/01/1952	IL 13	A	Cliftonville	D 2-2	S. Mitten; Currie
30/01/1952	IC rd1 rep	A	Distillery	D 1-1	J. Mitten
02/02/1952	IL 14	H	Bangor	W 4-0	J. Mitten 2; Johnston 2
04/02/1952	IC rd1 rep 2	N	Distillery	W 2-0	Johnston; J. Mitten
09/02/1952	IL 15	A	Crusaders	D 1-1	S. Mitten
16/02/1952	IC qf	A	Cliftonville	D 2-2	Lyness; S. Mitten
21/02/1952	IC qf rep	H	Cliftonville	W 2-0	Currie; S. Mitten
23/02/1952	IL 16	H	Linfield	W 2-0	Lyness; J. Mitten
01/03/1952	IL 17	A	Glentoran	W 3-1	S. Mitten; Cubitt; Lyness
08/03/1952	IL 18	H	Glenavon	L 0-1	-
15/03/1952	IC sf	N	Ards	L 1-3	Lyness
19/03/1952	CAS rd1	H	Feltonville	D 1-1	S. Mitten
22/03/1952	IL 19	A	Distillery	D 2-2	Lyness; Quinn
24/03/1952	CAS rd1 rep	H	Feltonville	W 5-0	Lyness 3; Cubitt; Fegan
29/03/1952	IL 20	H	Derry City	W 2-1	Elliott; J. Mitten
05/04/1952	IL 21	H	Ards	W 3-1	J. Mitten; Lyness; S. Mitten
12/04/1952	IL 22	A	Coleraine	L 1-5	Trevorrow
19/04/1952	CAS qf	H	Glentoran	D 1-1	Johnston
22/04/1952	CAS qf rep	A	Glentoran	L 0-3	-
28/04/1952	FBC po	H	Coleraine	W 3-2	Currie; Lyness 2
05/05/1952	FBC sf	N	Glentoran	W 1-0	Lyness
17/05/1952	FBC f	N	Crusaders	W 3-0	Lyness 2; Walsh

Notes

20/08/1951 v. Cliftonville: Match played at Windsor Park and competition held over from 1950/51 season

04/02/1951 v. Distillery: Match played at Windsor Park

15/03/1951 v. Ards: Match played at Windsor Park

05/05/1951 v. Glentoran: Match played at Windsor Park

17/05/1951 v. Crusaders: Match played at Solitude

Player Appearances and Goals

ANDERSON William	1	0	McCAIGE	1	0
BAILIE Oswald	26	0	McCAMBRIDGE Gerard	2	0
BARR Joseph	40	1	McGUIGAN J	2	0
CUBITT William	37	7	MITTEN John	52	13
CURRIE Jack	41	15	MITTEN Samuel	40	20
DOUGLAS Joseph	26	2	MORRISON Vincent	2	0
ELLIOTT Alfred	2	1	MULLEN James	13	7
FEGAN Gerald	42	2	MURPHY Martin	17	0
GAMBLE Samuel	1	0	MURPHY Harold	52	1
GEORGE Derek	1	0	QUINN William	13	1
HAMILTON J	9	0	RICE	1	0
JOHNSTON Ernest	29	6	RODGERS James	14	0
JORDAN	5	0	TREVORROW Eric	50	1
LONG Walter	9	0	WALSH Harold	1	1
LYNESS James	39	21	WILLIAMS Richard	3	0
McCAFFREY James	1	0			

Date	Comp	Venue	Opponents	Result	Scorers
16/08/1952	UC 1	A	Derry City	W 4-0	Trevorrow; Baker 3
19/08/1952	UC 2	H	Glentoran	W 4-2	Lyness; Edwards; Kelly 2
21/08/1952	UC 3	A	Cliftonville	W 5-2	S. Mitten 3; J. Mitten; Kelly
23/08/1952	UC 4	H	Crusaders	L 2-3	Edwards; J. Mitten
26/08/1952	UC 5	H	Coleraine	L 0-2	-
30/08/1952	UC 6	A	Glentoran	L 1-5	Kelly
02/09/1952	UC 7	A	Crusaders	L 1-3	S. Mitten
06/09/1952	UC 8	H	Derry City	D 2-2	J. Mitten; Baker
11/09/1952	UC 9	A	Coleraine	L 0-4	-
13/09/1952	CC 1	A	Distillery	L 0-2	-
16/09/1952	UC 10	H	Cliftonville	W 4-1	Cubitt; Currie; Johnston; Edwards
20/09/1952	CC 2	A	Cliftonville	W 2-1	J. Mitten; Lyness
27/09/1952	CC 3	H	Portadown	W 2-0	McMullen; S. Mitten
11/10/1952	CC 4	A	Glentoran	L 1-2	Lyness
18/10/1952	CC 5	H	Derry City	W 2-1	Baker; McMullen
25/10/1952	CC 6	A	Linfield	L 0-1	-
01/11/1952	CC 7	H	Crusaders	W 1-0	Currie
08/11/1952	CC 8	A	Glenavon	W 4-1	S. Mitten 4
15/11/1952	CC 9	H	Bangor	W 2-1	Simpson; Fulton og
22/11/1952	CC 10	H	Ards	W 2-1	Baker 2
29/11/1952	CC 11	A	Coleraine	L 0-3	-
06/12/1952	IL 1	H	Portadown	W 4-0	Baker; McMullen 2; Lyness
13/12/1952	IL 2	A	Ards	W 3-1	Baker 2; Johnston
20/12/1952	IL 3	H	Cliftonville	W 6-1	McMullen; Lyness; Trevorrow; Baker 2; McCleary og
25/12/1952	IL 4	A	Distillery	W 4-2	Johnston 2; Orr; Lyness
26/12/1952	IL 5	H	Linfield	D 2-2	Baker 2
27/12/1952	IL 6	A	Glenavon	L 2-5	Johnston; S. Mitten
03/01/1953	IL 7	H	Bangor	W 3-1	Baker 2; McMullen
10/01/1953	IL 8	H	Coleraine	D 1-1	Lyness
17/01/1953	IL 9	A	Glentoran	L 1-4	Lyness
24/01/1953	IL 10	H	Crusaders	W 5-3	Johnston; Baker 2; Lyness; Bonnar
31/01/1953	IL 11	A	Derry City	L 1-3	Lyness
07/02/1953	IC rd1	A	Coleraine	D 0-0	-
11/02/1953	IC rd1 rep	H	Coleraine	D 2-2	Baker; McMullen
18/02/1953	IC rd1 rep 2	A	Coleraine	L 1-2 (aet)	Bonnar
21/02/1953	IL 12	H	Ards	W 4-0	Johnston; Bonnar; White 2
28/02/1953	IL 13	H	Glenavon	W 4-1	Skelton; White; Bonnar; McMullen
07/03/1953	IL 14	A	Cliftonville	W 4-1	Bonnar 4
14/03/1953	IL 15	A	Crusaders	W 2-1	Skelton; Bonnar
18/03/1953	CAS rd1	H	Brantwood	D 2-2	Bonnar; Cubitt
21/03/1953	IL 16	A	Bangor	W 2-1	Bonnar; Murdough og
23/03/1953	CAS rd1 rep	A	Brantwood	D 3-3	McDowell og; White; McMullan
30/03/1953	CAS rd1 rep 2	H	Brantwood	W 2-1	Cubitt; Skelton
01/04/1953	CAS qf	H	Ards	D 0-0	-
04/04/1953	IL 17	H	Distillery	W 4-0	Skelton 2; Currie; McMullen
06/04/1953	IL 18	A	Portadown	D 1-1	Currie
07/04/1953	IL 19	A	Glentoran	L 0-1	-
11/04/1953	IL 20	H	Derry City	W 3-0	Skelton 2; White
13/04/1953	CAS qf rep	A	Ards	L 1-5	Currie
18/04/1953	IL 21	A	Coleraine	L 1-2	Currie
28/04/1953	IL 22	A	Linfield	L 0-3	-
05/05/1953	GC qf	H	Ards	L 0-1	-
08/05/1953	TEST	H	Huddersfield Town	D 4-4	Walker; Jones 3

Played: 52, won: 26, drawn: 9, lost: 17, goals scored: 107, goals conceded: 85

Irish League: 3rd; Irish Cup: Round 1; Gold Cup: Quarter-final; Ulster Cup: Group stage; City Cup: 3rd; County Antrim Shield: Quarter-final

Notes

08/05/1953 v. Huddersfield Town: Testimonial for Eric Trevorrow

Player Appearances and Goals

BAILIE Oswald	3	0	McCARTNEY James	4	0
BAKER James	22	19	McGREGOR Alexander	2	0
BONNAR Patrick	20	11	McMULLEN Charles	39	10
BOWERS John	3	0	MILLAR Robert	2	0
BROWN Desmond	40	0	MITTEN John	26	4
CUBITT William	50	3	MITTEN Samuel	18	10
CURRIE Jack	20	6	MURPHY Harold	51	0
EDWARDS	11	3	MURPHY Martin	3	0
GAMBLE Samuel	1	0	ORR Victor	5	1
HOSEY	3	0	SIMPSON James	46	1
HOUSTON	5	0	SKELTON Stanley	17	7
JOHNSTON Ernie	32	7	SMITH	1	0
KAVANAGH	1	0	SWANN John	1	0
KELLY James	8	4	TREVORROW Eric	51	2
LYNESS James	21	10	WALSH Harold	7	0
McCAFFREY James	20	0	WHITE James	12	5
McCANN John	27	0			

Played: 49, won: 19, drawn: 9, lost: 21, goals scored: 83, goals conceded: 93

Irish League: 4th; Irish Cup: Round 1; Gold Cup: Quarter-final; Ulster Cup: Group stage; City Cup: 9th; County Antrim Shield: Finalists

Date	Comp	Venue	Opponents	Result	Scorers
15/08/1953	UC 1	H	Derry City	W 6-0	McCall; Coulter; Coll; McMullen 2; Currie
18/08/1953	UC 2	A	Glentoran	L 1-5	Coll
20/08/1953	UC 3	H	Cliftonville	W 3-2	Currie 2; Coll
22/08/1953	UC 4	A	Crusaders	D 1-1	McMullen
26/08/1953	UC 5	A	Coleraine	L 0-3	-
29/08/1953	CC 1	A	Distillery	W 1-0	Johnston
01/09/1953	UC 6	H	Glentoran	D 1-1	Johnston
03/09/1953	UC 7	A	Derry City	L 1-3	Trevorrow
05/09/1953	CC 2	H	Cliftonville	W 1-0	Coll
08/09/1953	UC 8	A	Crusaders	L 1-2	Coll
10/09/1953	UC 9	H	Coleraine	L 1-2	Coll
12/09/1953	CC 3	A	Portadown	L 1-4	Coll
16/09/1953	UC 10	A	Cliftonville	L 1-2	Coll
19/09/1953	CC 4	H	Glentoran	L 0-3	-
26/09/1953	CC 5	A	Derry City	L 0-2	-
10/10/1953	CC 6	H	Linfield	L 0-2	-
17/10/1953	CC 7	A	Crusaders	W 3-0	McGuickan; Moody 2
24/10/1953	CC 8	H	Glenavon	L 0-2	-
31/10/1953	CC 9	A	Bangor	D 5-5	McMullen 2; Truesdale og; McGuickan; Trevorrow
07/11/1953	CC 10	A	Ards	D 1-1	Coll
14/11/1953	CC 11	H	Coleraine	L 1-4	McGarrity
21/11/1953	IL 1	H	Glentoran	L 1-4	Coll
28/11/1953	IL 2	A	Portadown	W 3-2	McMullen; McClure; Coll
05/12/1953	IL 3	A	Ards	W 2-1	Currie; McClure
12/12/1953	IL 4	H	Coleraine	W 5-1	McClure 2; Coll 2; Currie
19/12/1953	IL 5	A	Glenavon	W 2-1	McClure ; Coll
25/12/1953	IL 6	H	Distillery	D 1-1	McClure
26/12/1953	IL 7	A	Cliftonville	W 3-0	Coll 3
28/12/1953	IL 8	H	Cliftonville	W 2-0	Robinson; McGuickan
02/01/1954	IL 9	A	Linfield	D 3-3	Robinson; Currie; McClure
09/01/1954	IL 10	H	Derry City	W 5-2	McClure; McMullen 2; Coll 2
16/01/1954	IL 11	H	Bangor	W 2-0	McClure 2
23/01/1954	IL 12	H	Glenavon	D 4-4	Minford 2; Coll 2
06/02/1954	IC rd1	A	Derry City	L 0-1	-
13/02/1954	IL 13	A	Distillery	L 0-4	-
16/02/1954	IL 14	A	Bangor	L 1-2	Young
20/02/1954	IL 15	A	Derry City	W 3-1	Coll; Young 2
27/02/1954	IL 16	H	Linfield	D 2-2	McClure; McMillen og
13/03/1954	IL 17	H	Crusaders	L 1-2	Robinson
20/03/1954	IL 18	A	Glentoran	L 1-4	Coll
27/03/1954	GC rd1	A	Bangor	W 2-1	Moore; Coll
03/04/1954	IL 19	H	Portadown	L 1-4	Currie
07/04/1954	CAS qf	H	Linfield	W 1-0	Young
10/04/1954	IL 20	H	Ards	W 2-0	McGuickan; Currie
17/04/1954	IL 21	A	Coleraine	W 2-1	Bonnar; W. Brown
20/04/1954	IL 22	A	Crusaders	D 1-1	Coll
01/05/1954	CAS sf	N	Glentoran	W 3-2	Coll; Robinson; Currie
06/05/1954	GC qf	H	Glentoran	L 1-4	Coll
08/05/1954	CAS f	N	Distillery	L 0-1	-

Notes

01/05/1954 v. Glentoran: Match played at Solitude

08/05/1954 v. Distillery: Match played at Solitude

Player Appearances and Goals

BONNAR Patrick	7	1	McCURRY Harold	10	0
BOWERS John	1	0	McFARLANE James	6	0
BROWN Desmond	36	0	McGARRITY	1	1
BROWN W	4	1	McGUICKAN Robert	19	4
BURNETT	1	0	McMULLEN Charles	34	8
COLL Liam	49	27	MINFORD David	10	2
COULTER James	8	1	MOODY Frank	2	2
CURRIE Jack	39	9	MOORE	1	1
GAMBLE Samuel	1	0	MURPHY Harold	48	0
HARPER	2	0	NICHOLL	1	0
HICKS Ivan	5	0	PICKEN Samuel	14	0
HOUSTON Malcolm	49	0	ROBINSON Harold	11	4
JOHNSTON Ernie	15	2	SIMPSON James	4	0
KENNEDY Ronald	2	0	SMALL James	4	0
LIVINGSTONE Wilfred	3	0	TELFORD John	2	0
McCALL Joseph	22	1	TOLAND	2	0
McCANN John	19	0	TREVORROW Eric	48	2
McCARTNEY James	2	0	WASSON	1	0
McCLURE William	18	11	WHITE James	3	0
McCONKEY Liam	3	0	YOUNG Noel	27	4
McCURDY John	5	0			

1953/1954

Played: 49, won: 19, drawn: 9, lost: 21, goals scored: 83, goals conceded: 93

Irish League: 4th; Irish Cup: Round 1; Gold Cup: Quarter-final; Ulster Cup: Group stage; City Cup: 9th; County Antrim Shield: Finalists

1953/1954

Played: 46, won: 12, drawn: 10, lost: 24, goals scored: 70, goals conceded: 97

Irish League: 12th; Irish Cup: Round 1; Gold Cup: Semi-final; Ulster Cup: Group stage; City Cup: 5th; County Antrim Shield: Semi-final

Date	Comp	Venue	Opponents	Result	Scorers
21/08/1954	UC 1	H	Cliftonville	W 4-0	Barr; Fearon; Rickett; Coll
28/08/1954	UC 2	A	Crusaders	L 0-3	-
01/09/1954	UC 3	H	Glentoran	L 0-3	-
04/09/1954	UC 4	H	Coleraine	L 1-3	Burke
09/09/1954	UC 5	A	Derry City	L 1-3	Kernohan
11/09/1954	CC 1	H	Distillery	L 1-2	Fearon
18/09/1954	CC 2	A	Cliftonville	W 1-0	Edgar
25/09/1954	CC 3	H	Portadown	W 3-1	Barr; Rickett; Burke
09/10/1954	CC 4	A	Glentoran	L 1-6	Rickett
13/10/1954	GC qf	H	Portadown	D 0-0	-
16/10/1954	CC 5	H	Derry City	D 1-1	Thomson
23/10/1954	CC 6	A	Linfield	W 3-2	Rickett 2; Coll
28/10/1954	GC qf rep	A	Portadown	W 2-0	Coll; Thomson
30/10/1954	CC 7	H	Crusaders	W 3-1	Coll; Thomson 2
06/11/1954	CC 8	A	Glenavon	L 2-4	Rickett; Galbraith
13/11/1954	CC 9	H	Bangor	D 2-2	Currie; Rickett
20/11/1954	CC 10	H	Ards	W 4-3	Coll; McCormack; Thompson; Rickett
24/11/1954	GC sf	N	Glenavon	L 1-4	Currie
27/11/1954	CC 11	A	Coleraine	L 1-2	Fearon
04/12/1954	IL 1	H	Cliftonville	L 2-3	Coll 2
11/12/1954	IL 2	A	Linfield	L 0-2	-
18/12/1954	IL 3	H	Glenavon	L 2-3	Houston; Lawlor
25/12/1954	IL 4	A	Distillery	L 1-3	Brown
26/12/1954	IL 5	H	Derry City	W 2-1	Lawlor; Houston
01/01/1955	IL 6	H	Glentoran	L 0-4	-
08/01/1955	IL 7	A	Ards	L 3-4	Fearon; Moore; Lawlor
15/01/1955	IL 8	H	Portadown	D 3-3	Curtis; Moore; Lawlor
22/01/1955	IL 9	H	Coleraine	W 4-2	Fearon 2; Forsythe; Rickett
29/01/1955	IL 10	A	Bangor	D 2-2	Rickett; Lawlor
05/02/1955	IC rd1	H	Crusaders	L 1-2	Curtis
12/02/1955	IL 11	A	Crusaders	W 3-1	Lawlor; Galbraith; Burke
19/02/1955	IL 12	A	Cliftonville	L 0-1	-
12/03/1955	IL 13	A	Glenavon	L 1-3	Fearon
19/03/1955	IL 14	H	Distillery	D 2-2	Lawlor 2
23/03/1955	IL 15	H	Linfield	L 2-3	Burke; Fearon
02/04/1955	IL 16	A	Derry City	D 1-1	Fearon
06/04/1955	CAS qf	A	Cliftonville	D 0-0	-
09/04/1955	IL 17	A	Glentoran	L 1-4	Curtis
11/04/1955	IL 18	H	Ards	D 2-2	Curtis; Lawlor
12/04/1955	IL 19	A	Portadown	L 1-2	Wallace
16/04/1955	IL 20	A	Coleraine	L 0-3	-
19/04/1955	FR	H	Dundalk	W 5-2	Galbraith 4; Curtis
21/04/1955	CAS qf rep	H	Cliftonville	W 2-0	Lawlor 2
23/04/1955	IL	H	Crusaders	W 2-0	Wallace; Magee
30/04/1955	IL 22	H	Bangor	L 1-3	Magee
07/05/1955	CAS sf	N	Crusaders	D 1-1	Lawlor
09/05/1955	FR	H	Leeds United	L 2-6	Lawlor; Fearon
11/05/1955	CAS sf rep	N	Crusaders	L 0-2	-

Notes

24/11/1954 v. Glenavon: Match played at The Oval

07/05/1955 v. Crusaders: Match played at Grosvenor Park

11/05/1955 v. Crusaders: Match played at Grosvenor Park

Player Appearances and Goals

Player	Apps	Goals	Player	Apps	Goals
ADAIR Eric	6	0	HOLDEN	1	0
ALLEN Maurice	21	0	HOUSTON Malcolm	43	2
BABES John	2	0	KERNOHAN Sandy	21	1
BARR Hubert	6	2	LAWLOR Kit	22	12
BEGGS Samuel	4	0	MAGEE William	5	2
BOWERS John	4	0	McCAIGE J	2	0
BROLLY Robert	17	0	McCLINTON Eugene	2	0
BROWN Desmond	37	1	McCORMACK William	4	1
BURKE Robert	12	4	McCURDY Jim	5	0
CLARK James	17	0	McCURRY J	8	0
COLL Liam	20	7	MOORE	5	2
COLLINS Henry	8	0	MURPHY Harold	24	0
CONNOR	1	0	O'NEILL	1	0
CUMMINS Walter	1	0	RICKETT Walter	41	10
CURRIE Jack	10	2	ROONEY	1	0
CURTIS Patrick	11	4	THOMSON John	13	5
EDGAR Samuel	1	1	TREVORROW Eric	32	0
FEARON John	43	9	WALLACE	10	2
FORSYTHE Clifford	3	1	WATT Samuel	8	0
GALBRAITH Thomas	15	2	YOUNG Noel	19	0

Played: 46, won: 12, drawn: 10, lost: 24, goals scored: 70, goals conceded: 97

Irish League: 12th; Irish Cup: Round 1; Gold Cup: Semi-final; Ulster Cup: Group stage; City Cup: 5th; County Antrim Shield: Semi-final

Played: 41, won: 11, drawn: 2, lost: 28, goals scored: 62, goals conceded: 123

Irish League: 12th; Irish Cup: Round 1; Gold Cup: Round 1; Ulster Cup: Group stage; City Cup: 9th; County Antrim Shield: Quarter-final

Date	Comp	Venue	Opponents	Result	Scorers
20/08/1955	UC 1	A	Cliftonville	L 0-2	-
27/08/1955	UC 2	H	Crusaders	L 0-1	-
31/08/1955	UC 3	A	Glentoran	L 0-3	-
03/09/1955	UC 4	A	Coleraine	L 1-3	Murphy
07/09/1955	UC 5	H	Derry City	W 3-2	Galbraith 2; McCartney
10/09/1955	CC 1	A	Distillery	L 2-3	McMillan; Smith
21/09/1955	GC rd1	H	Linfield	L 0-3	-
24/09/1955	CC 2	A	Portadown	W 3-2	McCartney 2; Barr
28/09/1955	CC 3	H	Cliftonville	L 0-4	-
01/10/1955	CC 4	H	Glentoran	W 2-1	Smith 2
15/10/1955	CC 5	A	Derry City	D 3-3	Thomson 2; H. Baxter
22/10/1955	CC 6	H	Linfield	L 1-4	McCartney
29/10/1955	CC 7	A	Crusaders	L 1-3	Barr
05/11/1955	CC 8	H	Glenavon	D 3-3	Galbraith; McCartney 2
12/11/1955	CC 9	A	Bangor	L 1-2	Thomson
19/11/1955	CC 10	A	Ards	W 3-1	McCartney; Watt; Thomson
26/11/1955	CC 11	H	Coleraine	L 2-3	Watt; McCartney
03/12/1955	IL 1	H	Linfield	L 1-3	McCartney
10/12/1955	IL 2	A	Glenavon	L 1-3	Haslett
17/12/1955	IL 3	H	Derry City	L 1-3	Thomson
24/12/1955	IL 4	A	Bangor	L 2-6	Corry og; Coulter
26/12/1955	IL 5	H	Distillery	W 3-1	McMillan; Barr 2
27/12/1955	IL 6	A	Cliftonville	L 1-3	Barr
31/12/1955	IL 7	H	Portadown	L 1-4	Coulter
07/01/1956	IL 8	A	Ards	L 3-4	Watt; Thomson
14/01/1956	IL 9	H	Glentoran	W 4-1	Haslett; Thomson; Watt
21/01/1956	IL 10	A	Coleraine	L 1-5	Haslett
28/01/1956	IL 11	A	Crusaders	L 0-6	-
04/02/1956	IC rd1	H	Glentoran	L 0-4	-
11/02/1956	IL 12	H	Crusaders	W 2-1	McMillan; Haslett
18/02/1956	IL 13	H	Glenavon	L 1-4	Galbraith
25/02/1956	IL 14	A	Linfield	W 2-1	Barr; Thomson
03/03/1956	IL 15	H	Cliftonville	L 1-2	Thomson
10/03/1956	IL 16	H	Bangor	L 2-3	McMillan 2
24/03/1956	IL 17	H	Coleraine	L 0-4	-
31/03/1956	IL 18	A	Distillery	L 1-5	Barr
03/04/1956	IL 19	A	Derry City	W 2-1	Dubois; McReynolds
07/04/1956	IL 20	A	Portadown	L 1-5	McMillan
11/04/1956	CAS qf	A	Linfield	L 1-7	Haslett
14/04/1956	IL 21	H	Ards	W 3-2	Norris; Haslett; McReynolds
28/04/1956	IL 22	A	Glentoran	W 3-2	Haslett 2; Barr

Notes

20/08/1955 v. Cliftonville: Match played at Celtic Park

Player Appearances and Goals

ALLEN Maurice	32	0	MALONE George	5	0
BARR George	24	8	McCARTNEY David	13	9
BAXTER Harry	28	1	McCORMACK William	4	0
BAXTER T	2	0	McMILLAN Donald	38	6
BEGGS Samuel	3	0	McREYNOLDS J	4	2
BROWN Desmond	22	0	MULLAN Kevin	1	0
COULTER	6	2	MUNSTER Patrick	3	0
CUBITT William	41	0	MURPHY Harold	39	1
CUNNINGHAM Hugh	7	0	NORRIS J	4	1
DUBOIS James	4	1	SMITH	8	3
FULLERTON	2	0	STARRETT	1	0
GALBRAITH Anthony	14	4	STIRLING Donald	15	0
HALE Edward	2	0	SWANN Harold	1	0
HASLETT Frank	22	9	THOMSON John	30	9
INGLIS James	1	0	TREVORROW Eric	38	0
KERNOHAN	3	0	WATT Samuel	34	5

Played: 49, won: 12, drawn: 7, lost: 30, goals scored: 82, goals conceded: 137

Irish League: 11th; Irish Cup: Round 1; Gold Cup: Round 1; Ulster Cup: 5th; City Cup: 10th; County Antrim Shield: Semi-final

Date	Comp	Venue	Opponents	Result	Scorers
18/08/1956	UC 1	H	Linfield	D 1-1	Cubitt
22/08/1956	UC 2	A	Crusaders	L 2-4	McGhee; Walker
25/08/1956	UC 3	H	Glenavon	W 3-2	McGhee; Walker; McCartney
28/08/1956	UC 4	A	Distillery	D 1-1	McCartney
01/09/1956	UC 5	A	Bangor	L 0-4	-
06/09/1956	UC 6	A	Derry City	L 1-2	Swann
08/09/1956	UC 7	A	Ards	W 4-1	Walker; McCartney 2; McGhee
11/09/1956	UC 8	H	Glentoran	W 3-2	McGhee 2; McCartney
15/09/1956	UC 9	H	Coleraine	W 3-1	McGhee 3
22/09/1956	UC 10	A	Portadown	L 0-2	-
29/09/1956	UC 11	H	Cliftonville	W 2-1	McCartney; Walker
13/10/1956	IL 1	A	Crusaders	L 1-3	Gough og
20/10/1956	IL 2	H	Glentoran	L 1-3	McGhee
27/10/1956	IL 3	A	Distillery	L 1-5	D. Brown
03/11/1956	IL 4	H	Portadown	W 6-1	McCartney 4; Walker 2
10/11/1956	IL 5	A	Coleraine	L 1-4	McGhee
17/11/1956	IL 6	H	Ards	L 0-5	-
24/11/1956	IL 7	A	Bangor	D 1-1	McGhee
01/12/1956	IL 8	H	Glenavon	L 0-4	-
08/12/1956	IL 9	A	Linfield	L 1-3	McCartney
15/12/1956	IL 10	H	Derry City	L 1-2	Murray
22/12/1956	IL 11	H	Cliftonville	W 4-3	McGhee 2; T. Stewart; Hedley
29/12/1956	IL 12	H	Distillery	L 2-4	T. Stewart 2
05/01/1957	IL 13	A	Portadown	D 3-3	Brady; T. Stewart 2
12/01/1957	IL 14	H	Coleraine	D 1-1	T. Stewart
19/01/1957	IL 15	A	Ards	L 1-2	McGhee
26/01/1957	IL 16	H	Bangor	L 2-3	Higginson; T. Stewart
02/02/1957	IC rd1	A	Portadown	D 1-1	McCartney
06/02/1957	IC rd1 rep	H	Portadown	L 2-3	Murray; Dornan
09/02/1957	IL 17	A	Glenavon	L 0-5	-
16/02/1957	IL 18	H	Linfield	L 1-6	McGhee
23/02/1957	IL 19	A	Derry City	L 0-3	-
02/03/1957	IL 20	H	Crusaders	W 5-2	Dillon 2; Dickson 2; Watt
09/03/1957	IL 21	A	Cliftonville	L 1-2	Dickson
13/03/1957	IL 22	A	Glentoran	L 2-7	T. Stewart; Brady
16/03/1957	CC 1	H	Distillery	L 2-5	McGhee; McCartney
23/03/1957	CC 2	H	Bangor	W 4-0	T. Stewart 3; McGhee
30/03/1957	CC 3	A	Cliftonville	L 1-3	Brady
06/04/1957	CC 4	H	Portadown	W 3-1	McGhee 2; Walker
11/04/1957	CAS qf	A	Linfield	W 1-0	T. Stewart
17/04/1957	GC rd1	H	Bangor	L 0-2	-
20/04/1957	CC 5	A	Glentoran	L 2-4	McGhee 2
23/04/1957	CC 6	A	Derry City	L 2-4	T. Stewart 2
25/04/1957	CAS sf	N	Distillery	L 2-3	Walker; T. Stewart
27/04/1957	CC 7	A	Linfield	L 2-7	Cubitt; McGhee
04/05/1957	CC 8	H	Crusaders	W 4-2	Higginson 2; T. Stewart 2
06/05/1957	CC 9	H	Ards	D 1-1	T. Stewart
09/05/1957	CC 10	A	Coleraine	L 0-4	-
11/05/1957	CC 11	A	Glenavon	L 0-4	-

Notes

28/08/1956 v. Distillery: Match played at Windsor Park

27/10/1956 v. Distillery: Match played at Windsor Park

25/04/1957 v. Distillery: Match played at Solitude

Player Appearances and Goals

Player	Apps	Goals	Player	Apps	Goals
ALEXANDER Samuel	1	0	MATHER Harold	3	0
ASTON Thomas	2	0	McCARTNEY David	29	12
BOYD Desmond	7	0	McCAUL Liam	4	0
BRADY Arthur	41	3	McGHEE James	42	22
BROWN Desmond	42	1	MURPHY Harold	5	0
BROWN Norman	18	0	MURRAY Thomas	13	2
BURNS Ronald	3	0	NICHOLL Trevor	1	0
CAMPBELL Robert	12	0	O'HANLON Jim	2	0
CARLISLE Arnold	1	0	PATTERSON M	2	0
COARD Ernest	22	0	QUINN Sydney	7	0
CUBITT William	41	2	STEWART Brian	1	0
DICKSON Victor	4	3	STEWART Thomas	25	19
DILLON Ronald	11	2	STIRLING Donald	17	0
DORNAN Alan	14	1	SWANN Harold	16	1
FRY Reggie	1	0	TONER George	3	0
GRAHAM Alan	3	0	TREVORROW Eric	36	0
HEDLEY Joseph	1	1	WALKER Thomas	25	8
HIGGINSON William	13	3	WALLACE Robert	1	0
HINTON Edward	36	0	WATT Samuel	11	1
LOGAN George	1	0	WATTON W	1	0
LUNEY Jim	1	0	WILSON Alexander	2	0
LYNCH Howard	18	0			

Played: 48, won: 23, drawn: 6, lost: 19, goals scored: 101, goals conceded: 94

Irish League: 3rd; Irish Cup: Winners; Gold Cup: Quarter-final; Ulster Cup: Group stage; City Cup: 7th; County Antrim Shield: Semi-final

Date	Comp	Venue	Opponents	Result	Scorers
17/08/1957	UC 1	H	Crusaders	D 1-1	McGhee
21/08/1957	UC 2	A	Glentoran	L 2-3	Smyth; McGhee
24/08/1957	UC 3	H	Cliftonville	L 1-2	McGhee
29/08/1957	UC 4	A	Derry City	L 1-2	Houston og.
31/08/1957	UC 5	A	Coleraine	L 2-4	G. Barr; McQuaid
04/09/1957	GC rd1	H	Cliftonville	D 1-1	Twinem
07/09/1957	CC 1	A	Distillery	L 0-5	-
10/09/1957	GC rd1 rep	A	Cliftonville	W 5-3	McGhee 3; G. Barr; W. Brown
14/09/1957	CC 2	H	Cliftonville	L 1-4	W. Brown
18/09/1957	GC qf	H	Ards	L 3-5	McCrae; Cubitt 2
21/09/1957	CC 3	A	Portadown	W 4-0	McGhee 3; O'Kane
28/09/1957	CC 4	H	Glentoran	L 2-3	Twinem; McCartney
12/10/1957	CC 5	A	Derry City	D 2-2	W. Glass; McGhee
19/10/1957	CC 6	H	Linfield	L 0-3	-
26/10/1957	CC 7	A	Ards	W 4-1	McGhee 2; Egan; McCrae
02/11/1957	CC 8	A	Crusaders	W 2-0	McGhee; Small
09/11/1957	CC 9	H	Coleraine	W 4-2	W. Glass 2; McGhee; Egan
16/11/1957	CC 10	H	Glenavon	L 0-3	-
23/11/1957	CC 11	A	Bangor	L 0-5	-
30/11/1957	IL 1	H	Linfield	W 3-1	O'Kane; McCrae 2
07/12/1957	IL 2	H	Bangor	L 1-3	Forsyth
14/12/1957	IL 3	A	Derry City	W 2-1	McCrae; Forsyth
21/12/1957	IL 4	H	Cliftonville	W 4-0	Twinem 2; McGhee; McCrae
25/12/1957	IL 5	A	Crusaders	L 2-5	Russell; McCrae
26/12/1957	IL 6	H	Glentoran	W 5-1	McGhee 2; Small; McCrae 2
28/12/1957	IL 7	A	Distillery	W 5-0	Cubitt; Forsyth 2; Russell; McCrae
04/01/1958	IL 8	H	Portadown	W 1-0	McGhee
11/01/1958	IL 9	A	Coleraine	L 2-4	McGhee; McCrae
18/01/1958	IL 10	H	Ards	D 1-1	Lowry
01/02/1958	IC rd1	H	Dundela	W 5-0	Russell; Forsyth 2; Cubitt; McGhee
08/02/1958	IL 11	A	Bangor	W 2-0	Small; McGhee
15/02/1958	IL 12	A	Linfield	L 1-5	McGhee
22/02/1958	IL 13	H	Derry City	W 2-1	Forsyth; McCrae
01/03/1958	IC qf	A	Ards	W 3-1	McGhee 2; Lowry
08/03/1958	IL 14	A	Cliftonville	W 4-2	McGhee 3; Trevorrow
15/03/1958	IL 15	H	Crusaders	W 4-2	Forsyth; McCrae 2; McGhee
22/03/1958	IC sf	N	Derry City	W 3-0	Lowry; McGhee; Egan
29/03/1958	IL 16	A	Glentoran	L 1-3	McGhee
05/04/1958	IL 17	H	Distillery	W 3-2	Forsyth; McGhee; Egan
08/04/1958	IL 18	A	Portadown	W 2-1	McCrae; Egan
12/04/1958	IL 19	H	Coleraine	D 2-2	McGhee; Egan
16/04/1958	CAS qf	A	Bangor	D 0-0	-
19/04/1958	IL 20	A	Ards	L 0-3	-
21/04/1958	CAS qf rep	H	Bangor	W 1-0	Wilson
26/04/1958	IC f	N	Linfield	W 2-0	McGhee; Russell
28/04/1958	IL 21	H	Glenavon	W 3-2	McGhee; Stewart; Forsyth
01/05/1958	IL 22	A	Glenavon	L 1-2	Murray
03/05/1958	CAS sf	N	Distillery	L 1-3	Forsyth
08/05/1958	TEST	H	All Star XI	L 2-5	Corr; Russell

Notes

22/03/1958 v. Derry City: Match played at Solitude

26/04/1958 v. Linfield: Match played at The Oval

03/05/1958 v. Distillery: Match played at Windsor Park

08/05/1958 v. All Star XI: Testimonial for Des Brown

Player Appearances and Goals

BARR George	4	2	McCARTNEY David	2	1
BLACK John	2	0	McCRAE Alexander	35	15
BOND Harold	46	0	McGHEE James	38	34
BOYD Desmond	5	0	McQUAID Thomas	4	1
BROWN Desmond	27	0	MULGREW Andrew	13	0
BROWN William	3	2	MURRAY David	5	1
COARD Ernest	5	0	O'KANE Edward	8	2
CUBITT William	48	4	QUINN Sidney	5	0
EGAN John	27	6	RUSSELL Edward	20	4
FORSYTH William	27	11	SMALL James	17	3
GLASS Cecil	9	0	SMYTH John	15	1
GLASS Wallace	13	3	STEWART Arthur	5	1
JOHNSTON Edward	20	0	TREVORROW Eric	41	1
KIRK Robert	2	0	TWINEM William	18	4
LOWRY Thomas	42	3	WILSON Alexander	18	1
MACKLIN Arthur	2	0	WORTHINGTON	2	0

Played: 49, won: 24, drawn: 5, lost: 20, goals scored: 110, goals conceded: 103

Irish League: 5th; Irish Cup: Finalists; Gold Cup: Round 1; Ulster Cup: Group stage; City Cup: 8th; County Antrim Shield: Semi-final

Date	Comp	Venue	Opponents	Result	Scorers
16/08/1958	UC 1	A	Crusaders	L 3-5	McCrae 2; Forsyth
20/08/1958	UC 2	H	Glentoran	W 3-2	Lowry 2; Russell
23/08/1958	UC 3	A	Cliftonville	L 1-3	Welsh
27/08/1958	UC 4	H	Derry City	W 4-1	Montgomery 2; Welsh; Forsyth
30/08/1958	UC 5	H	Coleraine	W 5-3	Welsh; McGhee 3; Trevorrow
04/09/1958	GC rd1	H	Glenavon	L 3-4	McCrae; McGhee; Forsyth
06/09/1958	CC 1	H	Distillery	L 1-4	McCrae
13/09/1958	CC 2	A	Cliftonville	W 5-1	Russell; Forsyth; McCrae 2; Clarke
20/09/1958	CC 3	H	Portadown	W 4-2	Russell; Clarke; Forsyth; Welsh
27/09/1958	CC 4	A	Glentoran	L 3-4	Trevorrow; Lowry; Welsh
11/10/1958	CC 5	H	Derry City	W 3-2	Welsh 2; Clarke
18/10/1958	CC 6	A	Linfield	L 1-3	Russell
25/10/1958	CC 7	H	Ards	W 5-1	McGhee 2; Clarke; Lowry; Russell
01/11/1958	CC 8	H	Crusaders	L 0-4	-
08/11/1958	CC 9	A	Coleraine	L 1-3	Mullen
15/11/1958	CC 10	A	Glenavon	L 0-3	-
22/11/1958	CC 11	H	Bangor	L 1-2	McGhee
29/11/1958	IL 1	H	Linfield	W 2-1	Russell; Forsyth
06/12/1958	IL 2	A	Bangor	W 2-0	McGhee 2
13/12/1958	IL 3	A	Glenavon	L 1-3	Clarke
20/12/1958	IL 4	H	Cliftonville	W 5-0	McGhee 3; Brown; Walsh
25/12/1958	IL 5	H	Crusaders	W 4-1	Welsh; McGhee 2; Lowry
26/12/1958	IL 6	A	Glentoran	L 0-4	-
27/12/1958	IL 7	H	Portadown	L 1-3	Lowry
03/01/1959	IL 8	A	Ards	W 4-1	Welsh; Russell 2; McGhee
24/01/1959	IL 9	A	Derry City	W 4-1	McGhee 2; Clarke; Russell
31/01/1959	IC rd1	H	Coleraine	W 4-2	Welsh; McGhee; A. Stewart; McCrae
07/02/1959	IL 10	H	Glentoran	L 2-3	McCrae; Russell
09/02/1959	IL 11	A	Distillery	W 4-3	McCrae 2; Welsh; Clarke
14/02/1959	IL 12	A	Coleraine	L 0-4	-
21/02/1959	IL 13	H	Distillery	W 4-2	McEvoy 2; Russell; Welsh
28/02/1959	IC qf	A	Portadown	D 1-1	Clarke
04/03/1959	IC qf rep	H	Portadown	W 1-0	Clarke
07/03/1959	IL 14	H	Derry City	L 2-3	McEvoy; Russell
14/03/1959	IL 15	A	Linfield	L 0-5	-
16/03/1959	CAS rd1	H	Larne	W 5-0	McGhee 2; Trevorrow; Clarke; T. Stewart
21/03/1959	IC sf	N	Linfield	W 2-1	McGhee; Russell
25/03/1959	IL 16	H	Coleraine	W 4-2	Clarke 2; A. Stewart; McEvoy
28/03/1959	IL 17	H	Glenavon	D 0-0	-
30/03/1959	IL 18	A	Portadown	W 4-3	T. Stewart 2; Russell 2
31/03/1959	IL 19	H	Ards	D 3-3	A. Stewart; Forsyth; McEvoy
04/04/1959	IL 20	H	Bangor	W 2-0	Trevorrow 2
11/04/1959	IL 21	A	Crusaders	W 2-0	McEvoy; McCrae
18/04/1959	IC f	N	Glenavon	D 1-1	Lowry
21/04/1959	CAS qf	A	Cliftonville	W 2-0	Russell; Lowry
25/04/1959	IL 22	A	Cliftonville	L 1-4	Welsh
29/04/1959	IC f rep	N	Glenavon	L 0-2	-
02/05/1959	CAS sf	N	Linfield	D 0-0	-
05/05/1959	CAS sf rep	N	Linfield	L 0-3	-

Notes

21/03/1959 v. Linfield: Match played at The Oval

18/04/1959 v. Glenavon: Match played at Windsor Park

29/04/1959 v. Glenavon: Match played at Windsor Park

02/05/1959 v. Linfield: Match played at Solitude

05/05/1959 v. Linfield: Match played at Solitude

Player Appearances and Goals

Player	Apps	Goals	Player	Apps	Goals
BLACK Gordon	5	0	McCRAE Alexander	34	11
BOND Harold	35	0	McEVOY Jack	9	6
BROWN Desmond	34	1	McGHEE James	34	21
CLARKE Norman	38	12	MOLYNEAUX Samuel	4	0
CUBITT William	47	0	MONTGOMERY Cyril	4	2
CURRIE Alan	3	0	MULLEN James	4	1
DOHERTY Alexander	12	0	MURPHY Michael	11	0
FORSYTH William	24	7	RUSSELL Edward	40	16
FRIEL Eamonn	2	0	SMALL James	8	0
HOUSTON Alexander	2	0	STEWART Arthur	12	3
JOHNSTON Edward	38	0	STEWART Thomas	6	3
KIRK Samuel	1	0	TREVORROW Eric	45	5
LOWRY Thomas	44	8	WADE	1	0
MACKLIN Arthur	2	0	WALSH William	40	14

Played: 45, won: 21, drawn: 7, lost: 17, goals scored: 94, goals conceded: 87

Irish League: 5th; Irish Cup: Quarter-final; Gold Cup: Semi-final; Ulster Cup: Group stage; City Cup: 5th; County Antrim Shield: Quarter-final

1959/1960

Date	Comp	Venue	Opponents	Result	Scorers
15/08/1959	UC 1	H	Crusaders	L 0-3	-
19/08/1959	UC 2	A	Glentoran	D 1-1	Barr
22/08/1959	UC 3	H	Cliftonville	W 4-2	Maguire 2; Lowry; Russell
25/08/1959	UC 4	A	Derry City	W 3-0	Barr; Smyth; Russell
28/08/1959	UC 5	A	Coleraine	W 2-1	Barr; Russell
05/09/1959	CC 1	A	Distillery	L 1-4	Barr
12/09/1959	CC 2	H	Cliftonville	W 2-0	Barr; Russell
16/09/1959	GC qf	A	Glenavon	W 5-4	Barr 2; Maguire 2; Lowry
19/09/1959	CC 3	A	Portadown	W 3-2	Maguire 2; Barr
26/09/1959	CC 4	H	Glentoran	W 4-0	Russell; McCrae 2; Stewart
10/10/1959	CC 5	A	Derry City	W 3-2	McCrae; Cubitt; Barr
17/10/1959	CC 6	H	Linfield	W 2-1	Maguire; Barr
21/10/1959	FR	A	Falkirk	L 1-4	McCrae
24/10/1959	CC 7	A	Ards	W 2-1	Maguire; Barr
28/10/1959	GC sf	N	Linfield	D 1-1	McCrae
31/10/1959	CC 8	A	Crusaders	L 0-2	-
05/11/1959	GC sf rep	N	Linfield	L 1-3	Russell
07/11/1959	CC 9	H	Coleraine	D 0-0	-
14/11/1959	CC 10	H	Glenavon	L 2-3	Lowe; Barr
21/11/1959	CC 11	A	Bangor	L 0-3	-
28/11/1959	IL 1	H	Derry City	W 2-0	Smyth; Small
05/12/1959	IL 2	A	Ards	D 1-1	Russell
12/12/1959	IL 3	H	Glenavon	L 0-4	-
19/12/1959	IL 4	A	Linfield	L 1-4	Barr
25/12/1959	IL 5	A	Crusaders	L 2-3	Smyth; Barr
26/12/1959	IL 6	H	Distillery	L 1-3	Fullerton
02/01/1960	IL 7	A	Coleraine	W 5-2	Maguire; Barr; Russell; Cubitt; McCrae
09/01/1960	IL 8	H	Glentoran	W 5-3	Clarke; Barr; McCrae 2; Smyth
16/01/1960	IL 9	A	Bangor	L 0-1	-
23/01/1960	IL 10	A	Cliftonville	W 4-0	Barr 2; Smyth 2
30/01/1960	IC rd1	H	Cliftonville	D 2-2	Clarke; McKinley og
04/02/1960	IC rd1 rep	H	Cliftonville	W 4-0	Clarke; Barr 2; Smyth
06/02/1960	IL 11	H	Portadown	D 2-2	Smyth; Barr
13/02/1960	IL 12	A	Derry City	L 1-6	Lynch
27/02/1960	IC qf	A	Distillery	L 3-5	Barr 3
02/03/1960	IL 13	H	Ards	W 2-1	Lynch; Barr
05/03/1960	IL 14	A	Glenavon	W 4-1	Russell; Lynch 3
12/03/1960	IL 15	H	Linfield	L 2-4	Barr 2
19/03/1960	IL 16	H	Crusaders	L 1-2	Barr
02/04/1960	IL 17	A	Glentoran	L 0-2	-
09/04/1960	IL 18	H	Bangor	W 2-0	Russell; Lynch
13/04/1960	CAS qf	A	Glentoran II	L 0-1	-
16/04/1960	IL 19	H	Portadown	W 5-1	Barr 3; Smyth; Russell
18/04/1960	IL 20	A	Distillery	W 2-1	Barr 2
21/04/1960	IL 21	H	Coleraine	D 4-4	Russell; Barr 2; Clarke
23/04/1960	IL 22	H	Cliftonville	W 3-1	Russell 3
27/04/1960	FR	H	Falkirk	W 3-0	Barr 3

Notes

28/10/59 v. Linfield: Match played at Grosvenor Park

05/11/59 v. Linfield: Match played at Grosvenor Park

Player Appearances and Goals

BARR Hubert	40	35	McCRAE Alexander	24	7
BOND Harold	44	0	McCULLOUGH Cecil	1	0
BROWN Desmond	5	0	McKILLEN Hugh	1	0
CLARKE Norman	32	4	MOLYNEAUX Samuel	1	0
CUBITT William	43	2	PATTERSON Herbert	2	0
CURRIE Alan	1	0	RUSSELL Edward	38	15
FULLERTON Jim	2	1	SMALL James	20	1
JOHNSTON Edward	44	0	SMYTH John	30	9
LOWE James	33	1	STEWART Arthur	39	1
LOWRY Thomas	14	2	STEWART Thomas	6	0
LYNCH Michael	10	6	TREVORROW Eric	20	0
MAGUIRE Vincent	28	9	TWENTYMAN Geoff	7	0
McAULEY Thomas	1	0	WALSH William	9	0

Played: 46, won: 27, drawn: 8, lost: 11, goals scored: 118, goals conceded: 72

Irish League: 5th; Irish Cup: Quarter-final; Gold Cup: Quarter-final; Ulster Cup: Winners; City Cup: Runners-up; County Antrim Shield: Semi-final

Date	Comp	Venue	Opponents	Result	Scorers
20/08/1960	UC 1	A	Crusaders	W 3-0	Mitchell 2; Smyth
24/08/1960	UC 2	H	Glentoran	D 1-1	Russell
27/08/1960	UC 3	A	Cliftonville	W 4-1	Mitchell 2; N. Clarke; Smyth
31/08/1960	UC 4	H	Derry City	W 3-0	Smyth 2; Mitchell
03/09/1960	UC 5	H	Coleraine	W 2-0	McDermott og; Mitchell
10/09/1960	CC 1	H	Ards	W 4-3	Barr; N. Clarke; Smyth 2
14/09/1960	GC rd1	H	Bangor	W 5-2	Barr 3; Smyth; Russell
17/09/1960	CC 2	A	Distillery	L 1-3	Mitchell
24/09/1960	CC 3	H	Crusaders	W 2-0	Smith 2
28/09/1960	GC qf	A	Glentoran	L 1-3	Smyth
01/10/1960	CC 4	A	Portadown	D 1-1	Smyth
07/10/1960	UC f	N	Glenavon	W 3-1	Barr 2; McKinstry og
15/10/1960	CC 5	H	Coleraine	W 5-2	Smith; Barr 2; Russell; Mitchell
22/10/1960	CC 6	A	Glentoran	L 0-3	-
29/10/1960	CC 7	H	Linfield	W 4-2	Twentyman; Barr; Russell; Stewart
05/11/1960	CC 8	A	Cliftonville	W 6-0	Russell; Barr; Waring og; Neill
12/11/1960	CC 9	H	Glenavon	D 3-3	Russell 2; Smith
19/11/1960	CC 10	A	Derry City	W 4-1	Smith 2; Barr 2
26/11/1960	CC 11	H	Bangor	W 3-1	Cubitt; N. Clarke; Mulholland og
03/12/1960	IL 1	A	Derry City	W 3-1	Small 3
10/12/1960	IL 2	A	Glenavon	D 1-1	Barr
17/12/1960	IL 3	H	Glentoran	W 2-1	Small 2
24/12/1960	IL 4	A	Distillery	W 4-3	Barr; Twentyman; Small 2
26/12/1960	IL 5	H	Crusaders	D 1-1	Smith
27/12/1960	IL 6	A	Ards	D 1-1	Smith
31/12/1960	IL 7	H	Coleraine	L 1-3	Barr
07/01/1961	IL 8	A	Portadown	L 3-4	Barr 3
14/01/1961	IL 9	H	Linfield	W 2-1	N. Clarke; Barr
21/01/1961	IL 10	A	Cliftonville	W 3-1	N. Clarke 2; Smyth
28/01/1961	IL 11	H	Bangor	W 5-2	Barr 3; Smith; Twentyman
11/02/1961	IL 12	A	Crusaders	L 0-1	-
18/02/1961	IL 13	H	Ards	D 1-1	Neill
25/02/1961	IC rd1	H	Derry City	W 2-1	Barr
01/03/1961	IL 14	H	Distillery	L 1-5	Mitchell
04/03/1961	IL 15	A	Coleraine	W 1-0	N. Clarke
11/03/1961	IC qf	A	Ballyclare Comrades	L 1-3	Stewart
15/03/1961	CAS rd1	H	Linfield Swifts	W 8-2	Barr 5; Stewart; Neill; Smith
18/03/1961	IL	H	Portadown	D 3-3	Barr; Stewart 2
29/03/1961	CAS qf	H	Crusaders	W 1-0	Johnston
01/04/1961	IL 17	A	Linfield	W 2-1	Small; Neill
04/04/1961	IL 18	H	Cliftonville	W 8-2	Stewart; Small 2; Neill 2; Waring og; Barr 2
08/04/1961	IL 19	A	Bangor	L 0-2	-
15/04/1961	IL 20	H	Derry City	W 3-0	Neill; Small; Stewart
21/04/1961	IL 21	A	Glentoran	L 0-4	-
29/04/1961	IL 22	H	Glenavon	W 6-0	Small 2; Smith; Barr; Neill; Kinkead og
05/05/1961	CAS sf	N	Glentoran	L 0-1	-

Notes

07/10/1960 v. Glenavon: Match played at Grosvenor Park

05/05/1961 v. Glentoran: Match played at Solitude

Player Appearances and Goals

BARR Hubert	38	34	MOFFETT Edward	7	0
BOND Harold	45	0	MOLYNEAUX Samuel	2	0
CLARKE Charles	2	0	MONTGOMERIE Jack	4	0
CLARKE Norman	46	7	NEILL Derek	19	8
CLARKE Robert	4	0	RUSSELL Edward	19	8
CUBITT William	38	1	SMALL James	13	13
DEMPSTER James	1	0	SMITH John Eric	39	11
DOBBIN Roy	10	0	SMYTH John	34	10
JOHNSTON Edward	40	1	STEWART Arthur	44	7
McAULEY Thomas	1	0	TREVORROW Eric	37	0
McCRACKEN Fred	2	0	TWENTYMAN Geoff	41	3
MITCHELL Peter	19	9	WILSON Alexander	1	0

Played: 43, won: 17, drawn: 11, lost: 15, goals scored: 89, goals conceded: 71

Irish League: 3rd; Irish Cup: Round 1; Gold Cup: Round 1; Ulster Cup: Group Stage; City Cup: 8th; County Antrim Shield: Semi-final

1961/1962

Date	Comp	Venue	Opponents	Result	Scorers
19/08/1961	UC 1	H	Crusaders	D 2-2	Twentyman; Emery
22/08/1961	UC 2	A	Glentoran	L 2-3	Twentyman; Smith
26/08/1961	UC 3	H	Cliftonville	D 1-1	Neill
31/08/1961	UC 4	A	Derry City	W 2-1	Tickell 2
02/09/1961	UC 5	A	Coleraine	L 1-3	Clarke
05/09/1961	GC rd1	A	Glentoran	L 1-4	Clarke
09/09/1961	CC 1	A	Ards	W 5-2	Twentyman; Smith; Clarke; Neill; Greenfield
16/09/1961	CC 2	H	Distillery	D 0-0	-
23/09/1961	CC 3	A	Crusaders	L 0-1	-
30/09/1961	CC 4	H	Portadown	L 0-1	-
14/10/1961	CC 5	A	Coleraine	L 1-4	McInnes
21/10/1961	CC 6	H	Glentoran	L 1-3	Smith
28/10/1961	CC 7	A	Linfield	L 0-1	-
04/11/1961	CC 8	H	Cliftonville	W 8-1	Clarke; Greenfield 2; Small 3; Russell; Smith
11/11/1961	CC 9	A	Glenavon	L 1-3	Tickell
18/11/1961	CC 10	H	Derry City	W 7-0	Clarke; Small; Russell; Tickell 2; Smith
25/11/1961	CC 11	A	Bangor	W 2-0	Tickell 2
02/12/1961	IL 1	A	Glentoran	W 2-1	Small; Tickell
09/12/1961	IL 2	H	Ards	L 1-2	Small
16/12/1961	IL 3	A	Coleraine	W 1-0	Small
23/12/1961	IL 4	H	Portadown	L 1-3	Clarke
25/12/1961	IL 5	A	Bangor	W 4-0	Small 3; Clarke
26/12/1961	IL 6	H	Linfield	W 4-2	Small 2; Clarke; Twentyman
30/12/1961	IL 7	A	Distillery	W 4-1	Small 2; Emery; Clarke
06/01/1962	IL 8	H	Glenavon	D 3-3	Cubitt; Moffett; Emery
13/01/1962	IL 9	A	Derry City	D 0-0	-
20/01/1962	IL 10	H	Cliftonville	W 7-0	Clarke; Moffett 4; Small; Twentyman
27/01/1962	IL 11	H	Crusaders	D 1-1	Small
03/02/1962	IL 12	A	Glenavon	D 2-2	Woodall; Small
10/02/1962	IL 13	H	Derry City	W 2-0	Small 2
17/02/1962	IL 14	A	Cliftonville	W 3-1	Patterson 2; Smith
24/02/1962	IC rd1	H	Crusaders	L 2-3	Woodall; Small
03/03/1962	IL 15	A	Crusaders	W 2-1	Halliday ; Woodall
10/03/1962	CAS qf	H	Distillery	D 2-2	Moffett; Woodall
17/03/1962	IL 16	H	Glentoran	D 1-1	Woodall
24/03/1962	IL 17	H	Distillery	W 3-2	Hughes 2; Twentyman
31/03/1962	IL 18	A	Ards	D 1-1	Hughes
02/04/1962	CAS qf rep	H	Distillery	W 3-1	Watters; Russell 2
07/04/1962	IL 19	H	Coleraine	D 1-1	Halliday
21/04/1962	IL 20	A	Linfield	L 1-6	Woodall
23/04/1962	IL 21	H	Bangor	W 2-1	Smyth; Russell
28/04/1962	IL 22	A	Portadown	L 1-3	Small
05/05/1962	CAS sf	N	Linfield	L 1-3	Russell

Notes

05/05/1962 v. Linfield: Match played at Grosvenor Park

Player Appearances and Goals

Name	Apps	Goals	Name	Apps	Goals
ALLISON Thomas	2	0	MOFFATT Edward	29	6
BOND Harold	42	0	NEILL Derek	9	2
CLARKE Norman	28	10	PATTERSON John	2	2
CLARKE Robert	4	0	ROBINSON Donald	1	0
CUBITT William	34	1	RUSSELL Edward	42	6
DOBBIN Roy	41	0	SMALL James	33	22
EMERY Jim	9	3	SMITH John	41	6
GREENFIELD Cyril	10	3	SMYTH Thomas	6	1
HALLIDAY Kenneth	5	2	TICKELL Brian	11	8
HUGHES Gavin	6	3	TREVORROW Eric	41	0
HUTCHINSON Thomas	9	0	TWENTYMAN Geoff	41	6
McGREEVEY	1	0	WATTERS Derek	6	1
McINNES Hugh	3	1	WOODALL Stanley	16	6
MITCHELL Peter	1	0			

Date	Comp	Venue	Opponents	Result	Scorers
18/08/1962	UC 1	A	Crusaders	W 2-1	McDowell; Burke
22/08/1962	UC 2	H	Glentoran	L 1-4	Blake
24/08/1962	UC 3	A	Cliftonville	D 2-2	Keenan; McDowell
29/08/1962	UC 4	H	Derry City	L 1-3	Keenan
01/09/1962	UC 5	H	Coleraine	D 2-2	T. Smyth; McDowell
08/09/1962	CC 1	H	Ards	W 4-2	McNamara; Halliday; Twentyman; Patterson og
15/09/1962	CC 2	A	Distillery	L 2-6	Halliday 2
22/09/1962	CC 3	H	Crusaders	L 3-4	Twentyman; Halliday 2
24/09/1962	GC qf	A	Cliftonville	W 2-0	Keenan; Halliday
27/09/1962	CC 4	A	Portadown	D 2-2	Russell; Moffatt
06/10/1962	CC 5	H	Coleraine	L 2-3	Callan; Keenan
13/10/1962	CC 6	A	Glentoran	D 1-1	Halliday
27/10/1962	CC 7	H	Linfield	W 3-2	Callan; Russell; Halliday
03/11/1962	CC 8	A	Cliftonville	W 3-0	Halliday; McDowell; Dobbin
10/11/1962	CC 9	H	Glenavon	D 1-1	J. Smith
15/11/1962	GC sf	N	Derry City	L 0-5	-
17/11/1962	CC 10	A	Derry City	D 0-0	-
24/11/1962	CC 11	H	Bangor	W 3-2	Halliday; Burke; Callan
01/12/1962	IL 1	A	Bangor	D 2-2	Burke; Halliday
08/12/1962	IL 2	H	Glenavon	D 1-1	Twentyman
15/12/1962	IL 3	A	Linfield	D 1-1	Callan
22/12/1962	IL 4	H	Derry City	W 5-2	Halliday 2; Russell; Callan; Burke
25/12/1962	IL 5	A	Crusaders	L 1-4	Halliday
26/12/1962	IL 6	H	Glentoran	W 4-3	McDowell 2; Fulton; Twentyman
29/12/1962	IL 7	A	Ards	D 2-2	McDowell 2
05/01/1963	IL 8	H	Portadown	D 2-2	Twentyman; McDowell
12/01/1963	IL 9	A	Distillery	L 1-6	McDowell
26/01/1963	IL 10	A	Cliftonville	W 1-0	Halliday
02/02/1963	IL 11	A	Glenavon	D 1-1	Russell
09/02/1963	IL 12	H	Linfield	D 1-1	Halliday
16/02/1963	IL 13	A	Derry City	D 1-1	McDowell
23/02/1963	IC rd1	H	Portadown	W 4-1	Burke 2; J. Smith; Russell
02/03/1963	IL 14	H	Crusaders	W 2-1	Campbell og; Halliday
09/03/1963	IC qf	H	Glentoran	W 3-1	Twentyman; Halliday; McDowell
16/03/1963	IL 15	A	Glentoran	L 1-5	Halliday
23/03/1963	IC sf	N	Distillery	L 1-3	Burke
27/03/1963	CAS rd1	A	Ballyclare Comrades	W 1-0	Burke
30/03/1963	IL 16	H	Ards	D 0-0	-
06/04/1963	IL 17	A	Portadown	D 1-1	Burke
10/04/1963	CAS qf	A	Distillery	L 1-4	Burke
13/04/1963	IL 18	H	Distillery	W 3-1	J. Smith; Halliday; Fulton
16/04/1963	IL 19	A	Coleraine	L 0-3	-
25/04/1963	IL 20	H	Bangor	W 4-2	Burke 2; McMaster; J. Smith
27/04/1963	IL 21	H	Cliftonville	W 5-1	Halliday 3; McDowell 2
30/04/1963	IL 22	H	Coleraine	D 2-2	Halliday; J. Smith

Played: 45, won: 16, drawn: 17, lost: 12, goals scored: 85, goals conceded: 91

Irish League: 5th; Irish Cup: Semi-final; Gold Cup: Semi-final; Ulster Cup: Group stage; City Cup: 5th; County Antrim Shield: Quarter-final

Notes

15/11/1962 v. Derry City: Match played at Coleraine Showgrounds
23/03/1962 v. Distillery: Match played at Windsor Park

Player Appearances and Goals

Player	Apps	Goals	Player	Apps	Goals
BECKETT Armstrong	1	0	McKEE Alexander	14	0
BLAKE Liam	5	2	McKINNEY Montgomery	25	0
BROWNLEES William	12	0	McMASTER Samuel	6	1
BURKE Robert	27	11	McNAMARA Tony	2	1
CALLAN Brian	28	5	MILLAR Harold	1	0
CUBITT William	35	0	MOFFATT Edward	10	1
DOBBIN Roy	31	1	MULDOON Oliver	2	0
FULTON Samuel	12	2	RUSSELL Edward	34	5
GARRETT Hugh	16	0	SHIELS Jim	35	0
GORDON David	10	0	SMITH John Eric	44	5
HALLIDAY Kenneth	36	24	SMYTH Thomas	12	1
HUNTER Ian	1	0	TWENTYMAN Geoff	35	6
KEARNEY Gerald	11	0	TWINEM Kenneth	3	0
KEENAN William	15	4	WILSON Carl	3	0
McDOWELL Jack	29	14			

Played: 48, won: 16, drawn: 9, lost: 23, goals scored: 96, goals conceded: 117

Irish League: 6th; Irish Cup: Round 1; Gold Cup: Quarter-final; Ulster Cup: Group stage; City Cup: 11th; County Antrim Shield: Semi-final

Date	Comp	Venue	Opponents	Result	Scorers
14/08/1963	FR	H	Port Vale	L 1-2	McDowell
17/08/1963	UC 1	H	Crusaders	L 1-10	Burke
21/08/1963	UC 2	A	Linfield	L 2-3	Burke; McDowell
24/08/1963	UC 3	H	Cliftonville	W 3-2	Neill 2; J.E. Smith
27/08/1963	UC 4	A	Derry City	D 2-2	Neill; McDowell
30/08/1963	UC 5	A	Coleraine	L 3-4	Doherty; J.E. Smith ; McDowell
07/09/1963	CC 1	A	Ards	L 2-4	Cowan; McDowell
11/09/1963	GC rd1	H	Cliftonville	D 1-1	McCabe
14/09/1963	CC 2	H	Distillery	L 0-3	-
18/09/1963	GC rd1 rep	A	Cliftonville	W 1-0	McKeown
21/09/1963	CC 3	A	Crusaders	L 0-2	-
28/09/1963	CC 4	H	Portadown	L 1-2	T. Smyth
05/10/1963	CC 5	A	Coleraine	L 1-3	Moffatt
09/10/1963	GC qf	H	Glentoran	D 3-3	McDowell 2; McKeown
16/10/1963	GC qf rep	A	Glentoran	D 2-2	McDonnell; McDowell
19/10/1963	CC 6	H	Glentoran	L 0-2	-
23/10/1963	GC qf rep 2	H	Glentoran	L 1-4	McDonnell
26/10/1963	CC 7	A	Linfield	L 0-3	-
02/11/1963	CC 8	H	Cliftonville	W 3-0	Russell; Fulton; T. Smyth
09/11/1963	CC 9	A	Glenavon	L 1-2	McDowell
16/11/1963	CC 10	H	Derry City	D 1-1	Russell
23/11/1963	CC 11	A	Bangor	W 4-1	Cloughley; Moffatt; Bryceland; Russell
30/11/1963	IL 1	A	Coleraine	L 0-1	-
07/12/1963	IL 2	H	Ards	D 3-3	Moffatt; Hickson 2
14/12/1963	IL 3	A	Portadown	L 3-4	Moffatt; Hickson; Russell
21/12/1963	IL 4	A	Bangor	W 3-2	Moffatt 2; Hickson
25/12/1963	IL 5	H	Linfield	L 1-4	Moffatt
26/12/1963	IL 6	A	Glentoran	L 2-3	Moffatt 2
28/12/1963	IL 7	A	Derry City	D 5-5	Moffatt; Russell; McDowell 3
04/01/1964	IL 8	H	Glenavon	W 3-2	Hickson; McDowell 2
11/01/1964	IL 9	A	Cliftonville	W 6-0	Cloughley; McDowell 3; Hickson; McDonnell
18/01/1964	IL 10	A	Distillery	L 2-5	Russell; Cloughley
25/01/1964	IL 11	H	Crusaders	W 3-2	McDowell 2; McDonnell
01/02/1964	IL 12	A	Glenavon	L 3-5	Hickson; McDowell; T. Smyth
08/02/1964	IL 13	A	Cliftonville	W 3-1	Hickson 2; Cloughley
15/02/1964	IL 14	H	Distillery	W 2-1	Moffatt 2
22/02/1964	IC rd1	A	Distillery	D 1-1	Russell
26/02/1964	IC rd1 rep	A	Distillery	L 1-2	McCabe
29/02/1964	IL 15	A	Crusaders	W 2-0	McDonnell 2
07/03/1964	IL 16	H	Bangor	L 1-2	Russel
14/03/1964	IL 17	H	Coleraine	W 2-1	McDonnell; Moffatt
28/03/1964	IL 18	A	Ards	W 3-2	McDonnell; Russell
31/03/1964	IL 19	H	Portadown	W 4-2	T. Smyth; McDonnell 2; Cloughley
11/04/1964	IL 20	A	Linfield	W 3-1	Russell; T. Smyth; McDonnell
18/04/1964	IL 21	H	Glentoran	L 0-3	-
21/04/1964	CAS qf	H	Crusaders	D 2-2	McDonnell; Patterson og
24/04/1964	CAS qf rep	A	Crusaders	W 4-1	Moffatt; McDonnell 3
29/04/1964	IL 22	H	Derry City	L 1-3	T. Smyth
01/05/1964	CAS sf	N	Distillery	L 1-5	Moffatt

Player Appearances and Goals

Player	Apps	Goals	Player	Apps	Goals
BECKETT Armstrong	10	0	LARMOUR	1	0
BONE	3	0	LINTON Samuel	8	0
BRYCELAND Hugh	10	1	McBRIDE Alexander	5	0
BUCHANAN Hugh	25	0	McCABE Robin	4	2
BURKE Robert	12	2	McCREE James	2	0
CASSIDY	1	0	McDONNELL Malachy	22	16
CHAMBERS	6	0	McDOWELL Jack	32	19
CLOUGHLEY David	48	5	McKEE Alexander	4	0
CORBETT	1	0	McKEOWN Terence	5	2
COWAN Wallace	6	1	McKINNEY Montgomery	1	0
CRAIG Samuel	1	0	MILLAR Harold	1	0
CUBITT William	46	0	MOFFATT Edward	37	15
DOBBIN Roy	40	0	NEILL Derek	8	3
DOHERTY Thomas	5	1	RUSSELL Edward	45	10
FULTON Samuel	3	1	SMITH John	1	0
GARRETT Hugh	13	0	SMITH John Eric	15	2
GORDON David	1	0	SMYTH Thomas	35	6
HICKSON David	22	9	STEWART Allen	2	0
HOUSTON Thomas	1	0	TURKINGTON Mervyn	8	0
KEARNEY Gerry	14	0	WALSH Sean	24	0

Played: 46, won: 18, drawn: 9, lost: 19, goals scored: 105, goals conceded: 100

Irish League: 6th; Irish Cup: Round 1; Gold Cup: Quarter-final; Ulster Cup: Group stage; City Cup: 8th; County Antrim Shield: Semi-final

Date	Comp	Venue	Opponents	Result	Scorers
07/08/1964	FR	H	Stoke City	L 0-6	-
15/08/1964	UC 1	H	Coleraine	L 0-4	-
20/08/1964	UC 2	H	Derry City	L 2-6	Pike; Thomas
22/08/1964	UC 3	A	Cliftonville	W 3-0	Hickson; Pike; Thomas
26/08/1964	UC 4	H	Glentoran	L 3-4	Thomas 3
28/08/1964	UC 5	A	Crusaders	W 4-0	Thomas 2; Bell; Tom. Smyth
02/09/1964	GC rd1	A	Portadown	W 2-1	Pike; Tom. Smyth
05/09/1964	CC 1	H	Ards	W 7-3	Hickson 4; Thomas 2; Tom. Smyth
09/09/1964	GC qf	A	Coleraine	D 1-1	Bell
12/09/1964	CC 2	A	Distillery	L 2-6	Thomas 2
19/09/1964	CC 3	H	Crusaders	L 3-4	E. Russell; Thomas 2
24/09/1964	GC qf rep	H	Coleraine	L 2-4	Bell; Cloughley
26/09/1964	CC 4	A	Portadown	L 3-4	Thomas; Tom. Smyth; E. Russell
10/10/1964	CC 5	H	Coleraine	L 0-1	-
17/10/1964	CC 6	A	Glentoran	L 1-3	Thomas
24/10/1964	CC 7	H	Linfield	L 0-1	-
31/10/1964	CC 8	A	Cliftonville	W 7-2	Thomas 3; E. Russell 2; Hickson; Tom. Smyth
07/11/1964	CC 9	H	Glenavon	W 4-1	Kearney 2; Thomas; Bell
14/11/1964	CC 10	A	Derry City	D 2-2	Thomas; Hickson
21/11/1964	CC 11	H	Bangor	W 3-1	Thomas 2; McDonnell
28/11/1964	IL 1	A	Glentoran	L 2-3	Thomas; Tonge
05/12/1964	IL 2	H	Cliftonville	W 3-1	Tonge; E. Russell; Hickson
12/12/1964	IL 3	A	Glenavon	W 2-1	E. Russell; John Murphy og.
19/12/1964	IL 4	H	Portadown	L 0-1	-
25/12/1964	IL 5	A	Coleraine	D 2-2	Tonge; Stewart
26/12/1964	IL 6	H	Bangor	W 3-0	Thomas; McDonnell 2
02/01/1965	IL 7	A	Derry City	D 3-3	Stewart; Thomas; McDonnell
09/01/1965	IL 8	H	Distillery	D 1-1	Thomas
16/01/1965	IL 9	A	Crusaders	D 0-0	-
30/01/1965	IL 10	H	Coleraine	L 0-4	-
06/02/1965	IL 11	A	Bangor	L 2-4	Thomas; Tonge
13/02/1965	IL 12	H	Linfield	W 3-2	Thomas; McDonnell; G. Smith
20/02/1965	IC rd1	H	Coleraine	L 1-3	Taggart
27/02/1965	IL 13	H	Derry City	L 3-5	Thomas; McDonnell 2
06/03/1965	IL 14	A	Ards	W 3-2	Thomas; G. Smith; Bell
13/03/1965	IL 15	A	Distillery	W 2-1	McCabe; McDonnell
20/03/1965	IL 16	H	Crusaders	W 1-0	McDonnell
27/03/1965	IL 17	H	Ards	W 4-1	Thomas 3; G. Smith
07/04/1965	IL 18	A	Linfield	L 2-5	Thomas; McDonnell
10/04/1965	IL 19	H	Glentoran	L 0-2	-
14/04/1965	CAS qf	A	Linfield	W 2-1	G. Smith 2
17/04/1965	IL 20	A	Cliftonville	W 8-2	G. Smith 2; Tonge; Kearney; Thomas; McDonnell 3
19/04/1965	IL 21	A	Portadown	D 3-3	Thomas 3
20/04/1965	IL 22	H	Glenavon	W 3-1	Tom. Smyth; McConaghie; Thomas
30/04/1965	CAS sf	N	Larne	D 1-1 (aet)	Thomas
06/05/1965	CAS sf rep	N	Larne	D 1-1 (aet)	McDonnell
08/05/1965	CAS sf rep 2	N	Larne	L 1-2 (aet)	G. Smith

Notes

30/04/1965 v. Larne: Match played at Solitude

06/05/1965 v. Larne: Match played at Solitude

08/05/1965 v. Larne: Match played at Solitude

Player Appearances and Goals

BARR Jim	1	0	McCONAGHIE Samuel	1	1
BECKETT Armstrong	2	0	McDONNELL Malachy	27	15
BELL David	19	5	McKEE Alex	1	0
BUCHANAN Hugh	1	0	McKINNEY Montgomery	3	0
BURNSIDE Victor	4	0	OWENS Leslie	5	0
CLOUGHLEY David	40	1	PIKE Joseph	10	3
COWAN Wallace	13	0	RUSSELL David	1	0
CRAIG Samuel	1	0	RUSSELL Edward	42	6
CUBITT William	25	0	SMITH George	15	8
DAVIES	1	0	SMITH Tony	23	0
DOBBIN Roy	42	0	SMYTH Thomas	33	6
HICKSON David	17	8	STEWART Alan	8	2
HUXLEY Derek	2	0	TAGGART George	16	1
KEARNEY Gerry	30	3	THOMAS Arthur	41	39
LINTON Uel	2	0	TONGE Jeffery	18	5
LUNN Kenneth	5	0	TURKINGTON Mervyn	16	0
McCABE Robin	2	1	WALSH Sean	39	0

Played: 57, won: 24, drawn: 16, lost: 17, goals scored: 123, goals conceded: 104

Irish League: 4th; Irish Cup: Quarter-final; Gold Cup: Quarter-final; Ulster Cup: 6th; City Cup: 8th; County Antrim Shield: Finalists; Top Four Trophy: Semi-final

Date	Comp	Venue	Opponents	Result	Scorers
07/08/1965	UC 1	H	Cliftonville	W 4-1	McDonnell 2; Thomas 2
11/08/1965	UC 2	A	Coleraine	L 0-3	-
14/08/1965	UC 3	H	Distillery	W 5-2	Thomas; Russell; J. Smith; G. Smith 2
18/08/1965	UC 4	A	Portadown	W 5-1	McDonnell; G. Smith; Thomas 2; J. Smith
21/08/1965	UC 5	H	Ards	W 7-3	Thomas 4; Russell; McDonnell: G. Smith
25/08/1965	UC 6	A	Glentoran	L 1-4	G. Smith
27/08/1965	UC 7	H	Crusaders	L 1-2	Thomas
01/09/1965	TEST	H	Harryville Amateurs	W 6-5	Aiken 3, Dobbin 2, McCabe
04/09/1965	UC 8	H	Linfield	D 2-2	Thomas; G. Smith
08/09/1965	UC 9	A	Glenavon	D 2-2	Nixon og; Craig
11/09/1965	UC 10	H	Bangor	W 2-0	J. Smith; Aiken
15/09/1965	UC 11	A	Derry City	L 0-3	-
18/09/1965	IL 1	H	Cliftonville	W 8-0	Thomas 3; Brannigan; McDonnell 2; J. Smith 2
24/09/1965	IL 2	A	Glentoran	D 0-0	-
01/10/1965	GC rd1	H	Bangor	W 4-3	Thomas; McDonnell; Cloughey; J. Smith
09/10/1965	IL 3	A	Bangor	D 0-0	-
13/10/1965	GC qf	H	Crusaders	D 3-3	Cloughey; McDonnell; G. Smith
16/10/1965	IL 4	H	Coleraine	L 1-2	G. Smith
21/10/1965	GC qf rep	A	Crusaders	L 0-3	-
23/10/1965	IL 5	A	Portadown	L 1-2	Russell
30/10/1965	IL 6	H	Crusaders	W 5-2	G. Smith; Thomas 2; Robinson; Russell
06/11/1965	IL 7	A	Distillery	D 1-1	McDonnell
13/11/1965	IL 8	A	Linfield	L 2-5	Dobbin; McDonnell
20/11/1965	IL 9	H	Derry City	L 3-4	McDonnell; Hutchinson; Burke
27/11/1965	IL 10	A	Ards	W 2-1	McDonnell; Aiken
04/12/1965	IL 11	H	Glenavon	D 5-5	J. Smith 2; McDonnell 2; Cairns
11/12/1965	IL 12	A	Cliftonville	W 5-1	McDonnell; Aiken 2; Cairns 2
18/12/1965	IL 13	H	Glentoran	W 2-1	Cairns; McDonnell
25/12/1965	IL 14	H	Bangor	W 2-0	McDonnell; Aiken
27/12/1965	IL15	A	Coleraine	W 3-1	McDonnell; Cairns; J. Smith
01/01/1966	IL 16	H	Portadown	W 1-0	Cairns
08/01/1966	IL 17	A	Crusaders	W 3-1	Cairns; Hutchinson; McDonnell
15/01/1966	IL 18	H	Distillery	W 3-0	Cairns; McDonnell; Russell
22/01/1966	IL 19	H	Linfield	D 0-0	-
29/01/1966	IL 20	A	Derry City	L 1-5	McDonnell
05/02/1966	IL 21	H	Ards	D 2-2	McDonnell 2
12/02/1966	IC rd1	A	Derry City	D 2-2	J. Smith; Cloughley
16/02/1966	IC rd1 rep	H	Derry City	W 3-1	McDonnell 2; Cairns
19/02/1966	IL 22	A	Glenavon	W 1-0	Cairns
26/02/1966	CC 1	A	Bangor	W 3-1	Pike; J. Smith; McDonnell
05/03/1966	IC qf	H	Coleraine	D 1-1	Coyle
10/03/1966	IC qf rep	A	Coleraine	D 2-2	J. Smith; Cairns
12/03/1966	CC 2	H	Glenavon	L 2-5	Stewart; McDonnell
16/03/1966	IC qf rep 2	N	Coleraine	L 1-2	Aiken
19/03/1966	CC 3	A	Linfield	L 0-5	-
30/03/1966	TFT sf	A	Linfield	D 2-2	McDonnell; Russell
02/04/1966	CC 4	H	Derry City	W 3-2	McDonnell; Cloughley; Cairns
09/04/1966	CC 5	H	Glentoran	D 1-1	J. Smith
11/04/1966	CC 6	A	Cliftonville	W 5-1	McDonnell 4; T. Smith
13/04/1966	TFT sf rep	H	Linfield	L 0-1	-
16/04/1966	CC 7	H	Portadown	W 4-2	Brannigan; Cairns 2; McDonnell
20/04/1966	CC 8	A	Distillery	L 1-2	J. Smith
26/04/1966	CC 9	H	Coleraine	D 1-1	Aiken
28/04/1966	CAS qf	A	Cliftonville	W 2-1	Cairns 2
30/04/1966	CC 10	A	Ards	D 1-1	Cloughley
04/05/1966	CAS sf	N	Ards	W 1-0	Cairns
14/05/1966	CAS f	N	Linfield	L 0-4	-
18/05/1966	CC 11	A	Crusaders	L 1-2	Aiken

Notes

01/09/1965 v. Harryville Amateurs: Testimonial for Billy Cubitt

16/03/1966 v. Coleraine: Match played at The Oval

04/05/1966 v. Ards: Match played at The Oval

14/05/1966 v. Linfield: Match played at Solitude

Player Appearances and Goals

AIKEN Thomas	54	8	McDONNELL Malachy	49	34
BARR Jim	3	0	McKEE Alex	11	0
BRANNIGAN Thomas	56	2	PATTERSON Alex	6	0
BURKE Robin	37	1	PIKE Joseph	3	1
BURNSIDE Victor	3	0	ROBINSON Martin	4	1
CAIRNS David	32	17	RUSSELL Edward	53	6
CLOUGHLEY David	51	5	RYLES James	5	0
COYLE John	21	1	SMITH George	18	9
CRAIG Samuel	2	1	SMITH John	49	14
DOBBIN Roy	29	1	SMITH Tony	42	1
HOGG Len	1	0	STEWART Allen	10	1
HUTCHINSON Charles	6	2	THOMAS Arthur	15	17
LINTON Uel	6	0	TRAYNOR Seamus	4	0
LOGAN James	1	0	TURKINGTON Mervyn	1	0
McCABE Robin	3	0	WALSH Sean	51	0
McCONAGHIE Samuel	1	0			

Played: 57, won: 24, drawn: 16, lost: 17, goals scored: 123, goals conceded: 104

Irish League: 4th; Irish Cup: Quarter-final; Gold Cup: Quarter-final; Ulster Cup: 6th; City Cup: 8th; County Antrim Shield: Finalists; Top Four Trophy: Semi-final

Played: 47, won: 18, drawn: 11, lost: 18, goals scored: 103, goals conceded: 98

Irish League: 7th; Irish Cup: Round 1; Gold Cup: Quarter-final; Ulster Cup: 5th; City Cup: 6th; County Antrim Shield: Round 1

Date	Comp	Venue	Opponents	Result	Scorers
06/08/1966	UC 1	A	Cliftonville	W 5-0	Aiken; McDonnell 2; Cloughley; Cairns
10/08/1966	UC 2	H	Coleraine	L 1-3	Cloughley
13/08/1966	UC 3	A	Distillery	D 1-1	MacColl
17/08/1966	UC 4	H	Portadown	W 4-2	Broad; MacColl 2; McDonnell
20/08/1966	UC 5	A	Ards	W 4-2	Cairns 3; McDonnell
24/08/1966	UC 6	H	Glentoran	L 1-2	A. Stewart
26/08/1966	UC 7	A	Crusaders	L 2-6	McDonnell 2
31/08/1966	UC 8	H	Derry City	D 4-4	Broad; A. Stewart 2; McDonnell
03/09/1966	UC 9	A	Linfield	W 2-1	Brannigan; McDonnell
07/09/1966	UC 10	H	Glenavon	D 1-1	Broad
10/09/1966	UC 11	A	Bangor	W 3-2	McDonnell; MacColl; Broad
17/09/1966	IL 1	A	Linfield	L 1-2	Broad
24/09/1966	IL 2	H	Glentoran	L 2-3	Broad; Cairns
01/10/1966	IL 3	A	Cliftonville	D 1-1	Aiken
08/10/1966	IL 4	A	Derry City	L 1-2	Broad
15/10/1966	IL 5	H	Ards	D 1-1	Broad
21/10/1966	GC qf	A	Glentoran	L 3-7	Cairns; McDonnell 2
29/10/1966	IL 6	H	Portadown	W 4-1	McDonnell 2; T. Stewart ; Broad
05/11/1966	IL 7	A	Distillery	D 1-1	McDonnell
12/11/1966	IL 8	A	Coleraine	W 2-1	McDonnell 2
19/11/1966	IL 9	H	Bangor	W 5-1	McDonnell 3; T. Stewart 2
26/11/1966	IL 10	H	Crusaders	W 7-3	T. Stewart; McDonnell 3; Broad; J. Smith
03/12/1966	IL 11	A	Glenavon	D 4-4	McDonnell; T. Stewart; Broad; Brannigan
10/12/1966	IL 12	H	Cliftonville	W 2-1	McDonnell ; Cloughley
17/12/1966	IL 13	A	Glentoran	L 2-5	Broad; McDonnell
24/12/1966	IL 14	H	Linfield	L 2-4	Brannigan 2
27/12/1966	IL 15	A	Bangor	W 2-0	Cloughley; Aiken
31/12/1966	IL 16	H	Coleraine	D 4-4	T. Stewart; Cairns 2; A. Stewart
07/01/1967	IL 17	H	Distillery	W 4-0	Cairns 2; Clarke; T. Stewart
14/01/1967	IL 18	A	Portadown	L 1-4	T. Stewart
21/01/1967	IL 19	H	Derry City	L 1-2	Rankin
28/01/1967	IL 20	A	Ards	W 2-1	Crothers og; Broad
04/02/1967	IL 21	A	Crusaders	L 3-4	T. Stewart; Brannigan; Clarke
11/02/1967	IL 22	H	Glenavon	W 2-0	Clarke; Cairns
18/02/1967	IC rd1	A	Distillery	L 0-3	-
25/02/1967	CC 1	H	Bangor	W 5-0	Burke; T. Stewart; Aiken; Broad
04/03/1967	CC 2	A	Glenavon	L 0-1	-
11/03/1967	CAS rd1	A	Larne	L 0-2	-
18/03/1967	CC 3	H	Linfield	W 3-1	T. Stewart; Clarke; Broad
25/03/1967	CC 4	A	Derry City	L 1-2	Cairns
27/03/1967	CC 5	H	Crusaders	D 2-2	Cairns 2
08/04/1967	CC 6	A	Glentoran	L 0-4	-
11/04/1967	CC 7	H	Ards	D 2-2	Aiken; Cairns
15/04/1967	CC 8	A	Portadown	L 0-2	-
19/04/1967	CC 9	H	Distillery	D 2-2	Broad; Aiken
27/04/1967	CC 10	A	Coleraine	W 2-1	Broad; Dobbin
29/04/1967	CC 11	H	Cliftonville	W 1-0	Wylie

Player Appearances and Goals

Player	Apps	Goals	Player	Apps	Goals
AIKEN Thomas	39	6	McDONNELL Malachy	24	26
BRANNIGAN Thomas	45	5	McFADDEN Victor	5	0
BROAD Christopher	34	17	McKEE Alexander	3	0
BURKE Robin	38	1	RANKIN Raymond	2	1
CAIRNS David	29	15	REID Willard	2	0
CLARKE Norman	28	4	RYLES Jim	1	0
CLOUGHLEY David	43	4	SMITH John Eric	22	1
CLUNIE Jim	4	0	SMITH Tony	33	0
CRAIG Samuel	5	0	STEWART Allen	23	4
CURRAN William	9	0	STEWART Thomas	34	12
DOBBIN Roy	23	1	TURKINGTON Mervyn	4	0
HOGG Len	1	0	WALKER John	5	0
KANE Andrew	1	0	WALSH Sean	41	0
LINTON Samuel	1	0	WILSON William	6	0
MacCOLL Duncan	11	4	WRIGHT Ronald	1	0
McCUSKER James	1	0	WYLIE Derek	2	1

Played: 48, won: 17, drawn: 9, lost: 22, goals scored: 100, goals conceded: 116

Irish League: 7th; Irish Cup: Round 1; Gold Cup: Round 1; Ulster Cup: 7th; City Cup: 7th; County Antrim Shield: Quarter-final

Date	Comp	Venue	Opponents	Result	Scorers
01/08/1967	FR	H	Southport	L 3-6	Aiken; McDonnell; Hogg
05/08/1967	UC 1	H	Crusaders	W 6-5	McDonnell 2; Burke; Treacey; Aiken 2
08/08/1967	UC 2	A	Derry City	L 2-3	McDonnell ; Broad
12/08/1967	UC 3	H	Linfield	L 2-5	Treacey; Broad
16/08/1967	UC 4	A	Glenavon	L 1-2	McDonnell
19/08/1967	UC 5	H	Bangor	W 2-1	McDonnell 2
23/08/1967	UC 6	H	Cliftonville	W 2-1	W. Reid; Wylie
25/08/1967	UC 7	A	Coleraine	W 4-1	McDonnell 3; Clarke
30/08/1967	UC 8	H	Distillery	D 2-2	W. Reid 2
02/09/1967	UC 9	A	Portadown	L 0-2	-
09/09/1967	UC 10	H	Ards	W 3-2	McDonnell 3
12/09/1967	GC rd1	A	Glenavon	L 1-8	Brannigan
16/09/1967	UC 11	A	Glentoran	L 1-6	McDonnell
23/09/1967	IL 1	A	Bangor	D 4-4	Hickson; Paterson; Aiken; McDonnell
30/09/1967	IL 2	H	Distillery	W 3-1	McDonnell; Hickson; Aiken
07/10/1967	IL 3	A	Portadown	L 1-2	Hickson
14/10/1967	IL 4	H	Coleraine	L 3-7	Hickson 2; Cairns
28/10/1967	IL 5	A	Linfield	L 1-3	McDonnell
04/11/1967	IL 6	A	Ards	L 1-3	McDonnell
11/11/1967	IL 7	H	Glenavon	W 4-3	Hickson; Aiken; Kay; Patterson og
18/11/1967	IL 8	A	Crusaders	L 1-3	McDonnell
25/11/1967	IL 9	H	Glentoran	L 2-5	McDonnell; Hickson
02/12/1967	IL 10	A	Derry City	L 1-5	W. Reid
16/12/1967	IL 11	H	Bangor	W 3-1	Clarke 2; Cairns
23/12/1967	IL 12	A	Distillery	W 2-0	Clarke; McDonnell
25/12/1967	IL 13	H	Portadown	W 5-2	McDonnell 2; W. Reid 2; Clarke
26/12/1967	IL 14	A	Coleraine	L 2-7	McDonnell; Clarke
30/12/1967	IL 15	H	Linfield	L 4-5	McDonnell; Treacey 2; Clarke
06/01/1968	IL 16	H	Ards	W 3-1	Treacey 2; Kay
13/01/1968	IL 17	A	Glenavon	L 1-3	Clarke
20/01/1968	IL 18	H	Crusaders	D 2-2	McDonnell ; Torrens
27/01/1968	IL 19	A	Glentoran	D 2-2	McDonnell; Cairns
03/02/1968	IL 20	H	Derry City	L 0-1	-
10/02/1968	IL 21	A	Cliftonville	W 5-1	McDonnell 3; W. Reid 2
17/02/1968	IC rd1	A	Crusaders	L 0-1	-
24/02/1968	IL 22	H	Cliftonville	W 5-2	Cairns 2; Treacey; Dobbin; Paterson
02/03/1968	CC 1	A	Linfield	L 0-1	-
09/03/1968	CAS rd1	H	Albert Foundry	W 3-0	Clarke; T. Stewart; McDonnell
16/03/1968	CC 2	H	Glenavon	D 1-1	McDonnell
23/03/1968	CC 3	A	Bangor	W 4-0	Cairns; McGowan; T. Stewart; McDonnell
30/03/1968	CAS qf	A	Larne	L 0-1	-
02/04/1968	CC 4	A	Cliftonville	D 2-2	Clarke; Cairns
06/04/1968	CC 5	H	Coleraine	D 1-1	Cairns
11/04/1968	CC 6	A	Ards	D 1-1	T. Stewart
13/04/1968	CC 7	H	Glentoran	D 1-1	Murray
15/04/1968	CC 8	H	Derry City	W 3-1	Cairns; Clarke; McGowan
16/04/1968	CC 9	A	Crusaders	L 0-2	-
20/04/1968	CC 10	A	Distillery	L 0-2	-
24/04/1968	CC 11	H	Portadown	W 3-1	Cairns 2; McDonnell

Player Appearances and Goals

Player	Apps	Goals	Player	Apps	Goals
AIKEN Thomas	20	5	McFADDEN Victor	1	0
BEERS Stanley	7	0	McGOWAN Michael	10	2
BRANNIGAN Thomas	48	1	McKEE Alexander	10	0
BROAD Christopher	2	2	McKENZIE	1	0
BURKE Robin	28	1	MURRAY Daniel	4	1
CAIRNS David	18	11	OLIVER Ian	1	0
CAMPBELL Mervyn	1	0	PARKER Alexander	18	0
CLAPPERTON Albert	1	0	PATERSON Raymond	15	2
CLARKE Norman	40	11	REID Stewart	3	0
DOBBIN Roy	45	1	REID Willard	17	8
HICKSON David	10	7	SMALLWOOD	1	0
HOBBS	8	0	SMITH Tony	37	0
HUNTER Hugh	4	0	SMYLIE Mervyn	1	0
KAY Len	11	2	STASIAK Eskild	4	0
LINTON Samuel	1	0	STEWART Allen	8	0
LOWRY Thomas	3	0	STEWART Thomas	34	3
McALLISTER Hopkins	7	0	TORRENS Roy	24	1
McAULEY	9	0	TREACEY Frank	13	7
McCUSKER James	7	0	WALSH Sean	25	0
McDONNELL Malachy	44	33	WYLIE Derek	5	1

1968/1969

Played: 48, won: 14, drawn: 11, lost: 23, goals scored: 85, goals conceded: 98

Irish League: 7th; Irish Cup: Quarter-final; Gold Cup: Round 1; Ulster Cup: 11th; City Cup: 9th; County Antrim Shield: Quarter-final

1968/1969

Date	Comp	Venue	Opponents	Result	Scorers
27/07/1968	FR	H	Rotherham United	L 0-2	-
01/08/1968	FR	H	Kilmarnock	L 3-4	Martin 2; Arthur
03/08/1968	UC 1	H	Coleraine	L 1-3	McGowan
06/08/1968	UC 2	A	Distillery	L 1-3	Martin
10/08/1968	UC 3	H	Portadown	D 2-2	Cairns 2
12/08/1968	TEST	H	Dundela	D 2-2	Dobbin 2
15/08/1968	UC 4	A	Ards	L 1-3	Brannigan
17/08/1968	UC 5	H	Glentoran	L 0-2	-
20/08/1968	UC 6	A	Crusaders	L 1-3	Martin
24/08/1968	UC 7	H	Derry City	D 2-2	Cairns; Martin
27/08/1968	UC 8	A	Linfield	L 1-4	Martin
31/08/1968	UC 9	H	Glenavon	L 1-4	McGowan
04/09/1968	UC 10	A	Bangor	L 0-2	-
07/09/1968	UC 11	A	Cliftonville	W 5-2	Chambers; McDonnell 3; Martin
11/09/1968	GC rd1	A	Distillery	L 1-3	McDonnell
14/09/1968	IL 1	H	Crusaders	L 1-3	Martin
21/09/1968	IL 2	A	Linfield	L 1-3	Martin
28/09/1968	IL 3	H	Derry City	W 5-3	McDonnell 3; Erwin; Martin
05/10/1968	IL 4	A	Portadown	W 1-0	Erwin
12/10/1968	IL 5	H	Bangor	W 3-0	Martin 2; Erwin
19/10/1968	IL 6	A	Coleraine	W 6-1	Erwin; McDonnell 4; Coyle
26/10/1968	IL 7	H	Cliftonville	W 2-1	Coyle; Dobbin
09/11/1968	IL 8	H	Distillery	W 2-1	Erwin 2
14/11/1968	IL 9	A	Glentoran	L 1-2	Erwin
16/11/1968	IL 10	A	Ards	L 3-4	McDonnell; Martin; Erwin
23/11/1968	IL 11	A	Glenavon	D 2-2	Erwin; McDonnell
30/11/1968	IL 12	A	Linfield	L 1-2	Erwin
07/12/1968	IL 13	A	Derry City	L 1-5	Erwin
14/12/1968	IL 14	A	Crusaders	L 1-2	Martin
21/12/1968	IL 15	H	Portadown	W 3-2	Averell; Martin; Erwin
25/12/1968	IL 16	H	Bangor	D 1-1	Martin
26/12/1968	IL 17	H	Coleraine	W 5-0	McGowan 2; Brown 2; Russell
04/01/1969	IL 18	H	Glentoran	D 2-2	Fullerton; Hutton og
11/01/1969	IL 19	A	Distillery	D 2-2	Martin; Averell
18/01/1969	IL 20	H	Ards	L 1-4	McCall
22/01/1969	IL 21	A	Cliftonville	W 3-0	Erwin 2; Russell
25/01/1969	IL 22	H	Glenavon	D 1-1	McGowan
01/02/1969	CC 1	A	Glentoran	L 1-3	Erwin
22/02/1969	CC 2	H	Distillery	D 0-0	-
26/02/1969	IC rd1	H	Carrick Rangers	W 2-0	Light; Erwin
01/03/1969	CC 3	A	Portadown	D 3-3	Martin; Larmour; Erwin
08/03/1969	IC qf	H	Distillery	L 1-2	Parker
15/03/1969	CC 4	H	Ards	W 3-0	Martin 2; Fullerton
22/03/1969	CC 5	A	Coleraine	L 0-2	-
29/03/1969	CC 6	H	Crusaders	W 3-1	Averell; Coyle; Erwin
02/04/1969	CAS qf	A	Crusaders	L 1-4	Averell
05/04/1969	CC 7	H	Cliftonville	D 0-0	-
07/04/1969	CC 8	H	Bangor	L 0-1	-
12/04/1969	CC 9	A	Glenavon	L 3-5	Fullerton 2; Martin
23/04/1969	CC 10	H	Linfield	D 1-1	Erwin
26/04/1969	CC 11	A	Derry City	W 3-2	Stewart; Fullerton 2

Notes

12/08/1968 v. Dundela: Testimonial for Roy Dobbin

Player Appearances and Goals

Player	Apps	Goals	Player	Apps	Goals
AVERELL Robert	44	4	LIGHT Dennis	7	1
BARR	6	0	MARCUS Samuel	2	0
BRANNIGAN Thomas	13	1	MARTIN Jim	44	19
BROWN Barry	5	2	McALLISTER Hopkins	4	0
CAIRNS David	9	3	McAULEY	2	0
CHAMBERS John	3	1	McCALL Alexander	3	1
CLARKE Norman	16	0	McDONNELL Malachy	16	13
COYLE Roy	38	3	McFADDEN Victor	9	0
CRAIG	2	0	McGOWAN Michael	36	5
DOBBIN Roy	36	1	PARKER Alexander	26	1
DUERDON Derek	2	0	PLATT Jim	17	0
ERWIN Gary	35	19	RUSSELL Edward	37	2
FERGUSON William	6	0	SMITH Tony	22	0
FULLERTON Jackie	33	6	SMYLIE Mervyn	2	0
GREENE Tony	11	0	STEWART	1	1
HOPKINS Mel	2	0	TORRENS Roy	36	0
LARMOUR John	3	1	WALSH Sean	18	0

Played: 47, won: 15, drawn: 9, lost: 23, goals scored: 62, goals conceded: 80

Irish League: 10th; Irish Cup: Finalists; Gold Cup: Semi-final; Ulster Cup: Group Stage; City Cup: 4th;
County Antrim Shield: Quarter-final; Blaxnit All-Ireland Cup: Round 1

Date	Comp	Venue	Opponents	Result	Scorers
26/07/1969	FR	H	Peterborough Utd	L 1-6	Martin
29/07/1969	FR	H	Mansfield Town	L 1-3	Martin
01/08/1969	FR	A	Drumcondra	L 2-6	Unknown
09/08/1969	UC 1	H	Cliftonville	W 4-0	Fleming 2; Martin; Herron
13/08/1969	UC 2	A	Coleraine	L 0-2	-
16/08/1969	UC 3	H	Distillery	W 3-0	Herron 2; O'Rourke
21/08/1969	UC 4	A	Portadown	D 1-1	Martin
23/08/1969	UC 5	H	Ards	W 5-1	Herron 3; Ferguson; Martin
27/08/1969	UC 6	H	Crusaders	W 2-1	Ferguson; Herron
30/08/1969	UC 7	A	Glentoran	L 2-3	Herron; Erwin
04/09/1969	UC 8	A	Derry City	L 1-2	Erwin
06/09/1969	UC 9	H	Linfield	L 1-2	Fullerton
13/09/1969	UC 10	A	Glenavon	L 0-2	-
17/09/1969	UC 11	H	Bangor	W 3-0	Fullerton; Herron; Erwin
20/09/1969	CC 1	A	Cliftonville	W 2-1	Fullerton; McGowan
27/09/1969	CC 2	H	Derry City	L 0-1	-
30/09/1969	GC qf	A	Glenavon	D 2-2	Martin 2
04/10/1969	CC 3	H	Glentoran	L 0-3	-
08/10/1969	GC qf rep	H	Glenavon	W 2-1	Herron; Fleming
11/10/1969	CC 4	A	Crusaders	D 2-2	Martin; Fleming
18/10/1969	CC 5	H	Coleraine	L 0-2	-
25/10/1969	IL 1	A	Distillery	L 0-1	-
01/11/1969	IL 2	H	Ards	L 1-2	Porter
08/11/1969	IL 3	A	Coleraine	L 0-3	-
15/11/1969	IL 4	H	Portadown	L 1-3	Moore
22/11/1969	IL 5	A	Bangor	W 4-3	Martin; Porter 3
26/11/1969	GC sf	N	Coleraine	L 1-3	Martin
29/11/1969	IL 6	A	Linfield	L 0-1	-
06/12/1969	IL 7	H	Derry City	L 3-4	Ryles 3
13/12/1969	IL 8	A	Crusaders	D 1-1	Martin
20/12/1969	IL 9	H	Glenavon	W 3-1	Ferguson; Ryles; Moore
26/12/1969	IL 10	H	Glentoran	L 0-3	-
27/12/1969	IL 11	A	Cliftonville	W 1-0	Martin
03/01/1970	IL 12	H	Distillery	D 0-0	-
10/01/1970	IL 13	A	Ards	L 1-4	Cooke
17/01/1970	IL 14	H	Coleraine	L 1-5	Martin
24/01/1970	IL 15	A	Portadown	D 1-1	Fleming
31/01/1970	IC rd1	A	Glentoran	W 2-0	Martin 2
07/02/1970	IL 16	H	Bangor	D 2-2	Martin; McAllister og
14/02/1970	IL 17	H	Linfield	L 0-4	-
25/02/1970	IC qf	H	Crusaders	W 2-1	Martin; McGowan
28/02/1970	IL 18	A	Derry City	W 2-0	Martin; M. Collins
14/03/1970	IC sf	N	Coleraine	W 2-0	B. Nicholl; McGowan
21/03/1970	IL 19	A	Glenavon	L 0-3	-
25/03/1970	IL 20	H	Crusaders	W 2-1	Jackson; Martin
28/03/1970	IL 21	H	Glentoran	D 0-0	-
30/03/1970	IL 22	H	Cliftonville	D 1-1	B. Nicholl
04/04/1970	IC f	N	Linfield	L 1-2	Fleming
07/04/1970	CAS qf	A	Larne	L 0-2	-
24/04/1970	AIC rd1	A	Sligo Rovers	L 0-3	-

Notes

26/11/1969 v. Coleraine: Match played at The Oval

14/03/1970 v. Coleraine: Match played at Windsor Park

04/04/1970 v. Linfield: Match played at Solitude

Player Appearances and Goals

Name	Apps	Goals	Name	Apps	Goals
AVERELL Robert	43	0	MARTIN Jim	44	17
COLLINS Michael	3	1	McFALL Quinton	23	0
COLLINS Raymond	1	0	McGOWAN Michael	22	3
COOKE Andrew	7	1	MOORE Brian	7	2
EASTON George	1	0	NICHOLL Brian	6	2
ELLISON Fred	1	0	NICHOLL Malcolm	14	0
ERWIN Gary	42	3	O'ROURKE James	14	1
FERGUSON William	31	3	PARKER Alexander	17	0
FLEMING Victor	33	6	PLATT James	40	0
FULLERTON Jack	16	3	PORTER Lynn	21	4
GREENE Tony	14	0	RICHARDSON William	23	0
GREGG Ian	4	0	RUSSELL Edward	41	0
HERRON James	18	10	RYLES James	5	4
JACKSON David	3	1	SIMPSON Robert	7	0
MARCUS Samuel	1	0	TORRENS Roy	36	0

Irish League: 5th; Irish Cup: Quarter-final; Gold Cup: Round 1; Ulster Cup: 6th; City Cup: 9th; County Antrim Shield: Semi-final

Played: 52, won: 18, drawn: 15, lost: 19, goals scored: 75, goals conceded: 70

Date	Comp	Venue	Opponents	Result	Scorers
0Star5/08/1970	FR	H	St. Johnstone	L 0-3	-
15/08/1970	UC 1	A	Cliftonville	W 1-0	Sterratt
18/08/1970	UC 2	H	Coleraine	D 0-0	-
22/08/1970	UC 3	A	Distillery	D 3-3	Fleming 3
27/08/1970	UC 4	A	Ards	D 2-2	Martin 2
29/08/1970	UC 5	H	Portadown	L 2-4	Fleming; Sterrett
02/09/1970	UC 6	H	Glentoran	W 2-1	Martin; McFall
05/09/1970	UC 7	A	Crusaders	L 0-3	-
09/09/1970	UC 8	H	Derry City	L 1-2	Stewart
12/09/1970	UC 9	A	Linfield	W 5-0	Stewart; Martin 3; Vincent
16/09/1970	UC 10	H	Glenavon	D 1-1	Frickelton
19/09/1970	UC 11	A	Bangor	W 2-1	Sterratt; Frickelton
26/09/1970	CC 1	A	Derry City	W 1-0	Frickelton
03/10/1970	CC 2	H	Linfield	L 1-4	McGowan
07/10/1970	GC rd1	A	Cliftonville	D 2-2	Cooke; Vincent
10/10/1970	CC 3	A	Glenavon	L 0-2	-
14/10/1970	GC rd1 rep	H	Cliftonville	D 0-0	-
17/10/1970	CC 4	H	Bangor	L 0-3	-
21/10/1970	GC rd1 rep 2	A	Cliftonville	D 0-0	-
24/10/1970	CC 5	H	Cliftonville	W 4-0	Orr 2; Averell; McFall
28/10/1970	GC rd1 rep 3	H	Cliftonville	L 1-2	Martin
31/10/1970	CC 6	A	Coleraine	L 0-2	-
07/11/1970	CC 7	H	Distillery	L 1-2	Jackson
14/11/1970	CC 8	A	Portadown	W 3-1	Vincent; Conlon og; McIlreavy
21/11/1970	CC 9	H	Ards	D 2-2	Vincent; Gregg
28/11/1970	CC 10	A	Glentoran	L 0-2	-
05/12/1970	CC 11	H	Crusaders	W 2-1	Martin; Platt
12/12/1970	IL 1	A	Derry City	D 2-2	McFall; Vincent
19/12/1970	IL 2	H	Bangor	W 4-0	Vincent; Martin; Frickelton; Platt
26/12/1970	IL 3	A	Cliftonville	D 2-2	Martin; Vincent
28/12/1970	IL 4	H	Linfield	L 1-2	McIlreavey
02/01/1971	IL 5	A	Glentoran	W 2-0	Martin; Vincent
09/01/1971	IL 6	H	Coleraine	L 1-2	Martin
16/01/1971	IL 7	A	Ards	W 1-0	Frickelton
23/01/1971	IL 8	H	Portadown	D 1-1	Stewart
30/01/1971	IL 9	H	Crusaders	D 1-1	Vincent
06/02/1971	IL 10	A	Glenavon	L 1-2	Aiken
13/02/1971	IC rd1	A	Glentoran	W 1-0	Martin
20/02/1971	IL 11	H	Distillery	D 2-2	Stewart; Martin
27/02/1971	IC qf	A	Coleraine	L 0-2	-
06/03/1971	IL 12	H	Derry City	W 3-1	Frickelton; Russell 2
13/03/1971	CAS qf	H	Islandmagee	W 3-0	Vincent; Donald; Martin
20/03/1971	IL 13	A	Bangor	D 1-1	Vincent
27/03/1971	IL 14	H	Cliftonville	W 2-1	Vincent 2
07/04/1971	IL 15	A	Linfield	L 0-3	-
10/04/1971	IL 16	H	Glentoran	L 0-2	-
12/04/1971	IL 17	A	Coleraine	W 2-0	Stewart ; Vincent
17/04/1971	IL 18	H	Ards	L 0-1	-
20/04/1971	IL 19	A	Portadown	W 3-1	Donald 2; McFall
24/04/1971	IL 20	A	Crusaders	L 0-1	-
28/04/1971	IL 21	H	Glenavon	W 4-2	Russell; Donald 2; Vincent
01/05/1971	IL 22	A	Distillery	D 1-1	Martin
06/05/1971	CAS sf	N	Crusaders	L 1-3	Sterrett

Notes

06/05/1971 v. Crusaders: Match played at The Oval

Player Appearances and Goals

AIKEN Thomas	10	1	McFALL Quinton	27	4
AVERELL Robert	40	1	McGOWAN Michael	4	1
CALVIN Nelson	1	0	McILREAVEY Kenneth	15	2
COOKE Andrew	38	1	McKINNEY Montgomery	40	0
DONALD Alexander	20	5	O'HARA William	11	0
ERWIN Gary	7	0	ORR Des	2	2
FLEMING Victor	4	4	PLATT John	31	2
FRICKELTON Samuel	38	6	RICHARDSON William	25	0
GOWDY Thomas	40	0	RUSSELL Edward	26	3
GREGG Ian	9	1	STERRETT Raymond	31	4
HENRY Thomas	2	0	STEWART Arthur	52	5
JACKSON William	7	1	TORRENS Roy	28	0
MARTIN Jim	38	16	VINCENT Stanley	42	15
McAFEE Jack	1	0			

Played: 52, won: 18, drawn: 15, lost: 19, goals scored: 75, goals conceded: 70

Irish League: 5th; Irish Cup: Quarter-final; Gold Cup: Round 1; Ulster Cup: 6th; City Cup: 9th; County Antrim Shield: Semi-final

Irish League: 7th; Irish Cup: Round 1; Gold Cup: Quarter-final; Ulster Cup: Round 1; Texaco Cup: Semi-final; City Cup: Winners; County Antrim Shield: Semi-final; Texaco Cup: Semi-final

Played: 53, won: 24, drawn: 12, lost: 17, goals scored: 90, goals conceded: 82

Date	Comp	Venue	Opponents	Result	Scorers
03/08/1971	FR	H	Beitar Tel Aviv	L 1-3	Martin
06/08/1971	TEST	H	Finn Harps	W 4-0	Averell; Frickelton 2; Donald
17/08/1971	UC 1	A	Coleraine	W 3-1	Gowdy; Davey og; B.Nicholl
21/08/1971	UC 2	H	Distillery	L 0-2	-
26/08/1971	UC 3	H	Ards	L 1-2	Aiken
28/08/1971	UC 4	A	Portadown	L 0-7	-
01/09/1971	UC 5	H	Cliftonville	W 2-1	Russell; Aiken
04/09/1971	UC 6	A	Glentoran	D 0-0	-
08/09/1971	UC 7	H	Crusaders	W 5-1	Aiken 2; Averell; Russell; Martin
11/09/1971	UC 8	A	Derry City	W 1-0	B. Nicholl
15/09/1971	TXC rd1 leg1	H	Waterford United	W 3-2	Martin 2; Frickelton
18/09/1971	UC 9	A	Glenavon	W 2-1	B. Nicholl; Martin
25/09/1971	UC 10	H	Bangor	W 2-1	Martin 2
30/09/1971	TXC rd1 leg2	A	Waterford United	D 3-3	Frickelton; Martin 2
02/10/1971	CC 1	A	Cliftonville	W 3-0	Martin 3
06/10/1971	UC 11	H	Linfield	W 2-0	Martin 2
09/10/1971	CC 2	H	Derry City	W 4-3	Martin 2; Aiken 2
16/10/1971	CC 3	H	Glentoran	W 3-1	Martin; Stewart; McFall
20/10/1971	TXC qf leg1	H	Shamrock Rovers	W 4-1	Martin 2; Averell; Frickelton
23/10/1971	CC 4	A	Crusaders	D 1-1	Martin
30/10/1971	CC 5	H	Coleraine	W 2-1	Martin 2
03/11/1971	TXC qf leg2	A	Shamrock Rovers	D 1-1	Martin
06/11/1971	IL 1	A	Portadown	L 0-2	-
13/11/1971	IL 2	H	Distillery	D 0-0	-
24/11/1971	TXC sf leg1	A	Airdrie	L 0-3	-
27/11/1971	IL 3	H	Crusaders	W 4-2	Martin 2; Blair 2
04/12/1971	CC f	N	Ards	W 1-0	Averell
08/12/1971	TXC sf leg2	A	Airdrie	L 3-4	Stewart; Martin; McFall
11/12/1971	IL 4	A	Bangor	W 1-0	Martin
18/12/1971	IL 5	H	Glentoran	L 1-2	Gorman og
25/12/1971	IL 6	H	Cliftonville	W 2-0	Martin; McFall
27/12/1971	IL 7	A	Linfield	D 2-2	Martin 2
01/01/1972	IL 8	H	Coleraine	W 3-2	Aiken; Martin 2
08/01/1972	IL 9	A	Glenavon	W 4-1	Gaston; McFall; Aiken; Martin
15/01/1972	IL 10	H	Derry City	D 1-1	Gaston
22/01/1972	IL 11	A	Crusaders	L 1-2	Martin
29/01/1972	IL 12	A	Ards	L 0-1	-
05/02/1972	IC rd1	A	Crusaders	L 0-1	-
12/02/1972	IL 13	H	Glenavon	L 2-3	Martin 2
19/02/1972	IL 14	A	Glentoran	L 0-1	-
26/02/1972	IL 15	H	Bangor	W 2-1	Stewart; Martin
11/03/1972	IL 16	A	Cliftonville	D 0-0	-
25/03/1972	IL 17	H	Linfield	W 2-1	Frickelton; Martin
29/03/1972	CAS qf	A	Chimney Corner	W 2-0	Frickelton; Martin
01/04/1972	IL 18	H	Portadown	L 1-6	Young
08/04/1972	GC rd1	A	Derry City	D 0-0	-
12/04/1972	GC rd1 rep	H	Derry City	D 4-4	Gowdy; Martin 3
15/04/1972	IL 19	A	Coleraine	L 2-4	Aiken; Davidson
17/04/1972	GC rd1 rep 2	A	Derry City	W 2-1	Davidson; Frickelton
19/04/1972	IL 20	H	Ards	D 1-1	Martin
21/04/1972	IL 21	A	Derry City	W 5-0	Donald; Martin 2; Davidson; Stewart
25/04/1972	GC qf	A	Portadown	L 1-3	Davidson
27/04/1972	IL 22	A	Distillery	L 0-2	-
29/04/1972	CAS sf leg 1	H	Ards	L 0-2	-
03/05/1972	CAS sf leg 2	A	Ards	D 1-1	Frickelton

Notes

06/08/1971 v. Finn Harps: Testimonial for Eddie Russell

30/09/1971 v. Waterford United: Ballymena United won 6-5 on aggregate

03/11/1971 v. Shamrock Rovers: Ballymena United won 5-2 on aggregate

24/11/1971 v. Airdrie: Match played at Stair Park

04/12/1971 v. Ards: Match played at The Oval

08/12/1971 v. Airdrie: Ballymena United lost 7-3 on aggregate

03/05/1972 v. Ards: Ballymena United lost 3-1 on aggregate

Player Appearances and Goals

Player	Apps	Goals	Player	Apps	Goals
AIKEN Thomas	50	9	McCONAGHIE Hugh	6	0
AVERELL Robert	39	3	McFALL Quinton	51	4
BLAIR George	8	2	McKINNEY Montgomery	44	0
BROWN Jim	8	0	NICHOLL Brian	14	3
CALVIN Nelson	7	0	NICHOLL Malcolm	1	0
COOKE Andrew	7	0	ORR Des	1	0
DAVIDSON Jim	15	4	RUSSELL Edward	50	2
DONALD Alexander	38	1	SAVAGE Vincent	2	0
DONNELL John	42	0	SIMPSON Robert	3	0
FRICKELTON Samuel	36	7	STARRETT Raymond	9	0
GASTON Raymond	9	2	STEWART Arthur	53	4
GOWDY Thomas	53	2	WHITE John	9	0
GREGG Ian	1	0	YOUNG Jim	7	1
MARTIN Jim	48	44			

Played: 53, won: 24, drawn: 12, lost: 17, goals scored: 90, goals conceded: 82

Irish League: 7th; Irish Cup: Round 1; Gold Cup: Quarter-final; Ulster Cup: Runners-up; City Cup: Winners; County Antrim Shield: Semi-final; Texaco Cup: Semi-final

1971/1972

Played: 43, won: 15, drawn: 9, lost: 19, goals scored: 67, goals conceded: 78

Irish League: 9th; Irish Cup: Round 1; Gold Cup: Quarter-final; Ulster Cup: 6th; City Cup: Group stage;
County Antrim Shield: Quarter-final; Carlsberg Cup: Round 2

Date	Comp	Venue	Opponents	Result	Scorers
04/08/1972	CBC rd1	H	Cliftonville	W 3-1	Davidson; Frickelton 2
08/08/1972	CBC rd2	H	Ards	L 0-6	-
19/08/1972	UC 1	A	Cliftonville	W 4-0	Davidson; McFall; Frickelton 2
22/08/1972	UC 2	H	Coleraine	D 2-2	Erwin; Russell
26/08/1972	UC 3	H	Distillery	D 2-2	Davidson; Brown
31/08/1972	UC 4	A	Ards	L 1-5	Davidson
02/09/1972	UC 5	A	Portadown	W 3-0	Erwin; Stewart; Davidson
09/09/1972	UC 6	H	Glentoran	W 2-1	Erwin; McFall
16/09/1972	UC 7	A	Crusaders	W 2-1	Erwin; Frickelton
23/09/1972	UC 8	H	Derry City	W 1-0	Frickelton
30/09/1972	UC 9	A	Linfield	L 2-3	Dixon; Frickelton
07/10/1972	UC 10	H	Glenavon	W 5-0	McFall; Russell; Frickelton 2; Brown
14/10/1972	UC 11	A	Bangor	L 0-1	-
21/10/1972	CC 1	H	Cliftonville	W 4-0	Erwin 3; Frickelton
04/11/1972	CC 2	A	Linfield	L 1-4	Frickelton
11/11/1972	CC 3	H	Crusaders	D 1-1	Stewart
18/11/1972	CC 4	A	Coleraine	L 1-3	Frickelton
25/11/1972	IL 1	H	Portadown	W 3-1	Erwin; Frickelton
02/12/1972	IL 2	A	Distillery	W 2-1	Scott; Erwin
09/12/1972	IL 3	H	Ards	L 0-2	-
16/12/1972	IL 4	A	Cliftonville	L 0-1	-
23/12/1972	IL 5	H	Bangor	W 1-0	Donald
26/12/1972	IL 6	A	Linfield	L 0-2	-
30/12/1972	IL 7	H	Coleraine	L 2-4	McFall; Brown
06/01/1973	IL 8	A	Crusaders	L 0-3	-
13/01/1973	IL 9	H	Larne	D 2-2	Kirk; Donald
25/01/1973	IL 10	A	Glentoran	W 1-0	Averell
27/01/1973	IL 11	H	Glenavon	D 1-1	Kirk
03/02/1973	IL 12	H	Crusaders	D 1-1	Kirk
10/02/1973	IC rd1	H	Glenavon	D 1-1	Kirk
17/02/1973	IL 13	A	Coleraine	L 1-2	Brown
19/02/1973	IC rd1 rep	A	Glenavon	L 0-2	-
24/02/1973	IL 14	H	Linfield	D 0-0	-
03/03/1973	IL 15	H	Distillery	W 2-1	Young 2
10/03/1973	IL 16	A	Bangor	L 0-1	-
17/03/1973	IL 17	H	Cliftonville	W 2-1	McFall; Kirk
24/03/1973	IL 18	A	Portadown	L 0-2	-
31/03/1973	IL 19	A	Ards	L 1-3	Young
04/04/1973	CAS qf	A	Glentoran	L 5-5 (aet)	Todd 2; Stewart; Brown; Young
14/04/1973	IL 20	A	Larne	D 2-2	Todd; Mawhinney og
18/04/1973	IL 21	H	Glentoran	W 4-1	Todd 2; O'Kane; Young
21/04/1973	IL 22	A	Glenavon	L 1-4	Brown
17/05/1973	GC qf	A	Portadown	L 1-5	O'Kane

Notes

04/04/1973 v. Glentoran: Ballymena United lost 5-3 on penalties

Player Appearances and Goals

AVERELL Robert	15	1	McAULEY Samuel	40	0
BLAIR Geoff	4	0	McCALL Len	1	0
BLAIR George	2	0	McFALL Quinton	38	5
BROWN Jim	37	6	McKINNEY Montgomery	36	0
DAVIDSON	16	5	O'KANE Sean	3	2
DIXON Thomas	24	1	RUSSELL Edward	37	2
DONALD Alexander	14	2	SCOTT Samuel	32	1
DONNELL John	5	0	SIMPSON Robert	2	0
ERWIN Gary	17	9	SLOAN John	3	0
FRICKELTON Samuel	17	14	SPENCE Henry	3	0
GLENDINNING Noel	7	0	STEWART Arthur	40	3
GOWDY Thomas	35	0	TODD Brian	7	5
KIRK Paul	15	5	TORRINGTON Roy	3	0
KIRKPATRICK Andrew	5	0	WHITE John	7	0
McAULEY Robert	1	0	YOUNG James	17	5

Played: 51, won: 24, drawn: 9, lost: 18, goals scored: 93, goals conceded: 79

Irish League: 6th; Irish Cup: Finalists; Gold Cup: Semi-final; Ulster Cup: 5th; City Cup: Group stage; County Antrim Shield: Round 1; Carlsberg Cup: Round 1; Blaxnit All-Ireland Cup: Finalists

Date	Comp	Venue	Opponents	Result	Scorers
28/07/1973	FR	A	Finn Harps	D 3-3	Kirk, Blair, J. Brown
04/08/1973	CBC rd1	A	Ards	L 0-5	-
18/08/1973	UC 1	H	Cliftonville	W 3-0	Todd 2, Young
21/08/1973	UC 2	A	Coleraine	L 0-3	-
25/08/1973	UC 3	A	Distillery	L 0-4	-
30/08/1973	UC 4	H	Ards	L 3-4	J. Brown; Todd 2
01/09/1973	UC 5	A	Portadown	L 0-3	-
08/09/1973	UC 6	A	Glentoran	W 2-1	Russell; Todd
15/09/1973	UC 7	H	Crusaders	W 2-0	J. Brown; George Blair
22/09/1973	UC 8	A	Larne	W 2-1	Stewart; Kirk
26/09/1973	GC qf	H	Linfield	W 1-1 (pen)	Orr
29/09/1973	UC 9	H	Linfield	D 3-3	Stewart; Kirk; Todd
06/10/1973	UC 10	A	Glenavon	W 4-2	McFall; Kirk 2; J. Brown
11/10/1973	GC sf	A	Bangor	L 0-0 (pen)	-
13/10/1973	UC 11	H	Bangor	D 1-1	Averell
20/10/1973	CC 1	A	Cliftonville	W 6-0	McFall; Kirk 3; Todd; George Blair
27/10/1973	CC 2	A	Larne	W 4-2	Kirk 2; Todd 2
03/11/1973	CC 3	H	Glentoran	D 2-2	Todd; Donald
10/11/1973	CC 4	A	Crusaders	W 3-2	Todd 2; Kirk
17/11/1973	CC 5	H	Coleraine	L 1-2	Todd
24/11/1973	IL 1	A	Glentoran	W 2-0	Kirk; Orr
01/12/1973	IL 2	H	Cliftonville	D 2-2	Averell; Kirk
08/12/1973	IL 3	A	Portadown	L 0-3	-
15/12/1973	IL 4	H	Distillery	W 6-0	Scott og; Kirk 3; Todd 2
22/12/1973	IL 5	A	Bangor	W 2-1	McFall; Todd
26/12/1973	IL 6	A	Linfield	W 3-2	Todd 3
29/12/1973	IL 7	H	Glenavon	L 0-1	-
12/01/1974	IL 8	H	Ards	W 1-0	Erwin
19/01/1974	IL 9	H	Crusaders	W 1-0	E. Russell
24/01/1974	IL 10	A	Larne	L 0-1	-
26/01/1974	IL 11	A	Cliftonville	D 1-1	Kirk
02/02/1974	IL 12	H	Portadown	D 1-1	Erwin
09/02/1974	IC rd1	A	Linfield	W 2-1	Erwin; Donald
16/02/1974	IL 13	A	Distillery	W 5-1	Frickelton; Kirk; Todd 2; Erwin
23/02/1974	IL 14	H	Bangor	L 1-2	McFall
02/03/1974	IC qf	H	Crusaders	W 7-1	Kirk 2; Orr; Todd; McFall; Erwin; Russell
09/03/1974	IL 15	A	Coleraine	L 2-3	Averell; McNutt og
16/03/1974	IL 16	H	Linfield	W 1-0	Kirk
23/03/1974	IC sf	N	Larne	D 1-1	Kirk
27/03/1974	IC sf rep	N	Larne	D 1-1	Frickelton
30/03/1974	IL 17	A	Glenavon	W 1-0	Kirk
03/04/1974	IC sf rep2	N	Larne	W 2-2 (aet)	Kirk 2
06/04/1974	IL 18	H	Larne	W 2-0	J. Brown; Kirk
09/04/1974	AIC qf	H	Athlone Town	W 4-2	Kirk 4
13/04/1974	IL 19	A	Ards	L 0-1	-
15/04/1974	IL 20	A	Crusaders	L 1-2	Erwin
20/04/1974	IL 21	H	Glentoran	L 1-2	Kirk
22/04/1974	IL 22	H	Coleraine	D 1-1	Sloan
27/04/1974	IC f	N	Ards	L 1-2	Sloan
01/05/1974	AIC Cup sf	H	Glenavon	W 3-1	Donald 3
03/05/1974	CAS rd1	A	Crusaders	L 0-5	-
07/05/1974	AIC Cup f	N	Ards	L 1-3	Todd

Notes

26/09/1973 v. Linfield: Ballymena United won 9-8 on penalties

11/10/1973 v. Bangor: Ballymena United lost 3-0 on penalties

23/03/1974 v. Larne: Match played at Seaview

27/03/1974 v. Larne: Match played at Seaview

03/04/1974 v. Larne: Match played at Seaview and Ballymena United won 4-3 on penalties

27/04/1974 v. Ards: Match played at Windsor Park

07/05/1974 v. Ards: Match played at Windsor Park

Player Appearances and Goals

AVERELL Robert	41	3	McKENZIE Robert	22	0
BLAIR Geoff	13	2	McKINNEY Montgomery	4	0
BLAIR George	5	0	O'KANE Sean	1	0
BROWN Jim	35	4	ORR Des	31	3
BROWN Robert	25	0	PARKER John	1	0
DONALD Alexander	38	5	RUSSELL Edward	33	3
ERWIN Gary	27	6	SLOAN John	8	2
FRICKELTON Samuel	16	2	SPENCE Kenneth	1	0
GLENDINNING Noel	1	0	STEWART Arthur	50	2
GOWDY Thomas	48	0	TODD Brian	41	23
KIRK Paul	40	30	TORRINGTON Roy	3	0
McAULEY Samuel	51	0	WHITE John	2	0
McFALL Quinton	40	5	YOUNG James	10	1

Played: 43, won: 19, drawn: 10, lost: 14, goals scored: 80, goals conceded: 59

Irish League: 4th; Irish Cup: Round 1; Gold Cup: Winners; Ulster Cup: 7th; City Cup: Group stage; County Antrim Shield: Round 1

Date	Comp	Venue	Opponents	Result	Scorers
03/08/1974	FR	A	Stranraer	D 1-1	Kirk
17/08/1974	UC 1	A	Cliftonville	W 4-1	Gowdy; Kirk; McFall; Averell
21/08/1974	UC 2	H	Coleraine	L 0-2	-
24/08/1974	UC 3	H	Distillery	W 3-1	Kirk; Averell; McFall
29/08/1974	UC 4	A	Ards	W 2-1	Barr; Kirk
31/08/1974	UC 5	H	Portadown	L 1-2	McAuley
07/09/1974	UC 6	H	Glentoran	L 0-1	-
14/09/1974	UC 7	A	Crusaders	L 1-2	Sloan
21/09/1974	UC 8	H	Larne	D 1-1	Kirk
25/09/1974	GC qf	H	Linfield	W 2-0	Kirk; Porter og
28/09/1974	UC 9	A	Linfield	L 0-1	-
05/10/1974	UC 10	H	Glenavon	W 3-1	Sloan; Erwin 2
09/10/1974	GC sf	H	Coleraine	W 5-1	Sloan; J. Brown; McLaughlin; Erwin; McAuley
12/10/1974	UC 11	H	Bangor	D 1-1	Hume og
19/10/1974	CC 1	H	Cliftonville	W 2-1	Russell; Stewart
26/10/1974	CC 2	H	Larne	W 4-1	Erwin 2; J. Brown; McFall
02/11/1974	CC 3	A	Linfield	L 0-2	-
09/11/1974	CC 4	H	Crusaders	L 0-2	-
13/11/1974	GC f	N	Glentoran	W 3-2	J. Brown; Orr; McFall
16/11/1974	CC 5	A	Coleraine	D 1-1	Orr
23/11/1974	IL 1	A	Glentoran	D 1-1	Sloan
07/12/1974	IL 2	A	Coleraine	L 1-3	Sloan
14/12/1974	IL 3	H	Ards	L 1-3	McFall
21/12/1974	IL 4	A	Glenavon	W 3-2	J. Brown 2; Erwin
26/12/1974	IL 5	A	Cliftonville	W 4-0	Erwin 3; McLaughlin
28/12/1974	IL 6	H	Crusaders	D 0-0	-
01/01/1975	IL 7	A	Portadown	W 2-0	Stewart ; Sloan
04/01/1975	IL 8	H	Bangor	L 1-2	Erwin
11/01/1975	IL 9	A	Larne	W 1-0	McLaughlin
18/01/1975	IL 10	H	Linfield	D 1-1	Averell
01/02/1975	IL 11	A	Distillery	W 2-0	B. Brown; Erwin
08/02/1975	IC rd1	A	Glentoran	L 3-6	B. Brown 2; Erwin
15/02/1975	IL 12	H	Coleraine	W 2-1	J. Brown; Erwin
22/02/1975	IL 13	A	Ards	D 0-0	-
01/03/1975	IL 14	H	Portadown	W 2-0	B. Brown; Erwin
08/03/1975	IL 15	H	Glenavon	W 8-0	Barr; McFall; B. Brown 3; Erwin 2; Patton og
15/03/1975	IL 16	H	Cliftonville	D 3-3	Erwin; Sloan; B. Brown
26/03/1975	IL 17	A	Distillery	D 1-1	J. Brown
29/03/1975	IL 18	A	Crusaders	W 2-1	Sloan; Orr
02/04/1975	IL 19	H	Glentoran	L 1-2	Sloan
05/04/1975	IL 20	A	Bangor	D 2-2	J. Brown; Sloan
12/04/1975	IL 21	H	Larne	W 4-2	Sloan 2; Erwin; McFall
25/04/1975	IL 22	A	Linfield	L 1-2	Averell
30/04/1975	CAS rd1	H	Glentoran II	L 1-3	B. Brown

Notes

13/11/1974 v. Glentoran: Match played at Windsor Park

Player Appearances and Goals

AVERELL Robert	42	4	McFALL Quinton	34	7
BARR William	20	2	McLAUGHLIN Eamon	26	3
BROWN Barry	12	9	McMASTER Ivan	1	0
BROWN Jim	40	8	O'KANE Derek	1	0
BROWN Robert	43	0	ORR Des	37	3
CONVERY Gerard	4	0	PARKER John	2	0
DONALD Alexander	12	0	RUSSELL Edward	2	1
ERWIN Gary	31	18	RUSSELL Kenneth	2	0
GOWDY Thomas	42	1	SLOAN John	43	12
KIRK Paul	9	5	STEWART Arthur	42	2
McAULEY Samuel	43	2			

Played: 47, won: 19, drawn: 9, lost: 19, goals scored: 82, goals conceded: 70

Irish League: 6th; Irish Cup: Round 1; Gold Cup: Finalists; Ulster Cup: 10th; City Cup: Group stage; County Antrim Shield: Winners

Date	Comp	Venue	Opponents	Result	Scorers
09/08/1975	FR	H	Nottingham Forest	L 0-3	-
16/08/1975	UC 1	H	Cliftonville	W 4-0	B. Brown 2; Stewart, Malcolmson
19/08/1975	UC 2	A	Coleraine	L 0-3	-
23/08/1975	UC 3	A	Distillery	L 1-2	McLaughlin
28/08/1975	UC 4	H	Ards	L 0-1	-
30/08/1975	UC 5	A	Portadown	D 1-1	B. Brown
06/09/1975	UC 6	A	Glentoran	L 1-3	Malcolmson
10/09/1975	GC rd1	H	Portadown	W 4-2	Sloan; Martin 3
13/09/1975	UC 7	H	Crusaders	L 1-2	Malcolmson
20/09/1975	UC 8	A	Larne	L 2-4	Martin 2
25/09/1975	GC qf	H	Distillery	W 6-0	Sloan 2; Martin 2; B. Brown; White og
27/09/1975	UC 9	H	Linfield	W 1-0	B. Brown
04/10/1975	UC 10	A	Glenavon	L 1-2	B. Brown
08/10/1975	GC sf	H	Glenavon	W 4-1	Martin 3; B. Brown
11/10/1975	UC 11	H	Bangor	W 1-0	B. Brown
18/10/1975	CC 1	H	Glentoran	L 1-2	B. Brown
25/10/1975	CC 2	A	Larne	D 1-1	B. Brown
01/11/1975	CC 3	A	Cliftonville	D 2-2	Stewart; Barr
08/11/1975	CC 4	H	Coleraine	D 1-1	B. Brown
13/11/1975	GC f	H	Coleraine	L 1-2	B. Brown
15/11/1975	CC 5	A	Crusaders	W 2-1	Martin 2
22/11/1975	IL 1	H	Glentoran	L 1-2	Martin
29/11/1975	IL 2	A	Ards	D 1-1	Averell
06/12/1975	IL 3	H	Glenavon	W 4-1	Martin 3; B. Brown
13/12/1975	IL 4	A	Crusaders	L 0-2	-
20/12/1975	IL 5	H	Coleraine	W 5-1	B. Brown 3; Martin 2
26/12/1975	IL 6	A	Larne	W 1-0	Martin
27/12/1975	IL 7	H	Portadown	D 1-1	B. Brown
01/01/1976	IL 8	A	Distillery	W 3-1	O'Kane; B. Brown 2
03/01/1976	IL 9	H	Cliftonville	W 1-0	O'Kane
10/01/1976	IL 10	H	Bangor	W 4-1	B. Brown 2; Martin; Barr
17/01/1976	IL 11	A	Linfield	L 1-2	Martin
24/01/1976	IL 12	A	Glentoran	L 2-5	Sloan; Stewart
31/01/1976	IC rd1	H	Carrick Rangers	L 2-3	Sloan 2
07/02/1976	IL 13	H	Ards	L 0-1	-
14/02/1976	IL 14	A	Glenavon	D 1-1	B. Brown
06/03/1976	IL 15	A	Coleraine	L 2-4	Stewart 2
13/03/1976	IL 16	H	Crusaders	L 2-3	B. Brown; Martin
20/03/1976	IL 17	H	Larne	W 3-2	Martin; Russell; Sloan
27/03/1976	IL 18	A	Portadown	L 1-3	Sloan
03/04/1976	IL 19	H	Distillery	W 1-0	Russell
14/04/1976	CAS rd1	H	Dundela	W 2-1	Russell; B. Brown
17/04/1976	IL 20	A	Cliftonville	L 0-2	-
20/04/1976	IL 21	A	Bangor	D 1-1	B. Brown
24/04/1976	IL 22	H	Linfield	D 1-1	Averell
30/04/1976	CAS qf	H	Chimney Corner	W 1-1 (aet)	B. Brown
03/05/1976	CAS sf	H	Linfield	W 2-0	Averell; Russell
07/05/1976	CAS f	N	Distillery	W 4-0	Martin; Russell; Brown 2

Notes

30/04/1976 v. Chimney Corner: Ballymena United won 3-1 on penalties

07/05/1976 v. Distillery: Match played at Inver Park

Player Appearances and Goals

AVERELL Robert	44	3	McAULEY Samuel	45	0
BARR William	20	1	McCALL Joseph	1	0
BROWN Barry	46	28	McFALL Quinton	37	0
BROWN Robert	20	0	McLAUGHLIN Eamon	25	2
DONALD Alexander	6	0	O'KANE Derek	11	2
DUNLOP George	27	0	ORR Des	31	0
GOWDY Thomas	45	0	RUSSELL Kenneth	17	5
HAZLETT Stephen	11	0	SLOAN John	41	8
HENDERSON Thomas	1	0	SPENCE Kenneth	24	0
MALCOLMSON David	14	3	STEWART Arthur	35	5
MARTIN Jim	41	24			

Played: 40, won: 5, drawn: 7, lost: 28, goals scored: 36, goals conceded: 82

Irish League: 9th; Irish Cup: Round 1; Gold Cup: Group stage; Ulster Cup: 12th; County Antrim Shield: Round 1

Date	Comp	Venue	Opponents	Result	Scorers
21/08/1976	UC 1	A	Ards	L 1-3	Martin
25/08/1976	UC 2	H	Coleraine	L 1-2	Moore
28/08/1976	UC 3	A	Distillery	D 1-1	Orr
31/08/1976	UC 4	A	Larne	L 1-2	Donald
04/09/1976	UC 5	H	Glenavon	L 0-2	-
07/09/1976	UC 6	A	Cliftonville	L 0-2	-
11/09/1976	UC 7	H	Linfield	L 3-4	Martin; Donald; Barclay og
18/09/1976	UC 8	A	Glentoran	L 1-4	Orr
25/09/1976	UC 9	H	Portadown	L 1-4	McKay
02/10/1976	UC 10	H	Bangor	D 0-0	-
09/10/1976	UC 11	A	Crusaders	L 0-1	-
16/10/1976	GC 1	A	Linfield	L 0-2	-
23/10/1976	GC 2	H	Larne	L 2-3	Orr; Martin
30/10/1976	GC 3	H	Cliftonville	L 1-3	Malcolmson
06/11/1976	GC 4	A	Coleraine	L 0-4	-
13/11/1976	GC 5	H	Crusaders	L 2-3	O'Connell; McFall
20/11/1976	IL 1	A	Glentoran	L 1-3	Orr
27/11/1976	IL 2	H	Ards	W 1-0	Flanaghan og
04/12/1976	IL 3	A	Glenavon	L 0-1	-
11/12/1976	IL 4	H	Crusaders	L 0-2	-
18/12/1976	IL 5	A	Larne	L 0-1	-
25/12/1976	IL 6	H	Coleraine	L 2-3	Brown; Kenny
28/12/1976	IL 7	A	Portadown	D 1-1	Martin
01/01/1977	IL 8	H	Distillery	W 2-0	Martin; Brown
08/01/1977	IL 9	A	Cliftonville	W 1-0	Kingon
15/01/1977	IL 10	A	Bangor	D 1-1	O'Connell
22/01/1977	IL 11	H	Linfield	D 1-1	Martin
05/02/1977	IC rd1	A	Distillery	L 1-4	Kingon
12/02/1977	IL 12	A	Ards	L 0-2	-
19/02/1977	IL 13	H	Glenavon	W 1-0	Kingon
26/02/1977	IL 14	H	Glentoran	L 0-4	-
05/03/1977	IL 15	A	Crusaders	L 1-4	Kenny
12/03/1977	IL 16	H	Larne	W 4-1	Kingon; Barr 3
19/03/1977	IL 17	A	Cliftonville	L 0-1	-
26/03/1977	IL 18	A	Coleraine	L 2-3	Orr; Donald
02/04/1977	IL 19	H	Portadown	L 2-4	Kenny; Russell
09/04/1977	IL 20	A	Distillery	D 0-0	-
16/04/1977	IL 21	H	Bangor	L 0-2	-
30/04/1977	IL 22	A	Linfield	D 0-0	-
03/05/1977	CAS rd1	A	Ards II	L 1-2	Russell

Player Appearances and Goals

Player	Apps	Goals	Player	Apps	Goals
AVERELL Robert	13	0	McCALL Joseph	9	1
BARR William	21	3	McFALL Quinton	23	1
BROWN Barry	17	2	McKAY Michael	4	1
DONALD Alexander	31	3	McLAUGHLIN Eamon	7	0
DONNELL John	9	0	McQUILLAN Alexander	8	0
DUNLOP George	35	0	McVICKER Samuel	3	0
FULLERTON George	2	0	MEARNS William	1	0
GOWDY Thomas	36	0	MOORE Terence	10	1
HUGHES Anthony	2	0	MORRISON Ronald	16	0
JOHNSTON Donald	7	0	O'CONNELL Jim	17	2
KENNY David	14	3	ORR Des	34	5
KINGON Terrence	21	4	RUSSELL Kenneth	18	1
MALCOLMSON David	32	1	SEYMOUR Byron	5	0
MARTIN Jim	27	6	SLOAN John	6	0
McAULEY Samuel	36	0	SPENCE Henry	4	0

Date	Comp	Venue	Opponents	Result	Scorers
20/08/1977	UC 1	H	Distillery	W 2-0	Cooke; Kenny
23/08/1977	UC 2	A	Ards	D 3-3	Ba. Brown 2; Malcolmson
27/08/1977	UC 3	H	Glenavon	D 1-1	Kenny
30/08/1977	UC 4	A	Larne	L 0-1	-
03/09/1977	UC 5	H	Linfield	L 1-3	Kenny
10/09/1977	UC 6	A	Coleraine	D 2-2	Ba. Brown; McAuley
17/09/1977	UC 7	H	Bangor	W 1-0	Ba. Brown
24/09/1977	UC 8	A	Portadown	L 1-6	Cooke
01/10/1977	UC 9	H	Cliftonville	W 1-0	Ba. Brown
08/10/1977	UC 10	A	Glentoran	L 1-4	-
15/10/1977	UC 11	H	Crusaders	W 2-0	Ba. Brown 2
22/10/1977	GC 1	H	Glentoran	W 2-1	McAvoy 2
29/10/1977	GC 2	A	Larne	L 0-2	-
05/11/1977	GC 3	A	Cliftonville	W 2-1	Kingon; Ba. Brown
12/11/1977	GC 4	H	Coleraine	L 1-2	Simpson
19/11/1977	GC 5	A	Crusaders	W 2-0	Simpson; T. Sloan
26/11/1977	IL 1	H	Glenavon	L 0-1	-
03/12/1977	IL 2	A	Ards	L 1-2	Ba. Brown
10/12/1977	IL 3	H	Glentoran	L 0-2	-
17/12/1977	IL 4	H	Crusaders	L 1-2	McAvoy
24/12/1977	IL 5	H	Larne	L 2-3	Simpson; Ba. Brown
27/12/1977	IL 6	A	Coleraine	L 0-3	-
31/12/1977	IL 7	H	Linfield	L 0-3	-
02/01/1978	IL 8	A	Distillery	D 2-2	Ba. Brown 2
07/01/1978	IL 9	H	Cliftonville	L 1-2	Kenny
14/01/1978	IL 10	H	Bangor	W 1-0	McAvoy
21/01/1978	IL 11	A	Portadown	L 0-3	-
28/01/1978	IL 12	A	Glenavon	L 1-2	McPartland
04/02/1978	IC rd1	H	Downpatrick Rec.	W 6-2	Nelson 2; McAuley; J. Sloan; McAvoy; McPartland
11/02/1978	IL 13	A	Ards	L 1-3	J. Sloan
25/02/1978	IC qf	H	Ards	W 1-0	McAvoy
04/03/1978	IL 14	H	Crusaders	W 2-1	J. Sloan; Johnston
07/03/1978	IL 15	A	Glentoran	L 0-2	-
11/03/1978	IL 16	A	Larne	L 1-2	Johnston
18/03/1978	IC sf	N	Crusaders	D 1-1	Nelson
21/03/1978	IC sf rep	N	Crusaders	D 1-1	McAvoy
28/03/1978	IL 17	A	Linfield	L 1-2	Nelson
01/04/1978	IL 18	H	Distillery	W 3-1	McAleese; J. Sloan; Johnston
04/04/1978	IC sf rep 2	N	Crusaders	W 1-1 (aet)	J. Sloan
08/04/1978	IL 19	A	Cliftonville	L 0-3	-
13/04/1978	IL 20	H	Coleraine	W 2-0	Simpson; McClean
15/04/1978	IL 21	A	Bangor	D 2-2	McClean; Johnston
20/04/1978	CAS rd1	H	Chimney Corner	L 0-1	-
22/04/1978	IL 22	H	Portadown	L 1-3	J. Sloan
29/04/1978	IC f	N	Linfield	L 1-3	McClean

Notes

18/03/1978 v. Crusaders: Match played at Windsor Park

21/03/1978 v. Crusaders: Match played at Windsor Park

18/03/1978 v. Crusaders: Match played at Windsor Park and Ballymena United won 4-1 on penalties

29/04/1978 v. Linfield: Match played at The Oval

Player Appearances and Goals

AVERELL Robert	7	0	McAVOY William	24	7
BROWN Barry	24	13	McCALL Joseph	3	0
BROWN Robert	31	0	McCULLOUGH Ronald	36	0
BUTCHER Ronald	17	0	McLEAN Jack	6	3
CATHCART Stephen	2	0	McPARTLAND James	11	2
COOKE Drew	16	2	McQUILLAN Alexander	2	0
DONALD Alexander	35	0	MORRISON Ronald	4	0
JACKSON David	18	0	NELSON Jim	41	4
JOHNSTON Geoff	13	4	QUINN Michael	1	0
KENNY David	15	4	RAFFERTY Philip	14	0
KINGON Terence	17	1	SIMPSON Alan	28	4
MALCOLMSON David	14	1	SLOAN John	27	6
MARTIN Shaun	8	0	SLOAN Thomas	40	1
McALEESE Michael	9	1	SPENCE Kenneth	24	0
McAULEY Samuel	38	2	WORTHINGTON Nigel	1	0

Played: 45, won: 15, drawn: 9, lost: 21, goals scored: 61, goals conceded: 79

Irish League: 11th; Irish Cup: Quarter-final; Gold Cup: Group stage; Ulster Cup: 3rd; County Antrim Shield: Quarter-final;
UEFA Cup Winners' Cup: Round 1

Date	Comp	Venue	Opponents	Result	Scorers
31/07/1978	FR	H	Carlisle United	L 0-2	-
04/08/1978	FR	H	Crewe Alexandra	W 4-2	McClean 2; McQuiston; Mullan
19/08/1978	UC 1	A	Distillery	W 2-0	Johnston; Butcher
23/08/1978	UC 2	H	Ards	W 2-1	McClean; Jackson
26/08/1978	UC 3	A	Glenavon	D 2-2	Mullan; McQuiston
29/08/1978	UC 4	H	Larne	W 1-0	McClean
02/09/1978	UC 5	A	Linfield	W 2-1	Mullan; Jess
09/09/1978	UC 6	H	Coleraine	W 3-2	Simpson; McClean 2
13/09/1978	ECWC rd1 leg 1	A	KSK Beveren	L 0-3	-
16/09/1978	UC 7	A	Bangor	W 4-1	McQuiston 2; Jackson; Jess
23/09/1978	UC 8	H	Portadown	D 1-1	McQuiston
27/09/1978	ECWC rd1 leg 2	H	KSK Beveren	L 0-3	-
30/09/1978	UC 9	A	Cliftonville	L 1-3	McClean
07/10/1978	UC 10	H	Glentoran	L 1-2	Mullan
14/10/1978	UC 11	A	Crusaders	L 0-1	-
21/10/1978	GC 1	H	Larne	W 4-1	McQuiston; McCullough; Devine; Sloan
28/10/1978	GC 2	A	Glentoran	L 0-3	-
04/11/1978	GC 3	A	Coleraine	W 3-2	Sloan 2; McQuiston
11/11/1978	GC 4	H	Crusaders	L 0-2	-
18/11/1978	GC 5	H	Cliftonville	W 3-1	Mullan; Jess; Sloan
25/11/1978	IL 1	H	Portadown	W 1-0	Sloan
09/12/1978	IL 2	H	Glentoran	W 5-1	McQuiston 2; Mullan 2; McCullough
16/12/1978	IL 3	A	Cliftonville	L 0-5	-
20/12/1978	IL 4	A	Bangor	D 0-0	-
23/12/1978	IL 5	H	Larne	L 1-3	McQuiston
26/12/1978	IL 6	A	Linfield	L 1-6	McQuiston
30/12/1978	IL 7	A	Coleraine	D 1-1	McClean
06/01/1979	IL 8	A	Crusaders	L 0-4	-
20/01/1979	IL 9	A	Glenavon	L 2-3	Murray; Mullan
24/01/1979	IL 10	A	Distillery	L 2-4	McAvoy; Murray
08/02/1979	IC rd1	H	Crusaders	W 2-0	McQuiston 2
10/02/1979	IL 11	A	Portadown	L 0-2	-
17/02/1979	IL 12	H	Bangor	D 1-1	Devine
24/02/1979	IC qf	H	Portadown	D 0-0	-
28/02/1979	IC qf rep	A	Portadown	L 1-2	McQuiston
03/03/1979	IL 13	A	Glentoran	L 0-2	-
07/03/1979	IL 14	H	Glenavon	L 0-2	-
10/03/1979	IL 15	H	Cliftonville	D 1-1	McCall
17/03/1979	IL 16	H	Ards	L 1-3	Jess
24/03/1979	IL 17	A	Larne	L 1-2	McQuiston
31/03/1979	IL 18	H	Linfield	L 1-2	Devine
07/04/1979	IL 19	H	Coleraine	W 2-1	McQuiston 2
14/04/1979	IL 20	H	Distillery	W 2-0	McClean 2
17/04/1979	IL 21	H	Crusaders	D 0-0	-
21/04/1979	IL 22	A	Ards	D 3-3	Gibson og; McQuiston; Sloan
27/04/1979	CAS rd1	H	Carrick Rangers	W 3-0	McCullough; Sloan; McQuiston
05/05/1979	CAS qf	A	Ballyclare Comrades	L 1-2	Murray

Notes

27/09/1978 v. KSK Beveren: Ballymena United lost 6-0 on aggregate

Player Appearances and Goals

BROWN Robert	30	0	McCULLOUGH Ronald	44	3
BUTCHER Liam	12	1	McCLEAN Jack	19	8
COOKE Drew	5	0	McQUILLAN Alexander	15	0
DEVINE Fred	20	3	McQUISTON Samuel	44	18
DONALD Alexander	40	0	MULLAN Gerard	36	7
GRIMSHAW Anthony	4	0	MURRAY Ivan	28	3
JACKSON David	27	2	QUINN Michael	1	0
JESS Brian	41	4	RAFFERTY Philip	15	0
JOHNSTON Geoff	1	1	SCOTT Mervyn	11	0
KENNY David	4	0	SHAW David	8	0
MARSHALL Mervyn	3	0	SIMPSON Alan	21	2
McAULEY Samuel	1	0	SLOAN John	38	7
McAVOY William	6	1	SPENCE Kenneth	4	0
McCALL Anthony	11	0	WORTHINGTON Nigel	31	0

Played: 47, won: 29, drawn: 11, lost: 7, goals scored: 101, goals conceded: 43

Irish League: 2nd; Irish Cup: Semi-final; Gold Cup: Finalists; Ulster Cup: 3rd; County Antrim Shield: Winners

Date	Comp	Venue	Opponents	Result	Scorers
28/07/1979	FR	N	Carlisle	L 1-2	Dickson
01/08/1979	FR	N	Southampton	L 0-4	-
18/08/1979	UC 1	A	Portadown	W 1-0	G. Mullan
22/08/1979	UC 2	A	Glentoran	W 2-1	McQuiston; Fox
25/08/1979	UC 3	A	Distillery	W 5-0	Malone 2; G. Mullan 2; McQuiston
28/08/1979	UC 4	A	Cliftonville	D 1-1	McQuiston
01/09/1979	UC 5	A	Ards	W 1-0	Malone
08/09/1979	UC 6	A	Glenavon	L 1-2	McQuiston
15/09/1979	UC 7	A	Linfield	D 1-1	Jess
22/09/1979	UC 8	A	Crusaders	D 2-2	McQuiston; Sloan
29/09/1979	UC 9	A	Coleraine	W 1-0	Tully
06/10/1979	UC 10	A	Larne	W 2-1	McQuiston; Malone
13/10/1979	UC 11	A	Bangor	D 1-1	P. Mullan
20/10/1979	GC 1	A	Cliftonville	W 3-0	Malone; P. Mullan; Tully
27/10/1979	GC 2	H	Coleraine	W 4-2	Malone; Fox; Jackson; McQuiston
03/11/1979	GC 3	A	Crusaders	W 3-1	McCall; Jess; G. Mullan
10/11/1979	GC 4	H	Glentoran	W 4-0	McQuiston 2; G. Mullan 2
17/11/1979	GC 5	A	Larne	W 2-0	G. Mullan; Malone
24/11/1979	IL 1	H	Portadown	W 2-1	Tully; McQuiston
27/11/1979	GC f	A	Linfield	L 1-2	McQuiston
01/12/1979	IL 2	A	Glentoran	L 0-2	-
08/12/1979	IL 3	H	Distillery	W 8-0	Sloan 3; Tully; Malone 3; Beattie
15/12/1979	IL 4	A	Cliftonville	L 1-2	Jess
22/12/1979	IL 5	H	Ards	W 2-0	McQuiston 2
26/12/1979	IL 6	A	Glenavon	D 1-1	Malone
29/12/1979	IL 7	H	Linfield	W 5-0	McQuiston 2; Malone 3
01/01/1980	IL 8	A	Crusaders	D 1-1	Jess
05/01/1980	IL 9	H	Coleraine	W 5-0	Malone 3; McQuiston; Jess
12/01/1980	IL 10	H	Larne	W 4-0	McQuiston; Neill; G. Mullan; Malone
23/01/1980	IL 11	A	Bangor	W 3-2	Beattie; Sloan; Scott
26/01/1980	IL 12	A	Portadown	W 5-2	McQuiston 2; P. Mullan; Malone; G. Mullan
02/02/1980	IC rd1	H	Bangor	D 1-1	McQuiston
06/02/1980	IC rd1 rep	A	Bangor	W 2-0	McQuiston; G. Mullan
09/02/1980	IL 13	H	Glentoran	D 1-1	Scott
16/02/1980	IL 14	A	Distillery	W 3-1	McQuiston 2; Malone
23/02/1980	IC qf	H	Portadown	W 3-2	Malone 2; McQuiston
01/03/1980	IL 15	H	Cliftonville	D 1-1	Malone
08/03/1980	IL 16	A	Ards	W 3-1	Breen; McQuiston; Malone
15/03/1980	IL 17	H	Glenavon	L 0-1	-
22/03/1980	IC sf	N	Linfield	L 0-1	-
29/03/1980	IL 18	A	Linfield	L 1-4	McCullough
05/04/1980	IL 19	H	Crusaders	W 2-1	McCullough; G. Mullan
07/04/1980	IL 20	A	Coleraine	D 1-1	Malone
12/04/1980	IL 21	A	Larne	D 1-1	Malone
14/04/1980	CAS rd1	A	Glentoran II	W 1-0	McCullough
19/04/1980	IL 22	H	Bangor	W 2-0	Malone; P. Mullan
01/05/1980	CAS qf	H	Barn United	W 4-2 (aet)	Millar og; G.Mullan 2; Sloan
09/05/1980	CAS sf	H	Larne	W 3-0	Malone; McCullough; McQuiston
13/05/1980	CAS f	N	Crusaders	W 0-0 (aet)	-

Notes

28/07/1979 v. Carlisle United: Match played at Coleraine Showgrounds
01/08/1979 v. Southampton: Match played at Coleraine Showgrounds
22/03/1980 v. Linfield: Match played at The Oval
13/05/1980 v. Crusaders: Match played at The Oval

Player Appearances and Goals

BEATTIE George	34	2	McQUISTON Samuel	45	26
BREEN Shane	10	1	McQUILLAN Alexander	1	0
BUTCHER Liam	6	0	MULLAN Gerry	31	13
DONALD Alec	7	0	MULLAN Patrick	38	4
FOX Graham	44	2	NEILL David	6	1
HUSTON Thomas	1	0	SCOTT Mervyn	8	2
JACKSON David	38	1	SLOAN John	47	6
JESS Brian	32	5	TULLY Brendan	18	4
MALONE Paul	44	28	WHITE Brian	47	0
McCALL Tony	31	1	WORTHINGTON Nigel	10	0
McCULLOUGH Ronnie	42	4			

Played: 47, won: 26, drawn: 10, lost: 11, goals scored: 92, goals conceded: 58

Irish League: 3rd; Irish Cup: Winners; Gold Cup: Group stage; Ulster Cup: Winners; County Antrim Shield: Quarter-final; Tyler All-Ireland Cup: Round 1; UEFA Cup: Round 1

Date	Comp	Venue	Opponents	Result	Scorers
26/07/1980	TC rd1	H	Shamrock Rovers	L 0-2	-
16/08/1980	UC 1	H	Portadown	W 6-2	Sloan 2; McQuiston; Neill 2; Malone
19/08/1980	UC 2	A	Glentoran	L 0-2	-
23/08/1980	UC 3	H	Distillery	W 5-0	Sloan 3; McQuiston; Malone
26/08/1980	UC 4	A	Cliftonville	W 2-1	McQuiston; Sloan
29/08/1980	UC 5	H	Ards	D 2-2	McQuiston; Malone
06/09/1980	UC 6	A	Glenavon	W 2-1	G. Mullan; Neill
13/09/1980	UC 7	H	Linfield	D 1-1	Sloan
17/09/1980	UEFA rd1 leg 1	H	FC Vorwaerts	W 2-1	McQuiston; Sloan
27/09/1980	UC 8	H	Coleraine	W 3-1	Malone; G. Mullan 2
01/10/1980	UEFA rd1 leg 2	A	FC Vorwaerts	L 0-3	-
04/10/1980	UC 9	H	Larne	W 4-0	McQuiston; McManus og; Malone; G. Mullan
08/10/1980	UC 10	A	Crusaders	W 5-0	G. Mullan 2; Malone 2; Sloan
11/10/1980	UC 11	A	Bangor	W 5-1	Neill; G. Mullan; Sloan; McQuiston; Malone
18/10/1980	GC 1	H	Cliftonville	D 1-1	Worthington
25/10/1980	GC 2	A	Coleraine	D 2-2	Malone; Sloan
01/11/1980	GC 3	H	Crusaders	D 3-3	McQuiston 2; Sloan
08/11/1980	GC 4	A	Glentoran	L 1-2	Malone
15/11/1980	GC 5	H	Larne	W 4-2	Malone 2; McCall; McCusker
22/11/1980	IL 1	A	Portadown	W 1-0	Sloan
29/11/1980	IL 2	H	Glentoran	L 1-2	Worthington
06/12/1980	IL 3	A	Distillery	W 2-1	McCusker; Malone
13/12/1980	IL 4	H	Cliftonville	W 4-3	Sloan; Neill; Malone; Worthington
20/12/1980	IL 5	A	Ards	W 1-0	McCusker
26/12/1980	IL 6	H	Glenavon	D 1-1	P. Mullan
27/12/1980	IL 7	A	Linfield	L 0-1	-
01/01/1981	IL 8	H	Crusaders	D 1-1	McQuiston
03/01/1981	IL 9	A	Coleraine	D 0-0	-
10/01/1981	IL 10	A	Larne	W 3-0	Malone; McQuiston; Sloan
17/01/1981	IL 11	H	Bangor	W 5-1	Malone 4; Neill
24/01/1981	IL 12	H	Portadown	W 2-0	P. Mullan; Neill
31/01/1981	IC rd1	A	Coleraine	W 2-1	Neill; Elliott
07/02/1981	IL 13	A	Glentoran	L 0-2	-
14/02/1981	IL 14	H	Distillery	W 2-0	McQuiston; P. Mullan
21/02/1981	IC qf	A	Cliftonville	W 4-1	Sloan; Malone 3
28/02/1981	IL 15	A	Cliftonville	D 1-1	Neill
07/03/1981	IL 16	H	Ards	W 3-2	McCusker; McQuiston; Fox
14/03/1981	IL 17	A	Glenavon	L 1-2	McQuiston
21/03/1981	IC sf	N	Glentoran	D 2-2	Neill; Worthington
24/03/1981	IC sf rep	N	Glentoran	W 2-0	Malone 2
28/03/1981	IL 18	H	Linfield	W 1-0	Malone
04/04/1981	IL 19	A	Crusaders	L 0-1	-
11/04/1981	IL 20	H	Coleraine	W 2-0	Malone 2
14/04/1981	IL 21	A	Bangor	L 1-3	Penney
18/04/1981	IL 22	H	Larne	W 1-0	Sloan
23/04/1981	CAS qf	H	Linfield	L 0-6	-
02/05/1981	IC f	N	Glenavon	W 1-0	McQuiston

Notes

01/10/1980 v. FC Vorwaerts: Ballymena United lost 4-2 on aggregate

21/03/1981 v. Glentoran: Match played at Windsor Park

24/03/1981 v. Glentoran: Match played at Windsor Park

02/05/1981 v. Glenavon: Match played at Windsor Park

Player Appearances and Goals

Player	Apps	Goals	Player	Apps	Goals
BEATTIE George	36	0	McDOWELL Maurice	2	0
DONALD Alexander	10	0	McQUILLAN Alexander	2	0
ELLIOTT Alexander	13	1	McQUISTON Samuel	39	15
FOX Graham	42	1	MULLAN Gerard	15	7
HENRY Kyle	2	0	MULLAN Patrick	27	3
HUSTON Thomas	15	0	NEILL David	45	10
JUSTIN David	1	0	PENNEY Stephen	3	1
KERNOHAN Harold	4	0	RODGERS Ian	1	0
MADILL John	2	0	SCOTT Mervyn	5	0
MALONE Paul	43	27	SLOAN John	44	17
MATTHEWS Denis	25	0	SMYTH David	3	0
McCALL Anthony	26	1	WHITE Brian	22	0
McCULLOUGH Ronald	38	0	WORTHINGTON Nigel	40	4
McCUSKER Peter	28	4			

Played: 45, won: 14, drawn: 11, lost: 20, goals scored: 52, goals conceded: 64

Irish League: 7th; Irish Cup: Round 1; Gold Cup: Finalists; Ulster Cup: 9th; County Antrim Shield: Semi-final;
UEFA Cup Winnres' Cup: Round 1

Date	Comp	Venue	Opponents	Result	Scorers
04/08/1981	FR	H	Tranmere Rovers	L 2-5	McCusker, Malone
15/08/1981	UC 1	A	Linfield	L 1-2	Malone
18/08/1981	UC 2	H	Distillery	W 2-1	Fox; Neill
22/08/1981	UC 3	H	Glenavon	L 1-2	Neill
26/08/1981	UC 4	A	Crusaders	W 1-0	Neill
28/08/1981	UC 5	H	Ards	L 1-2	Neill
05/09/1981	UC 6	A	Glentoran	L 2-4	Malone 2
12/09/1981	UC 7	H	Cliftonville	D 1-1	Malone
16/09/1981	ECWC rd1 leg1	H	AS Roma	L 0-2	-
19/09/1981	UC 8	A	Coleraine	L 1-2	Malone
26/09/1981	UC 9	H	Larne	L 0-1	-
30/09/1981	ECWC rd1 leg2	A	AS Roma	L 0-4	-
03/10/1981	UC 10	A	Bangor	W 1-0	McCall
10/10/1981	UC 11	H	Portadown	L 1-4	McCusker
17/10/1981	GC 1	A	Cliftonville	W 1-0	Malone
22/10/1981	GC 2	H	Coleraine	W 2-0	Guy; Neill
31/10/1981	GC 3	A	Crusaders	D 1-1	Malone
07/11/1981	GC 4	H	Glentoran	D 1-1	Malone
14/11/1981	GC 5	A	Larne	W 2-0	Malone 2
21/11/1981	IL 1	A	Ards	D 0-0	-
28/11/1981	IL 2	H	Glenavon	D 0-0	-
05/12/1981	IL 3	A	Linfield	L 0-3	-
08/12/1981	GC f	A	Linfield	L 1-1 (aet)	Malone
26/12/1981	IL 4	H	Coleraine	W 4-2	McCusker 3; Malone
28/12/1981	IL 5	H	Crusaders	D 0-0	-
01/01/1982	IL 6	A	Bangor	W 3-1	Neill; McCusker; Malone
02/01/1982	IL 7	H	Portadown	L 1-3	Malone
16/01/1982	IL 8	H	Larne	W 2-0	Sloan; Malone
23/01/1982	IL 9	A	Cliftonville	D 1-1	Guy
30/01/1982	IC rd1	A	Distillery	L 2-3	Malone; McQuiston
06/02/1982	IL 10	H	Ards	W 2-1	Sloan; Malone
13/02/1982	IL 11	A	Glenavon	D 1-1	McQuiston
20/02/1982	IL 12	A	Glentoran	L 1-3	Sloan
27/02/1982	IL 13	H	Linfield	D 1-1	McCusker
06/03/1982	IL 14	A	Crusaders	L 1-2	Guy
13/03/1982	IL 15	H	Distillery	D 1-1	Guy
27/03/1982	IL 16	A	Coleraine	L 0-2	-
30/03/1982	CAS rd1	A	Ballyclare Comrades	W 2-1	McCall; Malone
03/04/1982	IL 17	H	Bangor	L 1-2	Sloan
06/04/1982	IL 18	A	Distillery	W 3-2	Sloan 2; Burns
10/04/1982	IL 19	A	Portadown	L 0-1	-
13/04/1982	IL 20	H	Glentoran	W 1-0	Burns
15/04/1982	CAS qf	H	Bangor	W 2-0	McQuiston; Malone
17/04/1982	IL 21	A	Larne	D 1-1	Malone
20/04/1982	IL 22	H	Cliftonville	L 1-3	McQuiston
22/04/1982	CAS sf	N	Distillery	L 1-2	Guy

Notes

30/09/1981 v. AS Roma: Ballymena United lost 6-0 on aggregate

08/12/1981 v. Linfield: Ballymena United lost 5-4 on penalties

22/04/1982 v. Distillery: Match played at Seaview

Player Appearances and Goals

BEATTIE George	34	0	McAULEY Samuel	18	0
BLAIR Jeff	11	0	McCALL Anthony	8	2
BURNS Ronald	7	2	McCULLOUGH Ronald	28	0
COOKE Joseph	4	0	McCUSKER Peter	41	6
ELLIOTT Alexander	2	0	McDOWELL Seamus	17	0
FEENEY Stephen	8	0	McGUIGAN Raymond	28	0
FOX Graham	19	1	McQUISTON Samuel	31	4
GRACEY Alan	15	0	MOFFATT Frank	11	0
GUY Michael	27	5	NEILL David	43	6
HUSTON Thomas	18	0	O'DOHERTY Anthony	11	0
HUTCHINSON Brian	2	0	PENNEY Stephen	4	0
KERNOHAN Harold	3	0	SLOAN John	43	6
MALONE Paul	42	20	SMYTH David	4	0
MATTHEWS Denis	43	0			

1982/1983

Played: 40, won: 16, drawn: 8, lost: 16, goals scored: 70, goals conceded: 72

Irish League: 8th; Irish Cup: Round 1; Gold Cup: Group stage; Ulster Cup: 4th; County Antrim Shield: Round 1

Date	Comp	Venue	Opponents	Result	Scorers
02/08/1982	FR	H	Southampton	L 2-4	Malone; Guy
21/08/1982	GC 1	H	Cliftonville	W 2-1	Malone; Hughes og
24/08/1982	GC 2	A	Coleraine	W 4-3	Guy 2; Malone 2
26/08/1982	GC 3	H	Crusaders	D 1-1	Penney
31/08/1982	GC 4	A	Glentoran	L 1-2	Malone
04/09/1982	GC 5	H	Larne	W 2-1	Malone; Neill
11/09/1982	UC 1	H	Linfield	L 1-2	Malone
18/09/1982	UC 2	A	Distillery	W 2-0	Penney; Guy
25/09/1982	UC 3	A	Glenavon	W 4-1	Guy 2; Neill; McCall
28/09/1982	FR	H	Motherwell	W 2-1	Best; Sloan
02/10/1982	UC 4	H	Crusaders	W 2-0	Blair; McDonald og
09/10/1982	UC 5	A	Ards	D 1-1	Malone
16/10/1982	UC 6	H	Glentoran	D 1-1	Malone
23/10/1982	UC 7	A	Cliftonville	W 5-0	Malone 3; Nicholl; Smyth
30/10/1982	UC 8	A	Coleraine	L 2-3	Malone; Blair
06/11/1982	UC 9	A	Larne	D 0-0	-
13/11/1982	UC 10	H	Bangor	W 5-1	Burns; Penney; Malone 2; Guy
20/11/1982	UC 11	A	Portadown	L 2-5	McQuiston 2
27/11/1982	IL 1	H	Ards	D 4-4	Penney 2; Malone; McCall
04/12/1982	IL 2	A	Glenavon	W 3-1	Malone; Burns 2
11/12/1982	IL 3	H	Linfield	L 0-2	-
27/12/1982	IL 4	H	Distillery	L 1-2	Penney
28/12/1982	IL 5	A	Coleraine	W 4-2	Guy; McQuiston 2; Penney
01/01/1983	IL 6	H	Bangor	D 1-1	McQuiston
03/01/1983	IL 7	A	Portadown	W 2-1	Malone; Smyth
08/01/1983	IL 8	H	Glentoran	L 1-3	Guy
12/01/1983	IL 9	A	Crusaders	L 0-6	-
15/01/1983	IL 10	A	Larne	W 2-1	Burns; Guy
22/01/1983	IC rd1	A	Glentoran	L 0-4	-
29/01/1983	IL 11	H	Cliftonville	W 1-0	McQuiston
05/02/1983	IL 12	A	Ards	L 0-4	-
12/02/1983	IL 13	A	Bangor	W 3-0	McQuiston; Malone; Sloan
19/02/1983	IL 14	H	Glenavon	W 2-0	Guy; Malone
26/02/1983	IL 15	A	Linfield	L 1-4	Malone
12/03/1983	IL 16	H	Crusaders	D 0-0	-
19/03/1983	IL 17	A	Distillery	L 1-2	Malone
26/03/1983	CAS rd1	H	Cliftonville	L 3-5	McQuiston; Sloan 2
02/04/1983	IL 18	H	Coleraine	L 2-4	Malone; McQuiston
09/04/1983	IL 19	H	Portadown	D 0-0	-
16/04/1983	IL 20	A	Glentoran	L 0-1	-
23/04/1983	IL 21	H	Larne	W 4-2	Crockard; Penney; Guy; Malone
26/04/1983	IL 22	A	Cliftonville	L 0-1	-

Player Appearances and Goals

Player	Apps	Goals	Player	Apps	Goals
BEATTIE George	28	0	McCREERY Robert	25	0
BLAIR Jeff	24	2	McCUSKER Peter	12	0
BURNS Ronald	26	4	McGUIGAN Raymond	18	0
COOK Joseph	6	0	McQUISTON Samuel	22	7
CROCKARD Brian	16	1	NEILL David	6	2
GUY Michael	32	11	NICHOLL Alistair	19	1
HARBINSON Liam	1	0	PENNEY Stephen	32	8
HUSTON Thomas	23	0	SHIELDS Warren	4	0
HUTCHINSON Brian	14	0	SLOAN John	40	5
MALONE Paul	38	23	SMYTH Roy	9	2
MATTHEWS Denis	26	0	WRIGHT Jeffery	3	0
McCALL Tony	33	2			

1982/1983

Played: 47, won: 20, drawn: 12, lost: 15, goals scored: 67, goals conceded: 60

Irish League: 6th; Irish Cup: Winners; Gold Cup: Group stage; Ulster Cup: Group Stage; County Antrim Shield: Quarter-final

Date	Comp	Venue	Opponents	Result	Scorers
05/08/1983	FR	A	Queen of the South	L 0-3	-
20/08/1983	GC 1	A	Coleraine	W 1-0	McCurry
23/08/1983	GC 2	H	Larne	W 2-1	Crockard; McAuley og
26/08/1983	GC 3	A	Carrick Rangers	D 0-0	-
30/08/1983	GC 4	H	Distillery	W 3-1	Sloan; Quinn og; Penney
03/09/1983	GC 5	A	Crusaders	L 1-4	Penney
06/09/1983	GC 6	H	Linfield	L 1-2	Penney
10/09/1983	GC 7	A	Cliftonville	L 1-3	Sloan
17/09/1983	UC 1	H	Linfield	L 0-3	-
24/09/1983	UC 2	A	Distillery	D 3-3	Leslie og; McCurry; Malone
01/10/1983	UC 3	H	Carrick Rangers	W 2-0	Crockard; Haugh og
08/10/1983	UC 4	A	Carrick Rangers	L 1-2	Malone
15/10/1983	UC 5	A	Glentoran	L 0-1	-
22/10/1983	UC 6	H	Distillery	D 0-0	-
29/10/1983	UC 7	A	Crusaders	D 1-1	Malone
05/11/1983	IL 1	H	Ards	W 2-0	R. Smyth 2
12/11/1983	IL 2	A	Portadown	D 1-1	R. Smyth
19/11/1983	IL 3	A	Carrick Rangers	L 0-1	-
26/11/1983	IL 4	H	Cliftonville	D 0-0	-
03/12/1983	IL 5	A	Distillery	W 1-0	Malone
10/12/1983	IL 6	H	Glentoran	L 1-4	Wright
17/12/1983	IL 7	A	Glenavon	W 3-1	Guy; R. Smyth; Sloan
24/12/1983	IL 8	H	Bangor	D 1-1	Malone
26/12/1983	IL 9	A	Coleraine	D 0-0	-
31/12/1983	IL 10	H	Larne	W 2-1	Speak; Wright
02/01/1984	IL 11	A	Crusaders	L 1-2	Wright
07/01/1984	IL 12	H	Newry Town	W 2-0	Speak 2
14/01/1984	IL 13	A	Linfield	L 0-1	-
04/02/1984	IL 14	A	Ards	L 0-3	-
09/02/1984	IC rd1	A	Tobermore United	W 7-0	Guy 2; Sloan; Speak 2; Crockard; R. Smyth
11/02/1984	IL 15	A	Portadown	W 2-1	Malone; Wright
18/02/1984	IC rd2	H	Dundela	W 2-1	Crockard; Malone
25/02/1984	IL 16	H	Carrick Rangers	D 2-2	Speak; Wright
03/03/1984	IL 17	A	Cliftonville	W 3-0	Guy; R. Smyth; Wright
10/03/1984	IC qf	H	Linfield	W 2-1	Sloan; Speak
17/03/1984	IL 18	H	Distillery	L 0-2	-
24/03/1984	IL 19	A	Glentoran	D 0-0	-
26/03/1984	CAS rd1	H	Ards	W 2-2 (aet)	R. Smyth; Wright
28/03/1984	IL 20	H	Linfield	L 1-3	Wright
31/03/1984	IL 21	H	Glenavon	D 2-2	Speak; Rice
07/04/1984	IC sf	N	Cliftonville	W 2-1	Guy; Speak
12/04/1984	CAS qf	A	Crusaders	L 1-2 (aet)	Harrison
14/04/1984	IL 22	A	Bangor	W 2-1	Fox; Shiels
17/04/1984	IL 23	H	Coleraine	L 1-2	Crockard
21/04/1984	IL 24	A	Larne	W 1-0	Speak
24/04/1984	IL 25	H	Crusaders	W 2-1	R. Smyth; Shiels
28/04/1984	IL 26	A	Newry Town	D 2-2	Ring; Harrison
05/05/1984	IC f	N	Carrick Rangers	W 4-1	Fox; Crockard; Harrison; Speak

Notes

26/03/1984 v. Ards: Ballymena United won 5-4 on penalties

07/04/1984 v. Cliftonville: Match played at The Oval

05/05/1984 v. Carrick Rangers: Match played at Windsor Park

Player Appearances and Goals

BEATTIE George	13	0	McGUIGAN Raymond	6	0
BUCHANAN James	2	0	McMULLAN Trevor	2	0
BURNS Ronald	39	0	O'NEILL Kevin	10	0
COOK Joseph	7	0	PENNEY Stephen	15	3
CROCKARD Brian	43	6	PLATT Jim	46	0
FOX Graham	38	2	RICE Arthur	10	1
GORDON Adrian	1	0	RING Michael	3	1
GUY Michael	35	5	SHIELDS Warren	2	0
HARRISON Alan	41	3	SHIELS Kenneth	8	2
HUSTON Thomas	8	0	SLOAN John	45	5
HUTCHINSON Brian	2	0	SMYTH Michael	5	0
MALONE Paul	27	7	SMYTH Roy	25	8
McALLISTER Donald	2	0	SPEAK Jonathan	21	11
McCREERY Robert	40	0	WRIGHT Jeffery	25	8
McCURRY Ciaran	25	2			

Played: 48, won: 18, drawn: 10, lost: 20, goals scored: 66, goals conceded: 65

Irish League: 8th; Irish Cup: Semi-final; Gold Cup: Group stage; Ulster Cup: Semi-final; County Antrim Shield: Round 1; UEFA Cup Winners' Cup: Round 1

Date	Comp	Venue	Opponents	Result	Scorers
03/08/1984	FR	H	Brighton & HA	L 0-1	-
18/08/1984	GC 1	H	Coleraine	L 1-2	Wright
21/08/1984	GC 2	A	Larne	L 1-3	Crockard
24/08/1984	GC 3	H	Carrick Rangers	D 1-1	Clark
29/08/1984	GC 4	A	Distillery	D 1-1	R. Smyth
01/09/1984	GC 5	H	Crusaders	W 2-0	Campbell; R. Smyth
04/09/1984	GC 6	A	Linfield	L 1-4	McAllister
08/09/1984	GC 7	H	Cliftonville	W 2-0	O'Neill 2
15/09/1984	UC 1	A	Linfield	D 1-1	O'Neill
19/09/1984	ECWC rd1 leg1	H	Hamrun Spartans	L 0-1	-
22/09/1984	UC 2	H	Distillery	L 1-2	Harrison
26/09/1984	ECWC rd1 leg2	A	Hamrun Spartans	L 1-2	Beattie
29/09/1984	UC 3	A	Carrick Rangers	W 3-1	Crockard 2; Campbell
06/10/1984	UC 4	H	Carrick Rangers	W 2-1	Sloan; Guy
13/10/1984	UC 5	H	Glentoran	W 3-0	Campbell; Beattie; Stewart og
20/10/1984	UC 6	A	Distillery	W 2-0	Sloan; Fox
27/10/1984	UC 7	H	Crusaders	L 0-2	-
03/11/1984	IL 1	A	Ards	W 2-1	Crockard; Campbell
10/11/1984	IL 2	H	Portadown	W 2-0	Campbell 2
17/11/1984	IL 3	H	Carrick Rangers	D 1-1	Campbell
21/11/1984	UC sf	N	Larne	L 1-3	Crockard
24/11/1984	IL 4	A	Cliftonville	W 2-0	Guy; Campbell
01/12/1984	IL 5	H	Distillery	W 3-0	Harrison; Campbell 2
08/12/1984	IL 6	A	Glentoran	L 0-1	-
15/12/1984	IL 7	H	Glenavon	W 3-1	Conville 2; Campbell
22/12/1984	IL 8	A	Bangor	L 0-1	-
26/12/1984	IL 9	H	Coleraine	D 2-2	Conville 2
29/12/1984	IL 10	A	Larne	W 3-0	Sloan 2; Guy
01/01/1985	IL 11	H	Crusaders	D 0-0	-
05/01/1985	IL 12	H	Newry Town	D 2-2	Harrison; McAllister
12/01/1985	IL 13	A	Linfield	D 0-0	-
26/01/1985	IL 14	H	Linfield	L 0-3	-
28/01/1985	IC rd1	H	Michelin	W 3-0	Crockard; Daly; Campbell
02/02/1985	IL 15	H	Ards	L 1-3	Harrison
09/02/1985	IL 16	A	Portadown	L 0-1	-
16/02/1985	IC rd2	H	Killyleagh YC	W 2-0	Crockard 2
23/02/1985	IL 17	A	Carrick Rangers	D 2-2	Guy; Sloan
02/03/1985	IL 18	H	Cliftonville	W 2-0	Guy; O'Neill
09/03/1985	IC qf	A	Ards	W 1-0	Sloan
16/03/1985	IL 19	A	Distillery	L 1-2	Speak
20/03/1985	CAS rd1	H	Ards	L 0-2	-
23/03/1985	IL 20	H	Glentoran	L 1-3	O'Neill
27/03/1985	IL 21	A	Crusaders	W 3-0	Campbell; Speak 2
30/03/1985	IC sf	N	Linfield	L 0-3	-
06/04/1985	IL 22	A	Glenavon	D 2-2	Speak; Harrison
09/04/1985	IL 23	H	Bangor	L 1-3	Speak
13/04/1985	IL 24	A	Coleraine	L 0-3	-
20/04/1985	IL 25	H	Larne	W 3-2	Campbell 2; Speak
27/04/1985	IL 26	A	Newry Town	L 1-3	Daly

Notes

26/09/1984 v. Hamrun Spartans: Ballymena United lost 3-1 on aggregate

21/11/1984 v. Larne: Match played at Windsor Park

30/03/1985 v. Linfield: Match played at The Oval

Player Appearances and Goals

Player	Apps	Goals	Player	Apps	Goals
BEATTIE George	21	2	HERRON Garry	1	0
BUCHANAN James	6	0	HUTCHINSON Brian	35	0
BURNS Ronald	15	0	KERNOHAN George	3	0
BURRELL Joseph	3	0	McALLISTER Donald	12	2
CAMPBELL Alan Jnr	44	15	McCREERY Robert	35	0
CARLETON Melvyn	13	0	McGEE Paul	2	0
CLARK Timothy	5	1	O'NEILL Colin	38	5
CONVILLE Steven	24	4	SLOAN John	48	6
CROCKARD Brian	39	8	SMYTH Michael	13	0
DALY Owen	31	2	SMYTH Roy	15	2
FOX Graham	34	1	SPEAK Jonathan	18	6
GRAHAM John	3	0	TENNYSON Brian	18	0
GUY Michael	34	5	WRIGHT Jeffery	12	1
HARRISON Alan	38	5			

Date	Comp	Venue	Opponents	Result	Scorers
09/08/1985	FR	H	UCD	W 2-0	Conville; Sloan
17/08/1985	UC 1	H	Newry Town	L 1-3	McAlinden
20/08/1985	UC 2	A	Dundela	D 0-0	-
22/08/1985	CAS rd1	H	Larne	W 2-1	Harrison; O'Neill
24/08/1985	UC 3	A	Portadown	L 2-3	Speak; Burns
30/08/1985	GC 1	A	Bangor	W 1-0	Dugan
03/09/1985	CAS qf	A	Distillery II	W 4-2	O'Neill; Speak 2; Daly
07/09/1985	GC 2	H	Larne	L 1-4	Dugan
14/09/1985	GC 3	H	Cliftonville	D 0-0	-
21/09/1985	GC 4	A	Distillery	D 2-2	Dugan; Burns
28/09/1985	GC 5	H	Crusaders	W 5-1	Sloan 2; O'Neill 2; Dugan
05/10/1985	GC 6	A	Glentoran	L 1-2	Hamilton
12/10/1985	GC 7	H	Coleraine	L 1-3	Burns
15/10/1985	CAS sf	N	Dundela	W 3-1	Speak; Dugan; O'Neill
19/10/1985	GC 8	H	Ards	L 1-3	Hamilton
26/10/1985	GC 9	H	Newry Town	W 2-1	Gorman; Daly
29/10/1985	CAS f	N	Distillery	L 1-3	Speak
02/11/1985	GC 10	A	Portadown	W 5-2	O'Neill 2; McAlinden; Harrison; Sloan
09/11/1985	GC 11	H	Linfield	L 0-2	-
16/11/1985	GC 12	A	Glenavon	L 2-3	Dugan; Harrison
30/11/1985	GC 13	H	Carrick Rangers	L 2-4	Dugan; Donaghy
07/12/1985	IL 1	H	Newry Town	W 3-1	Crockard: Speak; Tennyson
14/12/1985	IL 2	A	Crusaders	D 0-0	-
21/12/1985	IL 3	H	Carrick Rangers	W 7-1	Speak 3; Smyth; Dugan; Sloan; Wright
26/12/1985	IL 4	A	Ards	L 0-1	-
28/12/1985	IL 5	A	Larne	D 0-0	-
01/01/1986	IL 6	H	Glentoran	L 0-1	-
04/01/1986	IL 7	A	Glenavon	W 2-0	Speak; O'Neill
11/01/1986	IL 8	H	Distillery	W 3-1	Wright; McAlinden; Tennyson
18/01/1986	L 9	A	Cliftonville	L 0-1	-
25/01/1986	IL 10	H	Bangor	W 2-1	Speak; McAlinden
01/02/1986	IC rd1	H	Institute	W 5-1	Speak; Wright; McAlinden 3
08/02/1986	IL 11	A	Coleraine	L 1-2	Wright
15/02/1986	IL 12	H	Linfield	D 1-1	Sloan
22/02/1986	IC qf	A	Coleraine	L 1-2	O'Neill
01/03/1986	IL 13	A	Linfield	L 1-5	McAlinden
08/03/1986	IL 14	H	Portadown	L 0-1	-
22/03/1986	IL 15	A	Newry Town	W 6-1	Daly; McAlinden; Wright; Speak 2; Scott
29/03/1986	IL 16	H	Crusaders	D 0-0	-
05/04/1986	IL 17	A	Bangor	W 2-0	McAlinden 2
08/04/1986	IL 18	H	Ards	W 1-0	Speak
12/04/1986	IL 19	H	Larne	L 0-2	-
19/04/1986	IL 20	H	Glenavon	D 3-3	Dugan 3
22/04/1986	IL 21	A	Distillery	D 1-1	Scott
26/04/1986	IL 22	H	Cliftonville	W 4-2	Dougherty; Dugan 2; Burns
29/04/1986	IL 23	A	Carrick Rangers	W 4-0	Burns; Speak; Conville; Dougherty
06/05/1986	IL 24	A	Portadown	D 1-1	Speak
09/05/1986	IL 25	H	Coleraine	L 1-2	Speak
13/05/1986	IL 26	A	Glentoran	L 0-2	-

Notes
15/10/1985 v. Dundela: Match played at The Oval
29/10/1985 v. Distillery: Match played at The Oval

Player Appearances and Goals

Player	Apps	Goals	Player	Apps	Goals
ADAIR Richard	29	0	HAMILTON Ian	17	2
ADAMS Mark	2	0	HARRISON Alan	20	3
BURNS Ronald	44	5	HERON John	12	0
CATHCART George	2	0	McALINDEN David	22	11
COBURN Thomas	1	0	McALLISTER	1	0
CONVILLE Steven	48	1	McGAUGHEY Philip	1	0
CROCKARD Brian	30	1	O'NEILL Colin	38	9
DALY Owen	15	3	QUINN Sean	4	0
DONAGHY Martin	3	1	SCOTT James	16	2
DOUGHERTY David	5	2	SLOAN John	45	5
DUGAN David	34	13	SMYTH Michael	31	1
EACHUS Stephen	15	0	SPEAK Jonathan	46	18
FELLOWES Roy	11	0	TENNYSON Brian	15	2
FOX Graham	7	0	WRIGHT Jeffery	30	5
GORMAN John	12	1			

Played: 48, won: 18, drawn: 10, lost: 20, goals scored: 85, goals conceded: 73

Irish League: 7th; Irish Cup: Quarter-final; Gold Cup: 11th; Ulster Cup: Group stage; County Antrim Shield: Finalists

1985/1986

Played: 42, won: 17, drawn: 12, lost: 13, goals scored: 73, goals conceded: 69

Irish League: 6th; Irish Cup: Round 1; Gold Cup: Group stage; League Cup: Round 2; Ulster Cup: Semi-final; County Antrim Shield: Quarter-final

Date	Comp	Venue	Opponents	Result	Scorers
02/08/1986	FR	H	Shamrock Rovers	L 2-4	Donnelly; Wright
09/08/1986	CAS rd1	A	Carrick Rangers	W 3-0	Speak; Dougherty; Donnelly
12/08/1986	CAS qf	H	Linfield	L 0-2	-
16/08/1986	UC 1	H	Dundela	W 3-0	Speak 2; Hayes
19/08/1986	UC 2	A	Ards	D 2-2	Speak 2
23/08/1986	UC 3	H	Glenavon	W 3-1	Dougherty; O'Neill 2
26/08/1986	UC qf	H	Crusaders	W 3-0 (aet)	Totten og; McAlinden; O'Neill
30/08/1986	IL 1	A	Linfield	L 0-3	-
02/09/1986	UC sf	N	Linfield	L 1-2	Burns
06/09/1986	IL 2	H	Coleraine	W 2-1	Speak; Pyper
13/09/1986	IL 3	A	Bangor	W 1-0	McAlinden
20/09/1986	IL 4	H	Cliftonville	D 1-1	Garrett
27/09/1986	IL 5	A	Distillery	L 1-3	Conville
04/10/1986	IL 6	H	Glenavon	D 1-1	Speak
11/10/1986	IL 7	A	Glentoran	L 2-7	Speak; Smyth
18/10/1986	IL 8	H	Larne	D 1-1	Dougherty
25/10/1986	IL 9	H	Ards	W 2-1	Pyper; Dougherty
01/11/1986	IL 10	A	Carrick Rangers	L 2-3	Conville; Pyper
08/11/1986	IL 11	H	Crusaders	L 2-3	Speak; Pyper
22/11/1986	IL 12	H	Portadown	D 0-0	-
29/11/1986	IL 13	A	Portadown	W 2-1	Dougherty; O'Neill
06/12/1986	IL 14	A	Linfield	D 0-0	-
13/12/1986	IL 15	A	Coleraine	D 2-2	Speak; Hamilton
20/12/1986	IL 16	H	Bangor	W 4-3	McKee; Wright; Speak; O'Neill
26/12/1986	IL 17	A	Cliftonville	L 1-3	Wright
27/12/1986	IL 18	H	Distillery	W 2-0	Tully og; Donnelly
01/01/1987	IL 19	A	Glenavon	W 2-1	Pyper; Scott
03/01/1987	IL 20	H	Glentoran	W 2-0	Dougherty 2
10/01/1987	IL 21	A	Larne	W 2-1	Dougherty; Barnes
17/01/1987	IL 22	A	Ards	D 1-1	Speak
24/01/1987	IL 23	H	Carrick Rangers	W 3-0	Logan og; Burns; Speak
31/01/1987	IL 24	A	Newry Town	W 5-1	Pyper 2; Speak 2; Dougherty
07/02/1987	IL 25	A	Crusaders	D 3-3	Pyper; Smyth; Scott
14/02/1987	IL 26	H	Newry Town	L 1-2	Scott
21/02/1987	IC rd1	A	Larne	L 0-2	-
28/02/1987	GC 1	H	Linfield	D 1-1	Scott
07/03/1987	GC 2	A	Coleraine	D 3-3	Nicholl; Pyper; Dougherty
14/03/1987	LC rd1	H	Milford Everton	W 8-1	Hamilton 2; Dougherty 3; Smyth; Speak; McKee
21/03/1987	GC 3	A	Larne	L 0-2	-
28/03/1987	LC rd2	H	Linfield	L 1-6	Dougherty
11/04/1987	GC 4	A	Carrick Rangers	W 3-1	Speak; Quinn; Dougherty
14/04/1987	GC 5	A	Crusaders	D 0-0	-
18/04/1987	GC 6	H	Cliftonville	L 0-4	-

Notes

02/09/1986 v. Linfield: Match played at The Oval

Player Appearances and Goals

ADAIR Richard	40	0	HERON John	5	0
Averell Richard	2	0	McALINDEN David	11	2
BARNES Stephen	11	1	McGAUGHEY Philip	2	0
BURNS Ronald	36	2	McKEE Stephen	23	2
CARSON Robert	2	0	NICHOLL Michael	9	1
CONVILLE Steven	41	2	O'NEILL Pat	23	5
DONAGHY Derek	5	0	PYPER William	28	9
DONNELLY Brian	40	2	QUINN Sean	3	1
DOUGHERTY David	38	15	SCOTT James	26	4
DUGAN David	3	0	SMYTH Michael	40	3
GARRETT John	16	1	SPEAK Jonathan	42	17
HAMILTON Ian	37	3	WRIGHT Jeffery	19	2
HAYES Norman	13	1	YOUNG Thomas	1	0

Played: 52, won: 21, drawn: 11, lost: 20, goals scored: 66, goals conceded: 68

Irish League: 7th; Irish Cup: Semi-final; Gold Cup: Group stage; League Cup: Quarter-final; Ulster Cup: Group stage; County Antrim Shield: Finalists; Floodlit Cup: Quarter-final; County Antrim Centenary Chalice: Finalists

Date	Comp	Venue	Opponents	Result	Scorers
01/08/1987	FR	A	UCD	W 4-2	O'Neill; Elliott; Averell 2
11/08/1987	CAS qf	A	Cliftonville	W 1-0	Pyper
15/08/1987	UC 1	A	Distillery	D 0-0	-
18/08/1987	UC 2	H	Coleraine	L 1-5	Speak
22/08/1987	UC 3	H	Bangor	L 0-1	-
29/08/1987	GC 1	A	Linfield	L 0-1	-
05/09/1987	GC 2	H	Coleraine	L 0-2	-
12/09/1987	GC 3	A	Larne	L 1-4	Simpson
19/09/1987	GC 4	H	Ards	W 1-0	Pyper
26/09/1987	GC 5	H	Carrick Rangers	W 3-2	Dougherty 2; Pyper
03/10/1987	GC 6	A	Portadown	L 0-1	-
06/10/1987	CAS sf	A	Glentoran	W 1-0	Conville
10/10/1987	GC 7	H	Crusaders	W 2-1	Pyper; Scott
17/10/1987	LC rd1	H	Brantwood	W 3-1	Dougherty; Simpson; Conville
24/10/1987	IL 1	H	Linfield	L 1-4	Morwood og
31/10/1987	IL 2	A	Coleraine	D 5-5	Dougherty; Simpson 2; Pyper; Conville
04/11/1987	LC rd2	A	Bangor	L 1-2	Pyper
07/11/1987	IL 3	H	Bangor	W 1-0	Conville
18/11/1987	LC qf	A	Larne	L 2-3	Garrett; Scott
21/11/1987	IL 4	A	Cliftonville	D 1-1	Dougherty
25/11/1987	CAS f	N	Newry Town	L 1-2	Dougherty
27/11/1987	FC rd1	A	Newry Town	W 1-1 (aet)	Dougherty
02/12/1987	FC rd2	A	Bangor	L 0-2	-
05/12/1987	IL 5	H	Distillery	W 2-1	Scott; Simpson
12/12/1987	IL 6	A	Glenavon	L 0-1	-
19/12/1987	IL 7	H	Glentoran	W 3-2	S. Young 2; Conville
26/12/1987	IL 8	A	Larne	L 0-1	-
28/12/1987	IL 9	A	Ards	W 1-0	Dougherty
01/01/1988	IL 10	H	Carrick Rangers	W 1-0	Dougherty
02/01/1988	IL 11	A	Crusaders	D 0-0	-
09/01/1988	IL 12	H	Newry Town	L 3-4	Donaghy; Donnelly; Conville
30/01/1988	IL 13	A	Bangor	D 1-1	Simpson
06/02/1988	IL 14	H	Cliftonville	D 1-1	Conville
13/02/1988	IL 15	A	Distillery	W 5-0	S. Young; McDonald; Conville; Smyth; Boyd
20/02/1988	IC rd1	H	Dunmurry Rec.	W 4-0	Dougherty; Conville; Pyper; Simpson
27/02/1988	IL 16	A	Glenavon	D 1-1	Smyth
01/03/1988	IL 17	A	Portadown	D 0-0	-
05/03/1988	IL 18	A	Glentoran	L 0-3	-
12/03/1988	IC qf	H	Distillery	D 0-0	-
19/03/1988	IL 19	H	Larne	L 0-1	-
22/03/1988	IC qf rep	A	Distillery	W 3-0	Pyper; McDonald; Conville
26/03/1988	IL 20	A	Carrick Rangers	W 2-1	McDonald; Conville
30/03/1988	CAC rd1	H	Crusaders	W 3-0	Scott; McDonald; Greer og
02/04/1988	IL 21	H	Crusaders	D 0-0	-
05/04/1988	IL 22	A	Newry Town	L 0-1	-
08/04/1988	IC sf	N	Glenavon	L 0-2	-
12/04/1988	IL 23	H	Ards	D 1-1	Pyper
16/04/1988	IL 24	H	Portadown	W 2-1	Simpson; Scott
18/04/1988	IL 25	H	Coleraine	W 2-1	Dougherty; Hamilton
20/04/1988	CAC qf	H	Cliftonville	W 0-0 (aet)	-
23/04/1988	IL 26	A	Linfield	L 1-3	Smyth
26/04/1988	CAC sf	A	Distillery	W 2-0	Pyper 2
07/05/1988	CAC f	N	Glentoran	L 2-4	Pyper 2

Notes

04/11/1987 v. Bangor: Bangor disqualified from League Cup after fielding an ineligible player

25/11/1987 v. Newry Town: Match played at The Oval

27/11/1987 v. Newry Town: Ballymena United won 7-6 on penalties

08/04/1988 v. Glenavon: Match played at The Oval

20/04/1988 v. Cliftonville: Ballymena United won 6-5 on penalties

07/05/1988 v. Glentoran: Match played at Windsor Park

Player Appearances and Goals

BARNES Stephen	5	0	McDONALD Michael	18	4
BOYD Alan	15	1	McGAUGHEY Philip	22	0
CARSON Robert	7	0	NICHOLL Michael	26	0
CONVILLE Steven	51	11	O'NEILL Colin	4	0
DONAGHY Derek	22	1	PYPER William	47	13
DONNELLY Brian	41	1	QUINN Sean	8	0
DOUGHERTY David	48	11	SCOTT James	50	5
ELLIOTT Lexie	12	0	SHIELS Samuel	1	0
GARRETT John	37	1	SIMPSON Richard	44	8
GRANT Damien	30	0	SMYTH Michael	45	3
HAMILTON Ian	29	1	SPEAK Jonathan	5	1
HERON John	9	0	YOUNG Stephen	37	3
KERNOHAN George	7	0	YOUNG Tom	4	0
LOVE Peter	6	0			

Played: 50, won: 18, drawn: 16, lost: 16, goals scored: 74, goals conceded: 70

Irish League: 9th; Irish Cup: Winners; Gold Cup: Group stage; League Cup: Round 2; Ulster Cup: Group stage; County Antrim Shield: Semi-final; Floodlit Cup: Round1

Date	Comp	Venue	Opponents	Result	Scorers
06/08/1988	FR	H	Partick Thistle	L 0-2	-
20/08/1988	UC 1	A	Ballyclare Comrades	L 0-1	-
23/08/1988	UC 2	H	Coleraine	L 1-3	Conville
26/08/1988	UC 3	H	Ards	W 3-2	Hardy; Donnelly og; Heron
03/09/1988	GC 1	A	Coleraine	W 2-0	McKee; Wood
10/09/1988	GC 2	H	Linfield	L 1-4	Simpson
17/09/1988	GC 3	H	Larne	L 0-2	-
24/09/1988	GC 4	A	Ards	D 2-2	Pyper; Smyth
01/10/1988	GC 5	A	Carrick Rangers	W 3-0	Pyper 2; S. Young
08/10/1988	GC 6	H	Portadown	D 1-1	Fullerton
11/10/1988	GC 7	A	Crusaders	D 0-0	-
15/10/1988	LC rd1	H	Armagh City	W 2-0	Conville; Hardy
22/10/1988	LC rd2	A	Cliftonville	L 0-1	-
29/10/1988	IL 1	A	Linfield	L 0-1	-
05/11/1988	IL 2	H	Coleraine	W 2-0	Hardy; Smyth
12/11/1988	IL 3	A	Bangor	D 1-1	Hardy
19/11/1988	IL 4	H	Cliftonville	D 3-3	Hardy 2; Loughery
26/11/1988	IL 5	A	Distillery	D 2-2	Loughery; Doherty
03/12/1988	IL 6	H	Glenavon	L 0-3	-
10/12/1988	IL 7	A	Glentoran	L 2-3	Loughery; Hardy
17/12/1988	IL 8	H	Larne	D 0-0	-
26/12/1988	IL 9	A	Carrick Rangers	D 0-0	-
31/12/1988	IL 10	H	Crusaders	D 1-1	Heron
02/01/1989	IL 11	A	Newry Town	W 3-2	Curry; S. Young; Pyper
07/01/1989	IL 12	H	Portadown	W 3-1	McKee; Pyper; Loughery
10/01/1989	IL 13	H	Ards	W 3-2	Curry; Doherty; S. Young
14/01/1989	IL 14	A	Coleraine	L 1-4	Pyper
17/01/1989	IL 15	A	Cliftonville	L 1-4	Pyper
28/01/1989	IC rd5	A	Distillery	W 4-1	Curry; Pyper; McKee; Simpson
01/02/1989	FC rd1 leg 1	A	Bangor	W 2-1	Curry; Loughery
04/02/1989	IL 16	H	Distillery	W 3-0	Curry; Loughery; Doherty
11/02/1989	FC rd1 leg 2	H	Bangor	L 0-2	-
18/02/1989	IC rd6	A	Ballyclare Comrades	D 2-2	Hardy; Pyper
01/03/1989	IC rd6 rep	H	Ballyclare Comrades	W 5-1	Pyper 2; Hardy; McKee; Doherty
04/03/1989	IL 17	H	Glentoran	L 1-2	Hardy
11/03/1989	IC qf	A	Crusaders	W 3-2	Curry 2; Hardy
18/03/1989	IL 18	A	Larne	D 1-1	Loughery
25/03/1989	IL 19	A	Ards	D 0-0	-
28/03/1989	IL 20	H	Carrick Rangers	L 1-2	Hardy
30/03/1989	CAS rd1	H	Linfield	W 3-0	Pyper; Curry; Hardy
01/04/1989	IL 21	A	Crusaders	D 0-0	-
08/04/1989	IC sf	N	Linfield	D 1-1	Hardy
12/04/1989	IC sf rep	N	Linfield	W 2-1	Doherty; Hardy
15/04/1989	IL 22	H	Newry Town	D 2-2	Hardy; Curry
19/04/1989	CAS qf	A	Cliftonville	W 3-0	McKee; Hardy 2
22/04/1989	IL 23	A	Portadown	D 0-0	-
24/04/1989	IL 24	H	Bangor	W 2-1	Hardy; Loughery
27/04/1989	IL 25	A	Glenavon	L 1-2	Hardy
29/04/1989	IL 26	H	Linfield	L 0-4	-
06/05/1989	IC f	N	Larne	W 1-0	Hardy
10/05/1989	CAS sf	N	Glentoran	L 0-2	-

Notes

11/02/1989 v. Bangor: Ballymena United lost 3-2 on aggregate

08/04/1989 v. Linfield: Match played at The Oval

12/04/1989 v. Linfield: Match played at The Oval

06/05/1989 v. Larne: Match played at The Oval

10/05/1989 v. Glentoran: Match played at Seaview

Player Appearances and Goals

Player	Apps	Goals	Player	Apps	Goals
AVERELL Richard	4	0	LOUGHERY Des	34	8
BOYD Alan	2	0	McELDOWNEY Rory	3	0
BROWN Paul	2	0	McENHILL Dominic	2	0
CARSON Robert	1	0	McERLEAN Joseph	1	0
CONVILLE Steven	13	2	McKEE John	49	5
CURRY Lindsay	31	9	NICHOLL Michael	9	0
DOHERTY Dermot	31	5	PYPER William	42	12
DONNELLY Brian	1	0	SCOTT James	27	0
FULLERTON Neill	7	1	SIMPSON Richard	24	2
GARRETT John	49	0	SMYTH Michael	49	2
GRANT Damien	47	0	WOOD Alun	10	1
HAMILTON Ian	36	0	YOUNG Stephen	39	3
HARDY Paul	38	21	YOUNG Thomas	6	0
HERON John	46	2			

Date	Comp	Venue	Opponents	Result	Scorers
08/08/1989	FR	H	Limerick City	W 4-0	Curry 3; Loughery
19/08/1989	UC 1	A	Linfield	L 0-2	-
22/08/1989	UC 2	H	Ards	L 2-3	Curry; Hardy
25/08/1989	UC 3	A	Glenavon	L 1-2	Curry
02/09/1989	GC 1	A	Cliftonville	D 1-1	Young
09/09/1989	GC 2	H	Bangor	D 0-0	-
13/09/1989	ECWC rd1 leg 1	A	RSC Anderlecht	L 0-6	-
16/09/1989	GC 3	H	Linfield	L 1-2	Loughery
23/09/1989	IL 1	H	Cliftonville	L 1-2	Hardy
27/09/1989	ECWC rd1 leg 2	H	RSC Anderlecht	L 0-4	-
30/09/1989	IL 2	A	Glentoran	L 0-1	-
07/10/1989	IL 3	A	Carrick Rangers	W 1-0	Simpson
14/10/1989	LC rd1	A	Brantwood	L 1-2 (aet)	Curry
04/11/1989	IL 4	A	Newry Town	D 3-3	Hardy; Curry
08/11/1989	IL 5	H	Glenavon	W 3-1	Loughery; Curry 2
11/11/1989	IL 6	H	Ards	D 0-0	-
18/11/1989	IL 7	A	Linfield	W 2-1	Loughery; Young
25/11/1989	IL 8	H	Bangor	W 1-0	Doherty
02/12/1989	IL 9	A	Portadown	L 0-1	-
09/12/1989	IL 10	H	Distillery	W 2-1	Hardy; Loughery
23/12/1989	FC rd1 leg 1	H	Portadown	L 0-1	-
26/12/1989	IL 11	H	Coleraine	D 1-1	Curry
30/12/1989	IL 12	A	Crusaders	W 2-0	Curry 2
01/01/1990	FC rd1 leg 2	A	Portadown	W 2-0	Pyper; Curry
06/01/1990	IL 13	H	Glentoran	D 1-1	Heron
09/01/1990	IL 14	A	Larne	W 2-1	Young; Curry
13/01/1990	IL 15	H	Carrick Rangers	W 3-1	Curry; Doherty; Loughery
20/01/1990	IC rd5	H	Dungannon Swifts	D 1-1	Loughery
31/01/1990	IC rd5 rep	A	Dungannon Swifts	L 1-1 (aet)	Curry
03/02/1990	IL 16	H	Newry Town	L 1-3	Sloan
07/02/1990	FC qf	A	Glenavon	L 1-2 (aet)	Pyper
10/02/1990	IL 17	A	Ards	W 2-0	Sloan 2
21/02/1990	IL 18	A	Glenavon	L 1-2	Candlish
24/02/1990	CAS rd1	A	Newry Town	L 1-3	Garrett
03/03/1990	IL 19	H	Linfield	W 5-1	Candlish; Pyper 2; Curry; Hamilton
17/03/1990	IL 20	A	Bangor	W 1-0	Candlish
24/03/1990	IL 21	H	Portadown	L 2-3	McKee; Sloan
31/03/1990	IL 22	A	Distillery	D 1-1	Pyper
14/04/1990	IL 23	H	Larne	D 0-0	-
17/04/1990	IL 24	A	Coleraine	W 2-0	Pyper; M. Smyth
21/04/1990	IL 25	H	Crusaders	D 0-0	-
28/04/1990	IL 26	A	Cliftonville	L 0-1	-

Played: 41, won: 13, drawn: 10, lost: 18, goals scored: 49, goals conceded: 55

Irish League: 5th; Irish Cup: Round 5; Gold Cup: Group stage; League Cup: Round 1; Ulster Cup: Group stage; County Antrim Shield: Round 1; Floodlit Cup: Quarter-final; UEFA Cup Winners' Cup: Round 1

1989/1990

Notes

27/09/1989 v. RSC Anderlecht: Ballymena United lost 10-0 on aggregate

01/01/1990 v. Portadown: Ballymena United won 2-1 on aggregate

31/01/1990 v. Dungannon Swifts: Ballymena United lost 4-2 on penalties

Player Appearances and Goals

Player	Apps	Goals	Player	Apps	Goals
CANDLISH Neil	10	3	McERLEAN Joseph	6	0
CURRY Lindsay	34	14	McGARRY Michael	1	0
DOHERTY Dermot	21	2	McKEE John	18	1
DONNELLY Brian	3	0	O'NEILL Kevin	11	0
FULLERTON Neil	3	0	PYPER William	32	6
GARRETT John	41	1	SAUNDERS Patrick	3	0
GRANT Damien	31	0	SCOTT Jim	22	0
GRIBBEN Paul	1	0	SIMPSON Richard	12	1
HAMILTON Ian	29	1	SLOAN Thomas	34	4
HARDY Paul	28	5	SMYTH David	26	0
HERON John	41	1	SMYTH Michael	41	1
LOUGHERY Des	25	6	YOUNG Stephen	38	3

Played: 45, won: 17, drawn: 11, lost: 17, goals scored: 73, goals conceded: 77

Irish League: 8th; Irish Cup: Round 5; Gold Cup: Quarter-final; League Cup: Round 2; Ulster Cup: Quarter-final; County Antrim Shield: Round 1; Floodlit Cup: Semi-final

Date	Comp	Venue	Opponents	Result	Scorers
04/08/1990	FR	H	Sligo Rovers	W 2-0	Sloan; Lenaghan
06/08/1990	FR	H	Motherwell	L 1-4	Pyper
18/08/1990	UC 1	A	Crusaders	L 1-2	M. Smyth
21/08/1990	UC 2	H	Portadown	L 0-4	-
24/08/1990	UC 3	H	Larne	W 5-0	Hardy; Loughery 2; M. Smyth; Heron
29/08/1990	UC qf	A	Glenavon	L 0-4	-
01/09/1990	GC 1	A	Cliftonville	D 1-1	Loughery
08/09/1990	GC 2	H	Ards	W 3-2	S. Young; Loughery; Pyper
15/09/1990	GC 3	A	Coleraine	L 0-1	-
22/09/1990	IL 1	A	Crusaders	D 0-0	-
27/09/1990	IL 2	H	Carrick Rangers	W 2-1	M. Smyth; Hardy
06/10/1990	IL 3	A	Larne	W 2-1	Hardy; Pyper
09/10/1990	GC qf	A	Portadown	L 1-3	S. Young
13/10/1990	IL 4	H	Portadown	L 0-2	-
20/10/1990	FC rd1	H	Distillery	W 2-1	S. Young; Sloan
27/10/1990	IL 5	A	Glenavon	L 1-3	Simpson
03/11/1990	IL 6	H	Linfield	D 2-2	S. Smyth; Simpson
06/11/1990	FC qf	H	Bangor	W 0-0 (aet)	-
10/11/1990	IL 7	A	Glentoran	D 0-2	-
17/11/1990	IL 8	H	Omagh Town	W 2-0	Loughery 2
24/11/1990	IL 9	A	Newry Town	D 0-3	-
28/11/1990	FC sf	N	Portadown	L 2-2 (aet)	S. Smyth 2
01/12/1990	IL 10	H	Ballyclare Comrades	D 1-1	Sloan
08/12/1990	IL 11	A	Distillery	L 0-2	-
22/12/1990	IL 12	A	Bangor	D 2-2	Candlish; S. Smyth
26/12/1990	IL 13	A	Coleraine	W 1-0	S. Smyth
12/01/1991	IL 14	A	Carrick Rangers	L 1-2	Loughery
19/01/1991	IC rd5	A	Omagh Town	L 2-3	Loughery; S. Smyth
22/01/1991	IL 15	H	Ards	W 4-1	S. Smyth; Simpson; Candlish; Pyper
26/01/1991	IL 16	H	Larne	D 4-4	Heron 2; Loughery; Simpson
29/01/1991	LC rd1	H	Chimney Corner	W 2-1 (aet)	Loughery 2
06/02/1991	IL 17	H	Cliftonville	D 1-1	S. Smyth
09/02/1991	IL 18	H	Glenavon	W 4-3	Heron; S. Smyth 2; Loughery
12/02/1991	LC rd2	A	Glentoran	L 2-4 (aet)	Candlish; Simpson
23/02/1991	IL 19	A	Linfield	L 0-3	-
02/03/1991	IL 20	H	Glentoran	L 2-3	S. Smyth; Heron
05/03/1991	CAS rd1	H	RUC	L 3-3 (aet)	Hamilton; Candlish; Lenaghan
12/03/1991	IL 21	A	Portadown	L 0-4	-
16/03/1991	IL 22	A	Omagh Town	D 1-1	S. Smyth
23/03/1991	IL 23	H	Newry Town	W 2-1	Loughery; Candlish
26/03/1991	IL 24	A	Ballyclare Comrades	W 5-1	Lenaghan; Loughery; S. Smyth 2; Pyper
30/03/1991	IL 25	H	Distillery	L 1-2	Simpson
10/04/1991	IL 26	H	Coleraine	W 4-0	Hardy; Loughery; Candlish; Pyper
13/04/1991	IL 27	A	Ards	D 0-0	-
16/04/1991	IL 28	H	Crusaders	W 1-0	Simpson
20/04/1991	IL 29	H	Bangor	W 3-0	Candlish 2; Pyper
27/04/1991	IL 30	A	Cliftonville	W 3-1	Hardy 2; Candlish

Notes

06/11/1990 v. Bangor: Ballymena United won 5-4 on penalties

28/11/1990 v. Portadown: Match played at Seaview and Ballymena United lost 5-3 on penalties

05/03/1991 v. RUC: Ballymena United lost 4-1 on penalties

Player Appearances and Goals

Name	Apps	Goals	Name	Apps	Goals
CANDLISH Neil	27	9	McGARRY Michael	5	0
DONNELLY Brian	12	0	McKEE John	27	0
FULLERTON Neill	3	0	PYPER William	43	6
GARRETT John	33	0	SAUNDERS Patrick	1	0
GRANT Damien	39	0	SCOTT James	27	0
GRIBBEN Paul	3	0	SIMPSON Richard	33	7
HAMILTON Ian	39	1	SLOAN Thomas	28	2
HARDY Paul	24	6	SMYTH David	22	0
HERON John	43	5	SMYTH Michael	11	3
JAMISON Blair	2	0	SMYTH Samuel	32	14
LENAGHAN Kevin	18	2	YOUNG Stephen	25	3
LOUGHERY Des	39	15	YOUNG Thomas	8	0
McELDOWNEY Rory	1	0			

Date	Comp	Venue	Opponents	Result	Scorers
17/08/1991	UC 1	A	Coleraine	L 1-2	Candlish
20/08/1991	UC 2	H	Portadown	W 2-0	Hardy 2
24/08/1991	UC 3	H	Ards	W 4-1	Pyper 3; S. Young
28/08/1991	UC qf	H	Crusaders	L 1-1 (aet)	S. Young
30/09/1991	GC 1	H	Cliftonville	W 1-0	Loughery
07/09/1991	GC 2	A	Ards	W 2-0	Candlish; Hardy
14/09/1991	GC 3	A	Coleraine	W 4-0	Candlish 2; Loughery; Hardy
21/09/1991	FC rd1	H	Crusaders	W 5-3	Loughery 2; Candlish 3
25/09/1991	GC qf	H	Distillery	W 5-0	Loughery 2; Hardy; Candlish 2
28/09/1991	IL 1	H	Larne	D 1-1	S. Young
05/10/1991	IL 2	A	Carrick Rangers	D 1-1	S. Young
08/10/1991	FC qf	A	Omagh Town	L 0-1	-
12/10/1991	IL 3	H	Crusaders	L 1-3	Hardy
19/10/1991	IL 4	A	Portadown	W 2-0	Candlish 2
26/10/1991	IL 5	H	Glenavon	L 1-2	Loughery
30/10/1991	GC sf	N	Glentoran	L 1-2	M. Smyth
02/11/1991	IL 6	A	Linfield	L 0-1	-
09/11/1991	IL 7	H	Glentoran	W 2-1	Loughery; Simpson
16/11/1991	IL 8	A	Omagh Town	W 2-0	Loughery 2
23/11/1991	IL 9	H	Newry Town	L 0-2	-
26/11/1991	CAS rd1	A	Linfield	L 0-1	-
30/11/1991	IL 10	A	Ballyclare Comrades	W 5-2	Hardy; Loughery; Tannock 2; M. Smyth
07/12/1991	IL 11	H	Distillery	D 0-0	-
14/12/1991	IL 12	A	Ards	L 1-6	Heron
21/12/1991	IL 13	H	Bangor	D 2-2	Heron; Hannan
26/12/1991	IL 14	H	Coleraine	D 1-1	Candlish
28/12/1991	IL 15	A	Cliftonville	D 0-0	-
01/01/1992	IL 16	A	Crusaders	W 2-1	Candlish; McConkey
04/01/1992	IL 17	H	Carrick Rangers	D 3-3	Loughery 2; Carson
11/01/1992	IL 18	A	Larne	L 1-3	Candlish
18/01/1992	IC rd5	A	Dundela	W 5-2	M. Smyth; Hardy 2; Loughery; McConkey
25/01/1992	IL 19	H	Portadown	L 0-6	-
01/02/1992	IL 20	A	Glenavon	L 0-2	-
04/02/1992	LC rd1	A	Ballymoney United	W 2-1 (aet)	Gilmore; Heron
08/02/1992	IL 21	H	Linfield	D 2-2	Gilmore; Candlish
15/02/1992	IC rd6	A	Omagh Town	D 1-1	Craig
18/02/1992	IC rd6 rep	H	Omagh Town	W 3-0	Gilmore; Candlish; Connolly
22/02/1992	IL 22	A	Glentoran	L 0-4	-
25/02/1992	LC rd2	H	Newry Town	W 3-0	Hardy; Craig; Moore
29/02/1992	IL 23	H	Omagh Town	D 1-1	Hardy
14/03/1992	IL 24	A	Newry Town	W 4-1	Craig 2; Gilmore; Candlish
17/03/1992	IC qf	H	Oxford United Stars	W 4-0	M. Smyth; Collet og; Craig; S. Young
19/03/1992	LC qf	A	Larne	L 0-3	-
21/03/1992	IL 25	H	Ballyclare Comrades	W 2-0	Hamilton; Millar
28/03/1992	IL 26	A	Distillery	D 0-0	-
03/04/1992	IC sf	N	Glenavon	L 1-3	Candlish
11/04/1992	IL 27	H	Ards	L 1-2	Mellon
18/04/1992	IL 28	A	Bangor	L 0-2	-
21/04/1992	IL 29	A	Coleraine	W 1-0	Fullerton
25/04/1992	IL 30	H	Cliftonville	D 1-1	Hardy

Notes

28/08/1991 v. Crusaders: Ballymena United lost 4-2 on penalties

30/10/1991 v. Glentoran: Match played at Seaview

03/04/1992 v. Glenavon: Match played at Windsor Park

Player Appearances and Goals

AITCHESON Des	3	0	LENAGHAN Kevin	22	0
CANDLISH Neil	44	18	LOUGHERY Des	32	14
CARSON Robert	10	1	McCONKEY Harry	14	2
CONNOLLY Timothy	9	1	McGARRY Michael	4	0
CRAIG Robert	16	5	McQUILLAN Shane	5	0
CURRY Paul	1	0	MELLON Graham	4	1
FULLERTON Neil	3	1	MILLAR Ian	7	1
GARRETT John	1	0	MOORE Colin	6	1
GILMORE Jason	26	4	PYPER William	17	3
GRANT Damien	43	0	SCOTT James	8	0
HAGAN James	35	0	SIMPSON Richard	10	1
HAMILTON Ian	45	1	SMYTH David	37	0
HANNAN Norman	5	1	SMYTH Michael	49	4
HARDY Paul	49	12	TANNOCK Ross	6	2
HERON John	45	3	YOUNG Stephen	47	5
HUXLEY Alan	3	0	YOUNG Thomas	2	0

Played: 50, won: 20, drawn: 12, lost: 18, goals scored: 82, goals conceded: 71

Irish League: 10th; Irish Cup: Semi-final; Gold Cup: Semi-final; League Cup: Quarter-final; Ulster Cup: Quarter-final; County Antrim Shield: Round 1; Floodlit Cup: Quarter-final

1991/1992

Played: 48, won: 20, drawn: 6, lost: 22, goals scored: 70, goals conceded: 77

Irish League: 10th; Irish Cup: Round 6; Gold Cup: Semi-final; League Cup: Quarter-final; Ulster Cup: Group stage;
County Antrim Shield: Round 1; Floodlit Cup: Finalists

Date	Comp	Venue	Opponents	Result	Scorers
15/08/1992	UC 1	A	Distillery	W 1-0	Hardy
18/08/1992	UC 2	H	Portadown	L 1-3	Candlish
22/08/1992	UC 3	H	Ards	L 0-6	-
28/08/1992	GC 1	A	Crusaders	L 0-1	-
05/09/1992	GC 2	H	Larne	W 4-0	Connolly; Loughery 2; Speak
12/09/1992	GC 3	A	Carrick Rangers	W 3-1	Loughery 2; Young
19/09/1992	FC rd1	H	Omagh Town	W 2-0	Hardy; Loughery
26/09/1992	IL 1	A	Bangor	L 2-3	Loughery; Hardy
03/10/1992	IL 2	H	Carrick Rangers	W 2-1	Speak 2
06/10/1992	GC qf	A	Distillery	W 2-0	Hardy 2
10/10/1992	IL 3	H	Distillery	W 4-1	Hardy; Speak; Candlish; Loughery
17/10/1992	IL 4	A	Linfield	D 1-1	Loughery
24/10/1992	IL 5	H	Glenavon	L 0-5	-
27/10/1992	GC sf	N	Cliftonville	L 1-2	Loughery
31/10/1992	IL 6	A	Newry Town	W 1-0	Speak
07/11/1992	IL 7	H	Crusaders	W 1-0	Speak
14/11/1992	IL 8	A	Larne	L 0-1	-
21/11/1992	IL 9	H	Ards	L 3-4	Speak 2; Loughery
24/11/1992	FC qf	A	Crusaders	W 3-2 (aet)	Speak 3
28/11/1992	IL 10	A	Omagh Town	L 0-2	-
02/12/1992	FC sf	N	Distillery	W 0-0 (aet)	-
05/12/1992	IL 11	H	Ballyclare Comrades	D 2-2	Candlish; Ritchie
08/12/1992	CAS rd1	H	Carrick Rangers	L 1-3	Ritchie
12/12/1992	IL 12	A	Glentoran	W 4-1	Hardy; Burn; Candlish 2
15/12/1992	FC f	N	Portadown	L 1-3	Candlish
19/12/1992	IL 13	H	Portadown	L 0-2	-
26/12/1992	IL 14	A	Coleraine	W 3-1	Candlish 2; Ritchie
28/12/1992	IL 15	H	Cliftonville	L 0-1	-
01/01/1993	IL 16	H	Bangor	L 0-1	-
02/01/1993	IL 17	A	Carrick Rangers	D 3-3	McQuillan 3
09/01/1993	IL 18	A	Distillery	L 0-1	-
16/01/1993	IL 19	H	Linfield	L 1-2	Candlish
23/01/1993	IC rd5	A	Glenavon	W 3-0	Candlish 3
30/01/1993	IL 20	A	Glenavon	W 2-0	Candlish 2
02/02/1993	LC rd1	H	Chimney Corner	W 7-0	Speak 2; Craig 2; Young; Burn; Loughery
06/02/1993	IL 21	H	Newry Town	W 3-2	Kearney; Speak; Loughery
09/02/1993	LC rd2	A	Cliftonville	W 1-1 (aet)	Burn
13/02/1993	IL 22	A	Crusaders	L 0-1	-
20/02/1993	IC rd6	A	Cliftonville	L 0-2	-
27/02/1993	IL 23	H	Larne	W 2-1	Spiers og; Magill
02/03/1993	LC qf	H	Bangor	L 0-2	-
06/03/1993	IL 24	A	Ards	D 0-0	-
20/03/1993	IL 25	H	Omagh Town	L 0-1	-
27/03/1993	IL 26	A	Ballyclare Comrades	W 3-2	Gordon og; Loughery; Speak
10/04/1993	IL 27	H	Glentoran	L 2-8	Speak 2
13/04/1993	IL 28	A	Portadown	L 0-2	-
17/04/1993	IL 29	H	Coleraine	D 1-1	Magill
24/04/1993	IL 30	A	Cliftonville	D 1-1	Gilmore

Notes

27/10/1992 v. Cliftonville: Match played at Windsor Park

02/12/1992 v. Distillery: Match played at Solitude and Ballymena United won 4-2 on penalties

15/12/1992 v. Portadown: Match played at Windsor Park

09/02/1993 v. Cliftonville: Ballymena United won 4-2 on penalties

Player Appearances and Goals

AITCHESON Des	2	0	HUXLEY Alan	4	0
BURN Philip	30	3	KEARNEY Gregory	10	1
CANDLISH Neil	40	14	LOUGHERY Des	36	13
CARLISLE Mark	48	0	MAGILL Darryn	31	2
CONNOLLY Timothy	39	1	McCONKEY Harry	4	0
CRAIG Robert	18	2	McGARRY Michael	6	0
CURRY Paul	1	0	McNEILL William	1	0
DOHERTY Dermot	8	0	McQUILLAN Shane	21	3
DUFFY Seamus	18	0	MOORE Colin	5	0
ELLIOTT Nigel	1	0	RITCHIE Robert	14	3
FULLERTON Neill	12	0	SMYTH Michael	4	0
GILMORE Jason	23	1	SPEAK Jonathan	34	17
GRANT Damien	37	0	WHEATLEY Martin	1	0
HAGAN James	32	0	WYLIE Keith	6	0
HARDY Paul	34	7	YOUNG Stephen	45	2
HERON John	25	0			

Date	Comp	Venue	Opponents	Result	Scorers
31/07/1993	FR	A	Derry City	L 1-4	Johnston
14/08/1993	UC 1	A	Newry Town	W 2-1	Doherty; Loughery
17/08/1993	UC 2	A	Glenavon	L 0-2	-
28/08/1993	UC 3	H	Crusaders	D 1-1	Speak
27/08/1993	GC 1	H	Glentoran	L 0-1	-
04/09/1993	GC 2	H	Larne	W 2-0	Johnston; Loughery
11/09/1993	GC 3	A	Portadown	L 1-5	McCabe
18/09/1993	IL 1	A	Carrick Rangers	W 5-2	Speak; McCabe 3; Hardy
22/09/1993	UC qf	A	Linfield	L 0-1	-
25/09/1993	IL 2	H	Ballyclare Comrades	L 2-3	Loughery; Speak
02/10/1993	IL 3	A	Ards	W 2-1	McConville; McCabe
09/10/1993	IL 4	H	Glentoran	W 3-2	Burn; Speak; Gilmore
16/10/1993	IL 5	H	Glenavon	L 1-3	McCabe
23/10/1993	IL 6	A	Linfield	L 1-2	McCabe
30/10/1993	IL 7	A	Larne	L 1-5	Loughery
06/11/1993	IL 8	H	Omagh Town	L 1-3	Young
09/11/1993	FC rd1	H	Larne	L 1-2	Speak
13/11/1993	IL 9	H	Cliftonville	W 2-1	Speak; McCabe
20/11/1993	IL 10	A	Distillery	L 1-4	Heron
27/11/1993	IL 11	H	Crusaders	D 0-0	-
30/11/1993	CAS rd1	H	Glenavon	L 1-1 (aet)	Speak
04/12/1993	IL 12	H	Bangor	L 1-2	Speak
11/12/1993	IL 13	A	Portadown	L 0-5	-
18/12/1993	IL 14	H	Newry Town	D 0-0	-
27/12/1993	IL 15	A	Coleraine	L 2-5	McCabe; Speak
30/12/1993	IL 16	H	Carrick Rangers	L 0-2	-
08/01/1994	IL 17	H	Ards	L 0-3	-
11/01/1994	IL 18	A	Ballyclare Comrades	D 1-1	Loughery
15/01/1994	IL 19	A	Glentoran	D 1-1	McConville
22/01/1994	IC rd5	H	Carrick Rangers	L 0-3	-
29/01/1994	IL 20	A	Glenavon	L 2-3	Speak; McCreadie
05/02/1994	LC rd1	H	Tobermore United	L 0-0 (aet)	-
12/02/1994	IL 21	H	Linfield	L 0-1	-
10/03/1994	IL 22	H	Larne	W 2-0	Gilmore; Speak
19/03/1994	IL 23	A	Cliftonville	W 2-0	Burn; Speak
29/03/1994	IL 24	A	Distillery	D 1-1	O'Hagen
02/04/1994	IL 25	A	Crusaders	L 0-1	-
04/04/1994	IL 26	A	Bangor	L 0-1	-
08/04/1994	IL 27	A	Omagh Town	W 2-1	McGlinchey; Loughery
16/04/1994	IL 28	H	Portadown	D 1-1	McCreadie
23/04/1994	IL 29	A	Newry Town	W 2-1	McCreadie; Speak
30/04/1994	IL 30	H	Coleraine	W 1-0	McCreadie

Played: 41, won: 11, drawn: 7, lost: 23, goals scored: 45, goals conceded: 72

Irish League: 11th; Irish Cup: Round 5; Gold Cup: Group stage; League Cup: Round 1; Ulster Cup: Quarter-final; County Antrim Shield: Round 1; Floodlit Cup: Round 1

Notes

30/11/1993 v. Glenavon: Ballymena United lost 5-4 on penalties

05/02/1994 v. Tobermore United: Ballymena United lost 5-4 on penalties

Player Appearances and Goals

Player	Apps	Goals	Player	Apps	Goals
BURN Philip	36	2	McCONKEY Harry	1	0
CARLISLE Mark	40	0	McCONVILLE Fintan	32	2
CONNOLLY Timothy	11	0	McCREADIE Barry	11	4
CRAIG Robert	10	0	McGLINCHEY Kieran	9	1
DAVIDSON Roy	9	0	McILVEEN Alan	6	0
DOHERTY Dermot	23	1	McQUILLAN Shane	1	0
FERGUSON Gareth	1	0	O'HAGAN Michael	14	1
FULLERTON Neill	12	0	REA James	2	0
GILMORE Jason	17	2	RITCHIE Robert	6	0
GRANT Damien	10	0	SMYTH Dean	22	0
HAGAN Jim	4	0	SPEAK Jonathan	40	13
HARDY Paul	16	1	TULLY Ciaran	6	0
HERON John	34	1	TULLY Michael	16	0
HUXLEY Alan	8	0	WHEATLEY Martin	1	0
JOHNSTON Samuel	11	1	WOODS Colin	5	0
KEARNEY Gregory	13	0	WYLIE Keith	5	0
LOUGHERY Des	24	6	YOUNG Stephen	32	1
McCABE David	20	9			

Played: 43, won: 10, drawn: 10, lost: 23, goals scored: 54, goals conceded: 72

Irish League: 12th (Relegated); Irish Cup: Round 5; Gold Cup: Quarter-final; League Cup: Round 2; Ulster Cup: Group stage; County Antrim Shield: Round 1; Floodlit Cup: Round 1

Date	Comp	Venue	Opponents	Result	Scorers
13/08/1994	UC 1	A	Larne	D 1-1	Cowan
16/08/1994	UC 2	A	Distillery	L 0-1	-
20/08/1994	UC 3	H	Glenavon	L 0-5	-
27/08/1994	GC 1	A	Omagh Town	W 2-1	Tully; Speak
03/09/1994	GC 2	H	Portadown	L 1-2	Patton
10/09/1994	GC 3	H	Bangor	W 2-0	Burn; Speak
17/09/1994	IL 1	H	Carrick Rangers	D 2-2	Loughery; McMullan
24/09/1994	IL 2	A	Ballyclare Comrades	W 3-1	Speak 3
01/10/1994	IL 3	H	Ards	L 1-2	Tully
08/10/1994	IL 4	A	Glentoran	L 0-2	-
11/10/1994	GC qf	H	Coleraine	L 0-1	-
15/10/1994	IL 5	A	Glenavon	L 1-3	Speak
22/10/1994	IL 6	H	Linfield	W 2-1	Burn; Crainie
29/10/1994	IL 7	H	Larne	D 0-0	-
01/11/1994	FC rd1	H	Ballyclare Comrades	L 0-1	-
05/11/1994	IL 8	A	Omagh Town	W 2-1	Loughery; Powell
12/11/1994	IL 9	A	Cliftonville	L 0-1	-
19/11/1994	IL 10	H	Distillery	L 2-3	Patton 2
26/11/1994	IL 11	A	Crusaders	L 1-2	Hall
29/11/1994	CAS rd1	A	Carrick Rangers	L 2-4	McMullan; Patton
03/12/1994	IL 12	A	Bangor	W 3-2	Patton; McMullan; Lynch
10/12/1994	IL 13	H	Portadown	W 3-2	Tlemo og; Burn; McMullan
17/12/1994	IL 14	A	Newry Town	W 8-0	Burn; Loughery; Speak 2; Patton 2; Lynch; Crainie
26/12/1994	IL 15	H	Coleraine	D 1-1	Heron
31/12/1994	IL 16	A	Carrick Rangers	L 1-2	McMullan
02/01/1995	IL 17	H	Ballyclare Comrades	D 2-2	Patton 2
07/01/1995	IL 18	A	Ards	L 1-4	Patton
14/01/1995	IL 19	H	Glentoran	D 3-3	Loughery; Patton; McCloy
24/01/1995	IC rd5	A	Omagh Town	D 0-0	-
28/01/1995	IL 20	H	Glenavon	L 0-1	-
30/01/1995	IC rd5 rep	H	Omagh Town	L 0-1	-
04/02/1995	LC rd1	H	Ballinamallard Utd	W 2-0	McMullan; Lynch
11/02/1995	IL 21	A	Linfield	L 0-3	-
18/02/1995	LC rd2	H	Ballyclare Comrades	L 1-2	Burn
25/02/1995	IL 22	A	Larne	W 3-2	McMullan; Speak; Crainie
18/03/1995	IL 23	H	Cliftonville	L 0-1	-
22/03/1995	IL 24	H	Omagh Town	L 0-2	-
25/03/1995	IL 25	A	Distillery	L 1-2	Patton
01/04/1995	IL 26	H	Crusaders	L 0-2	-
15/04/1995	IL 27	A	Portadown	D 2-2	Burn; Patton
17/04/1995	IL 28	H	Bangor	L 0-3	-
22/04/1995	IL 29	H	Newry Town	D 1-1	Speak
29/04/1995	IL 30	A	Coleraine	D 0-0	-

Player Appearances and Goals

Player	Apps	Goals	Player	Apps	Goals
BROOKS Matthew	2	0	LOUGHERY Des	33	4
BURN Philip	32	6	LYNCH Stephen	18	3
CARLISLE Mark	39	0	McCLOSKEY Jim	17	0
COWAN Steven	9	1	McCLOY Steven	6	1
CRAIG Alan	6	0	McCONVILLE Fintan	37	0
CRAINIE Daniel	18	3	McGREEVY Michael	2	0
CURRY Lindsay	4	0	McMULLAN Trevor	42	7
DAVIDSON Roy	9	0	MUIR Paul	3	0
DOEY Stephen	11	0	O'NEILL Mark	6	0
DOHERTY Dermot	5	0	PATTON Barry	39	13
FARRINGTON Mark	1	0	POWELL Gary	5	1
FULLERTON Neill	2	0	SMYTH Dean	20	0
GILMORE Jason	6	0	SPEAK Jonathan	33	10
GRANT Damien	22	0	TULLY Michael	26	2
HALL Tony	40	1	WHEATLEY Martin	1	0
HERON John	37	1	WHELAN Stephen	2	0
HUXLEY Alan	3	0	WYLIE Keith	11	0
KING Adam	1	0			

Played: 46, won: 21, drawn: 11, lost: 14, goals scored: 57, goals conceded: 53

First Division: 2nd; Irish Cup: Quarter-final; Gold Cup: Quarter-final; League Cup: Round 2; Ulster Cup: Group Stage; County Antrim Shield: Semi-final; Floodlit Cup: Round 1

Date	Comp	Venue	Opponents	Result	Scorers
28/07/1995	FR	H	Airdrieonians	L 0-3	-
02/08/1995	FR	H	Finn Harps	W 2-1	C. Moore; Lynch
12/08/1995	LC rd1	A	Chimney Corner	W 1-0	McWalter
15/08/1995	LC rd2	H	Portadown	L 0-4	-
19/08/1995	UC 1	A	Larne	W 1-0	Loughery
26/08/1995	UC 2	A	Linfield	L 0-3	-
02/09/1995	UC 3	H	Ards	L 0-4	-
09/09/1995	GC 1	H	Coleraine	W 2-0	Patton; Burn
15/09/1995	GC 2	A	Bangor	L 0-1	-
21/09/1995	GC 3	A	Glenavon	L 0-3	-
30/09/1995	FD 1	H	Carrick Rangers	W 3-1	Loughery 2; Burn
07/10/1995	FD 2	A	Newry Town	W 2-1	McCourt; McWalter
14/10/1995	FD 3	A	Omagh Town	D 0-0	-
21/10/1995	FD 4	H	Distillery	L 0-1	-
28/10/1995	FD 5	A	Ballyclare Comrades	W 3-1	McWalter; Murray; Curry
04/11/1995	FD 6	H	Larne	D 0-0	-
11/11/1995	FD 7	A	Coleraine	D 1-1	Murray
18/11/1995	FD 8	A	Carrick Rangers	D 1-1	Burn
21/11/1995	CAS rd1	A	Bangor	W 5-3	Curry 2; McWalter 2; McGuinness og
25/11/1995	FD 9	H	Newry Town	D 0-0	-
02/12/1995	FD 10	H	Omagh Town	W 2-0	Murray; McWalter
06/12/1995	CAS qf	A	Glentoran	W 2-1	McWalter 2
09/12/1995	FD 11	A	Distillery	W 1-0	Murray
12/12/1995	FR	H	Derry City	W 3-1	Burn; Allen; Patton
16/12/1995	FD 12	H	Ballyclare Comrades	D 0-0	-
19/12/1995	CAS sf	N	Crusaders	L 0-2	-
01/01/1996	FD 13	H	Coleraine	L 1-2	McWalter
06/01/1996	FD 14	H	Carrick Rangers	L 1-2	Murray
13/01/1996	FD 15	A	Newry Town	L 0-1	-
17/01/1996	GC qf	A	Cliftonville	L 0-1	-
20/01/1996	IC rd5	A	Chimney Corner	W 1-0	Loughery
23/01/1996	FC rd1 leg1	H	Crusaders	L 0-2	-
31/01/1996	FD 16	A	Larne	D 0-0	-
03/02/1996	FD 17	H	Distillery	D 1-1	Steele
06/02/1996	FC rd1 leg2	A	Crusaders	W 1-0	McCourt
10/02/1996	FD 18	A	Ballyclare Comrades	W 1-0	McConnell
16/02/1996	FD 19	A	Larne	D 2-2	Loughery 2
24/02/1996	IC rd6	A	Armagh City	W 4-0	C. Moore 2; Loughery 2
27/02/1996	FD 20	A	Omagh Town	D 2-2	McConnell; McWalter
02/03/1996	FD 21	A	Coleraine	L 0-4	-
09/03/1996	IC qf	A	Glentoran	D 0-0	-
13/03/1996	IC qf rep	H	Glentoran	L 2-4	Moors; McConville
16/03/1996	FD 22	A	Carrick Rangers	W 2-0	Moors 2
23/03/1996	FD 23	H	Newry Town	W 3-0	Steele 2; C. Moore
30/03/1996	FD 24	H	Omagh Town	W 2-0	C. Moore; McWalter
06/04/1996	FD 25	A	Distillery	W 3-1	C. Moore; Murray; Burn
08/04/1996	FD 26	H	Ballyclare Comrades	W 2-1	McWalter; Allen
20/04/1996	FD 27	A	Larne	W 1-0	Loughery
27/04/1996	FD 28	H	Coleraine	W 4-3	Loughery; Burn; Allen; McWalter

Notes

19/12/1995 v. Crusaders: Match played at The Oval

06/02/1996 v. Crusaders: Ballymena United lost 2-1 on aggregate

Player Appearances and Goals

ALLEN Jason	44	2	MAY Dean	3	0
BEATTIE Mark	1	0	McCONNELL John	39	2
BECK Robert	30	0	McCONVILLE Fintan	36	1
BOOTH Geoff	1	0	McCOURT Tom	19	2
BOYD Nigel	39	0	McWALTER Mark	28	13
BURN Philip	32	5	MOORE Colin	19	5
CARLISLE Mark	28	0	MOORE David	24	0
CRAIG Alan	2	0	MOORS Chris	5	3
CURRY Lindsay	17	3	MUIR Paul	36	0
GILMORE Jason	14	0	MURRAY Peter	27	6
HERON John	3	0	PATTON Barry	13	1
KERR Matthew	1	0	SMYTH Dean	14	0
LOUGHERY Des	34	10	STEELE James	12	3
LYNCH Stephen	6	0	STEWART Stephen	32	0
MAUCHLEN Ally	24	0	WYLIE Keith	1	0

Played: 45, won: 28, drawn: 3, lost: 14, goals scored: 68, goals conceded: 38

First Division: Winners (Promoted); Irish Cup: Round 5; Gold Cup: Semi-final; League Cup: Round 1; Ulster Cup: Round 1;
County Antrim Shield: Finalists; Floodlit Cup: Round 1; Irish News Cup: Round 1

Date	Comp	Venue	Opponents	Result	Scorers
10/08/1996	LC rd1	A	Dungannon Swifts	L 0-1	-
17/08/1996	UC rd1 leg 1	H*	Crusaders	D 1-1	Murray
24/08/1996	UC rd1 leg 2	A	Crusaders	L 2-3	Boyd; Allen
07/09/1996	GC 1	A	Larne	W 2-1	Loughery; Elder og
14/09/1996	GC 2	H	Ards	W 3-0	Feehan: Murphy og; Loughery
21/09/1996	GC 3	A	Crusaders	L 1-2	Bustard
28/09/1996	FD 1	A	Bangor	W 3-0	Gilmore; Feehan; Smyth
12/10/1996	FD 2	H	Distillery	L 0-1	-
19/10/1996	FD 3	A	Newry Town	W 1-0	Feehan
22/10/1996	GC qf	H	Portadown	W 0-0 (aet)	-
26/10/1996	FD 4	H	Carrick Rangers	W 1-0	Loughery
29/10/1996	GC sf	N	Linfield	L 0-2	-
02/11/1996	FD 5	H	Larne	W 4-2	Murray; Smyth; Feehan; Patton
09/11/1996	FD 6	A	Omagh Town	W 1-0	Loughery
16/11/1996	FD 7	H	Ballyclare Comrades	W 4-1	Gilmore; Smyth; Loughery 2
19/11/1996	INC rd1 leg 1	A	Sligo Rovers	L 0-1	-
23/11/1996	FD 8	H	Bangor	W 2-1	Murray; Feehan
26/11/1996	CAS rd1	H	Carrick Rangers	W 2-0	Loughery; Patton
30/11/1996	FD 9	A	Distillery	L 0-1	-
03/12/1996	CAS qf	H	Chimney Corner	W 2-0	Loughery; Patton
07/12/1996	FD 10	H	Newry Town	W 2-0	Bustard; Loughery
14/12/1996	FD 11	A	Carrick Rangers	W 2-1	Murray; Boyd
17/12/1996	INC rd1 leg 2	H	Sligo Rovers	L 2-4	Patton; Loughery
21/12/1996	FD 12	A	Larne	W 3-1	Loughery: McConnell; Boyd
26/12/1996	FD 13	H	Omagh Town	W 3-1	Murray; Loughery; Patton;
30/12/1996	FC rd1 leg 1	H	Glenavon	L 1-2	Patton
01/01/1997	FD 14	A	Ballyclare Comrades	W 1-0	Stewart
04/01/1997	FD 15	A	Bangor	L 1-2	Murray
07/01/1997	FC rd1 leg 2	A	Glenavon	W 1-0 (aet)	Patton
11/01/1997	FD 16	H	Distillery	W 1-0	Patton
15/01/1997	CAS sf	N	Portadown	W 2-1 (aet)	Boyd; Feehan
18/01/1997	FD 17	A	Newry Town	L 0-1	-
25/01/1997	IC rd5	A	Bangor	L 0-3	-
01/02/1997	FD 18	H	Carrick Rangers	W 2-1	Patton; Knell
08/02/1997	FD 19	A	Larne	W 1-0	Muir
15/02/1997	FD 20	A	Omagh Town	W 4-0	Feehan 4
25/02/1997	CAS f	N	Cliftonville	L 0-0 (aet)	-
01/03/1997	FD 21	H	Ballyclare Comrades	W 3-0	Knell; Loughery; Feehan
08/03/1997	FD 22	H	Bangor	D 0-0	-
22/03/1997	FD 23	A	Distillery	W 1-0	Feehan
25/03/1997	FD 24	H	Newry Town	W 3-1	Loughery 2; Feehan
31/03/1997	FD 25	A	Carrick Rangers	W 2-0	McGreevy; Loughery
05/04/1997	FD 26	H	Larne	W 2-0	Feehan 2
19/04/1997	FD 27	H	Omagh Town	L 0-1	-
26/04/1997	FD 28	A	Ballyclare Comrades	D 2-2	Feehan; McAlea og
01/05/1997	TEST	H	Coleraine	W 5-1	Murray 3; Storey; Feehan

Notes

17/08/1996 v. Crusaders: Match played at Allen Park

24/08/1996 v. Crusaders: Ballymena United lost 4-3 on aggregate

22/10/1996 v. Portadown: Ballymena United won 3-2 on penalties

29/10/1996 v. Linfield: Match played at The Oval

07/01/1997 v. Ballymena United lost 3-2 on penalties after drawing 2-2 on aggregate

15/01/1997 v. Portadown: Match played at The Oval

25/02/1997 v. Cliftonville: Match played at Windsor Park and Ballymena United lost 5-4 on penalties

01/05/1997 v. Coleraine: Testimonial for Des Loughery

Player Appearances and Goals

ALLEN Jason	35	1	LOUGHERY Des	42	16
BECK Robert	33	0	McCONNELL John	31	1
BOYD Nigel	31	4	McDOWELL John	5	0
BUSTARD Ian	39	2	McGREEVY Declan	18	1
CARLISLE Mark	40	0	MOORE Colin	10	0
CRAIG Alan	4	0	MUIR Paul	36	1
CRAWFORD Darren	12	0	MURRAY Peter	39	6
CRAWFORD John	1	0	PATTON Barry	41	9
CURRY Lindsay	1	0	SMYTH John	39	3
FEEHAN Ciaran	39	16	STEWART Stephen	40	1
GILMORE Jason	30	2	STOREY Paul	1	0
KNELL Phillip	15	2	TELFORD Colin	2	0

Played: 45, won: 28, drawn: 3, lost: 14, goals scored: 68, goals conceded: 38

First Division: Winners (Promoted); Irish Cup: Round 5; Gold Cup: Semi-final; League Cup: Round 1; Ulster Cup: Round 1; County Antrim Shield: Finalists; Floodlit Cup: Round 1; Irish News Cup: Round 1

Played: 55, won: 22, drawn: 12, lost: 21, goals scored: 91, goals conceded: 86

Irish League: 5th; Irish Cup: Round 5; Gold Cup: Group stage; League Cup: Quarter-final; County Antrim Shield: Round 1;
Floodlit Cup: Semi-final; Irish News Cup: Finalists

Date	Comp	Venue	Opponents	Result	Scorers
09/08/1997	LC rd1	A	Dundela	W 4-1	Patton 3; Loughery
12/08/1997	LC rd2	A	Newry Town	W 1-1 (aet)	Patton
16/08/1997	IL 1	A	Cliftonville	W 2-0	Patton 2
23/08/1997	IL 2	A	Crusaders	L 2-4	McGreevy; Muir
29/08/1997	IL 3	H	Coleraine	W 1-0	McGreevy
01/09/1997	LC qf	A	Glenavon	L 1-6	Patton
09/09/1997	IL 4	A	Glenavon	W 2-1	Patton 2
13/09/1997	IL 5	A	Linfield	D 0-0	-
16/09/1997	GC 1	A	Ballyclare Comrades	L 0-1	-
20/09/1997	IL 6	A	Omagh Town	L 2-3	O'Connell; McDowell
23/09/1997	GC 2	H	Larne	L 0-2	-
27/09/1997	IL 7	H	Glentoran	L 0-2	-
29/09/1997	GC 3	A	Crusaders	L 2-3	Smyth; Patton
04/10/1997	IL 8	A	Portadown	D 1-1	Allen
07/10/1997	GC 4	A	Dungannon Swifts	W 5-2	Murray; Patton; Knell; Candlish 2
11/10/1997	IL 9	H	Ards	W 3-1	Knell 3
14/10/1997	GC 5	H	Glenavon	D 1-1	Patton
18/10/1997	IL 10	H	Cliftonville	W 2-0	Knell; Murray
25/10/1997	IL 11	H	Crusaders	L 2-3	Patton; Bustard
31/10/1997	IL 12	A	Coleraine	W 1-0	Patton
04/11/1997	IL 13	H	Glenavon	D 0-0	-
08/11/1997	IL 14	H	Linfield	D 1-1	Muir
15/11/1997	IL 15	H	Omagh Town	W 4-2	Patton; Murray 3
18/11/1997	CAS rd1	H	Ballyclare Comrades	L 2-3	O'Connell; Patton
22/11/1997	IL 16	A	Glentoran	W 2-1	Patton; Murray
25/11/1997	INC rd1	H	Limavady United	W 2-0	Candlish; McGreevy
29/11/1997	IL 17	H	Portadown	L 1-2	McGreevy
06/12/1997	IL 18	A	Ards	L 1-2	Muir
13/12/1997	IL 19	H	Cliftonville	W 4-0	Knell; Patton; O'Connell; Murray
20/12/1997	IL 20	A	Crusaders	W 4-3	Murray; Knell; Patton; Candlish
26/12/1997	IL 21	H	Coleraine	D 2-2	Knell; Patton
01/01/1998	IL 22	A	Glenavon	D 3-3	Knell; Boyd; Patton
03/01/1998	IL 23	H	Linfield	L 0-2	-
10/01/1998	IL 24	A	Omagh Town	L 0-3	-
13/01/1998	INC sf leg 1	A	Coleraine	W 5-2	Hunter 2; O'Connell 2; Loughery
17/01/1998	IL 25	H	Glentoran	L 1-2	Knell
24/01/1998	IC rd5	H	Glentoran	D 1-1	Patton
27/01/1998	IC rd5 rep	A	Glentoran	L 1-2	Candlish
31/01/1998	IL 26	A	Portadown	L 0-4	-
03/02/1998	FC rd1	A	Larne	W 3-2	Boyd 2; McGreevy
07/02/1998	IL 27	H	Ards	D 1-1	O'Connell
10/02/1998	INC sf leg 2	H	Coleraine	W 6-0	Hunter 2; Knell; Patton 2; Loughery
14/02/1998	IL 28	A	Cliftonville	L 2-5	Patton; Murray
28/02/1998	IL 29	H	Crusaders	W 1-0	Bustard
03/03/1998	FC qf	H	Coleraine	W 1-0	Knell
07/03/1998	IL 30	A	Coleraine	D 0-0	-
12/03/1998	INC f leg 1	A	Omagh Town	D 1-1	Loughery
18/03/1998	FC sf	N	Cliftonville	L 1-2	Loughery
21/03/1998	IL 31	H	Glenavon	W 2-1	Patton; Knell
28/03/1998	IL 32	A	Linfield	L 0-1	-
02/04/1998	INC f leg 2	H	Omagh Town	L 0-1	-
11/04/1998	IL 33	H	Omagh Town	W 2-1	Loughery; Candlish
14/04/1998	IL 34	A	Glentoran	D 2-2	Hunter; Candlish
18/04/1998	IL 35	H	Portadown	L 1-2	Carlisle
25/04/1998	IL 36	A	Ards	W 2-0	Muir; Loughery

Notes

12/08/1997 v. Newry Town: Ballymena United won 5-4 on penalties

06/02/1996 v. Crusaders: Ballymena United lost 2-1 on aggregate

10/02/1998 v. Coleraine: Ballymena United won 11-2 on aggregate

17/03/1998 v. Cliftonville: Match played at Windsor Park

02/04/1998 v. Omagh Town: Ballymena United lost 2-1 on aggregate

Player Appearances and Goals

ALLEN Jason	52	1	McCONNELL John	42	0
BECK Robert	26	0	McDOWELL John	35	1
BOYD Nigel	47	3	McGREEVY Declan	41	6
BUSTARD Ian	43	2	McKINNEY Richard	5	0
CALDERWOOD David	3	0	MUIR Paul	47	4
CANDLISH Neil	32	7	MURRAY Peter	40	9
CARLISLE Mark	45	1	O'CONNELL PJ	35	6
CRAWFORD Darren	24	0	PATTON Barry	53	26
HUNTER Glenn	22	5	SMYTH John	20	1
KNELL Phillip	45	13	STEWART Stephen	34	0
LOUGHERY Des	30	6	STOREY Paul	8	0
McAULEY Philip	3	0			

Played: 55, won: 22, drawn: 12, lost: 21, goals scored: 91, goals conceded: 86

Irish League: 5th; Irish Cup: Round 5; Gold Cup: Group stage; League Cup: Quarter-final; County Antrim Shield: Round 1; Floodlit Cup: Semi-final; Irish News Cup: Finalists

Played: 52, won: 19, drawn: 10, lost: 23, goals scored: 62, goals conceded: 62

Irish League: 6th; Irish Cup: Semi-final; Gold Cup: Quarter-final; League Cup: Round 1; County Antrim Shield: Quarter-final; Irish News Cup: Finalists

Date	Comp	Venue	Opponents	Result	Scorers
15/08/1998	IL 1	H	Glenavon	W 1-0	Hunter
22/08/1998	IL 2	A	Linfield	L 0-1	-
28/08/1998	IL 3	H	Omagh Town	D 0-0	-
01/09/1998	IL 4	A	Cliftonville	W 1-0	Loughery
05/09/1998	IL 5	H	Portadown	W 1-0	Bustard
08/09/1998	GC 1	A	Distillery	D 2-2	Patton; Knell
12/09/1998	IL 6	A	Glentoran	L 1-2	Loughery
19/09/1998	IL 7	H	Newry Town	D 1-1	Hunter
22/09/1998	GC 2	H	Carrick Rangers	W 1-0	Patton
26/09/1998	IL 8	A	Coleraine	L 1-2	Loughery
03/10/1998	IL 9	A	Crusaders	L 0-2	-
06/10/1998	IL 10	H	Linfield	W 1-0	Knell
13/10/1998	GC 3	A	Bangor	W 1-0	Hunter
17/10/1998	IL 11	A	Glenavon	D 0-0	-
24/10/1998	IL 12	A	Omagh Town	W 4-1	Patton; Parker; Hunter 2
27/10/1998	GC 4	H	Cliftonville	W 3-2	Loughery; O'Connell; Hunter
31/10/1998	IL 13	H	Cliftonville	L 1-2	Parker
07/11/1998	IL 14	H	Glentoran	D 1-1	Hunter
10/11/1998	GC 5	A	Coleraine	L 0-2	-
14/11/1998	IL 15	A	Portadown	W 3-1	Hunter; Loughery; Percy
21/11/1998	IL 16	A	Newry Town	D 0-0	-
24/11/1998	GC qf	A	Portadown	L 0-1	-
28/11/1998	IL 17	H	Coleraine	W 1-0	Percy
05/12/1998	IL 18	H	Crusaders	W 2-0	Knell 2
08/12/1998	INC qf	A	Institute	W 2-1	Loughery; Hunter
12/12/1998	IL 19	A	Linfield	L 1-4	Percy
19/12/1998	IL 20	H	Glenavon	L 0-1	-
22/12/1998	CAS qf	A	Glentoran	L 0-1	-
26/12/1998	IL 21	A	Coleraine	W 1-0	Loughery
30/12/1998	IL 22	H	Crusaders	L 1-2	Hunter
02/01/1999	IL 23	A	Cliftonville	L 0-1	-
09/01/1999	IL 24	H	Portadown	D 2-2	Knell; Percy
23/01/1999	IC rd5	H	Larne	W 3-1	O'Connell; Knell 2
26/01/1999	LC rd1	H	Linfield	L 2-3 (aet)	Hunter; Knell
30/01/1999	IL 25	H	Newry Town	D 0-0	-
06/02/1999	IL 26	A	Glentoran	L 0-1	-
13/02/1999	IL 27	H	Linfield	W 4-2	Loughery 2; O'Connell; Carlisle
20/02/1999	IC rd6	H	Ballyclare Comrades	W 3-0	McDowell; Hunter; Loughery
27/02/1999	IL 28	A	Glenavon	L 0-1	-
06/03/1999	IL 29	H	Coleraine	L 0-1	-
13/03/1999	IC qf	A	Distillery	D 1-1	Hunter
16/03/1999	IC qf rep	H	Distillery	W 2-1 (aet)	Knell; Patton
20/03/1999	IL 30	A	Crusaders	L 0-1	-
23/03/1999	IL 31	H	Cliftonville	D 2-2	Hunter; Boyd
30/03/1999	IL 32	A	Omagh Town	W 5-0	Calderwood; Hunter 2; O'Connell; Loughery
03/04/1999	IL 33	A	Portadown	L 1-2	Loughery
05/04/1999	IL 34	H	Omagh Town	L 1-2	Patton
10/04/1999	IC sf	N	Portadown	L 0-2	-
13/04/1999	INC sf	H	Omagh Town	W 2-1	Patton; Hunter
17/04/1999	IL 35	A	Newry Town	L 0-1	-
24/04/1999	IL 36	H	Glentoran	L 3-6	Hunter 2; Loughery
27/04/1999	INC f	A	Finn Harps	L 0-2	-

Notes

10/04/1999 v. Portadown: Match played at The Oval

Player Appearances and Goals

Player	Apps	Goals	Player	Apps	Goals
ALLEN Jason	42	0	McDOWELL John	25	1
BECK Robert	31	0	McGREEVY Declan	17	0
BOYD Nigel	31	1	McKINNEY Richard	22	0
BUSTARD Ian	38	1	MUIR Paul	42	0
CALDERWOOD David	22	1	MURRAY Peter	9	0
CANDLISH Neil	7	0	O'CONNELL PJ	44	4
CARLISLE Mark	51	1	O'HAGAN Kevin	18	0
DRUMMOND Scott	1	0	PARKER Darren	38	2
GILMORE Gavin	1	0	PATTON Barry	37	6
HANNA Steven	4	0	PERCY Keith	28	4
HUNTER Glenn	49	19	STEVENSON Jason	1	0
KNELL Phillip	47	9	STOREY Paul	7	0
LOUGHERY Des	47	13	TENNYSON Terry	4	0
McCONNELL John	35	0			

Date	Comp	Venue	Opponents	Result	Scorers
14/08/1999	IL 1	A	Glenavon	D 0-0	-
21/08/1999	IL 2	H	Lisburn Distillery	D 1-1	Hunter
28/08/1999	IL 3	A	Cliftonville	D 1-1	McGreevy
31/08/1999	IL 4	H	Coleraine	D 0-0	-
07/09/1999	IL 5	A	Newry Town	L 1-3	Hunter
11/09/1999	IL 6	A	Linfield	L 0-3	-
18/09/1999	IL 7	H	Glentoran	D 0-0	-
25/09/1999	IL 8	H	Crusaders	D 1-1	Drummond
02/10/1999	IL 9	A	Portadown	D 2-2	Parker; Hunter
05/10/1999	GC rd1	H	Crusaders	W 3-2	Hunter; Drummond; Gregg
09/10/1999	IL 10	H	Glenavon	L 0-3	-
16/10/1999	IL 11	A	Lisburn Distillery	W 4-3	Hunter 3; Gregg
23/10/1999	IL 12	H	Cliftonville	W 2-1	Culbertson; Knell
26/10/1999	GC qf	A	Linfield	L 1-3	Knell
30/10/1999	IL 13	A	Coleraine	D 1-1	Calderwood
06/11/1999	IL 14	H	Newry Town	D 2-2	Gregg; Knell
12/11/1999	IL 15	H	Linfield	L 1-3	Swalwell
20/11/1999	IL 16	A	Glentoran	L 1-3	Patton
27/11/1999	IL 17	A	Crusaders	L 0-3	-
01/12/1999	CAS rd1	A	Bangor	L 0-1	-
04/12/1999	IL 18	H	Portadown	D 1-1	Flynn
11/12/1999	IL 19	A	Newry Town	D 2-2	Knell; Hunter
18/12/1999	IL 20	H	Crusaders	D 2-2	Knell; Hunter
27/12/1999	IL 21	H	Coleraine	D 2-2	Knell; Stewart og
03/01/2000	IL 22	A	Linfield	L 2-3	Drummond; Hunter
08/01/2000	IL 23	H	Glenavon	W 2-0	Swalwell; Hunter
22/01/2000	IC rd5	A	Loughgall	W 1-0	Hunter
29/01/2000	IL 24	A	Cliftonville	L 2-3	Patton; Hunter
02/02/2000	LC rd1	H	Portadown	L 2-4	Drummond; Swalwell
05/02/2000	IL 25	A	Glentoran	L 2-3	Hunter 2
12/02/2000	IL 26	H	Portadown	L 2-4	Hunter; Patton
19/02/2000	IC rd6	H	Bessbrook United	W 2-1	Hunter; Patton
26/02/2000	IL 27	H	Newry Town	D 0-0	-
04/03/2000	IL 28	A	Crusaders	D 2-2	Hunter 2
11/03/2000	IC qf	A	Coleraine	L 0-1	-
18/03/2000	IL 29	A	Coleraine	L 0-1	-
25/03/2000	IL 30	H	Linfield	L 0-1	-
28/03/2000	IL 31	H	Lisburn Distillery	W 2-1	Hunter 2
01/04/2000	IL 32	A	Glenavon	L 0-2	-
15/04/2000	IL 33	A	Lisburn Distillery	L 1-2	Patton
18/04/2000	IL 34	H	Glentoran	W 2-1	Knell; Hunter
22/04/2000	IL 35	H	Cliftonville	D 2-2	Patton 2
29/04/2000	IL 36	A	Portadown	W 2-0	Hunter; Knell

Played: 43, won: 9, drawn: 16, lost: 18, goals scored: 54, goals conceded: 74

Irish League: 8th; Irish Cup: Quarter-final; Gold Cup: Quarter-final; League Cup: Round 1; County Antrim Shield: Round 1

Player Appearances and Goals

ALLEN Jason	30	0	McCONNELL John	38	0
ANDERSON Noel	1	0	McGREEVY Declan	5	1
BEGGS Geoffrey	2	0	McGUINNESS Raymond	20	0
BOYD Nigel	19	0	MUIR Paul	6	0
CALDERWOOD David	13	1	MULLAN Ollie	6	0
CALLAGHAN Paul	8	0	O'HAGAN Kevin	3	0
CARLISLE Mark	29	0	O'NEILL Dermot	34	0
CULBERTSON Richard	11	1	PARKER Darren	23	1
DRUMMOND Scott	38	4	PATTON Barry	28	7
FLYNN Gerry	34	1	RICE Paul	1	0
FULTON Gareth	24	0	SWALWELL Andrew	30	3
GREGG John	20	3	TENNYSON Terry	26	0
HUNTER Glenn	42	23	TUMILTY Barry	30	0
KNELL Phillip	28	8	WILKINS Ian	3	0
LOUGHRAN Kieran	7	0			

Played: 43, won: 11, drawn: 8, lost: 24, goals scored: 53, goals conceded: 81

Irish League: 10th (Relegated); Irish Cup: Round 7; Gold Cup: Round1; League Cup: Round 1; County Antrim Shield: Quarter-final

Date	Comp	Venue	Opponents	Result	Scorers
27/07/2000	FR	N	Shamrock Rovers	W 4-2	Hunter 2; Dillon 2
12/08/2000	IL 1	H	Cliftonville	D 2-2	Hunter; Loughran
19/08/2000	IL 2	A	Glentoran	D 1-1	Drummond
28/08/2000	IL 3	A	Coleraine	W 2-0	Drummond 2
05/09/2000	IL 4	H	Crusaders	W 2-1	Lyttle; Loughran
09/09/2000	IL 5	A	Glenavon	L 1-2	Drummond
15/09/2000	IL 6	H	Omagh Town	L 1-2	Burnside
23/09/2000	IL 7	A	Linfield	L 1-4	Drummond
30/09/2000	IL 8	H	Newry City	W 1-0	Drummond
03/10/2000	GC rd1	A	Dungannon Swifts	L 1-2	Rice og
10/10/2000	IL 9	A	Portadown	L 0-1	-
14/10/2000	IL 10	A	Cliftonville	D 2-2	McNicholl; Tumilty
21/10/2000	IL 11	H	Glentoran	L 0-3	-
28/10/2000	IL 12	H	Coleraine	L 0-1	-
04/11/2000	IL 13	A	Crusaders	W 3-2	Gregg; Allen; McNicholl
11/11/2000	IL 14	H	Glenavon	L 1-2	Scoullar
18/11/2000	IL 15	A	Omagh Town	L 0-4	-
25/11/2000	IL 16	H	Linfield	L 1-5	Lyttle
28/11/2000	CAS rd1	H	Ballymoney United	W 3-0	Burgess; Drummond; Scoullar
02/12/2000	IL 17	A	Newry Town	L 2-5	McDowell; Burgess
09/12/2000	IL 18	H	Portadown	D 1-1	Lyttle
13/12/2000	CAS qf	H	Linfield	L 1-3	Drummond
16/12/2000	IL 19	H	Cliftonville	W 2-1	T. Anderson; Burgess
23/12/2000	IL 20	A	Glentoran	L 1-2	Allen
26/12/2000	IL 21	A	Coleraine	L 0-1	-
01/01/2001	IL 22	A	Glenavon	L 0-4	-
06/01/2001	IL 23	H	Omagh Town	W 2-1	Loughran; Boyd
09/01/2001	IL 24	H	Crusaders	L 0-1	-
13/01/2001	IL 25	A	Linfield	D 2-2	Boyd; Tumilty
20/01/2001	IC r6	H	Lurgan Celtic	W 4-2	Boyd; Allen; Hunter 2
27/01/2001	IL 26	H	Newry Town	L 0-1	-
03/02/2001	IL 27	A	Portadown	L 2-3	Campbell; McDowell
06/02/2001	LC rd1	H	Ards	L 1-2	Loughran
10/02/2001	IL 28	A	Cliftonville	L 1-3	Tumilty
17/02/2001	IC rd7	H	Glenavon	D 1-1	Hunter
20/02/2001	IC rd7 rep	A	Glenavon	L 1-3	McNicholl
24/02/2001	IL 29	H	Glentoran	L 1-3	Brien
13/03/2001	IL 30	H	Coleraine	L 0-1	-
17/03/2001	IL 31	A	Crusaders	L 1-3	Dillon
31/03/2001	IL 32	H	Glenavon	W 1-0	Hunter
14/04/2001	IL 33	A	Omagh Town	W 1-0	Boyd
17/04/2001	IL 34	H	Linfield	D 1-1	Campbell
21/04/2001	IL 35	A	Newry Town	W 2-0	Allen; Campbell
28/04/2001	IL 36	H	Portadown	D 3-3	Boyd; Hunter 2

Notes

27/07/2000 v. Shamrock Rovers: Match played at Allen Park

Player Appearances and Goals

Player	Apps	Goals	Player	Apps	Goals
ALLEN Jason	38	4	GREGG John	16	1
ANDERSON Noel	3	0	HILL Gareth	1	0
ANDERSON Tony	13	1	HUNTER Glenn	16	7
BOYD Nigel	39	5	KERR Matthew	3	0
BRIEN Glen	9	1	LOUGHRAN Kieran	31	4
BURGESS Aaron	15	3	LYTTLE Gerard	31	3
BURNSIDE Gavin	7	1	McALINDEN David	8	0
CALDERWOOD David	21	0	McDOWELL John	35	2
CALLAGHAN Paul	15	0	McNICHOLL Simon	19	3
CAMPBELL Shea	13	3	MORRISROE Brian	4	0
CARLISLE Mark	37	0	O'LOUGHLIN John	8	0
CRAWFORD Darren	1	0	SCOULLAR Blair	19	2
CULBERTSON Richard	6	0	SPACKMAN Alex	9	0
DALTON Timothy	15	0	STEVENSON Jason	2	0
DILLON Michael	16	1	TENNYSON Terry	17	0
DRUMMOND Scott	28	8	TUMILTY Barry	38	3
FAGAN Tyrone	1	0	WARD Jonathan	1	0
FLYNN Gerry	32	0			

Date	Comp	Venue	Opponents	Result	Scorers
23/07/2001	FR	H	Partick Thistle	L 0-1	-
10/08/2001	FD 1	A	Carrick Rangers	W 2-0	Boyd; Moore
18/08/2001	FD 2	H	Dungannon Swifts	D 1-1	McDowell
24/08/2001	FD 3	A	Ballyclare Comrades	D 2-2	Campbell; McNicholl
31/08/2001	FD 4	H	Institute	L 2-5	McLernon; McNicholl
08/09/2001	FD 5	H	Limavady United	L 1-2	Withnell
11/09/2001	LC 1	A	Institute	L 0-2	-
15/09/2001	FD 6	A	Armagh City	D 0-0	-
22/09/2001	FD 7	H	Larne	W 2-1	Boyd; Withnell
29/09/2001	FD 8	A	Lisburn Distillery	L 0-4	-
01/10/2001	LC 2	H	Omagh Town	W 2-1	Campbell; McLernon
06/10/2001	FD 9	H	Bangor	W 3-2	McLernon; Withnell; Campbell
09/10/2001	LC 3	A	Coleraine	L 0-5	-
13/10/2001	FD 10	H	Carrick Rangers	W 3-1	Campbell; McDowell; McNicholl
20/10/2001	FD 11	A	Dungannon Swifts	D 2-2	Withnell; Campbell
22/10/2001	LC 4	H	Limavady United	W 2-1	Withnell 2
27/10/2001	FD 12	H	Ballyclare Comrades	W 2-0	McLernon; O'Neill
06/11/2001	CAS rd1	H	Donard Hospital	W 3-1	Duff; Browne; D. McAlinden
10/11/2001	FD 13	A	Limavady United	L 1-2	Withnell
17/11/2001	FD 14	H	Armagh City	W 2-1	Campbell; O'Neill
24/11/2001	FD 15	A	Larne	D 1-1	Campbell
01/12/2001	FD 16	H	Lisburn Distillery	L 0-1	-
04/12/2001	FD 17	A	Institute	D 1-1	Browne
08/12/2001	FD 18	A	Bangor	W 3-1	Withnell 2; Campbell
11/12/2001	CAS qf	H	Ards	W 2-1	Withnell; Campbell
15/12/2001	FD 19	A	Carrick Rangers	W 2-0	O'Loughlin; O'Neill
22/12/2001	FD 20	H	Dungannon Swifts	L 0-1	-
05/01/2002	FD 21	H	Limavady United	W 4-3	Campbell; O'Neill; D. McAlinden; Robinson
12/01/2002	FD 22	A	Armagh City	W 2-0	O'Loughlin; Campbell
19/01/2002	IC rd5	A	Omagh Town	D 0-0	-
26/01/2002	FD 23	H	Larne	D 4-4	Withnell 2; McLaughlin; D. McAlinden
30/01/2002	IC rd5 rep	H	Omagh Town	W 2-1	Boyd; Patrick
02/02/2002	FD 24	A	Lisburn Distillery	L 0-3	-
06/02/2002	CAS sf	N	Linfield	L 0-4	-
09/02/2002	FD 25	H	Bangor	W 1-0	Byrne
16/02/2002	IC rd6	H	Glenavon	L 0-3	-
23/02/2002	FD 26	H	Carrick Rangers	W 3-2	Byrne; Withnell; McLernon
02/03/2002	FD 27	A	Dungannon Swifts	L 1-3	Boyd
16/03/2002	FD 28	H	Ballyclare Comrades	D 2-2	McLernon; Gregg
19/03/2002	FD 29	A	Ballyclare Comrades	D 3-3	Withnell 2; Culbertson
23/03/2002	FD 30	A	Institute	L 1-2	Campbell
30/03/2002	FD 31	A	Limavady United	L 0-1	-
02/04/2002	FD 32	H	Armagh City	W 3-1	Campbell; Boyd; McLernon
05/04/2002	FD 33	H	Institute	W 2-0	Withnell; McGarvey og
13/04/2002	FD 34	A	Larne	D 1-1	O'Loughlin
20/04/2002	FD 35	H	Lisburn Distillery	L 1-2	Culbertson
27/04/2002	FD 36	A	Bangor	D 1-1	Gregg

Notes

06/02/2002 v. Linfield: Match played at Seaview

Player Appearances and Goals

ADDIS Stuart	14	0	McDOWELL John	34	2
BEESLEY Paul	5	0	McLAUGHLIN Gareth	7	1
BOYD Nigel	38	5	McLERNON Trevor	43	7
BROWNE Leon	13	2	McMENEMY Mark	21	0
BURNSIDE Paul	4	0	McNAMEE Darren	4	0
BYRNE Paul	21	2	McNICHOLL Mark	16	3
CAMPBELL Shea	41	13	MOORE Daryl	3	1
CARLISLE Mark	43	0	MURTAGH Conall	8	0
CRAWFORD Anthony	8	0	NEILL Alan	2	0
CRAWFORD Darren	17	0	NELSON Dwayne	8	0
CULBERTSON Richard	12	2	O'LOUGHLIN John	42	3
DILLON Michael	4	0	O'NEILL Stephen	13	4
DOBBIN Michael	1	0	PATRICK Lee	22	1
DUFF Kevin	29	1	ROBINSON Martin	9	1
GREGG Conor	6	2	TELFORD Andrew	4	0
HAMILTON Adam	7	0	TENNANT Paul	1	0
KENNEDY Donal	1	0	WATSON Albert	11	0
LOUGHRAN Kieran	22	0	WHITE Robert	6	0
McALINDEN David	27	3	WITHNELL Peter	30	16
McALINDEN Michael	2	0	WRIGHT Tommy	7	0

Played: 47, won: 27, drawn: 10, lost: 10, goals scored: 122, goals conceded: 66

First Division: 2nd (Promoted); Irish Cup: Round 5; League Cup: Semi-final; Ulster Cup: Runners-up; County Antrim Shield: Finalists

Date	Comp	Venue	Opponents	Result	Scorers
15/07/2002	FR	H	Scunthorpe United	L 0-1	-
10/08/2002	UC 1	H	Carrick Rangers	D 1-1	Withnell
17/08/2002	UC 2	A	Ballyclare Comrades	W 6-0	Campbell 3; Withnell; O. Kearney; Boyd
24/08/2002	UC 3	H	Dungannon Swifts	D 0-0	-
26/08/2002	LC 1	H	Institute	W 5-1	Boyd; Campbell; Stewart; McLaughlin; Gregg
02/09/2002	UC 4	H	Larne	W 1-0	Campbell
07/09/2002	UC 5	A	Bangor	W 5-1	McLernon; Campbell 3; Withnell
10/09/2002	LC 2	A	Omagh Town	D 0-0	-
14/09/2002	UC 6	H	Armagh City	W 4-1	McLernon; O. Kearney; Campbell; Millar
16/09/2002	FR	H	Bolton Wanderers	L 0-2	-
21/09/2002	UC 7	A	Limavady United	L 0-3	-
23/09/2002	LC 3	H	Coleraine	W 3-1	O. Kearney; McMullan; Withnell
28/09/2002	FD 1	H	Armagh City	D 2-2	Byrne; Campbell
05/10/2002	FD 2	A	Carrick Rangers	W 4-1	Withnell; Campbell 2
08/10/2002	LC 4	H	Limavady United	W 7-1	Campbell 3; McDowell; O'Loughlin; McLernon; Gray
12/10/2002	FD 3	H	Ballyclare Comades	W 3-0	Withnell; Campbell; Stewart
26/10/2002	FD 4	H	Larne	W 3-2	Campbell 2; Withnell
28/10/2002	CAS rd1	H	Ballymoney United	W 8-0	Campbell 2; O'Loughlin; McLaughlin; Withnell; O. Kearney; Burnside 2
02/11/2002	FD 5	H	Limavady United	W 4-1	Byrne; O. Kearney 2; Campbell
05/11/2002	LC qf	H	Crusaders	W 2-0	McLernon; Withnell
09/11/2002	FD 6	A	Bangor	W 2-0	Withnell; O. Kearney
12/11/2002	FD 7	A	Dungannon Swifts	D 2-2	McDowell; O'Loughlin
16/11/2002	FD 8	A	Armagh City	W 3-2	McLaughlin 2; McLernon
23/11/2002	FD 9	H	Carrick Rangers	W 6-1	McDowell; Campbell 2; Withnell 3
26/11/2002	LC sf	A	Glentoran	L 3-5	McMullan; Campbell; O'Loughlin
30/11/2002	FD 10	A	Larne	W 3-1	Campbell; Withnell; O. Kearney
07/12/2002	FD 11	H	Dungannon Swifts	W 5-2	Withnell 2; McLernon; Gray; O. Kearney
14/12/2002	FD 12	A	Ballyclare Comrades	W 3-0	Withnell 2; McLernon
21/12/2002	FD 13	H	Bangor	L 2-3	McLernon; Withnell
26/12/2002	FD 14	H	Limavady United	L 1-3	Gray
01/01/2003	FD 15	A	Limavady United	D 1-1	Withnell
14/01/2003	CAS qf	A	Lisburn Distillery	W 2-1	O. Kearney; Millar
18/01/2003	IC rd5	A	Portadown	D 1-1	Campbell
21/01/2003	IC rd5 rep	H	Portadown	L 0-6	-
25/01/2003	FD 16	H	Larne	W 1-0	Culbertson
01/02/2003	FD 17	H	Armagh City	L 2-3	O. Kearney; Campbell
08/02/2003	FD 18	A	Carrick Rangers	W 4-1	Campbell 3; O'Loughlin
18/02/2003	CAS sf	H	Chimney Corner	W 3-1	Evans; Gregg; Withnell
22/02/2003	FD 19	A	Bangor	D 1-1	Campbell
25/02/2003	FD 20	H	Ballyclare Comrades	W 3-0	O'Loughlin; Campbell 2
01/03/2003	FD 21	H	Carrick Rangers	W 3-2	Withnell 2; Evans
04/03/2003	CAS f	A	Glentoran	L 0-3	-
15/03/2003	FD 22	A	Armagh City	D 2-2	O. Kearney; Byrne
22/03/2003	FD 23	H	Dungannon Swifts	W 2-0	Campbell; O. Kearney
29/03/2003	FD 24	A	Ballyclare Comrades	W 4-2	Campbell 2; O. Kearney; Gray
04/04/2003	FD 25	A	Dungannon Swifts	L 2-3	Campbell; O. Kearney
12/04/2003	FD 26	A	Larne	L 1-2	O. Kearney
19/04/2003	FD 27	H	Bangor	D 1-1	Evans
21/04/2003	FD 28	A	Limavady United	L 1-2	Campbell

Notes

15/07/2002 v. Scunthorpe United: Match played at St. Patrick's Army Barracks

Player Appearances and Goals

Player	Apps	Goals	Player	Apps	Goals
BOYD Nigel	29	2	McALINDEN David	9	0
BURNSIDE Gavin	1	2	McDOWELL John	16	3
BYRNE Paul	30	3	McLAUGHLIN Gareth	17	4
CAMPBELL Shea	44	38	McLERNON Trevor	43	8
CARLISLE Mark	36	0	McMULLAN Trevor	42	2
CULBERTSON Richard	18	1	MILLAR Paul	24	2
DUFF Kevin	4	0	MULLAN Gareth	2	0
EVANS Paul	13	3	MURTAGH Conall	2	0
GORMLEY Eddie	5	0	NELSON Dwayne	24	0
GRAY Joe	35	4	O'LOUGHLIN John	33	6
GREGG Conor	12	2	PATRICK Lee	1	0
HENRY David	9	0	ROBINSON Robert	14	0
KEARNEY Gareth	30	0	STEWART Alfie	27	2
KEARNEY Oran	43	16	WATSON Albert	16	0
MARTIN David	6	0	WITHNELL Peter	34	24

Date	Comp	Venue	Opponents	Result	Scorers
16/07/2003	FR	H	Bolton Wanderers	L 1-7	Scates
18/07/2003	FR	H	Oldham Athletic	L 1-2	Scates
12/08/2003	FR	A	Carrick Rangers	W 2-0	McLernon; Feeney
19/08/2003	LC 1	A	Portadown	L 1-3	O. Kearney
23/08/2003	LC 2	H	Institute	L 1-3	McLaughlin
29/08/2003	LC 3	A	Glenavon	W 1-0	O. Kearney
06/09/2003	LC 4	H	Portadown	L 0-3	-
13/09/2003	LC 5	A	Institute	L 2-3	Ramsey; S. Campbell
16/09/2003	LC 6	H	Glenavon	L 1-3	Ramsey
20/09/2003	IL 1	A	Larne	W 2-1	O. Kearney 2
27/09/2003	IL 2	H	Cliftonville	L 0-1	-
04/10/2003	IL 3	A	Dungannon Swifts	D 0-0	-
18/10/2003	IL 4	H	Crusaders	D 1-1	O. Kearney
21/10/2003	IL 5	H	Glentoran	D 0-0	-
25/10/2003	IL 6	A	Lisburn Distillery	L 1-2	Jemson
28/10/2003	CAS rd1	H	Dunmurry YM	W 3-1	Marks; McBride; O. Kearney
01/11/2003	IL 7	H	Limavady United	L 0-3	-
08/11/2003	IL 8	A	Linfield	L 1-4	Bailie og
15/11/2003	IL 9	H	Glenavon	W 4-0	Jemson; O. Kearney 2; S. Campbell
18/11/2003	CAS qf	A	Crusaders	W 1-0	McBride
22/11/2003	IL 10	H	Ards	W 1-0	Jemson
06/12/2003	IL 11	H	Newry Town	W 4-0	McBride; O. Kearney 2; Jemson
13/12/2003	IL 12	A	Portadown	W 1-0	O. Kearney
16/12/2003	IL 13	A	Omagh Town	L 0-2	-
20/12/2003	IL 14	H	Institute	W 2-1	Evans; G. Kearney
26/12/2003	IL 15	A	Coleraine	L 0-4	-
01/01/2004	IL 16	H	Larne	D 1-1	Marks
03/01/2004	IL 17	A	Cliftonville	W 3-0	S. Campbell 2; Scates
10/01/2004	IL 18	H	Dungannon Swifts	W 1-0	Scates
17/01/2004	IC rd5	A	Glentoran	L 2-4	Jemson; S. Campbell
24/01/2004	IL 19	A	Glentoran	L 1-3	Jemson
03/02/2004	CAS sf	N	Ards	L 0-1	-
07/02/2004	IL 20	H	Lisburn Distillery	L 1-4	McBride
14/02/2004	IL 21	A	Crusaders	D 0-0	-
21/02/2004	IL 22	A	Limavady United	W 1-0	Simms
28/02/2004	IL 23	H	Linfield	D 0-0	-
13/03/2004	IL 24	A	Glenavon	W 3-0	Scates; S. Campbell; Jemson
27/03/2004	IL 25	H	Omagh Town	W 3-1	S. Campbell 3
06/04/2004	IL 26	A	Ards	D 1-1	McBride
10/04/2004	IL 27	A	Newry Town	D 1-1	S. Campbell
13/04/2004	IL 28	H	Portadown	L 1-4	Boyd
19/04/2004	IL 29	A	Institute	W 4-0	Simms; Jemson; S. Campbell 2
24/04/2004	IL 30	H	Coleraine	W 3-1	McBride; S. Campbell 2

Notes

18/07/2003 v. Oldham Athletic: Match played at St. Patrick's Army Barracks

22/07/2003 v Heart of Midlothian: Testimonial for Mark Carlisle

03/02/2004 v. Ards: Match played at Seaview

Player Appearances and Goals

BOYD Nigel	35	1	McCLEAN Ruari	16	0
BYRNE Paul	31	0	McDOWELL John	20	0
CAMPBELL Gareth	1	0	McLAUGHLIN Gareth	15	1
CAMPBELL Shea	32	14	McLERNON Trevor	14	0
DONAGHY Ciaran	37	0	MELLY Dominic	3	0
DUFF Kevin	5	0	MONTGOMERY Johnny	3	0
EVANS Paul	16	1	MORROW Andrew	4	0
GRAY Joe	32	0	NELSON Dwayne	11	0
GREGG Conor	5	0	O'LOUGHLIN John	22	0
JEMSON Nigel	26	8	RAMSEY Kevin	9	2
KEARNEY Gareth	11	1	ROBINSON Robert	29	0
KEARNEY Oran	36	11	SCATES Garth	18	3
MARKS Jamie	23	2	SIMMS Gordon	10	2
McALLISTER Noel	1	0	WATSON Albert	31	0
McBRIDE Justin	28	6			

Played: 45, won: 16, drawn: 17, lost: 12, goals scored: 58, goals conceded: 54

Irish League: 8th; Irish Cup: Semi-final; League Cup: Quarter-final; County Antrim Shield: Round 1; UEFA Intertoto Cup: Round 1

Date	Comp	Venue	Opponents	Result	Scorers
20/06/2004	INT rd 1 leg 1	A	Odense BK	D 0-0	-
26/06/2004	INT rd 1 leg 2	H	Odense BK	L 0-7	-
15/07/2004	FR	H	Blackpool	L 0-2	-
24/07/2004	FR	H	Dundee	W 1-0	Simms
14/08/2004	LC 1	A	Lisburn Distillery	D 2-2	Hamill; Gray
21/08/2004	LC 2	H	Larne	L 1-3	Hamill
28/08/2004	LC 3	H	Institute	W 3-0	Hamill; Hill; C. McLaughlin og
11/09/2004	LC 4	A	Institute	D 1-1	Hamill
18/09/2004	LC 5	A	Larne	W 1-0	Campbell
21/09/2004	LC 6	H	Lisburn Distillery	D 1-1	Hamill
25/09/2004	IL 1	A	Loughgall	L 0-1	-
28/09/2004	LC qf	A	Glentoran	L 0-1	-
02/10/2004	IL 2	H	Newry City	W 2-1	P. McLaughlin og; Simms
09/10/2004	IL 3	A	Dungannon Swifts	W 2-1	Hill; Simms
16/10/2004	IL 4	H	Institute	D 1-1	Hill
23/10/2004	IL 5	A	Linfield	W 1-0	Melly
26/10/2004	CAS rd1	H	Kilmore Rec.	L 0-1	-
30/10/2004	IL 6	H	Crusaders	D 1-1	McCann
06/11/2004	IL 7	A	Portadown	L 0-3	-
13/11/2004	IL 8	H	Ards	D 2-2	Simms; Smyth
20/11/2004	IL 9	A	Limavady United	L 1-2	McBride
27/11/2004	IL 10	A	Lisburn Distillery	W 2-0	Melly; Scates
04/12/2004	IL 11	H	Omagh Town	D 1-1	McBride
11/12/2004	IL 12	H	Cliftonville	D 1-1	Adams og
18/12/2004	IL 13	A	Larne	D 0-0	-
27/12/2004	IL 14	H	Coleraine	D 2-2	Hill; McBride
03/01/2005	IL 15	A	Loughgall	W 2-1	Smyth; Kearney
16/01/2005	IC rd5	H	Coagh United	W 1-0	Kearney
19/01/2005	IL 16	A	Glentoran	L 2-4	Boyd; Fitzgerald
22/01/2005	IL 17	H	Dungannon Swifts	L 1-2	Hamill
29/01/2005	IL 18	A	Institute	D 1-1	Hill
02/02/2005	IL 19	H	Linfield	L 3-4	Mullan; Smyth; Watson
12/02/2005	IC r6	H	Kilmore Rec.	W 4-1	Nolan 2; Melly; Kearney
19/02/2005	IL 20	A	Crusaders	W 3-2	Nolan 2; Kearney
26/02/2005	IL 21	H	Portadown	W 2-0	Smyth; Fitzgerald
01/03/2005	IL 22	A	Newry City	D 1-1	Nolan
05/03/2005	IC qf	H	HW Welders	D 0-0	-
08/03/2005	IC qf rep	H	HW Welders	W 4-0	Kearney; Fitzgerald; Nolan
12/03/2005	IL 23	A	Ards	D 1-1	Fitzgerald
19/03/2005	IL 24	H	Limavady United	W 2-1	Mullan; Watson
24/03/2005	IL 25	H	Lisburn Distillery	W 2-1	Kearney; Mullan
29/03/2005	IL 26	A	Omagh Town	W 2-0	Hamill; Kearney
02/04/2005	IC sf	N	Larne	L 0-1	-
09/04/2005	IL 27	A	Cliftonville	D 0-0	-
16/04/2005	IL 28	H	Glentoran	L 0-3	-
23/04/2005	IL 29	A	Coleraine	W 2-0	Watson; Mullan
30/04/2005	IL 30	H	Larne	D 0-0	-

Notes

20/06/2004 v. Odense BK: Match played at Odense Atletikstadion

26/06/2004 v. Odense BK: Ballymena United lost 7-0 on aggregate

02/04/2005 v. Larne: Match played at The Oval

Player Appearances and Goals

BOYD Nigel	30	1	McLAUGHLIN Gareth	5	0
CAMPBELL Shea	11	1	MELLY Dominic	32	3
DONAGHY Ciaran	44	0	MONTGOMERY Jonathan	2	0
FITZGERALD Darren	11	5	MULLAN Gareth	15	4
GRAY Joe	29	1	MURRAY Reece	2	0
HAMILL Rory	35	7	NOLAN Matthew	13	6
HILL Eddie	29	5	O'LOUGHLIN John	2	0
HUGHES Mark	4	0	REID Randal	1	0
KEARNEY Oran	42	7	ROBINSON Robert	36	0
MARKS Jamie	24	0	ROSBOTHAM Andrew	11	0
McBRIDE Justin	21	3	SCATES Garth	34	1
McCABE Gerard	3	0	SIMMS Gordon	36	3
McCANN Tim	16	1	SMYTH Gary	40	4
McCLEAN Ruari	4	0	WATSON Albert	39	3
McFREDERICK William	9	0	YOULE Dean	4	0

Date	Comp	Venue	Opponents	Result	Scorers
13/08/2005	LC 1	A	Portadown	L 0-1	-
20/08/2005	LC 2	H	Newry City	L 1-2	Sweeney
25/08/2005	LC 3	H	Glenavon	W 1-0	Sweeney
30/08/2005	LC 4	A	Newry City	D 1-1	Hamill
10/09/2005	LC 5	A	Glenavon	W 2-1	Melly; Kelbie
17/09/2005	IL 1	H	Larne	W 1-0	Steele
20/09/2005	LC 6	H	Portadown	D 1-1	Aid. Watson
24/09/2005	IL 2	A	Newry City	L 0-2	-
01/10/2005	IL 3	H	Cliftonville	L 0-2	-
15/10/2005	IL 4	A	Loughgall	L 0-1	-
22/10/2005	IL 5	A	Armagh City	W 1-0	Sweeney
25/10/2005	CAS rd1	H	Wakehurst	W 3-1	Sweeney 2; Haveron
29/10/2005	IL 6	H	Linfield	L 0-2	-
05/11/2005	IL 7	H	Dungannon Swifts	W 4-3	Smyth; Rosbotham; Charnock; Hamill
12/11/2005	IL 8	A	Ards	W 3-1	Youle; Haveron; Sweeney
19/11/2005	IL 9	H	Limavady United	L 1-3	Sweeney
26/11/2005	IL 10	H	Lisburn Distillery	W 1-0	Rosbotham
29/11/2005	CAS qf	A	Cliftonville	W 2-0	Alb. Watson; Haveron
02/12/2005	IL 11	A	Portadown	L 1-6	Hamill
13/12/2005	IL 12	A	Glentoran	W 2-1	Sweeney: Kelbie
17/12/2005	IL 13	H	Glenavon	L 2-3	Sweeney; Kelbie
26/12/2005	IL 14	A	Coleraine	W 1-0	Sweeney
30/12/2005	IL 15	H	Institute	W 1-0	King
02/01/2006	IL 16	A	Larne	W 2-1	Sweeney; Melly
07/01/2006	IL 17	H	Newry City	D 0-0	-
14/01/2006	IC rd5	H	Kilmore Rec.	W 4-0	Aid. Watson 2; Scates; Haveron
21/01/2006	IL 18	A	Cliftonville	D 2-2	Scates; Kelbie
25/01/2006	CAS sf	A	Larne	W 3-0	Kelbie 3
28/01/2006	IL 19	H	Loughgall	W 3-2	Smyth 2; Kelbie
04/02/2006	IL 20	A	Armagh City	W 3-0	Kelbie 2; Sweeney
07/02/2005	CAS f	N	Linfield	L 1-2	Kelbie
11/02/2006	IC rd6	A	Lisburn Distillery	D 0-0	-
15/02/2006	IC rd6 rep	H	Lisburn Distillery	L 1-2	Brown
18/02/2006	IL 21	A	Linfield	L 2-3	Smyth; Rowe
24/02/2006	IL 22	A	Dungannon Swifts	D 2-2	King 2
11/03/2006	IL 23	H	Ards	D 1-1	Brown
18/03/2006	IL 24	A	Limavady United	D 2-2	Hamill 2
25/03/2006	IL 25	A	Lisburn Distillery	L 1-2	Kelbie
08/04/2006	IL 26	H	Portadown	L 2-3	Hamill; Kelbie
15/04/2006	IL 27	H	Coleraine	W 1-0	Kelbie
18/04/2006	IL 28	A	Glenavon	D 2-2	Kelbie; Hamill
22/04/2006	IL 29	H	Glentoran	L 0-4	-
29/04/2006	IL 30	A	Institute	W 1-0	Kelbie

Notes

07/02/2006 v. Linfield: Match played at Seaview

Player Appearances and Goals

ADDIS Stuart	4	0	MELLY Dominic	10	2
BOYD Nigel	19	0	MULLAN Gareth	1	0
BROWN Paul	10	2	REID Randal	2	0
CHARNOCK Phil	13	1	ROSBOTHAM Andrew	16	2
COLLIER Stephen	6	0	ROWE Gerard	17	1
DONAGHY Ciaran	37	0	SCATES Garth	39	2
HAMILL Rory	34	7	SHANNON Gregg	3	0
HAVERON Gary	43	4	SIMMS Gordon	18	0
KELBIE Kevin	31	16	SMYTH Gary	34	4
KING Stuart	35	3	STEELE Jonathan	6	1
McCABE Gerard	2	0	SWEENEY Vincent	42	12
McCLEAN Craig	33	0	WATSON Aidan	31	3
McDOWELL Paul	15	0	WATSON Albert	38	1
McFREDERICK William	36	0	YOULE Dean	3	1

Date	Comp	Venue	Opponents	Result	Scorers
18/07/2006	TEST	H	Motherwell	D 0-0	-
22/07/2006	FR	A	Stranraer	D 1-1	Kelbie
29/07/2006	FR	H	Airdrie United	W 2-1	Kelbie; Rosbotham
12/08/2006	LC 1	H	Crusaders	D 0-0	-
19/08/2006	LC 2	A	Portadown	L 1-3	Kelbie
25/08/2006	LC 3	A	Limavady United	L 1-2	Patrick
29/08/2006	FR	H	Manchester City	L 1-3	Haveron
31/08/2006	LC 4	H	Portadown	W 1-0	Patrick
09/09/2006	LC 5	A	Crusaders	L 1-2	Scates
16/09/2006	LC 6	A	Limavady United	D 3-3	Brown; Kelbie 2
23/09/2006	IL 1	H	Glenavon	W 4-2	Scates; D. Murphy; Kelbie; Picking
30/09/2006	IL 2	A	Glentoran	L 0-2	-
07/10/2006	IL 3	H	Crusaders	W 2-1	Haveron; Kelbie
14/10/2006	IL 4	A	Cliftonville	L 1-2	Alb. Watson
17/10/2006	CAS rd1	H	Dundela	L 1-3	Kelbie
21/10/2006	IL 5	H	Linfield	D 0-0	-
28/10/2006	IL 6	A	Portadown	L 1-2	Friel
04/11/2006	IL 7	H	Armagh City	D 2-2	Picking 2
11/11/2006	IL 8	A	Limavady United	D 1-1	Reid
18/11/2006	IL 9	A	Dungannon Swifts	L 0-1	-
25/11/2006	IL 10	H	Lisburn Distillery	L 0-1	-
01/12/2006	IL 11	A	Larne	W 1-0	Reid
09/12/2006	IL 12	H	Donegal Celtic	W 1-0	Fitzgerald
16/12/2006	IL 13	A	Loughgall	D 3-3	Fitzgerald; Picking; King
26/12/2006	IL 14	H	Coleraine	L 2-3	Picking; Patrick
30/12/2006	IL 15	A	Newry City	W 3-1	Reid; Picking; Haveron
02/01/2007	IL 16	H	Glentoran	W 3-2	Haveron; Kelbie 2
06/01/2007	IL 17	A	Glenavon	L 1-3	Charles og
13/01/2007	IC rd5	H	HW Welders	W 1-0	Scates
20/01/2007	IL 18	A	Crusaders	D 2-2	Kelbie; Patrick
27/01/2007	IL 19	H	Cliftonville	L 0-1	-
03/02/2007	IL 20	H	Portadown	W 2-0	Patrick; Brown
10/02/2007	IC rd6	H	Comber Rec.	W 1-0	Brown
17/02/2007	IL 21	A	Linfield	L 0-2	-
24/02/2007	IL 22	H	Dungannon Swifts	W 2-1	Brown; Kelbie
03/03/2007	IC qf	H	Linfield	D 1-1	O'Kane og
10/03/2007	IL 23	H	Limavady United	D 0-0	-
17/03/2007	IL 24	A	Armagh City	W 3-0	King; Alb. Watson; Scates
24/03/2007	IL 25	A	Lisburn Distillery	L 1-3	Kelbie
31/03/2007	IC qf rep	A	Linfield	L 2-4	Kelbie; Picking
07/04/2007	IL 26	H	Larne	W 3-0	Kelbie 3
10/04/2007	IL 27	A	Donegal Celtic	L 2-3	Fitzgerald; Haveron
14/04/2007	IL 28	A	Coleraine	W 1-0	Haveron
21/04/2007	IL 29	H	Loughgall	W 4-1	Kelbie 2; Scates; Kelly
28/04/2007	IL 30	H	Newry City	D 1-1	Scates

Notes

18/07/2006 v. Motherwell: Testimonial for Nigel Boyd

Player Appearances and Goals

BOYD Nigel	17	0	MELAUGH Gavin	7	0
BROWN Paul	23	4	MELLY Dominic	5	0
CALLAGHAN Aaron	39	0	MURPHY Darren	22	1
CARNDUFF Daley	1	0	MURPHY Paul	40	0
CUSHLEY David	6	0	O'NEILL Sean	1	0
FITZGERALD Darren	27	3	PATRICK Lee	25	5
FRIEL Austin	19	1	PICKING Mark	39	7
HAVERON Gary	34	5	REID Randal	13	3
KELBIE Kevin	39	17	ROSBOTHAM Andrew	3	0
KELLY Simon	13	1	SCATES Garth	38	6
KING Stuart	25	2	SIMMS Gordon	11	0
LOWRY Stephen	12	0	WATSON Aidan	29	0
McCLEAN Craig	26	0	WATSON Albert	38	2
McCONAGHIE Gareth	6	0			

Date	Comp	Venue	Opponents	Result	Scorers
20/07/2007	FR	A	Stranraer Athletic	W 1-0	Reid
21/07/2007	FR	A	Stranraer	L 1-3	Lowry
23/07/2007	FR	H	St. Johnstone	W 2-0	McClean; Kelly
28/07/2007	FR	H	Coventry City	L 0-6	-
11/08/2007	LC 1	A	Linfield	L 1-5	Fitzgerald
18/08/2007	LC 2	A	Glenavon	W 3-1	Picking; Scates 2
23/08/2007	LC 3	H	Dungannon Swifts	L 0-1	-
28/08/2007	CAS rd1	H	Orangefield OB	W 8-0	Reid; Walsh 3; King; Picking; Patrick; Fitzgerald
01/09/2007	LC 4	A	Glenavon	D 3-3	Picking; Walsh; Callaghan
11/09/2007	CAS qf	H	Donegal Celtic	W 2-0	Walsh; Picking
15/09/2007	LC 5	H	Linfield	L 0-3	-
22/09/2007	IL 1	A	Glenavon	W 2-1	Kelbie; Walsh
29/09/2007	IL 2	H	Glentoran	L 0-4	-
03/10/2007	CAS sf	H	Crusaders	L 1-2	Flynn
06/10/2007	IL 3	A	Crusaders	L 0-3	-
09/10/2007	LC 6	A	Dungannon Swifts	L 0-1	-
13/10/2007	IL 4	H	Cliftonville	L 0-1	-
20/10/2007	IL 5	A	Linfield	L 0-1	-
27/10/2007	IL 6	H	Portadown	W 2-1	Kelbie; Walsh
03/11/2007	IL 7	A	Armagh City	W 2-1	Walsh; Lowry
10/11/2007	IL 8	H	Limavady United	W 3-0	Walsh; Lowry; Kelbie
24/11/2007	IL 9	H	Dungannon Swifts	D 0-0	-
07/12/2007	IL 10	H	Larne	W 3-0	Kelbie; Fitzgerald; Cushley
15/12/2007	IL 11	A	Donegal Celtic	W 2-0	Alb. Watson; Scates
18/12/2007	IL 12	A	Lisburn Distillery	W 2-1	Kelbie; Cushley
22/12/2007	IL 13	H	Institute	W 2-1	Kelbie 2
26/12/2007	IL 14	A	Coleraine	D 1-1	Lowry
29/12/2007	IL 15	H	Newry City	W 2-1	Kelbie 2
01/01/2008	IL 16	A	Glentoran	W 4-2	Scates; Haveron; Melaugh; Kelbie
05/01/2008	IL 17	H	Glenavon	D 0-0	-
12/01/2008	IC rd5	A	Newry City	D 2-2	Kelly; Kelbie
19/01/2008	IL 18	H	Crusaders	D 2-2	Melaugh; Walsh
22/01/2008	IC rd5 rep	H	Newry City	L 0-0 (aet)	-
26/01/2008	IL 19	A	Cliftonville	L 2-3	Kelbie; Wray
01/02/2008	IL 20	A	Portadown	L 1-2	Kelbie
08/02/2008	FR	A	Derry City	L 0-1	-
16/02/2008	IL 21	H	Linfield	L 0-4	-
23/02/2008	IL 22	A	Dungannon Swifts	L 1-2	Melaugh
15/03/2008	IL 23	H	Armagh City	W 2-1	King; Kelbie
22/03/2008	IL 24	H	Lisburn Distillery	D 2-2	Kelly; Alb. Watson
25/03/2008	IL 25	A	Larne	L 1-2	Kelbie
28/03/2008	IL 26	A	Limavady United	L 1-3	Melaugh
05/04/2008	IL 27	H	Donegal Celtic	D 0-0	-
12/04/2008	IL 28	A	Coleraine	W 2-0	Wray 2
19/04/2008	IL 29	A	Institute	D 1-1	King
26/04/2008	IL 30	A	Newry City	D 2-2	Kelbie; McNeill

Played: 41, won: 15, drawn: 10, lost: 16, goals scored: 62, goals conceded: 60

Irish League: 6th; Irish Cup: Round 5; League Cup: Group stage; County Antrim Shield: Semi-final

Notes

Notes

20/07/2007 v. Stranraer Athletic: Match played at Stair Park

21/01/2008 v. Newry City: Ballymena United lost 4-2 on penalties

Player Appearances and Goals

Player	Apps	Goals	Player	Apps	Goals
BAIRD Gary	2	0	McNEILL Paul	6	1
BOYD Nigel	2	0	MELAUGH Gavin	33	4
BROWN Paul	6	0	MURPHY Paul	40	0
CALLAGHAN Aaron	13	1	O'NEILL Sean	1	0
COLLIGAN Lee	2	0	PATRICK Lee	27	1
CUSHLEY David	14	2	PICKING Mark	32	4
FITZGERALD Darren	15	3	POOLEY Dean	2	0
FLYNN Jonathan	15	1	REID Randal	14	1
HAVERON Gary	31	1	SCATES Garth	38	4
KELBIE Kevin	34	16	WALSH Davitt	24	10
KELLY Simon	29	2	WARD Michael	11	0
KING Stuart	30	3	WATSON Aidan	13	0
LOWRY Stephen	28	3	WATSON Albert	37	2
McCLEAN Craig	37	0	WRAY Thomas	22	3

Date	Comp	Venue	Opponents	Result	Scorers
17/07/2008	FR	H	Rangers XI	L 1-3	Teggart
19/08/2008	CAS rd1	H	Ballyclare Comrades	W 3-0	Walsh; Teggart 2
23/08/2008	IL 1	H	Cliftonville	L 1-5	Teggart
26/08/2008	IL 2	A	Newry City	D 2-2	Teggart; Haveron
30/08/2008	IL 3	H	Dungannon Swifts	L 0-3	-
06/09/2008	IL 4	A	Institute	D 1-1	Kelbie
09/09/2008	CAS qf	A	Glentoran	L 1-6	Simpson og
13/09/2008	IL 5	H	Glenavon	L 0-3	-
16/09/2008	IL 6	H	Lisburn Distillery	L 1-2	Teggart
20/09/2008	IL 7	A	Crusaders	L 0-2	-
23/09/2008	IL 8	A	Glentoran	L 1-4	Kelbie
27/09/2008	IL 9	H	Bangor	L 1-2	Mullan
04/10/2008	IL 10	A	Coleraine	D 1-1	Teggart
11/10/2008	IL 11	A	Linfield	W 2-0	Kelbie 2
18/10/2008	IL 12	H	Glentoran	D 1-1	Kelbie
25/10/2008	IL 13	A	Lisburn Distillery	L 0-1	-
29/10/2008	LC rd3 leg1	H	Glentoran	L 1-3	McNeill
01/11/2008	IL 14	A	Cliftonville	D 0-0	-
04/11/2008	LC rd3 leg2	A	Glentoran	W 2-1	Teggart; King
10/11/2008	IL 15	H	Newry City	L 2-3	Teggart 2
15/11/2008	IL 16	A	Dungannon Swifts	L 1-2	Teggart
22/11/2008	IL 17	A	Institute	L 0-1	-
29/11/2008	IL 18	A	Glenavon	W 3-1	King; Cushley; McNeill
09/12/2008	IL 19	H	Crusaders	W 1-0	King
13/12/2008	IL 20	A	Bangor	W 3-0	G. McDonnell; Ward 2
20/12/2008	IL 21	H	Glentoran	W 2-1	Deans; Kelbie
26/12/2008	IL 22	H	Coleraine	W 2-0	Crossan og; Kelbie
01/01/2009	IL 23	A	Linfield	L 0-1	-
03/01/2009	IL 24	H	Lisburn Distillery	W 1-0	Kelbie
10/01/2009	IL 25	H	Cliftonville	L 1-3	Ward
24/01/2009	IL 26	A	Newry City	W 1-0	Walsh
27/01/2009	IL 27	H	Dungannon Swifts	L 1-2	Muir
31/01/2009	IL 28	A	Institute	D 0-0	-
03/02/2009	IC rd4	A	Ballyclare Comrades	W 2-0	Kelbie; Colligan
14/02/2009	IC rd5	H	Crusaders	L 0-1	-
21/02/2009	IL 29	A	Crusaders	D 0-0	-
27/02/2009	IL 30	H	Bangor	W 2-0	Muir; Cushley
07/03/2009	IL 31	A	Glenavon	L 1-2	Kelbie
14/03/2009	IL 32	A	Coleraine	W 1-0	Muir
21/03/2009	IL 33	H	Linfield	L 0-3	-
11/04/2009	IL 34	H	Institute	W 1-0	Cushley
14/04/2009	IL 35	H	Newry City	L 0-4	-
18/04/2009	IL 36	A	Dungannon Swifts	L 3-4	Cushley; Colligan; Teggart
25/04/2009	IL 37	A	Glenavon	L 1-2	Teggart
02/05/2009	IL 38	A	Bangor	D 1-1	McNeill

Notes

04/11/2008 v. Glentoran: Ballymena United lost 4-3 on aggregate

Player Appearances and Goals

BLAYNEY Alan	38	0	McGINLAY Michael	4	0
BURKE Thomas	3	0	McNEILL Paul	16	3
COLLIGAN Lee	32	2	McVEIGH Dermot	1	0
CUSHLEY David	24	4	MELAUGH Gavin	33	0
DEANS Ryan	13	1	MUIR Paul	13	3
GETTY Christopher	2	0	MULLAN Liam	12	1
GRATTAN William	1	0	O'NEILL Sean	6	0
HAVERON Gary	28	1	PICKING Mark	17	0
HOGAN Liam	6	0	SMITH Michael	12	0
KELBIE Kevin	40	10	STEWART Aaron	18	0
KENNEDY Peter	4	0	TEGGART Neil	26	12
KING Stuart	22	3	WALSH Davitt	23	2
MAGILL Colin	2	0	WARD Michael	27	3
McCLEAN Craig	16	0	WATSON Aidan	34	0
McCONNELL Nathan	5	0	WATSON Albert	31	0
McDONNELL Gavin	36	1	WRAY Thomas	31	0
McDONNELL Joe	14	0	YOUNG George	5	0

Date	Comp	Venue	Opponents	Result	Scorers
01/08/2009	FR	H	Croydon Athletic	D 0-0	-
08/08/2009	IL 1	H	Cliftonville	L 0-1	-
11/08/2009	CAS rd1	H	HW Welders	W 4-0	P. Muir; Aid. Watson; A. Smith; Taggart
15/08/2009	IL 2	A	Dungannon Swifts	L 1-2	McConnell
18/08/2009	IL 3	A	Coleraine	L 2-3	Aid. Watson; Kelbie
22/08/2009	IL 4	H	Crusaders	L 1-2	Alb. Watson
26/08/2009	IL 5	A	Glentoran	W 2-1	Kelbie 2
01/09/2009	IL 6	H	Glenavon	L 0-3	-
05/09/2009	IL 7	A	Institute	W 1-0	Kelbie
12/09/2009	IL 8	H	Newry City	L 1-2	McConnell
15/09/2009	IL 9	A	Lisburn Distillery	W 2-0	Cushley; Lockhart
19/09/2009	IL 10	H	Portadown	W 2-1	Cushley; Kelbie
26/09/2009	IL 11	A	Linfield	L 0-1	-
29/09/2009	CAS qf	A	Donegal Celtic	W 4-1	Cushley 2; Anderson; Taggart
06/10/2009	IL 12	A	Cliftonville	W 2-0	McConnell; A. Smith
10/10/2009	IL 13	H	Dungannon Swifts	L 0-1	-
17/10/2009	IL 14	H	Coleraine	W 3-2	A. Smith; Anderson; Beverland og
20/10/2009	CAS sf	N	Crusaders	L 0-1	-
24/10/2009	IL 15	H	Crusaders	W 2-0	M. Smith; Cushley
27/10/2009	IL 16	H	Glentoran	L 2-3	McConnell 2
31/10/2009	LC rd3 leg1	A	Institute	L 1-2	M. Smith
07/11/2009	IL 17	A	Glenavon	D 2-2	A. Stewart; M. Smith
10/11/2009	LC rd3 leg2	H	Institute	L 1-2	M. Smith
14/11/2009	IL 18	H	Institute	D 1-1	Kelbie
28/11/2009	IL 19	H	Lisburn Distillery	L 0-1	-
03/12/2009	IL 20	A	Newry City	L 2-3	Colligan; A. Smith
12/12/2009	IL 21	A	Portadown	L 0-2	-
19/12/2009	IL 22	H	Linfield	W 2-0	Lockhart; Kelbie
16/01/2010	IC rd5	H	Ards	D 0-0	-
19/01/2010	IC rd5 rep	H	Ards	W 1-0 (aet)	Kelbie
23/01/2010	IL 23	A	Glentoran	L 0-3	-
26/01/2010	IL 24	A	Coleraine	L 1-3	Cushley
06/02/2010	IL 25	A	Institute	D 2-2	Lockhart; Wray og
09/02/2010	IL 26	H	Cliftonville	W 2-1	Kelbie; Surgenor
13/02/2010	IC rd6	H	Ballinamallard Utd	W 5-2	Surgenor; Kelbie 3; Haveron
16/02/2010	IL 27	H	Glenavon	W 1-0	Kelbie
23/02/2010	IL 28	A	Dungannon Swifts	L 1-2	Surgenor
27/02/2010	IL 29	H	Newry City	D 0-0	-
06/03/2010	IC qf	A	Glenavon	D 3-3	Kelbie; M. Smith; A. Smith
09/03/2010	IC qf rep	H	Glenavon	W 2-0	A. Smith; Anderson
13/03/2010	IL 30	H	Portadown	L 0-1	-
20/03/2010	IL 31	A	Linfield	L 0-1	-
25/03/2010	IL 32	A	Crusaders	D 2-2	A. Smith; Taggart
03/04/2010	IL 33	A	Lisburn Distillery	D 2-2	G. Muir; Kelbie
06/04/2010	IL 34	H	Coleraine	L 2-4	Lockhart; A. Smith
10/04/2010	IC sf	N	Portadown	L 1-1 (aet)	A. Smith
17/04/2010	IL 35	H	Institute	W 3-0	Surgenor; Colligan; A. Smith
20/04/2010	IL 36	A	Newry City	L 0-1	-
24/04/2010	IL 37	H	Lisburn Distillery	L 1-2	Anderson
01/05/2010	IL 38	A	Glenavon	D 1-1	Kelbie

Notes

20/10/2009 v. Crusaders: Match played at Solitude

10/11/2009 v. Institute: Ballymena United lost 4-2 on aggregate

10/04/2010 v. Portadown: Match played at Windsor Park and Ballymena United lost 4-3 on penalties

Player Appearances and Goals

ANDERSON Noel	32	4	NELSON Dwayne	33	0
CARSON Philip	22	0	NELSON Ross	1	0
COLLIGAN Lee	46	2	OKUNAIYA Ormon	17	0
CUSHLEY David	37	6	O'NEILL Sean	14	0
HAVERON Gary	24	1	RAMSEY Christopher	32	0
KELBIE Kevin	37	16	SMITH Andrew	39	10
KERR Aaron	2	0	SMITH Michael	48	5
LEMON Aaron	3	0	STEWART Aaron	40	1
LOCKHART Darren	34	4	STEWART George	11	0
McCAUGHREN Lee	2	0	SURGENOR Mark	40	4
McCONNELL Nathan	30	5	TAGGART Gavin	30	3
McLAUGHLIN James	7	0	WATSON Aidan	23	2
McNEILL Paul	11	0	WATSON Albert	32	1
MUIR Gary	13	1	YOUNG George	2	0
MUIR Paul	3	1			

Date	Comp	Venue	Opponents	Result	Scorers
10/07/2010	FR	H	Cowdenbeath	D 2-2	A. Smith; Berry
31/07/2010	FR	H	St. Mirren	L 0-2	-
07/08/2010	IL 1	A	Linfield	D 0-0	-
14/08/2010	IL 2	H	Donegal Celtic	L 0-4	-
21/08/2010	IL 3	A	Portadown	W 3-1	Surgenor; Hanley; McCutcheon
27/08/2010	IL 4	A	Glenavon	W 2-0	McCutcheon; Gibson
31/08/2010	IL 5	A	Crusaders	L 1-2	McCutcheon
04/09/2010	IL 6	H	Cliftonville	D 1-1	McCutcheon
07/09/2010	CAS qf	H	Crusaders	L 0-1	-
11/09/2010	IL 7	H	Newry City	W 1-0	Carson
18/09/2010	LC rd2	A	Banbridge Town	W 3-0	Carson; Murray; Stewart
21/09/2010	IL 8	A	Glentoran	W 2-1	Murray; Gibson
25/09/2010	IL 9	A	Coleraine	L 0-1	-
02/10/2010	IL 10	H	Dungannon Swifts	D 1-1	Murray
05/10/2010	IL 11	H	Lisburn Distillery	L 0-1	-
09/10/2010	IL 12	A	Donegal Celtic	W 3-2	Hanley; Murray; Gibson
16/10/2010	IL 13	H	Portadown	W 3-1	Gibson; Hanley; McCutcheon
23/10/2010	LC rd3	H	Ards	W 3-1	Spence og; Gibson; M. Smith
30/10/2010	IL 14	H	Linfield	D 3-3	Gibson; Surgenor 2
06/11/2010	IL 15	H	Glenavon	D 3-3	McCutcheon 2; Watson
09/11/2010	IL 16	A	Lisburn Distillery	D 1-1	Surgenor
13/11/2010	IL 17	A	Cliftonville	L 0-5	-
19/11/2010	IL 18	A	Newry City	W 4-0	McCutcheon; M. Smith; Murray; Hanley
27/11/2010	IL 19	H	Crusaders	D 1-1	Berry
11/12/2010	IL 20	A	Dungannon Swifts	W 2-1	McCutcheon 2
01/01/2011	IL 21	A	Glenavon	L 1-3	McCutcheon
04/01/2011	IL 22	H	Portadown	W 3-1	A. Smith; Murray 2
15/01/2011	IC rd5	H	Glentoran	D 1-1	Gage
18/01/2011	LC qf	H	Crusaders	L 0-2	-
24/01/2011	IC rd5 rep	A	Glentoran	L 2-3 (aet)	Murray; McCutcheon
29/01/2011	IL 23	A	Linfield	D 0-0	-
05/02/2011	IL 24	A	Cliftonville	D 2-2	Murray; M. Smith
08/02/2011	IL 25	H	Coleraine	L 0-1	-
14/02/2011	IL 26	H	Glentoran	L 0-2	-
19/02/2011	IL 27	H	Coleraine	D 1-1	Haveron
26/02/2011	IL 28	H	Donegal Celtic	L 0-3	-
01/03/2011	IL 29	H	Crusaders	L 0-3	-
05/03/2011	IL 30	A	Lisburn Distillery	W 1-0	McCutcheon
19/03/2011	IL 31	H	Glentoran	L 2-3	Surgenor; McCafferty
22/03/2011	IL 32	A	Dungannon Swifts	L 0-1	-
26/03/2011	IL 33	A	Newry City	D 1-1	A. Boyd
01/04/2011	IL 34	A	Coleraine	D 1-1	M. Smith
16/04/2011	IL 35	A	Donegal Celtic	D 3-3	A. Boyd; Murray; McCutcheon
23/04/2011	IL 36	H	Newry City	W 1-0	Berry
26/04/2011	IL 37	H	Dungannon Swifts	L 0-2	-
30/04/2011	IL 38	H	Glenavon	W 1-0	McCutcheon

Player Appearances and Goals

Player	Apps	Goals	Player	Apps	Goals
BERRY Ryan	17	2	McCUTCHEON Gary	44	15
BOYD Aaron	8	2	McDOWELL Maurice	16	0
BOYD Matthew	2	0	McLAUGHLIN James	1	0
BROWN Ryan	24	0	MURRAY Eamonn	38	10
CARSON Rory	14	2	NELSON Dwayne	21	0
COLLIGAN Lee	35	0	OKUNAIYA Ormon	1	0
DOWIE Christopher	1	0	REID David	1	0
GAGE Denver	35	1	SMITH Andrew	21	1
GIBSON Richard	24	6	SMITH Michael I	43	4
HANLEY Nathan	22	4	SMITH Michael II	3	0
HAVERON Gary	36	1	STEWART Aaron	37	1
LOWRY Neil	1	0	SURGENOR Mark	38	5
McAREAVEY Paul	3	0	TAGGART Gavin	28	0
McCAFFERTY Neil	15	1	WATSON Albert	43	1
McCAUGHERN Lee	2	0	YOUNG George	12	0

Date	Comp	Venue	Opponents	Result	Scorers
07/07/2011	FR	H	Kilmarnock	D 0-0	-
06/08/2011	IL 1	A	Lisburn Distillery	W 4-1	Teggart; McCutcheon 2; Baker
13/08/2011	IL 2	H	Glenavon	D 3-3	McCutcheon 2; Baker
20/08/2011	IL 3	H	Crusaders	L 0-3	-
26/08/2011	IL 4	A	Donegal Celtic	W 3-2	Baker 2; R. Black
30/08/2011	IL 5	H	Carrick Rangers	L 0-2	-
03/09/2011	IL 6	H	Linfield	L 1-2	McCutcheon
07/09/2011	CAS qf	H	Linfield	L 0-1	-
10/09/2011	IL 7	A	Cliftonville	W 4-3	Surgenor; Kane; McCutcheon 2
17/09/2011	IL 8	H	Coleraine	L 1-5	Stewart
20/09/2011	LC rd2	H	Chimney Corner	W 7-0	Vauls; Watson; Surgenor; Kane; McCutcheon 2; Ryles og
24/09/2011	IL 9	A	Glentoran	W 4-2	McCutcheon 3; Jenkins
01/10/2011	IL 10	H	Dungannon Swifts	D 1-1	McCutcheon
08/10/2011	IL 11	H	Portadown	L 2-4	Teggart; McCutcheon
12/10/2011	LC rd3	A	Bangor	W 2-0	Rafferty og; Boyd
15/10/2011	IL 12	A	Crusaders	L 2-3	Boyd; Munster
22/10/2011	IL 13	A	Carrick Rangers	W 2-0	Baker; McCutcheon
29/10/2011	IL 14	A	Lisburn Distillery	W 1-0	McCutcheon
05/11/2011	IL 15	A	Coleraine	L 0-1	-
12/11/2011	IL 16	A	Portadown	L 1-2	McCutcheon
16/11/2011	LC qf	A	Dergview	W 6-2	Baker; Jenkins; Teggart; McCutcheon 3
19/11/2011	IL 17	H	Cliftonville	L 3-7	McCutcheon; Jenkins 2
26/11/2011	IL 18	H	Donegal Celtic	W 2-0	McCutcheon; Boyd
03/12/2011	IL 19	A	Linfield	L 0-1	-
10/12/2011	IL 20	A	Glenavon	L 0-3	-
13/12/2011	LC sf	H	Crusaders	L 0-1	-
20/12/2011	IL 21	A	Dungannon Swifts	D 1-1	McCutcheon
26/12/2011	IL 22	A	Coleraine	L 0-2	-
31/12/2011	IL 23	H	Donegal Celtic	D 2-2	Munster; Stewart
07/01/2012	IL 24	H	Linfield	L 1-2	Jenkins
14/01/2012	IC rd5	A	Lisburn Distillery	W 2-1	McCutcheon; Teggart
17/01/2012	IL 25	H	Glentoran	L 0-3	-
20/01/2012	IL 26	A	Crusaders	D 2-2	McCutcheon; Munster
31/01/2012	IL 27	H	Portadown	L 1-2	Costello
04/02/2012	IL 28	H	Cliftonville	L 0-1	-
11/02/2012	IC rd6	H	Derriaghy CC	W 3-1	Teggart; Munster; Jenkins
17/02/2012	IL 29	A	Carrick Rangers	W 3-1	Jenkins; Carson; McCutcheon
25/02/2012	IL 30	A	Glenavon	W 2-0	McCutcheon 2
03/03/2012	IC qf	A	Newry City	W 2-1	McCutcheon; A. Davidson
10/03/2012	IL 31	H	Lisburn Distillery	D 2-2	A. Davidson; McCutcheon
17/03/2012	IL 32	H	Dungannon Swifts	D 1-1	McCutcheon
24/03/2012	IL 33	A	Glentoran	W 2-1	Jenkins 2
07/04/2012	IL 34	A	Donegal Celtic	W 3-0	Costello 2; A. Davidson
10/04/2012	IL 35	A	Dungannon Swifts	W 4-2	Teggart; McCutcheon; Costello; J. Davidson
14/04/2012	IL 36	H	Carrick Rangers	W 3-0	Costello 3
21/04/2012	IL 37	H	Glenavon	D 2-2	Costello; Taylor
28/04/2012	IL 38	A	Lisburn Distillery	W 3-2	Teggart; McCutcheon 2

Notes

03/03/2012 v. Newry City: Ballymena United expelled from Irish Cup after playing an ineligible player in Alan Davidson

Player Appearances and Goals

Player	Apps	Goals	Player	Apps	Goals
BAKER Jordan	32	6	McCUTCHEON Gary	46	34
BLACK Aaron	1	0	MUNSTER David	31	4
BLACK Ross	21	1	MURRAY Eamonn	12	0
BOYD Aaron	11	3	NELSON Dwayne	21	0
CAIRNS Mcauley	1	0	PRICE Corey	1	0
CARSON Rory	23	1	RODGERS Christopher	25	0
COSTELLO James	33	8	SMITH Michael	4	0
DAVIDSON Alan	9	3	STEWART Aaron	39	2
DAVIDSON Jamie	12	1	SURGENOR Mark	26	2
DOWNEY Conor	22	0	TAGGART Gavin	29	0
DRUMMOND Wayne	20	0	TAYLOR Jonathan	13	1
GAGE Denver	9	0	TEGGART Alan	42	7
JENKINS Allan	41	9	VAULS Richard	24	1
KANE Tony	28	2	WATSON Liam	12	1
KERR Aaron	4	0	WOODS Curtis	14	0
LOWRY Neil	12	0			

Date	Comp	Venue	Opponents	Result	Scorers
14/07/2012	FR	N	Port Talbot	W 1-1 (pens)	Cushley
15/07/2012	FR	A	St. James' Gate	W 2-0	Baker; Teggart
28/07/2012	FR	H	Dundalk	W 2-0	Teggart; J. Davidson
11/08/2012	IL 1	H	Linfield	W 2-0	J. Davidson 2
18/08/2012	IL 2	A	Crusaders	D 0-0	-
25/08/2012	IL 3	A	Ballinamallard United	D 0-0	-
27/08/2012	LC rd2	H	Lurgan Celtic	W 4-1	Lowry; Thompson; Jenkins; McCabe
31/08/2012	IL 4	H	Lisburn Distillery	W 2-0	Harkness og; Lowry
04/09/2012	IL 5	A	Cliftonville	L 1-2	Thompson
08/09/2012	IL 6	H	Donegal Celtic	D 3-3	Jenkins; Taylor; J. Davidson
15/09/2012	IL 7	H	Dungannon Swifts	D 1-1	Cushley
22/09/2012	IL 8	A	Coleraine	L 1-4	Thompson
25/09/2012	CAS qf	H	Cliftonville	W 1-0	Cushley
28/09/2012	IL 9	H	Glentoran	D 1-1	Thompson
06/10/2012	IL 10	A	Portadown	D 2-2	Surgenor; Teggart
09/10/2012	LC rd3	H	HW Welders	W 3-1	Teggart 2; Kane
13/10/2012	IL 11	H	Glenavon	W 2-1	McCashin og; Teggart
20/10/2012	IL 12	A	Lisburn Distillery	W 4-0	J. Davidson; Cushley; McCabe 2
27/10/2012	IL 13	H	Ballinamallard United	D 1-1	Teggart
30/10/2012	CAS sf	H	Donegal Celtic	W 2-0	A. Davidson; Thompson
03/11/2012	IL 14	A	Dungannon Swifts	W 3-1	A. Davidson; J. Davidson; Surgenor
05/11/2012	LC qf	H	Linfield	L 0-6	-
10/11/2012	IL 15	H	Crusaders	W 2-1	A. Davidson; Costello
17/11/2012	IL 16	H	Cliftonville	L 0-8	-
24/11/2012	IL 17	A	Linfield	L 1-2	Stewart
27/11/2012	CAS f	N	Linfield	W 1-1 (aet)	Munster
01/12/2012	IL 18	A	Donegal Celtic	L 0-1	-
08/12/2012	IL 19	H	Portadown	L 1-2	Rodgers
15/12/2012	IL 20	A	Glenavon	L 1-4	J. Davidson
26/12/2012	IL 21	H	Coleraine	L 0-2	-
29/12/2012	IL 22	H	Lisburn Distillery	D 3-3	Taggart; Cushley; Surgenor
04/01/2013	IL 23	H	Ballinamallard United	W 3-0	Rodgers; Dolan; Cushley
05/01/2013	FR	A	RSKV Leonidas	L 0-1	-
12/01/2013	IC rd5	H	Warrenpoint Town	W 2-1	Dolan; A. Davidson
15/01/2013	IL 24	A	Glentoran	W 2-1	Teggart; Kane
19/01/2013	IL 25	A	Crusaders	L 1-5	Teggart
29/01/2013	IL 26	A	Dungannon Swifts	D 0-0	-
02/02/2013	IL 27	A	Linfield	D 2-2	Cushley 2
09/02/2013	IC rd6	H	Coleraine	L 2-3	Taggart; Liggett
16/02/2013	IL 28	H	Coleraine	L 0-1	-
23/02/2013	IL 29	A	Glenavon	L 0-7	-
02/03/2013	IL 30	H	Donegal Celtic	D 2-2	Cushley; Kane
09/03/2013	IL 31	H	Glentoran	D 0-0	-
16/03/2013	IL 32	A	Portadown	D 0-0	-
30/03/2013	IL 33	A	Cliftonville	L 0-5	-
02/04/2013	IL 34	H	Portadown	W 6-1	Cushley 3; Surgenor; Liggett 2
13/04/2013	IL 35	A	Donegal Celtic	W 4-1	Burns og; Liggett; Dolan; Teggart
16/04/2013	IL 36	A	Lisburn Distillery	W 2-0	Liggett; A. Davidson
20/04/2013	IL 37	H	Glenavon	L 0-2	-
27/04/2013	IL 38	H	Dungannon Swifts	L 1-2	Taylor

Notes

14/07/2012 v Port Talbot: Ballymena United won 5-3 on penalties

27/11/2012 v Linfield: Match played at The Oval and Ballymena United won 4-3 on penalties

Player Appearances and Goals

ADDIS Stuart	6	0	MAHER Shaun	8	0
BAKER Jordan	2	0	McCABE James	23	3
BINGHAM William	4	0	McCULLAGH Mark	7	0
BLACK Ross	22	0	MUNSTER David	39	1
COSTELLO James	12	1	NELSON Dwayne	40	0
CUSHLEY David	41	11	PRICE Corey	1	0
DAVIDSON Alan	29	5	RODGERS Christopher	17	2
DAVIDSON Jamie	25	6	RUDDY Michael	21	0
DOLAN Shane	13	3	STEWART Aaron	35	1
DUFFIN Peter	9	0	SURGENOR Mark	30	4
FLEMING Jamie	1	0	TAGGART Gavin	32	2
GAGE Denver	1	0	TAYLOR Jonathan	18	2
JENKINS Allan	31	2	TEGGART Alan	36	8
KANE Tony	40	3	THOMPSON Gary	40	5
LIGGETT Gary	17	5	VAULS Richard	12	0
LOWRY Neil	20	2			

Date	Comp	Venue	Opponents	Result	Scorers
10/08/2013	IL 1	H	Glenavon	L 3-6	Lowry; Thompson; Taylor
17/08/2013	IL 2	A	Crusaders	W 2-1	Dolan; Liggett
24/08/2013	IL 3	H	Dungannon Swifts	W 2-1	Jenkins; Dolan
26/08/2013	LC rd2	H	Ballymoney United	W 2-2 (aet)	Stewart; T. Kane
30/08/2013	IL 4	A	Ards	L 0-2	-
03/09/2013	IL 5	H	Portadown	W 2-1	McLellan; Teggart
07/09/2013	IL 6	H	Cliftonville	L 0-1	-
14/09/2013	IL 7	A	Linfield	L 1-4	Liggett
21/09/2013	IL 8	A	Glentoran	D 0-0	-
24/09/2013	CAS qf	H	Donegal Celtic	W 1-0	Cushley
28/09/2013	IL 9	H	Warrenpoint Town	L 0-1	-
04/10/2013	IL 10	A	Ballinamallard United	L 0-1	-
08/10/2013	LC rd3	H	Ballinamallard United	W 3-0	Jenkins; Cushley; Dolan
12/10/2013	IL 11	H	Coleraine	D 2-2	Taylor 2
19/10/2013	IL 12	A	Dungannon Swifts	W 3-2	Liggett; Thompson; Jenkins
26/10/2013	IL 13	H	Linfield	L 1-4	Cushley
30/10/2013	CAS sf	A	Crusaders	L 0-1	-
02/11/2013	IL 14	H	Glentoran	L 3-4	Teggart 2; Liggett
09/11/2013	IL 15	A	Cliftonville	L 1-2	Cushley
12/11/2013	LC qf	H	Portadown	W 4-0	Cushley; Surgenor; Thompson; Teggart
16/11/2013	IL 16	H	Ards	W 4-2	Cushley; Thompson 2; Ruddy
23/11/2013	IL 17	A	Warrenpoint Town	W 2-0	Cushley; Jenkins
30/11/2013	IL 18	H	Ballinamallard United	W 2-0	Surgenor; Dolan
07/12/2013	IL 19	A	Portadown	L 0-1	-
14/12/2013	IL 20	A	Glenavon	D 0-0	-
17/12/2013	LC sf	A	Crusaders	L 3-4 (aet)	Cushley 3
21/12/2013	IL 21	H	Crusaders	W 1-0	Cushley
26/12/2013	IL 22	A	Coleraine	W 3-2	Teggart; Jenkins 2
01/01/2014	IL 23	A	Ards	D 0-0	-
04/01/2014	IL 24	H	Ballinamallard United	W 1-0	Cushley
11/01/2014	IC rd5	A	HW Welders	D 2-2	Simpson og; Boyce
14/01/2014	IL 25	A	Dungannon Swifts	W 3-2	Ervin; Jenkins; Boyce
18/01/2014	IL 26	H	Linfield	L 1-2	Teggart
21/01/2014	IC rd5 rep	H	HW Welders	W 1-0	Thompson
01/02/2014	IL 27	A	Portadown	L 0-1	-
04/02/2014	IL 28	H	Cliftonville	L 1-3	Devlin og
08/02/2014	IC rd6	A	Linfield	W 2-1	Jenkins; Cushley
15/02/2014	IL 29	H	Coleraine	D 2-2	McLellan; Teggart
22/02/2014	IL 30	H	Warrenpoint Town	W 3-2	Cushley 2; Boyce
01/03/2014	IC qf	H	Dungannon Swifts	W 4-1	Munster; Taylor; Boyce 2
07/03/2014	IL 31	A	Glentoran	L 0-3	-
15/03/2014	IL 32	A	Crusaders	L 0-1	-
22/03/2014	IL 33	H	Glenavon	W 2-1	Boyce 2
29/03/2014	IL 34	H	Dungannon Swifts	L 1-2	Gawley
05/04/2014	IC sf	N	Queen's University	W 3-0	A. Davidson 2; Kelly
12/04/2014	IL 35	A	Coleraine	D 1-1	Teggart
19/04/2014	IL 36	A	Ballinamallard United	D 0-0	-
22/04/2014	IL 37	A	Warrenpoint Town	L 0-1	-
26/04/2014	IL 38	H	Ards	D 1-1	McCabe
03/05/2014	IC f	N	Glenavon	L 1-2	Jenkins

Notes

26/08/2013 v Ballymoney United: Ballymena United won 5-3 on penalties

05/04/2014 v Queens University: Match played at The Oval

03/05/2014 v Glenavon: Match played at Windsor Park

Player Appearances and Goals

Player	App	Goals	Player	App	Goals
ADDIS Stuart	10	0	LACROIX Yohan	4	0
BLACK Nicholas	1	0	LIGGETT Gary	21	4
BOYCE Darren	16	7	LOUGHRAN Caolan	2	0
CAIRNS Macauley	3	0	LOWRY Neil	19	1
CARSON Jake	1	0	McBRIDE Stephen	20	0
CUSHLEY David	41	15	McCABE James	3	1
DAVIDSON Alan	29	2	McCULLAGH Mark	34	0
DOLAN Shane	20	4	McLELLAN Michael	24	2
DUFFIN Peter	2	0	McQUILLAN Cathal	1	0
ERVIN Jim	17	1	MILLAR Leroy	2	0
FERGUSON Matthew	1	0	MUNSTER David	33	1
GAWLEY Neal	11	1	NELSON Dwayne	18	0
GILLAN Eoin	1	0	ROBINSON Thomas	6	0
GRAHAM Jack	1	0	RUDDY Michael	26	1
HAMILL Steven	1	0	SHANAHAN Aaron	15	0
HARRIS Aaron	1	0	STEWART Aaron	39	1
JENKINS Allan	44	9	SURGENOR Mark	26	2
JOHNSTON Jason	1	0	TAGGART Gavin	24	0
KANE Eoin	2	0	TAYLOR Jonathan	38	4
KANE Tony	42	1	TEGGART Alan	43	8
KELLY Mark	6	1	THOMPSON Gary	39	6

Date	Comp	Venue	Opponents	Result	Scorers
02/08/2014	CS	A	Cliftonville	L 0-0 (aet)	
09/08/2014	IL 1	H	Warrenpoint Town	W 2-0	Cushley; Gawley
13/08/2014	IL2	A	Crusaders	D 2-2	Taggart; Taylor
16/08/2014	IL 3	H	Portadown	W 3-2	McVey; Jenkins; Boyce
23/08/2014	IL 4	A	Dungannon Swifts	W 3-0	Tipton 2; Cushley
25/08/2014	LC rd2	A	Newington YC	W 3-0	T. Kane; Boyce; Tipton
29/08/2014	IL 5	A	Glenavon	L 1-2	Cushley
02/09/2014	IL 6	H	Institute	W 2-1	Teggart 2
06/09/2014	IL 7	A	Ballinamallard United	L 0-3	-
13/09/2014	IL 8	H	Glentoran	D 2-2	Boyce; Thompson
20/09/2014	IL 9	A	Coleraine	W 2-1	Thompson; Ruddy
23/09/2014	CAS rd1	A	Donegal Celtic	W 3-1 (aet)	Cushley 3
27/09/2014	IL 10	H	Cliftonville	D 2-2	Tipton; Jenkins
04/10/2014	IL 11	A	Linfield	L 2-3	Taylor 2
07/10/2014	LC rd3	H	Ballyclare Comrades	W 3-1	Tipton 3
11/10/2014	IL 12	H	Dungannon Swifts	D 2-2	Jenkins; Teggart
18/10/2014	IL 13	A	Portadown	L 1-2	McVey
25/10/2014	IL 14	H	Glenavon	L 1-4	Jenkins
28/10/2014	CAS qf	H	Cliftonville	L 3-4	Boyce; Jenkins; Teggart
01/11/2014	IL 15	A	Glentoran	L 0-4	-
08/11/2014	IL 16	H	Coleraine	L 0-2	-
11/11/2014	LC qf	H	Dungannon Swifts	W 3-1	T. Kane; Gawley; Boyce
15/11/2014	IL 17	A	Warrenpoint Town	D 2-2	Tipton 2
22/11/2014	IL 18	H	Ballinamallard United	W 3-0	Surgenor 2; Shevlin
29/11/2014	IL 19	A	Cliftonville	L 0-7	-
06/12/2014	IL 20	H	Linfield	L 2-3	Jenkins; Tipton
13/12/2014	IL 21	H	Crusaders	L 0-2	-
16/12/2014	LC sf	A	Ballinamallard United	W 3-2	Jenkins; Tipton; Munster
20/12/2014	IL 22	A	Institute	W 2-1	Munster; Teggart
26/12/2014	IL 23	H	Coleraine	W 4-3	Boyce; Tipton 2; Jenkins
01/01/2015	IL 24	A	Warrenpoint Town	L 0-2	-
03/01/2015	IL 25	H	Glenavon	L 2-4	Boyce; McCutcheon
10/01/2015	IC rd5	H	Crumlin Star	W 4-0	Tipton; McCutcheon; Boyce 2
17/01/2015	IL 26	A	Portadown	D 5-5	Tipton 2; Boyce; Taylor; Jenkins
24/01/2015	LC f	N	Cliftonville	L 2-3	Cushley 2
31/01/2015	IL 27	A	Linfield	L 1-2	Cushley
07/02/2015	IC rd6	A	Cliftonville	W 2-1	Cushley 2
10/02/2015	IL 28	H	Glentoran	L 1-3	Kane
14/02/2015	IL 29	H	Institute	W 3-0	McCutcheon; Jenkins; McAllister
21/02/2015	IL 30	A	Cliftonville	L 0-1	-
28/02/2015	IC qf	A	HW Welders	W 3-2	Boyce; Tipton; Thompson
06/03/2015	IL 31	A	Dungannon Swifts	L 0-1	-
14/03/2015	IL 32	H	Crusaders	L 1-3	Jenkins
21/03/2015	IC sf	N	Portadown	L 1-3	Boyce
28/03/2015	IL 33	A	Ballinamallard United	W 3-1	Surgenor; Gawley; Tipton
04/04/2015	IL 34	A	Coleraine	W 1-0	Boyce
07/04/2015	IL 35	A	Warrenpoint Town	W 2-1	Tipton; Boyce
11/04/2015	IL 36	A	Institute	W 2-1	Teggart; Forker og
18/04/2015	IL 37	H	Ballinamallard United	W 2-1	Gawley; McAllister
25/04/2015	IL 38	H	Dungannon Swifts	W 1-0	Jenkins

Notes

24/01/2015 v Cliftonville: Match played at Windsor Park

21/03/2015 v Portadown: Match played at The Oval

Player Appearances and Goals

Player	Apps	Goals	Player	Apps	Goals
ADDIS Stuart	9	0	McCUTCHEON Gary	9	3
ALLEN Timothy	12	0	McNALLY Patrick	9	0
BOYCE Darren	47	14	McNEILL Jake	2	0
CUSHLEY David	37	11	McVEY Kyle	12	2
DAVIDSON Alan	8	0	MUNSTER David	24	2
ERVIN Jim	18	0	NELSON Dwayne	29	0
FERGUSON Matthew	5	0	NIXON Stewart	1	0
GARDNER Craig	2	0	RUDDY Michael	20	1
GAWLEY Neal	37	4	SHEVLIN Matthew	4	1
HARRIS Aaron	3	0	STEWART Aaron	14	0
JENKINS Allan	44	12	SURGENOR Mark	29	3
KANE Eoin	6	0	TAGGART Gavin	15	1
KANE Tony	43	3	TAYLOR Johnny	39	4
McALLISTER Eamonn	10	2	TEGGART Alan	40	6
McBRIDE Stephen	38	0	TIPTON Matthew	47	19
McCAUL Brian	17	0	THOMPSON Gary	34	3
McCULLAGH Mark	22	0			